Searching and Researching on the Internet and the World Wide Web

Ernest Ackermann
Mary Washington College

Karen Hartman
Mary Washington College

Franklin, Beedle & Associates, Inc.
8536 SW St. Helens Drive, Suite D
Wilsonville, OR 97070
503/682–7668
www.fbeedle.com

Dedication

To my family—Lynn, Karl and Oliver—and to the memory of my parents

Henry Ackermann (1904 – 1997)

Marie Ackermann (1914 – 1997)

always encouraging, always loving.

—E. A.

————————————

To Jack, Tracy, and Hilary

—K. H.

President and Publisher	Jim Leisy (jimleisy@fbeedle.com)
Manuscript Editor	Eve Kushner
Production	Tom Sumner
	Stephanie Welch
	Susan Skarzynski
Cover Design	Steve Klinetobe
Marketing Group	Victor Kaiser
	Cary Crossland
	Carrie Widman
	Jason Smith
	Marc Chambers
Order Processing	Chris Alarid
	Ann Leisy

cover image ©1997 PhotoDisc, Inc.

Printed in the U.S.A.

Rights and Permissions
Franklin, Beedle & Associates, Incorporated
8536 SW St. Helens Drive, Suite D
Wilsonville, Oregon 97070
http://www.fbeedle.com

Contents

Chapter 3
Using the World Wide Web for Research
page 67

Chapter 4
Directories and Virtual Libraries
page 103

Chapter 5

Search Strategies for
Search Engines
page 134

Chapter 6

Using Search Engines
page 168

Chapter 7

Specialized Databases
page 190

Chapter 8

Searching Library Catalogs
page 217

Chapter 9

FTP: Searching Archives, Downloading Files
page 243

Chapter 10

Finding Email Addresses, Phone Numbers, and Maps
page 270

Chapter 11

Searching Email Discussion Group Archives and Usenet Newsgroup Archives
page 287

Chapter 12

Evaluating Information Found on the WWW
page 318

Chapter 13

Citing Web and Internet Resources
page 344

Chapter 14

Putting It All Together:
Two Sample Research Projects
page 359

Preface

Intended Audience for This Book

This book was written for use in college-level Internet courses or for self-study. The topics address the research needs of students in a broad range of disciplines, as well as researchers, prospective and in-service teachers, and librarians. While writing this book, we became acquainted with college programs where the first Internet course is devoted to the research potential of the medium; other programs have decided to make the Internet research course the second in their sequence. Therefore, the book is written so that it is useful to people first learning about the Internet and the World Wide Web, as well as those with more online experience.

Certain assumptions are made about the reader of this book. We expect the reader to be acquainted with the fundamental operations of a personal computer, in particular the ability to launch and use applications software. Access to the Internet is equally important to successfully complete the activities in this book. You must have either an Internet account at your college or a dial-up account through an Internet service provider.

Important Features of This Book

The main topics of this book are formulating search strategies, understanding how to form search expressions, critically evaluating information, and citing resources. We carry these themes throughout the book. The 10-step search strategy developed in Chapter 5, for example, is applied to exercises in many of the subsequent chapters. This strategy, combined with the numerous step-by-step activities throughout the book, provides a variety of techniques and concepts that are useful to the beginner and the more advanced user. In reading the text and working through the activities, projects, and exercises, you will come to understand that for every research topic you need to go through an evaluation process to determine the most appropriate search strategy. This process of constructing searches guarantees a more precise result and is applicable to any search engine or database.

We give details for several step-by-step activities using many of the major search engines, directories, virtual libraries, and other information resources on the Web and the Internet. The demonstrations in the text were developed using Netscape Navigator 4 on a personal computer using Windows 95. (*Note:* Navigator is available for PCs and Macintosh computers and is functionally indistinguishable on either platform. You can therefore use this book successfully with either platform.) You'll find that the essential search skills, the ways to determine which type of resource to use, and the ways to evaluate and cite resources depend very little on the specific Web browser and computer system you use. After reading the text and working through the activities and exercises you'll be better prepared to effectively find what you need, determine the appropriate tools and resources to use, and be able to evaluate what you've found. Most importantly, enjoy yourself!

Some Thoughts about the Research Potential of the Internet and the World Wide Web

The Internet and the World Wide Web have had profound effects on the way we find information and do research. This is due in part to the astounding increase in the information resources and tools available for finding information. Soon after our initial experience in this book in using a Web browser, we will start discovering the wide range of information sources and the ways we can access them. Instead of spending hours combing through books, library catalogs, and indexes, making endless telephone calls, or traveling to far-off places, we can find an enormous amount of information on virtually any subject with a few clicks of the mouse.

The explosion in the number of information resources raises some important issues. First of all, we need to know how to search the World Wide Web effectively. Sometimes we get frustrated when using the Internet or the Web because there appears to be too much extraneous information, yet we are anxious to learn how to get as much good information as we can from the Web. Second, we need to know how the different search engines are constructed so that as we encounter new search engines we will have developed skills that enable us to search any database. Third, we need to know when a search engine isn't the most appropriate resource to use, in which case we will want to use a virtual library or a Web directory. Finally, with the varied information sources that make up the Web, we need to know how to evaluate sources we find.

Organization of This Book

This book is arranged so that the information presented is reinforced and built on in subsequent chapters. We start with an introduction to the Internet and the Web, cover using a browser, bookmarks, and other tools, and then move on to researching on the Web. In doing our research, a number of fundamental concepts and tactics for finding information on the Web are introduced. We then consider the resources we can browse: directories and virtual libraries. Next we cover the topics of developing a search strategy, constructing search expressions, and learning about the common features in various search engines and other searchable indexes. This is followed by numerous examples of using search engines and discussions of using specialized databases and library catalogs. We then turn our attention to the other resources for finding information—FTP archives, white page services, discussion groups, and Usenet newsgroups.

Evaluating resources and citing resources are considered next. The last chapter demonstrates, within the context of doing a research project, many of the concepts and techniques introduced and discussed in earlier chapters for acquiring, evaluating, and citing resources.

The book is organized as follows:

Chapters 1 and 2	Introduction to the Internet and the Web; techniques and intricacies of using a Web browser; keeping track of information with bookmarks
Chapter 3	Introduction to research skills and tools on the Web
Chapter 4	Directories and virtual libraries
Chapters 5, 6, 7, and 8	Search strategies and tools—search engines, meta-search engines, specialized databases, library catalogs
Chapters 9, 10, and 11	Other resources for information—FTP archives; white pages services: email addresses, street addresses, maps; email discussion groups and Usenet news archives
Chapter 12	Evaluating information found on the Internet and the Web
Chapter 13	Citing information for research
Chapter 14	Putting it all together—two sample research projects
Appendices A, B, and C	Annotated list of search engines, meta-search engines, and virtual libraries; charts comparing search engines
Appendix D	Keeping current—an annotated list of services and Web sites

The first two chapters in the book are designed to introduce the environment (Internet and WWW), the medium (a Web browser), and the media (Web pages, different file types) you'll be using for research. In those chapters we also discuss using bookmarks or lists of favorite sites as an aid in keeping track of your research and search activities. Chapter 3 introduces the fundamental issues related to using the Web for research; gives an overview of using directories, virtual libraries, search engines, and meta-search engines; and discusses different tactics for finding information on the Web. We take up the topics of directories and virtual libraries in Chapter 4. Developing a search strategy and using search engines, meta-search engines, specialized databases, and library catalogs are covered in Chapters 5, 6, 7, and 8. We then address other resources on the Internet and the Web: FTP resources, including finding and downloading freeware and shareware programs in Chapter 9; finding email and street addresses and maps in Chapter 10; and using email discussion groups, Usenet newsgroups, and their archives as resources in Chapter 11. Chapter 12 focuses on guidelines for evaluating information, and contains links to other evaluative guides on the Web. Chapter 13 addresses citing references for a research project and contains a list of formats to use for citing Web and Internet resources. The last chapter brings the concepts and techniques together by applying the research strategies to two sample research projects: finding resources for a research paper, and using the Internet for market research.

There are other ways to approach this material; however, we feel you should complete Chapter 3 before moving on to other chapters in the book. You may skip certain topics from the first two chapters if you feel a complete introduction to the Internet, the Web, a Web browser, and bookmarks isn't necessary. Chapter 5 is essential to the discussions about searching in the remainder of the text. If using library catalogs doesn't fit into your plans or syllabus then you may skip Chapter 8. If you're pressed for time and need to concentrate on research skills, you can skip Chapters 9 and 10 and may want to skip Chapter 11. Evaluating resources can be considered anytime after becoming experienced with the nature of information on the Internet, so you may want to cover some of the material in that chapter soon after Chapters 3, 4, and 5. The research projects in Chapter 14 deal with many of the tools and resources discussed in earlier chapters, but the projects are constructed in such a way that the reader can focus on individual portions of each.

Each of the chapters contains one or more step-by-step activities to demonstrate using the tools, services, and resources discussed in the text. Some of the text depends on the reader becoming a participant in the activities, or having other experiences using the Internet and the World Wide Web. By following the activities and trying them out, the reader/participant is guided through first-hand experience with searching on the Internet. Including these activities is a bit of a risk because of the dynamic nature of the Internet and the World Wide Web. Nothing is frozen in place and it may be that when you work with these exercises you'll see differences in the way information is displayed. Don't let that deter you. Using the World Wide Web and the Internet means you have to adapt to changes. Be persistent and use your skills to navigate a changing, but important, environment. One of the things that makes the Web exciting and vigorous is how it is changing to become more useful.

Each chapter contains several exercises or projects to help the reader better understand the tools and topics discussed. As using the World Wide Web is a hands-on activity, doing the exercises is an important part of learning. The exercises deal with topics drawn from a variety of areas, so doing the exercises exposes the participant to many of the types of resources that make up the World Wide Web.

Supplemental Materials

For teachers using this book, an instructor's guide is available from the publisher. A Web page is maintained to accompany this book at **http:// www.mwc.edu/ernie/search-web.html**. Hyperlinks to individual Web pages for each chapter and appendix are on that page. These individual pages contain up-to-date links to all the resources mentioned in the book and are periodically updated to keep the activities current. Furthermore, since the material at a Web site can change, these links provide access to the most recent Web versions of information resources mentioned in this book.

Accompanying the book is a CD-ROM with Netscape Navigator 4. If you choose to install the browser from the disc, your browser will be compatible with the activities, exercises, and figures that are in the book. Also included is a diskette that contains HTML versions of all the exercises and projects from the chapters. They appear as Web pages and can be used with any browser. All URLs embedded in the pages are hyperlinks to make it easier for the user to work on the projects. The disk also includes an HTML version of Chapter 2, "Browser Details and Bookmarks in Netscape Navigator 3," which you might want to consult to go over the details of using the browser and working with bookmarks if you're using version 3 of Navigator. The diskette also contains an interactive search quiz, the 10-step search strategy that is discussed throughout the book, and other useful Web pages. To use the disk, start your computer, put the disk in drive A:, click on **Start** on the desktop, click on **Run**, type **A:Readme.txt**, and press **Enter**. Instructions will be displayed on the screen.

About Us

The material in this book is derived directly from our teaching and training experiences. During the past several years we've been involved in teaching students about using the Internet and the Web as resources for research. We have also led workshops for librarians, teachers, and other groups of professionals interested in using the Internet resources in their work. We have conducted presentations about finding and evaluating resources on the Web. As a reference librarian and a professor of computer science, we work as researchers ourselves.

Acknowledgments

There are many people to thank for the encouragement, friendship, support, and help that carried us through the 14 months of work on this project. We owe our greatest thanks, as always, to our immediate and extended families. They, more than anyone else, have made it possible for us to complete this work. Ernie wishes to thank his wife Lynn for all her help, love, and support—reading drafts and making improvements; being encouraging and supportive always, especially when work-related and personal pressures built up; and (as she says) keeping herself amused. He also wants to thank his children, Karl and Oliver, for their special encouragement, interest, and advice, and for giving him the most important reasons for writing. Karen wishes to especially thank her husband, Jack, and their daughters Tracy and Hilary for their patience and support throughout the past year and two months while she worked on this book. They never complained that she was unavailable for conversation and help on most weekends and evenings.

We want to thank all the people who fall into the categories of friends, colleagues, and students in Fredericksburg, Virginia, and Mary Washington College who have given us their support, encouragement, help, and understanding. We also want to thank all the people involved with developing, producing, and improving the ways we can use the Web and the Internet for research and finding information.

Franklin, Beedle & Associates has been a very supportive and co-operative publisher and has helped us greatly throughout this project. The folks we have worked with most directly include Jim, Tom, Susan, Stephanie, Cary, Carrie, Vic, Jason, Marc, Sue, Chris, and Ann.

This book has been through several reviews and we want to thank our reviewers—Mimi Will of Foothill College, Kris Chandler of Pikes Peak Community College, Bill O'Connor of Western Montana College, UM, Lois Davis of Casper College, Kath Finney of Central Oregon Community College, and David Bullock of Portland State University—for their helpful, insightful, and frank comments and suggestions.

We especially want to thank Kris Chandler, who used a draft of this book for her course at Pikes Peak Community College during the summer of 1997. Her comments and the comments of her students were very useful to us.

We hope you like this book and find it useful. Please feel free to send us email to let us know your opinions, suggestions, or comments about our work. When you have the time, visit our home pages at **http://www.mwc.edu/ernie** and **http://library.mwc.edu/karen**.

Ernest Ackermann
Department of Computer Science
Mary Washington College
ernie@mwc.edu
http://www.mwc.edu/ernie

Karen Hartman
Simpson Library
Mary Washington College
khartman@mwc.edu
http://library.mwc.edu/karen

Manuscript Reviewers

Many thanks for the thoughtful feedback from the following reviewers:

Mimi Will, Foothill College
Kris Chandler, Pikes Peak Community College
Bill O' Connor, Western Montana College, UM
Lois Davis, Casper College
Kath Finney, Central Oregon Community College
David Bullock, Portland State University

Chapter 1

Introduction to the World Wide Web

Every day millions of people around the world use their computers to access the information that makes up the World Wide Web. They search for and retrieve information on all sorts of topics in a wide variety of areas, including the arts, business, government, humanities, news, politics, recreation, and the sciences. The information can appear in a variety of digital formats, such as text, images, audio, or video. It's becoming more the case that if something can be put into a digital format, then it can be shared through the Web. Individuals, companies, research labs, libraries, news organizations, television networks, governments, and other organizations all make resources available. People communicate with each other using electronic mail; they share information and make commercial and business transactions. All this activity is possible because tens of thousands of networks are connected to the Internet and exchange information in the same basic ways. The World Wide Web (WWW) is part of the Internet, but it's not a collection of networks. Rather, it's the information that is connected or linked in a sort of web. Never before has so much information from such a wide variety of sources and in so many formats been available to the public.

Using a Web browser—the computer program or software that lets you access the World Wide Web—you can find information on almost any topic with just a few clicks of your mouse button. Some of the resources on the Web have been classified into directories that you can easily browse by going from one category to another. Several search tools (programs that search the Web for resources) are readily available. When you type a keyword or phrase into a form and click on a button or icon on the screen, a list of items appears in the browser's window. You simply click on the ones you want to retrieve. The amount and variety of information available are astounding, but it's sometimes difficult to find appropriate material.

This chapter covers some of the basic information and concepts you need to begin finding information on the World Wide Web. The sections in this chapter are as follows:
* The World Wide Web as an Information Resource
* Hypertext and Hypermedia
* Key Terms and Concepts
* Information Sources Available on the Web

1

About This Book

This book is designed to help anyone who uses the WWW to find information or research a topic. We'll cover the tools and methods with which you search for resources on the World Wide Web, and we will explain how to access and use those tools. We'll go over the methods and techniques to use so you can be effective and efficient in your searching and researching. We'll also talk about how to evaluate and cite resources within the context of a research project. The text, activities, and exercises are designed to give you the experience you need to tap the cornucopia of information on the WWW, find the resources you want, and—just as important—evaluate the material you've found. Prior experience with the World Wide Web isn't necessary, but it will help you move through some of the material more quickly.

Each of the chapters contains at least one detailed activity in which you work with a Web browser to access information on the World Wide Web. These activities demonstrate concepts and techniques. As you read the activities and follow along, you'll receive step-by-step instructions for working with the World Wide Web. Remember, though, that these activities reflect the World Wide Web at the time of writing. Because some things change frequently, they may not appear to you on your screen as they do in this book. The World Wide Web and the Internet are constantly changing, but don't let that hold you back. Be persistent and use your skills to work in this important environment. Change is one of the things that make the Internet and the World Wide Web exciting, vigorous, and useful.

At the end of the chapter, we provide a chapter summary, a list of terms, and finally some exercises. The terms are defined in the chapter and also appear in the glossary at the back of the book. The exercises or projects will help you practice using the World Wide Web and will reinforce the concepts in the chapter. Take the time to do as many as you can.

Click and Double-Click

We'll be using the term *click on* regularly. To click on something, you use a mouse to point to it and then press the mouse button. If your mouse has two buttons, press on the left button. To double-click, press the (left) button twice in rapid succession without moving the mouse.

This book assumes you have Microsoft Windows. If you're in another windowed environment, on a workstation that uses X Windows, or on a Macintosh, you'll find that most of the instructions are the same.

The World Wide Web as an Information Resource

You can think of the **World Wide Web (WWW)** as a large collection of information that's accessible through the Internet. The **Internet** is a collection of tens of thousands of computer networks that exchange information according to some agreed-upon, uniform rules or protocols. Because of this uniformity, a computer connected to one of the Internet's networks can transport text and images and display them on a computer connected to another part of the Internet.

Whether you've worked on the WWW before or not, you'll be pleased with how easy it is to use. It's also enticing. The World Wide Web gives a uniform means of accessing all the different types of information on the Internet. Since you only need to know one way to get information, you concentrate on what you want, not on how to obtain it. The Internet is commonly used throughout the world, so the WWW gives us easy and relatively quick access to information on a global scale. That alone is remarkable, but it gets better. The information on the Web is often in a multimedia format called a *Web page*, which may combine text, images, audio, or video. This format lets us take advantage of modern computers' multimedia capabilities. A Web page can also contain links to other resources or information on the World Wide Web; these connections allow us to examine, work with, or explore related material. This is why it's called a web: one page contains links to another, and that one contains links to another, and so on. Since the information can be anywhere in the world, the term World Wide Web is most appropriate.

Tim Berners-Lee, credited with the concept of the WWW, made the following statement in the document "About the World Wide Web": "The World Wide Web (known as 'WWW', 'Web' or 'W3') is the universe of network—accessible information, the embodiment of human knowledge." (By the way, you can find that document on the WWW by using the URL **http://www.w3.org/hypertext/www/www**. We'll say more a little later about how to use URLs.) Berners-Lee has made a strong statement, but it's certainly true. There's a wide range of materials available on such subjects as art, science, humanities, politics, law, business, education, and government information. In each of these areas you can find scientific and technical papers, financial data, stock market reports, government reports, advertisements, and publicity and news about movies and other forms of entertainment. Through the WWW you can find information about many types of products, information about health and environmental issues, government documents, and tips and advice on recreational activities such as camping, cooking, gardening, and travel. You can tour museums, plan a trip, make reservations, visit gardens throughout the world, and so on. Just a little bit of exploring will show you the wide range and types of information available.

To access the Web, you start a program on your computer called a *Web browser*. The browser makes the connections to a specific WWW site, retrieves information from the site, and displays it in a window on your screen. The information in the window is often in multimedia format; it may have text, images, video, or audio. From there, you can go to other locations on the Internet to search for, browse, and retrieve information. You use a mouse to move a hand or pointer to an icon, menu item, region of a map or image, button, or underlined portion of the window, and click the mouse button (the left one if your mouse has more than one button). These items are called *hyperlinks*, or *links* for short. If you've clicked on a link in the document, the browser follows that link; the current document is replaced or another window pops up. Some Web pages, including those you'll use for searching and researching, have a place for you to type in a word or phrase, fill out a form, or check off options. Using a Web browser is a relatively easy way to work with information on the WWW.

Items that are accessible through the WWW give hypertext access to the Internet. In order for this to work, there are standard ways of specifying the links and creating documents that can be displayed as part of the WWW. Information is exchanged according to a specific set of rules, or *Hypertext Transfer Protocol (HTTP)*; each link has a particular format, or a *Uniform Resource Locator (URL)*; and Web pages are written using a language called *Hypertext Markup Language (HTML)*, which the browser can interpret.

The browser window also has text and icons in the borders, outside the portion of the window containing the Web page. Clicking on text or icons in the upper border of a window pops up a menu or a dialog box from which you can choose an action. Figure 1.1 shows these and other portions of a browser window.

Throughout this book, we'll use version 4 of Netscape Navigator as the browser. If you're using a different browser—such as an earlier version of Netscape Navigator, Microsoft Internet Explorer, or the AOL browser—you'll see lots of similarities. While your view might be slightly different, we've tried not to rely on any special features of Netscape Navigator 4. That way, the explanations and activities will be meaningful regardless of the browser you're using.

Figure 1.1 shows the home page for the Library of Congress. When a site has several Web pages available, as the Library of Congress's Web site does, the one that acts as the first or introductory page is called the *home page*. The term home page is used in other ways as well. Lots of people have Web pages that tell something about themselves; a page like that is called a personal home page. The first page you see when you start your browser is called the home page for the browser.

Hypertext and Hypermedia

When you use the WWW, you work in a hypertext or *hypermedia* environment. That means you move from item to item and back again without having to follow a predefined path. You follow hyperlinks according to your needs. Sometimes the items you select are part of other sentences or paragraphs; the links to other Internet resources are presented in context. The links can also be represented by icons or images,

Figure 1.1—Home Page for the Library of Congress

or they may be regions in a map or display. Working with hyperlinks is fundamental to using the World Wide Web effectively, so we'll go into a little bit of detail on this topic.

The term *hypertext* is used to describe text that contains links to other text. When the hypertext and links are from a variety of media (text, video, sound), as is the case in the WWW, we use the term hypermedia. On a screen or page, certain items will be boldfaced, underlined, or colored differently. Each one represents a link to another part of the current document, screen, page, file, image, or other Internet resource. Selecting one of these links allows you to follow or jump to the information the link represents. You can also return to a previous link. There's a definite starting point, but the path you take after that is your choice. You are not constrained by having to go in some sort of straight line; you can think of being able to move up, down, right, or left from any link.

As an example, we'll look at an excerpt from a hypertext glossary. The definitions and explanations in the glossary are connected through hypertext. The excerpt here comes from a glossary of Internet terms that accompanies the book *Learning to Use the World Wide Web*, by Ernest Ackermann. This glossary is available on the WWW in hypertext form. To see it, use the URL **http://www.mwc.edu/ernie/lrn-web-glossary.html**. Here's the excerpt:

> **Web Page** The information available and displayed by a **Web browser** as the result of opening a local file or opening a location (**URL**). The contents and format of the Web page are specified using **HTML**.

If you used your mouse to select one of the underlined words or phrases and if you clicked on it, you'd be taken to another part of the glossary. For example, choosing (**URL**) takes you to a definition of URL (Uniform Resource Locator). From there you could browse the glossary by following other links, or you could return to the entry for Web page. You could always follow the links back to the place you started. The information in the glossary wouldn't change, but the way you accessed it and the order in which you did so would change.

Before we discuss other concepts related to the World Wide Web, let's do an activity that shows what we might see when we start a Web browser and search for some information. We'll use Netscape Navigator, the most popular browser, for all the activities in the book. Except for some of the details we give in Chapter 2, we won't focus on the features of the Web browser you use. We hope that the explanations and activities will be meaningful to you regardless of your browser.

✳ Tip

This is the first of many activities in this book. You'll see that each activity is divided into two parts: "Overview" and "Details." In the first part, "Overview," we discuss what we'll be doing and enumerate the steps we'll follow. The section "Details" goes through the steps, shows the results we got when we tried the activity, and provides some discussion. Your results might be different from what's shown here, but that's part of the dynamic nature of the Web; things are always changing. Don't let those changes confuse you. Follow the steps, use what's here as a guide, and pay attention to what you see. As you work through this and other activities, ✳ Do It indicates something for you to do. These activities are meant to be teaching devices to help you learn fundamental skills that don't change, even though the number of results obtained or the actual screens may look very different.

✳

Activity 1.1   First Look at Using a Web Browser to Find Information on the Web

Overview

Here we're assuming the program is properly set up on your computer and that you have a way of connecting to the Internet.

In going through the steps of this activity, we'll start the browser, explain some of the items you'll see on your screen, and then look at a subject directory that gives you access to lots of information. Finally, we'll exit the Web browser. We'll follow these steps:

1. Start the Web browser.
2. Go to the Yahoo! directory.
3. Explore the WWW.
4. Exit the Web browser.

These steps will allow us to look at using a Web browser and Netscape Navigator and will set a context for some of the concepts and terms in this book. Now for the details.

Details

1   Start the Web browser.

You start the Web browser Netscape Navigator either by clicking on an icon labeled **Netscape** or choosing **Netscape** from a menu. In some cases you may have to select a program group from the list of programs you can run, or you may have a shortcut to Netscape on your desktop. If you're using a different browser, you'll probably start it in the same way but by clicking on another icon.

Suppose the Netscape icon is on your desktop.

✳️*Do It!* Double-click on the Netscape icon. Locate an icon that looks like one of the following:

Netscape
Communicator

Netscape
Communicator

Clicking this icon starts Netscape Navigator. A window similar to the one in Figure 1.1 will appear on your screen, although the contents will be different.

In some cases, clicking the icon will cause your computer to go through the steps necessary to connect to the Internet. If you use a modem to connect to the Internet, the program to use the modem will start, and the modem will dial a number to connect to the Internet.

If you're familiar with a windowed environment, you should feel very comfortable using a Web browser. You work with many of the items in this window in the same way as with any other window. You can resize the window or switch between the window and an icon that represents the window. The menu commands are listed across the top row. They include:

File   Edit   View   Go   Communicator   Help

The menu bar contains items (such as **File**, **Edit**, and **Help**) that are common to several windowed applications. Each command has a pulldown menu; click on the command and a menu will appear.

The browser's window also has several icons in the command toolbar, as we've pointed out in Figure 1.1. You can use them to go from one Web page to another, print a Web page, stop the current page that is loading, and so forth. For example, you click on the icon labeled **Back** to go to the previous Web page. Some of the icons take you to other Web pages or services. Click on the button labeled **Search** to get a Web page with hyperlinks to several search engines.

It's important for you to know how to get online help. As you may have guessed, one way is to use the pulldown menu item Help, which has a link to online help.

2   Go to the Yahoo! directory.

There's lots of information on the WWW, and it's just about impossible to keep track of it all. To assist you, some hyperlinks are arranged by category to create directories. One popular, large, and well-designed directory is named Yahoo! (You can get to that directory and some others by clicking on the button labeled **Search**.) Here we'll go directly to the home page for Yahoo! by typing its URL in the location field (also called the location box) of the browser window and then pressing the **Enter** key. The location field is shown in Figure 1.1. It should currently hold the URL of the current Web page. The field is labeled either **Location:** or **NetSite:**.

⟨Do It⟩ Use the mouse to point to the location field and click the (left) mouse button.

When you click on the location field, it changes color. By typing, you can replace the current URL.

⟨Do It⟩ Type **http://www.yahoo.com** in the location field and press **Enter**.

This URL brings you to the beginning of the Yahoo! directory—its home page. After you type new text into the location field, its label will change to **Go to:** as shown in Figure 1.2.

Type the URL http://www.yahoo.com
in the location field and press **Enter**

Figure 1.2—Location Field with the URL http://www.yahoo.com

When you press **Enter**, your Web browser sends a request to the Yahoo! Web server, the computer that makes Yahoo! Web pages available. The server then sends the Web page with the address (or URL) **http://www.yahoo.com**—the Yahoo! home page—to your computer. The Web page is sent across the Internet. If there aren't any problems and your Internet connection isn't too slow, you ought to have the Yahoo! home page on your screen in a few seconds. (Pretty neat, huh?) The home page for Yahoo! appears in Figure 1.3.

Figure 1.3—Home Page for Yahoo!

You don't have to type the complete URL in the location field when you're using Netscape Navigator version 2 or later. Omitting the leading **http://www.**, you can just type **yahoo.com** in the location field. The browser will retrieve the page whose full URL is **http:// www.yahoo.com**.

Another way to get to Yahoo! and other search services is to click on the directory button labeled **Net Search**. The contents of the browser window will be replaced by a Web page that lists several search services. If the **Yahoo!** directory doesn't appear at first, you can get to it by clicking on **Yahoo!** in the short list of directories near the top.

3   Explore the WWW.

An easy way to explore the WWW is to follow hyperlinks. When you start with a directory such as Yahoo!, you can do plenty of exploring. Clicking on the link **Science** as indicated in Figure 1.3 will take you to a window such as the one shown in Figure 1.4.

Do It! Use the mouse to point to the hyperlink **Science** and click on the (left) mouse button.

In Figure 1.4, we've pointed out an advertisement near the top of the window. You may come across these sorts of ads on lots of Web pages. If you click on the ad, the browser will bring up another Web page that's designed to inform you about or sell you a product or a service. Feel free to look, but remember that the advertisement is likely to be marketing something and will definitely take you away from the task at hand.

In the next step we're going to click on the hyperlink **Astronomy**. If that one isn't in your window, use the scroll bar to go down the page, as indicated in Figure 1.4.

Figure 1.4—Yahoo! Science

You can see that there are still many topics to explore. We will choose one.

✳️*Do It!* Use the mouse to point to the hyperlink **Astronomy** and click once with the (left) mouse button.

Figure 1.5 shows a portion of the Web page under the heading "Astronomy."

Figure 1.5—Yahoo! Science: Astronomy

There are lots of links to follow here, and you can follow these to explore the WWW. You'll find you can move from page to page easily with a little practice. Press the toolbar button **Back**, [icon], to go back through previous pages. Spend some time exploring these topics or others.

All pages from Yahoo! contain a search form that you can use to search for information. There are times you'll want to do a search rather than browse the directory, and we discuss that in Chapter 3. Before you start a search here or with other directories and search tools, be sure to read whatever online material is available about help, tips, or options. Learning how to use the search facilities of a directory or search engine will save you time later.

When you're ready, go on to the next step.

4   Exit the Web browser.

Of course, you can exit Netscape Navigator in the same way you exit most other windowed applications. You can do one of the following:

❋   Click on **File** in the menu bar and select **Exit**.
❋   Press [Alt] + **F** and then **X**.
❋   Double-click on the button in the upper-left corner of the window.

The window will close, and you will have ended this session with Netscape Navigator. If you're paying by the minute or hour for the connection and you want to stop working with the Internet for the time being, be sure your connection is terminated.

_____ End of Activity 1.1 _____

In Activity 1.1 we looked at starting the Web browser, browsing the Web directory Yahoo!, and ending a browser session.

We'll go over lots more details about using the browser in the next chapter. Now we'll go over some key terms and concepts related to the Web and the way information is presented on it.

Key Terms and Concepts

In this section we'll discuss some of the terms and concepts that are important to know about as you're working with the Internet and the Web. The topics we'll cover include:

❋   Client/Server
❋   HTTP (Hypertext Transfer Protocol)
❋   HTML (Hypertext Markup Language)
❋   URL (Uniform Resource Locator)
❋   Error Messages
❋   Bookmarks

❈ Common Types of Files on the Internet and the Web

❈ Sharing and Copying Information Found on the Internet and the World Wide Web

❈ Selected Web-based Guides to the Internet and the World Wide Web

Client/Server

When you start a WWW browser or follow a hyperlink, the browser sends a request to a site on the Internet. That site returns a file that the browser then has to display. This sort of interaction in which one system requests information and another provides it is called a ***client/server*** relationship. The browser is the client, and a computer at the site that provides the information is the server.

HTTP (Hypertext Transfer Protocol)

The documents or screens are passed from a server to a client according to specific rules for exchanging information. These rules are called protocols. The protocol used on the WWW is named HTTP, which stands for Hypertext Transfer Protocol, because the documents, pages, or other items passed from one computer to another are in hypertext or hypermedia form.

HTML (Hypertext Markup Language)

The rules for creating or writing a Web page are all specified as HTML— Hypertext Markup Language. This language provides the formal rules for marking text. The rules govern how text is displayed as part of a Web page. HTML would be used, for example, to mark text so that it appears in boldface or italics. In order for text or an icon to represent a hyperlink, it has to be marked as a link in HTML, and the URL has to be included. The URL doesn't appear, however, unless someone looks at the page with a browser. Web pages are usually stored in files with names that end in **.html** or **.htm**.

In order for you to see or hear what's in the file, the browser has to be able to interpret the file's contents. Depending on the type of file, the browser may display text, graphics, or images. If the file is written using HTML, the browser interprets the file so that graphics and images are displayed along with the text. Depending on the HTML code in the file, the text is displayed in different sizes and styles, and hyperlinks are represented on the page.

URL (Uniform Resource Locator)

The hyperlinks are represented in a specific format called a URL, or Uniform Resource Locator. The portion of the Netscape window labeled Location: holds the document's URL. Each Web page has a URL as its address. For example, the URL for the Library of Congress's home page is **http://www.loc.gov**.

The URLs that point to Web pages or home pages all start with **http://**, because they are all transmitted according to HTTP. You'll see something different for URLs that access information through other Internet services or protocols. ***FTP***, or ***File Transfer Protocol***, was one of the first protocols used on the Internet to exchange files. It's still in common use. For example, the URL for the NASA collection of space images is **ftp://ftp.jpl.nasa.gov/pub/images**.

You'll find it helpful to think of a URL as having the form:

```
how-to-get-there://where-to-go/what-to-get
```

You'll see in later chapters that URLs are used in the following ways:

❋ All hyperlinks on Web pages are represented as URLs.

❋ The entries in the bookmark and history file are stored as URLs.

❋ You type in a URL when you want to "open a location" (direct your browser to go to a specific Web page).

When you cite a resource on the World Wide Web, you include the URL for it. You'll also want to include the URL when you're telling someone else about a resource, such as in an email message. It's much more effective to include URLs. Here's an example:

A good resource for information about African studies is the "African Studies" page **http://www.vibe.com/history/africanstudies/africanwww.html** of the *World Wide Web Virtual Library* at **http://vlib.stanford.edu/Overview.html**

People reading this message can use their browsers to go directly to the items you mention.

We will now show you the different parts of a URL so that you have a better idea about the information a URL conveys:

Most URLs have this format. By indicating which Internet protocol to use, they tell you how to retrieve the information. By naming both the Web server and the file or directory holding the information, they tell you where the site is located. If only a server name is present and not a file name, as in **http://www.loc.gov**, you still retrieve a file; by default, the server passes along a certain file, usually named **index.html**. Sometimes you'll see URLs written without **http:** in front. You can safely omit **http:** when you open a Web page or location by typing the URL into the browser's location field.

As amazing as some computer systems are, they generally need very precise instructions. So you have to be careful about spacing (generally there aren't blank spaces in a URL), the symbols used (a slash and a period are not interchangeable), and the case of the letters. Here's an example:

The URL for the frequently asked questions (FAQ) for finding email addresses is **http://www.qucis.queensu.ca/FAQs/email/finding.html**. Replacing email with EMAIL, as in the URL **http://www.qucis.queensu.ca/FAQs/EMAIL/finding.html**, will cause the server to report an error back to the browser. The following will be displayed:

```
404 Not Found
The requested URL /FAQs/EMAIL/finding.html was not
found on this server.
```

The error message tells us that part of the URL was correct—the name of the Web server, **www.qucis.queensu.ca**—but that the Web server could not find the file on the server because there was something wrong with the rest of the URL.

Error Messages

A message such as this is called a 404 Error. You may see this error message if the URL is incorrect. Sometimes you'll also get this error message if a Web page has been removed from a Web server or is no longer available. If you click on a hyperlink and get a 404 error, you may have come upon what is sometimes called a dead link.

Here's another message you may see:

```
403 Forbidden
Your client does not have permission to get URL
/ernie/abc.html from this server.
```

That means the URL was correct and the file is on the server, but the file isn't available to the public.

If the URL contains the name of a Web server that your browser can't find, you'll see an error message such as this:

```
Host Name Lookup Problem
Check the spelling and try again.
```

Bookmarks

When you find a site on the Web that you'd like to visit again, you can save it for future reference, with what Netscape calls a ***bookmark***, to the site. A bookmark is a link to a Web page, and the collection of the bookmarks you've saved is called the ***bookmark list***. You'll find using bookmarks very useful. We show how you can manage the bookmark list in the next chapter.

To save a Web page as a bookmark, click on Bookmarks in the menu bar and then click on Add Bookmark. That puts the bookmark in the bookmark list. To visit a site you've saved as a bookmark, click on Bookmarks in the menu bar and then either click on a bookmark that's in the list or click on Go to Bookmarks to select one. Selecting Go to Bookmarks also lets you manage the bookmark list.

Common Types of Files on the Internet and the Web

Web pages can contain text, images, video, audio, and other types of information. Either these will be part of the Web page or there will be hyperlinks to information in a variety of formats. Although information can appear as text, it is sometimes stored in a compressed format (to save space) or in some other form. In many cases, the Web browser can display the information in the file if it's an image or a video, or it can convert the file's contents to sound if it's an audio file (and if your computer is equipped with a sound card and speakers or earphones). In other cases, you need to get the appropriate software so that your computer can deal with the files.

Sometimes you can tell the file type by its name. The letters at the end of a file name following a dot (**.**) are called the file extension portion of the file name. Files whose names end with **.txt** or **.text**, for example, usually contain only plain, printable characters.

We won't go into all the details here, but we will list some of the more common file formats. For more information about using different file formats, check the online help that comes with your browser—click on Help in the menu bar of Netscape Navigator—or use your browser to access the following two excellent resources (we list titles, authors, and URLs):

- ❀ *Common Internet File Formats*, Eric Perlman and Ian Kallen, **http://www.matisse.net/files/formats.html**
- ❀ *Multimedia File Formats on the Internet*, Allison Zhang, **http://rodent.lib.rochester.edu/multimed/ contents.htm**

Text Files

Plain text files contain plain printable characters, like the ones you see on this page, but without special fonts or typefaces, such as italic or bold. They're also called ASCII (rhymes with pass key) files. ASCII stands for American Standard Code for Information Interchange, and it is the standard code used to represent characters in digital format in a computer. All browsers can display these files, and they often appear as if they were typed on a typewriter or computer terminal. Files of this type usually have names that end with **.txt**, **.asc**, or **.doc**.

PostScript file format was invented by Adobe Systems. The files contain text but usually not in a readable format. The files also contain commands that a printer or display device interprets; the commands pertain to formatting, different fonts, font sizes, and images in the file. Files of this type usually have names that end with **.ps**.

Adobe Systems also invented PDF (Portable Document Format). These files contain instructions so that they can be displayed with different fonts and typefaces, different colors, and images. You can view these files on your computer if you have Adobe Acrobat software, which is free from the *Adobe Acrobat* Web site, **http://www.adobe.com/ prodindex/acrobat**.

Compressed Files

Files are compressed to save space on a server and to transfer a file over the Internet more quickly. There are many types of compressed files, but the most common are those ending with **.zip**. If you retrieve a file in compressed format, you'll need software to uncompress the file. Two popular shareware programs work with these types of files:

* PKZIP   **http://www.pkware.com**
* WinZip   **http://www.winzip.com**

The frequently asked questions (FAQ) for the Usenet newsgroup comp.compression, **http://www.cis.ohio-state.edu/hypertext/faq/ usenet/compression-faq/top.html**, contains lots of detailed questions and answers about compressed files.

Image Files

Graphic images are stored in files in a variety of formats. As a part of a Web page or on their own, most browsers can display images stored in GIF (Graphics Interchange Format) or JPEG (Joint Photographic Expert Group) format. Files with images in these formats have names ending with **.gif**, **.jpg**, or **.jpeg**. Another format, TIFF (Tagged Image File Format), can store high-quality images. Files with images in TIFF have names ending in **.tif** or **.tiff**. If your browser cannot display files in TIFF, you'll have to get some other software to display them. Two shareware programs can display images in various formats and can convert from one format to another:

* Lview Pro

  ftp://uiarchive.cso.uiuc.edu/pub/systems/pc/ simtelnet/win95/graphics/lview1d2.zip
* Paint Shop Pro

  http://www.jasc.com/psp.html

Audio Files

These files contain information that's in an audio or sound format. With a sound card and speakers, you can play such files on your computer. Audio files often have one of the following three formats:

* Next/Sun format (file names end with **.au**)
* Waveform audio format (WAV), a standard format for computers using Microsoft Windows (file names end with **.wav**)
* RealAudio format (file names end with **.ra**)

If you're using Netscape Navigator version 3 or later, the browser contains the software to deal with all three types. Next/Sun and WAV files tend to be very large and thus may take a long time to retrieve. The RealAudio format uses a different technology called streaming in which sound becomes available as it's transferred to your computer through the Internet. A free player for RealAudio files is available from the URL **http://www.real.com/products/playerdl.html**.

Multimedia Files

With these types of files, you can view video and hear accompanying sound. It's similar to viewing a movie or television. Two popular formats are MPEG (Moving Picture Expert Group) and QuickTime (created by Apple Computer). Netscape Navigator version 3 or later can display files in MPEG format. File names in this format end with **.mpg** or **.mpeg**. QuickTime file names end with **.mov** or .qt. A QuickTime player is available at no cost at **http://quicktime.apple.com/sw**.

Sharing and Copying Information Found on the Internet and the World Wide Web

Much of what you find on the WWW can be saved in a file on your computer, which makes it easy to share and distribute information on the Web. Exchanging information was one of the main reasons the WWW project (and the Internet) began. There's also a drawback to this. Free access to information makes it difficult to control unauthorized distribution of anything that's available through the WWW. Anyone with a Web browser can make an exact digital copy of information. This may be illegal. In many cases, documents on the Web come with statements explaining the rules for personal use. For example, here's a quote from **http://sunsite.unc.edu/expo/vatican.exhibit/exhibit/About.html** describing limitations to use of the materials in the exhibit **Rome Reborn** offered by the Library of Congress:

> The text and images in the Online Exhibit ROME RE-BORN: THE VATICAN LIBRARY AND RENAISSANCE CULTURE are for the personal use of students, scholars, and the public. Any commercial use or publication of them is strictly prohibited.

Remember that anything available in electronic form on the Internet or World Wide Web is a copyrighted work, and you need to treat it in the same way as a book, magazine, piece of art, play, or piece of recorded music. Just because something is available on the WWW doesn't mean that you may copy it. You are allowed to copy the material for personal use, but in almost every case, you cannot use it for commercial purposes without written permission from the copyright holder. The *Copyright Website*, **http://www.benedict.com**, by Benedict O'Mahoney, is a good resource for information about copyright issues.

Selected Web-based Guides to the Internet and the World Wide Web

Taking advantage of the resources on the World Wide Web, using a Web browser, and knowing about the Internet aren't difficult, but they require a lot of knowledge. If you're not familiar with the Web or the Internet, you may want to look at some Web-based guides. We will now present a list of some of the good ones available on the Web, giving you the name of the resource and its URL. To access any of these guides, double-click on the location field (it should turn blue), type the URL, and press Enter.

* *Getting Started on the Internet*

   http://www.imagescape.com/helpweb/welcome.html

* *Internet Web Text,* John December

   http://www.december.com/web/text

* *Library of Congress Brief Guides to the Internet*
   http://lcweb.loc.gov/loc/guides/aboutinet.html

* *Newbies Anonymous: A Newcomer's Guide to the Internet*

   http://www.geocities.com/thetropics/1945/ index1.htm

* *UCSD Science & Engineering Library—About the Net*
   http://scilib.ucsd.edu/aboutnet/aboutnet.html

There's a Web site to accompany the book you're reading, as well as some of our other books about using the Internet and the Web. Here's a list:

* *Learning to Use the Internet*

   http://www.mwc.edu/ernie/lrn-net.html

* *Learning to Use the World Wide Web*

   http://www.mwc.edu/ernie/Lrn-web.html

* *Searching and Researching on the Internet and the World Wide Web*

   http://www.mwc.edu/ernie/search-web.html

Information Sources Available on the Web

Because there's so much information available on the Web, it has to be organized so that you can find what you need. There must also be tools or programs to help you locate information. Throughout this book, we'll be discussing the major information sources on the Web.

Directories or Subject Catalogs

There are directories, arranged by subject, of a general collection of Internet and WWW resources. Several of the directories contain reviews or descriptions of the entries. We discuss them in detail in Chapter 4.

One way to access several of these is to go to the Web page with the URL **http://home.netscape.com/escapes/search** or to click on the button called Search in the command toolbar of Netscape Navigator 4. Another way is to go to the section "Searching the Internet" of the *Internet Scout Toolkit* at **http://www.cs.wisc.edu/scout/toolkit/search/index .html** and to click on "Subject Catalogs" or "Annotated Directories."

Search Engines

Search engines provide keyword searching capability. These are covered in Chapters 5 and 6.

One way to access several of these is to go to the Web page with the URL **http://home.netscape.com/escapes/search** or to click on the button Search in the command toolbar of Netscape Navigator 4. Another way is to go to the Web page for *Library of Congress Brief Guides to the Internet,* "Locating Information," **http://scout.cs.wisc.edu/scout/ toolkit**.

Meta-search Tools

Meta-search tools allow you to use several search engines. A meta-search tool usually allows you to search several search engines or directories simultaneously. Many meta-search tools take your query, search several databases or search engines simultaneously, and then integrate the results. Some meta-search tools are good places to find lists of specialized databases.

Examples of meta-search tools are MetaCrawler, **http://www .metacrawler.com**, and the Internet Sleuth, **http://www.isleuth.com**.

Virtual Libraries

Virtual libraries are directories or subject catalogs consisting of Web resources that librarians or other information specialists have selected and evaluated. Arranged by subject, these are directories of a general collection of Internet and WWW resources. Several of the directories contain reviews or descriptions of the entries. We discuss them in detail in Chapters 4 and 7.

Two excellent examples are *The Internet Public Library,* **http:// www.ipl.org**, and *Librarians' Index to the Internet,* **http://sunsite .berkeley.edu/internetindex**.

Specialized Databases

Specialized databases can be comprehensive collections of hyperlinks in a particular subject area or self-contained indexes that are searchable and available on the Web. We discuss specialized databases in Chapter 7.

The Internet Sleuth, **http://www.isleuth.com**, accesses more than fifteen hundred specialized databases and directories.

Library Catalogs Accessible on the World Wide Web

Libraries have often been at the forefront of making resources available through the Internet, and thousands of libraries allow Internet and Web access to their catalogs of holdings. We discuss searching library catalogs in Chapter 8.

Some resources for library catalogs accessible on the World Wide Web are *WebCATS*, **http://library.usask.ca/hywebcat**, and *Libweb*, **http://sunsite.berkeley.edu/libweb**.

FTP Archives

FTP stands for File Transfer Protocol. Dating back to the early 1970s, it's the original protocol used to share files among computers with access to the Internet. Before the appearance of the World Wide Web, FTP was the most popular and effective way of sharing information and resources. Naturally, people started collecting files and saving them in archives available to anyone with a connection to the Internet. There are thousands of FTP archives containing information in various formats, such as text, data, programs, images, and audio. We discuss using FTP and FTP archives in Chapter 9.

Several Web sites allow you to search FTP archives and make it relatively easy to retrieve files through FTP. One is *Filez*, **http://www.filez.com**.

Email Discussion Groups

Email discussion groups are sometimes called *interest groups, listserv,* or *mailing lists*. Internet users join, contribute to, and read messages to the entire group through email. Several thousand different groups exist. Individual groups may keep archives of the postings to the group, but most archives are arranged by date. In many cases, it's more appropriate to think of the group's members rather than the group's archives as a good resource for information. We discuss email discussion groups and archives in more detail in Chapter 11.

Several services let you search for discussion groups. One is Liszt, **http://www.liszt.com**.

Usenet Newsgroups

Usenet newsgroups are collections of group discussions, questions, answers, and other information shared through the Internet. The messages are called articles and are grouped into categories called newsgroups. The newsgroups number in the thousands, with tens of thousands of articles posted daily. We discuss Usenet and searching archives of Usenet articles in more detail in Chapter 11.

Many search engines include the option of searching archives of Usenet articles, and some services—such as Deja News, **http://www.dejanews.com**—keep large archives of Usenet articles.

Summary

Millions of people around the world use the Internet for communication, research, business, a source of information, and recreation. One of the most popular and effective ways to tap into its resources is through the World Wide Web (WWW). The WWW is a vast collection of information that's connected like a web. There is no beginning or end; the information is accessible in a nonlinear fashion through connections called hyperlinks. You view the resources on the WWW by using a program called a Web browser. This book concentrates on the Netscape Navigator browser. You navigate through the WWW by pointing to hyperlinks (underlined or boldfaced words or phrases, icons, or images) and clicking once with the mouse. To use the WWW and the Internet effectively, you need to know how to find and use the services, tools, and programs that give you access to their resources, as well as the sources of information.

It's possible to link information in almost any digital form on the World Wide Web. Text files, programs, charts, images, graphics files, digitized video, and sound files are all available. Not only can you find things from a variety of media, but you also get a great deal of information in many categories or topics.

When using the WWW, you work in a hypertext or hypermedia environment. Items, services, and resources are specified by a Uniform Resource Locator, or URL. Web browsers use these URLs to specify the type of Internet service or protocol needed and the location of the item. For example, the URL for the Web page "Explore the Internet" (Library of Congress) is **http://lcweb.loc.gov/global/explore.html**. The protocol or service in this case is HTTP, or Hypertext Transfer Protocol, and a Web browser using that URL would contact the Internet site **lcweb.loc.gov** and access the file **explore.html** in the directory named global.

The documents on the WWW are called Web pages. These are written and constructed using a language called Hypertext Markup Language (HTML).

A Web browser is used to access the information and resources on the World Wide Web. Whenever you start the browser or access a hyperlink, the browser—which is a computer program—sends a request to have a file transferred to it. The browser then interprets the information in the file so that it can be viewed in the browser's window, or in some cases viewed through another program. For example, if a hyperlink points to a text file, the file is then displayed in the window as ordinary text. If the hyperlink points to a document written in Hypertext Markup Language (HTML), then it's displayed by the browser. If the file is a sound file or an animation, then a program different from the browser is started so the file can be heard or seen. Most of the facilities and capabilities are built into the browser, but in some cases your computer needs to be equipped with special equipment or programs. For instance, if a hyperlink points to a sound file, your computer needs to have a sound card, speakers, and the software to play the sounds.

Starting a Web browser usually means first activating your connection to the Internet and then clicking on an icon or command to start Netscape Navigator. If the cost of using the Internet depends on how much time you spend on the Net, then be sure to terminate the Internet connection when the Web session is over.

A number of different types of information sources are available on the World Wide Web. Those include:

* Directories of a general collection of Internet and WWW resources, arranged by subject.

* Search engines, which are tools that provide keyword searching capability.

* Meta-search tools, which allow you to access databases from one place.

* Virtual libraries, which are directories or subject catalogs consisting of selected Web resources.

* Specialized databases, which contain comprehensive collections of hyperlinks in a particular subject area, or which are self-contained, searchable indexes made available on the Web.

* Library catalogs accessible on the World Wide Web.

* FTP archives, which are collections of files in various formats available on the Internet.

* Email discussion groups, of which several thousand groups exist to share opinions and experiences, ask and answer questions, or post information about a specific topic.

* Usenet newsgroups, which are collections of group discussions, questions, answers, and other information that have been shared through the Internet.

Selected Terms Introduced in This Chapter

bookmark
bookmark list
client/server
File Transfer Protocol
    (FTP)
home page
hyperlink
hypermedia
hypertext
HyperText Markup Language
    (HTML)

HyperText Transfer Protocol
    (HTTP)
Internet
Uniform Resource Locator
    (URL)
Web browser
Web page
World Wide Web
    (WWW)

Exercises and Projects

These exercises and projects are designed to help you become familiar with using your Web browser, to have you visit several types of resources on the Web, and to give you some experience using Web resources to gather information. As you work through these exercises and projects, you're likely to find sites to which you'd like to return. In those cases, add them to your bookmarks!

1. Take some time to become familiar with your browser and the way it's set up.
   a. What Web page is displayed when you start the browser? What's its URL?
   b. List the steps, in a way that's easy to follow, for starting the Web browser on your computer.

2. Type the URL **http://www.yahoo.com** in the location field as in Activity 1.1. Go to the section **Recreation**. Visit the Web pages of three amusement parks on three different continents. Which ones did you visit? Where? If money and time were no concern, which one would you travel to tomorrow?

3. Go to the home page for Yahoo! You can do this by clicking on the word **Yahoo!** at the top of any of the **Yahoo!** Web pages or by typing the URL **http://www.yahoo.com** in the location field.
   a. We're going to try the search feature in Yahoo! Before searching, click on the hyperlink **options** and then **Help on Search**. Take some time to read about searching, and then go back to the Yahoo! home page.
   b. Using Yahoo!'s search feature, find three Web sites that deal with bungee jumping.

4. Do you know the meaning of the words *singultus* and *mendacious*? What would you do if you were diagnosed with singultus? Would you be offended or pleased if someone described your behavior as mendacious? Before answering these questions, look up the meanings of the words in a dictionary—on the Web.
   a. Go to the home page for Yahoo! Select the category **Reference**, **Dictionaries**, and then **English**. Search for these terms using one of the online versions of *Webster's Dictionary*. What do they mean?

b. Let's look for some other dictionaries. We're going to use WebCrawler. To access it, click once on the location field, type **http://webcrawler.com**, and press **Enter**. Once you're using WebCrawler, click on **Reference** and then **Dictionaries**. Click on the hyperlink **Search the Web for more about Dictionaries** on that Web page. Look for the hyperlink **Dictionary Index**. Follow hyperlinks until you get to *A Web of Online Dictionaries* by R. Beard, **http://www.bucknell.edu/~rbeard/diction.html**.

Describe what you find there. Use one of the specialized dictionaries to find a definition of the financial term *price earnings ratio*. What does the term *Blue Heeler* mean in Australian slang?

c. See if you can find the same Web page, *A Web of Online Dictionaries* hosted at Bucknell University, using Yahoo! If you found it, describe how you came upon it, and if you didn't find it, explain why.

5. When you click on the **Search** button in Netscape Navigator, four or five search services are featured. The previous exercises gave you some experience using Yahoo! and WebCrawler.

a. Try the other three: Excite, Infoseek, and Lycos. Each has a hyperlink called **Travel**. Visit that section of each of the directories and describe what you find in each.

b. Suppose you were planning a trip to Buenos Aires. Which of the directories would you prefer to use to help you plan your trip? Why?

6. The Internet Sleuth lists more than fifteen hundred specialized databases and directories. Go to its Web page: Click on the location field (it should turn blue), type **http://www.isleuth.com**, and press **Enter**. You can find databases to search in many different categories. For each category given below, list the names and URLs of three databases.

a. Financial Aid (look in Business)
b. Employment
c. Earth Sciences
d. Airlines

7. Use the Internet Sleuth again, but this time pick one category of database. Pick three databases from that category and search each one using the same word or phrase. How do the results compare? Are you ready to choose one database over another? Explain.

8. Go to the Library of Congress, **http://www.loc.gov**.

a. What is "THOMAS" and how would you find it useful?
b. Follow the link to the American Memory Collection. What is it? What sorts of materials does it contain?

c.   Become familiar with the American Memory Collection and ways of searching it. Write a list of tips that would be useful to someone wanting to search or browse the collection.

9.   Go to the Internet Public Library, **http://www.ipl.org**. Type the URL in the location field.

a.   Describe the user interface. That is, tell what the home page looks like and how a user can access the other portions of the Web site. What's your opinion of the user interface? Why?

b.   Go to the Reference Collection (or Reference Center, as it's also called), then the section called Health & Medical Sciences, and then the section called Consumer Information. What do you find there?

c.   Describe some positive aspects about how information is arranged and displayed in the Internet Public Library.

10.   Now, let's pay a visit to another virtual library, *Librarians' Index to the Internet*. Its URL is **http://sunsite.berkeley.edu/internetindex**.

a.   Describe the user interface. That is, tell what the home page looks like and how a user can access the other portions of the Web site. What's your opinion of the user interface? Why?

b.   Go to the section called "Health, Medicine." What information does this library provide on consumer information within the areas of health and medicine?

c.   Describe some positive aspects about how information is arranged and displayed in the Librarians' Index to the Internet.

2
Chapter

Browser and
Bookmark Essentials

A Web browser helps you access the World Wide Web, the information on the Internet. In Chapter 1, we mentioned some details about using a browser. Chapter 2 will address the practical issues that arise when using a Web browser. This chapter will also explore the commands and tools that allow you to use the information and resources on the Web most effectively. We will focus on using Netscape Navigator version 4, but we'll do that in such a way that you'll be able to learn about other popular versions, such as Netscape Navigator 3 or Microsoft Internet Explorer. There are lots of similarities between all these versions.

We'll also cover the bookmark features of Netscape Navigator and discuss ways to manage bookmarks. You use bookmarks to save the locations, URLs, and names of useful and interesting Web pages or Web sites. With bookmarks, these sites will be easy to access whenever you're using a browser—they'll just be a click or two away.

The sections in this chapter are as follows:
* Surveying a Browser's Features
* Starting and Stopping the Web Browser
* Exploring the Web Browser's Window
* Using the Right Mouse Button
* Getting Around a Page and the World Wide Web
* Getting Help
* Saving, Printing, and Mailing Items from the WWW
* Using Bookmarks to Keep Track of Resources

Surveying a Browser's Features

Before we begin, let's discuss what you can expect from a Web browser. Of course, a Web browser will allow you to look at Web pages throughout the WWW or to connect to various sites to access information and explore resources. The Web browser will enable you to follow the hyperlinks on a Web page and to type in a URL for it to follow. The browser should have a number of other commands readily available through menus, icons, and buttons. And what about the times you need help? Your browser ought to include an easy way to find online help, as well as built-in links to other resources on the Web that can give you help or answers.

You'll definitely want a way to save links to sites you've visited on the WWW so you can return to them during other sessions. Web browsers meet this need in two ways—with a ***history list***, which keeps a record of the Web pages you've come across in recent sessions, and with a ***bookmark list***, which you use to note the WWW pages you want to access in the future. Some browsers call these bookmarked sites *favorites*. The name of the site and its URL are kept in these lists. The browser contains tools to manage and arrange the bookmark list. For example, you'll be able to sort bookmarks and organize them into folders.

Web browsers include the means for you to search for information on a current Web page. You'll be able to save a Web page on your computer, print the page, and email its contents to others.

Some Web pages are designed using ***frames***. This design allows for several independent Web pages—with their own scroll bars and URLs— to be displayed in one window. When a page is in a frame, the browser allows you to save, print, or email a particular frame. Take a look at *Wired Cybrarian,* **http://www.wired.com/cybrarian**, as an example of a site that uses frames.

When you use the Web for searching and researching, you may need to fill out a form or transmit some information in a secure manner. Your browser can correctly display and handle this sort of Web page.

World Wide Web pages can contain text and images, as well as hyperlinks to digital audio, digital video, or other types of information. Your Web browser is probably equipped to handle many of these types. But whether you can access something also depends on the software and hardware on your computer. If you don't have the programs and the hardware (a sound card and speakers) to play a sound file, then your Web browser will be unable to handle sound files.

Web browsers do let you add to the list of software they use to display or play different media, however. If you come across a file or hyperlink to something the Web browser isn't configured to handle, you can add ***helper applications*** or ***plug-ins***. These programs allow you to work with certain types of files. You do this by setting options or preferences for your browser. In setting preferences, you can choose the font and colors used for displaying text, set your email address, and select other items. We'll go over setting preferences and working with helpers when appropriate in this chapter.

Here's a list of sources for more complete and detailed information:

For Netscape Navigator version 4:

❋ The section "The Preference Panels" of online help. (Press 1, click on **About Navigator**, and then click on **The Preference Panels**.)

For Netscape Navigator version 3:

❋ *Learning to Use the World Wide Web: Academic Edition* by Ernest Ackermann.

❋ *Netscape Navigator Handbook*, available online with URL **http://home.netscape.com/eng/mozilla/3.0/handbook**.

Starting and Stopping the Web Browser

A Web browser is a computer program, or software, which is run on your computer. Just like other programs, it has to be started before you use it. When you're finished browsing the Web, you'll want to end the Web session by stopping the browser or exiting the program.

Starting the Web Browser

Before you can start the browser, you need access to the Internet. If your computer is directly connected to a network, you have access to the Internet. If you gain access to the Internet by using a modem, you likely have SLIP or PPP access to the Internet. *SLIP (Serial Line Internet Protocol)* and *PPP (Point-to-Point Protocol)* are standards for transmitting information on the Internet over serial lines. A *modem* is a serial device, meaning that information is transmitted one bit at a time. To activate your connection, it may be enough to start Netscape Communicator or Navigator. This will start a program that dials the correct number and then prompts you for a login name and password. If you have a network card in your computer and you connect to your local network or the Internet through a cable, then different protocols are used. There are other variations, so it's a good idea to check with the folks who provide your Internet connection for the exact details.

If you're using Communicator, you may have to set up or select a user profile before you access Navigator. The first time you set up a user profile, you'll need to supply your name and email address, so be sure you know an email address to use before you start. You'll also be asked for the Internet address of the SMTP gateway (the computer that sends your email out) and the Internet address of your POP or IMAP server (the computer that receives and sends email to your computer). SMTP? POP server? This may seem confusing, but don't worry! Just be sure to get that information from your Internet service provider (ISP) or the people who support your computer system.

To start a Netscape session, double-click on the Netscape icon. Look for an icon that looks like one of the following:

Ending a Session on the WWW; Stopping the Browser

Ending a session on the WWW means stopping or leaving the browser program. You may also have to terminate your connection to the Internet.

You stop the Web browser program in the same way that you end almost any other Windows program or application. Here are some ways to do that:

* Double-click on the upper-left corner.
* Click on the **X** in the upper-right corner.
* Click on **File** in the menu bar, and then click on **Exit**.
* Press $\boxed{\text{Alt}}$ + **F**, and then press **X**.

Here are some ways to end the modem session, in case that doesn't happen automatically when Netscape ends:

* Click on the button **Disconnect** in the dialog box or window that represents your dialup networking connection.
* Select a command from a pulldown menu that hangs up the phone (modem).
* Choose an item from a menu that starts a logout or bye program.

Just remember to terminate the connection so that you or someone else doesn't get an expensive bill from the company that provides your Internet services.

If there is more than one open window with a connection to the Internet, such as another browser window or an email window, then you can close the current window without disconnecting from the Web or Internet. Follow any of the first three steps above for stopping a Web browser program, or press $\boxed{\text{Alt}}$ + **F**, and then press **Q**.

Exploring the Web Browser's Window

When you start a WWW browser, a window opens on your screen. It's the Web browser's job to retrieve and display a file inside the window. What is in the window will change as you go from site to site, but each window has the same format. The items that help you work with the Web document in the window include the scroll bar, the menu bar, and the toolbar, which are the same every time you use the browser. The major components of a Web page are labeled in Figure 2.1. They include the following:

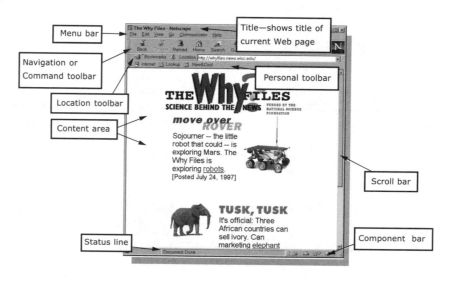

Menu bar

Title—shows title of current Web page

Navigation or Command toolbar

Personal toolbar

Location toolbar

Content area

Scroll bar

Status line

Component bar

Figure 2.1—Navigator Window with Major Components Labeled

Title

The title of the Web page is created when the page is written. A page's title is not the same as its URL, just as a book's title is different from its library call number.

Menu Bar

The *menu bar* near the top of the window includes:

File   Edit   View   Go   Communicator   Help

You choose any of these by moving the mouse pointer to the word and clicking on it. You can also activate one of these choices by using the **Alt** key along with the underlined letter. For example, to display the menu associated with **File**, use **Alt** + **F**.

Selecting an item from the menu bar brings forth a pulldown menu with several options. For example, if you click on **File**, you see the menu shown to the right:

Select any item in that menu either by clicking on it with the mouse or by pressing the underlined character in its name. To print the current Web page, you can click on **Print** in this menu or you can press **P** (upper- or lowercase). Some items on the menu are followed by Ctrl + a letter, such as the following:

Save As...   Ctrl + **S**

This means that to select the command from the menu, you can either click on **Save As** or use a keyboard shortcut, Ctrl + **S**. With this particular command, you save a copy of the Web page in a file on your computer.

When you select an item that's followed by **...**, as in **Save As...**, it brings up a dialog box. The box will request more information or will ask you to select additional options. If, for example, you select **Save As...**, you will then need to type in or select a file name. When you select an item that's followed by an arrow, as with **New**, it brings up another menu.

✴ Tip

Giving commands using the keyboard—keyboard shortcuts.

You can access all the commands for using a Web browser by pointing and clicking on a word, icon, or portion of the window, but sometimes you may want to give a command using the keyboard. To do this, use the keys labeled Ctrl or Alt, along with another key. For example, to mail a document to an Internet address, you can select **Mail** from a menu or use Ctrl+**M**. Using Ctrl+**M** means holding down the key labeled Ctrl, pressing the key labeled **M**, and then releasing them both. As another example, giving the command Alt+**H** will display a menu of items to select for helpful hints. You hold down the key labeled Alt, press **H**, and then release them both.

Here are some details about each of the pulldown menus:

File

Using the commands in the **File** menu, you can open a new browser window, send an email message, or open a page in the Web editor (Composer) that's part of Netscape Communicator. You can also use this menu to open a page in the browser—either a Web page (which you would open by giving its URL) or a file on your computer. You can go in "offline" mode, which means working with files or messages on your computer without being connected to the Internet. The menu options also allow you to print, mail, or save the current document into a file. One item related to printing lets you select a printer, and another lets you preview a document before it's printed. This menu has items that permit you to close the window, end the WWW session, or both. There are also menu items that let you work with frames if they're present.

Edit

Use the **Edit** menu to copy items from the current document to other applications, such as a word processor. You can also use **Copy** and **Paste** to copy URLs or email addresses from one window into the location field or address field of a message. In addition, the menu contains the item **Find**, which presents a dialog box that lets you search the current document for a word or phrase. The items **Search Internet** and **Search Directory** are used to search for items on the Internet or to search for email addresses or phone book information. **Preferences** brings up a screen through which you set preferences; these determine how the Web browser operates, what items appear in the window, and how a document looks. For example, you can set the programs that will be run to view images and play sound or video as part of a Web page. You can control what's shown on the screen and how Netscape works with your network and computer system. There's a separate item for the preferences that you must set to use email and Usenet news. These include the domain names or IP (Internet Protocol) addresses of the mail and news servers.

View

The items on the **View** menu change what you see and how you view those items. You can use this menu to hide any of the toolbars (or to show them if they're not in view) or to change the font size (the size of the letters in the Web page). You also use the **View** menu to reload a copy of the current document; this is useful if there have been some changes to the source page since it was originally loaded or if the images in a document were not loaded automatically. The menu has items to stop the current page from loading or to stop animations. The item **Page Source** lets you view the source version of the current page so you can see which HTML commands were used to create it. Selecting **Page Info** shows information about the current document, such as when it was last modified and whether it's a secure document (used for commercial or private transactions).

Go

Items in the **Go** menu take you to different documents or pages that you have viewed during the current Netscape session. Netscape keeps a list of the pages (the history list) you've traveled through to reach the current document. You can choose **Back** to return to the previous page or **Forward** to move to a page from which you've just come back. You can also go to the home page for that session or to any or the recent pages on the history list.

Communicator

An important use of the **Communicator** menu is to access the bookmark list. With that list, you can look up names of URLs that you've put in the list, add new items, and otherwise manage the bookmark list. The complete history list is available from this menu. You can also use this menu to reach the other components of Netscape Communicator, including the email system (Messenger Mailbox), Usenet newsreader (Collabra Discussion Groups), the Web page editor (Composer), Address Book, and others. Selecting **Security Info** gives information about the current Web page, including whether it was sent in a secure (encrypted) mode and the name of the Web server from which it was sent.

Help

Choose the **Help** menu to obtain information about using the Web browser. This menu includes a link to online help, product information and support (which itself has links to lots of helpful information), and information about netiquette, plug-ins or helpers, and other items.

Toolbars

Web browsers, like other Windows software, have one or more rows of icons called *toolbars* just below the menu bar. Each icon works like a button. When you press it with the mouse, some operation or action takes place. In some cases, a dialog box pops up. For example, if you click on the icon to print the current document, you can select a printer and specify whether you want to print the whole document or just a part of it. The icons give you a visual clue to the operation or action they represent. The commands they represent are all available through the items on the menu bar, but the icons give a direct path, a shortcut to the commands. There are three toolbars in Netscape Navigator version 4: the navigation toolbar (also called the command toolbar), the location toolbar, and the personal toolbar. You can hide each toolbar by clicking on its left edge, making it disappear from the browser window. Click on the edge again to make it reappear.

Navigation Toolbar

Table 2.1 explains all the icons in the navigation toolbar—also called the command toolbar.

Name	Icon	Explanation
Back, Forward		These two buttons with directional arrows move between documents or Web pages that you've already seen. **Back** takes you to the previous page, and **Forward** can only be used if you've previously used **Back**. To obtain a list of sites to go back to or forward to, put the mouse pointer on either of these icons and click the *right* mouse button.
Reload		This button reloads the current Web page from the source. If the page didn't load completely, if the loading process is disturbed in some way, or if the source has

changed since you last accessed it, you may want to reload the Web page.

Home

This button takes you to your home page, the one you first saw when you started Netscape.

Search

This button takes you to a Web page where you select a service to search the WWW. This is a good guide to different search services. For some items, you type in one or more keywords and wait for results. You'll get a Web page with hyperlinks to resources that match the keyword(s) you typed. This takes you to the same Web page as clicking on the directory button **Net Search** in previous versions of Netscape.

Images

This button appears only if Netscape Navigator has been set so that it will *not* automatically display images while loading a Web page. With that setting, Web pages load more quickly. To load the images, click on this button. To set a preference for automatically or not automatically loading images, select **Preferences** from **Edit** in the menu bar, then select **Advanced**, and finally click on the box next to **Automatically load images**.

Guide

This button represents a menu of several guides to Web or Internet resources and a hyperlink to the Netscape Web guide to sites, news and events on the Internet. Click with the mouse button to bring up the menu. The entries are as follows: **The Internet**, a guide to sites, news, and events on the Internet; **People**, a guide to white pages services for finding email and street addresses; **Yellow Pages**, a guide to businesses on the Web; and **What's New & What's Cool**, a guide to new and noteworthy Web sites. All of these options are available through the directory button in earlier versions of Netscape Navigator. Click with the left mouse button to go to Netscape's guide to the Internet. This guide of online resources is maintained by Yahoo!

<table>

Print		This button allows you to print the current document. You can specify whether you want to print all or some of the pages, as well as other options about the printing.
Security		This button displays the page dealing with security information. It brings up the same page you would see if you selected **Security Info** from the **Communicator** menu in the menu bar. You can use this option to check security, obtain encryption information about the current Web page, set a Netscape password for yourself, and perform other security-related tasks.
Stop		This button stops a current Web page from loading. This is useful if it's taking a long time to contact a site or load a page.

Table 2.1—Icons in a Netscape Navigator Window

Location Toolbar

The location toolbar includes the Bookmark Quickfile icon, which serves as a link to the bookmark list; the Page Proxy icon, which lets you add sites to the bookmark list, personal toolbar, or the desktop; and the location field, which holds the URL for the current Web page. We'll discuss the essential features of each.

The Bookmark Quickfile icon labeled **Bookmarks** is used to bring up a menu of items:

❄ The first item, **Add Bookmark**, lets you add the URL and title of the current Web page to the bookmark list. The title is what you see when you look through the list. Once something is in the bookmark list, you can access the Web page in one or two clicks. The bookmark list is therefore very useful when you're doing research.

❄ The last item, **Edit Bookmarks**, lets you arrange bookmarks into folders, rename items, delete items, and otherwise manage the list.

❄ The second item, **File Bookmark**, is used to highlight a folder in the list. It's used with the Page Proxy icon to the right of the Bookmark Quickfile icon.

You use the Page Proxy icon, or Page icon for short, to copy the URL of the current Web page. Move the mouse pointer over the icon and hold down the left mouse button. Then drag it to the desktop to make a shortcut to the Web page. Click on the shortcut and you'll go directly to the Web page. Alternately, drag it to the personal toolbar where it is added as an icon. As a third option, drag it to the Bookmarks icon and add it to the bookmark list, or click on **File Bookmark** and select the folder to which it will be added.

The location field holds the URL of the current Web page. In Activity 1.1, we showed how you can go directly to a Web page by clicking on the location field, typing in the URL, and pressing Enter. Clicking on the arrow displays a list of URLs for Web pages you've visited recently. Click on any one to go directly to it.

Personal Toolbar

The personal toolbar contains icons that represent Web pages. Clicking on an item takes you directly to that Web page. What you see the first time you use Netscape varies depending on what version you're using or whether someone else has used the browser. Figure 2.1 shows three icons in the personal toolbar. The one titled **Internet** is a hyperlink to the Netscape Internet guide. The others titled **Lookup** and **New&Cool** represent folders that contain several hyperlinks to Web sites.

There are two ways to put items in the personal toolbar. One way is to use the Page icon to place (drag and drop) an icon for the current Web page into the personal toolbar. In this way, the personal toolbar consists of hyperlinks to Web sites. Another way is to select a folder (a collection of bookmarks) in the bookmark list as the one that will be used for the personal toolbar entries. Check the online help for a way to do that, because it gives you quick access to a collection of bookmarks that might be useful when you're researching a topic.

Content Area or Document View

The *content area* is the portion of the window that holds the document, page, or other resource as your browser presents it. It can contain text or images. Sometimes the content area is divided into or consists of several independent portions called frames. Each frame has its own scroll bar, and you can move through one frame while staying in the same place in others.

The content area holds the Web page you're viewing, which likely contains hyperlinks in text or graphic format. Clicking on a hyperlink with the *left* mouse button allows you to follow the link. Clicking with the *right* mouse button (or holding down the mouse button without clicking if your mouse has only one button) brings up a menu that gives you options for working with a hyperlink. We discuss using the right mouse button in a later section.

Scroll Bar

Netscape has horizontal and vertical **scroll bars**. The horizontal one is at the bottom of the window, and the vertical one is at the right of the window. These scroll bars and their associated arrows help you move through the document. The scroll bars work the same way as those in common Microsoft Windows applications.

Status Line

When you are retrieving a document, opening a location, or following a hyperlink, the bar along the bottom of the window (the **status line**) holds the URL that's being used. It also lets you know whether a site is being contacted, if it's responding, and how the transmission is progressing. The bar on the left, called the *progress bar*, gives a graphical view of how much of the complete page has been received.

The icon on the left that looks like a lock is the Security icon. Clicking on it brings up the same window as clicking on the Security icon in the command toolbar. If it looks like the lock is open, then the document you're viewing has not passed through secure channels. If the lock is closed, then some security has been put in place during the transmission of the Web page or document.

Information available through the World Wide Web passes across the Internet. That means that any site on the path of the transmission can intercept the packets that make up the document or Web page. Thus, it's difficult to guarantee the security or privacy of information (such as a credit card number) exchanged on the WWW. We all face that same problem whenever we use a portable wireless telephone.

Netscape Communication Corporation and others provide the means to guarantee secure transmissions. If the document you're working with is secure, the lock will be closed. It's not a good idea to send sensitive or valuable information through the WWW if the lock isn't closed, but that's always up to you.

Component Bar

Netscape Communicator consists of several software tools for working on the Web and the Internet. The *component bar* gives quick access to some of these: Navigator for browsing the Web, Mailbox for working with email, discussion groups for working with Usenet news, and Composer for writing Web pages. Clicking on any of these takes you to them. If mail arrives while you're using Netscape, a green arrow appears as part of the mail icon.

Using the Right Mouse Button

Most of what we've said about using the mouse relates to using the *left* mouse button, but Netscape Navigator 4 takes advantage of the *right* mouse button as well. Some of these features are also available with Netscape Navigator 3. If your mouse has only one button, then holding it down is usually equivalent to pressing the right button on a mouse with two or more buttons.

Here are some of the ways to use the right mouse button:

* If the mouse pointer is on the **Back** or **Forward** icons, clicking the right mouse button brings up a list of sites; you can go backward or forward to these. Select one from the list and click on it.

* You can use the right mouse button to copy and paste information from a Web page, email, or other windowed source. Say that you're working with Netscape email or are in the content area of a Web page and are *not on a hyperlink*. Using the mouse, move the cursor or pointer to the beginning of the text you want to copy. Hold down the left mouse button, use the mouse to highlight the text, then click the right mouse button and select **Copy**. Now move the mouse pointer to where you want to paste the text— maybe you've copied a URL and want to put it in the location field. Press the right mouse button and select **Paste**. If you are pasting a URL into the location field or some other field in a form, be sure to click on the location field with the left mouse button first to highlight the text you want to replace.

* If the mouse pointer is in the content area but *not on a hyperlink*, clicking the right mouse button brings up a menu with several useful items, many of which appear as part of other menus or toolbars. These include items to go **Back** or **Forward** to a Web page and to **Reload** or **Stop** loading the current Web page. You can set the background image as wallpaper for your desktop, save the image in a file, add the current page to the bookmark list, create a desktop shortcut to the page, or send the Web page via email.

* If the mouse pointer is *on an image*, then you have the same choices as when it's in the content area and not on a hyperlink. In addition, you can view the image in a separate window, save the image in a file, or copy the URL for the image (in case you want to include it in a Web page you're constructing).

* If the mouse pointer is *on a hyperlink* (remember, when it's over a hyperlink, the pointer changes to a hand) and you click the right mouse button, then a menu appears with all the same items as when the pointer isn't on a hyperlink. In addition, the menu includes items to open the link in a new, separate window or to open it in Netscape Composer. You can also save the Web page represented by the link to a file, or you can copy the link, which means copying the URL for later use with the paste operation.

Getting Around a Page and the World Wide Web

You've probably spent some time browsing the World Wide Web and some of the resources and information it has to offer. In this section, we'll go over how to move around within a page and how to go from one page or location to another. Knowing this, you'll be able to get around the WWW effectively.

Moving Through a Page

When you start a WWW browser, you see a portion of a page or document in the window. As you may remember, the starting page is called the *home page*. Many of these pages contain more information than is immediately displayed, so you need to know how to move through a document. You can do this by using the scroll bars, using the keyboard, or searching for a specific word or phrase.

Using the Scroll Bars

You can move around or through a document by using the vertical and horizontal scroll bars on the right and bottom of the window. The scroll bars on a Netscape Navigator window are used the same way as on any other window.

Using the Keyboard

Pressing the up or down arrow will move you up or down one line. Pressing the **PgUp** key moves up one window length, and pressing **PgDn** moves down one window length. Pressing **Ctrl** + **Home** takes you to the beginning of the document, and pressing **Ctrl** + **End** takes you to its end.

Finding Text or Searching a Page

You can search a document for a word, portion of a word, phrase, or any string of characters. To find a string, you first have to bring up the dialog box labeled *Find*, as shown in Figure 2.2. There are two ways to do this—either select **Edit** from the menu bar and choose **Find in Page...**, or press **Ctrl** + **F** on the keyboard.

Figure 2.2—Find Box

Once the Find dialog box is up, type in a string (words or characters) and press **Enter** or click on the **Find Next** button. You can cancel a search by clicking on the **Cancel** button. You can search in one of two directions. **Down** searches from your current position to the end of the document. **Up** searches from the current position to the beginning of the document. Mark the **Match case** box if you want to match the capitalization in the string exactly.

Moving Between Pages

As you work with and browse the World Wide Web, you'll often go from one page to another. Much of the time, you do this by clicking on hyperlinks, but you can also go directly to a Web page, document, or location by typing its URL and then letting the browser retrieve it for you. To move between pages you've already visited, you can use the **Back** or **Forward** arrow icons on the toolbar to move between pages during a session. Web browsers also let you save URLs or titles of the pages you've visited in one session so that you can access them easily during that or any other session. This information is saved in the *history list* (a list of all sites visited during recent sessions) and in the *bookmark list* (a list of hyperlinks to sites you have explicitly saved from one session to the next).

✳ Tip

When you can't wait—breaking a connection or stopping a page.

Press the key labeled **Esc** or click on the **Stop** icon to stop a page from being loaded into your browser or to stop Netscape from trying to connect to a site. When you want to follow a link or go after a document, click on hypertext or an icon. Watch the *status bar* to see if the remote site holding the information has been contacted and if it's responding. Your Web browser will try for a certain amount of time (a minute or so) to contact the remote site. If you don't want to wait that long or you don't want to wait for the browser to display a complete page, press **Esc** or the **Stop** icon. This doesn't close the browser; it just interrupts the transmission or attempted connection.

✳

Going Directly to a Web Page

We'll describe two ways to go directly to a Web page, document, or location. In both cases, you type the URL and press **Enter**. The browser attempts to make the connection, and if it can retrieve the page, it will bring the page up on the window.

If the browser can't retrieve the page, check your typing to make sure you have the URL right. There could be other problems as well. If the page is not available to the public, you'll see the message "403 Forbidden" in the window. If the page doesn't exist, you'll get the message "404 Not Found." It could also be that the site is out of service or too busy to handle your request.

One way to go directly to a Web page is to click on the location field. After the pane changes color, type the URL and press **Enter**. We did that in Activity 1.1.

Another way to go directly to a Web page is to click on **File** in the menu bar and then to select **Open Page** (the keyboard shortcut is **Ctrl** + **O**). A dialog box labeled **Open Page** pops up on the screen, as shown in Figure 2.3. Type the URL of the site you want to go to, be sure you've selected Navigator as the way you want the page opened, and click on the button labeled **Open**. (Figure 2.3 shows the dialog box filled in with the URL for the *World Wide Web Virtual Library*, **http:// vlib.stanford.edu/Overview.html**. Why not try it and browse the library?) The Web browser then attempts to make the connection, and the page you've requested replaces the current one in the window. You can also use this method to view a local file—one that's on a disk drive on your computer or local network.

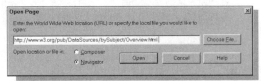

Figure 2.3—Dialog Box to Open a Page

Using Back and Forward

You can move to a previous Web page by clicking on either of the icons . You can also go back or forward by selecting either option from the **Go** menu in the menu bar. The keyboard shortcuts are **Alt** + **←** to move backward and **Alt** + **→** to go forward. You can also move in these directions by pressing the right mouse button (while the pointer is on a Web page) and then selecting **Back** or **Forward** from the menu that pops up on the screen.

Keeping Track—The History List

The Web browser keeps a record of the path you've taken to get to the current location. To see the path and select a site from it, click on **Go** in the menu bar. The browser keeps track of all the Web pages visited recently in the *history list*. The number of days an item may be kept on the list is set in the Preference panel category titled Navigator. To get to the spot where you can set it, click on **Edit** in the menu bar, select **Preferences**, and then click on **Navigator**. You can use this list to go directly to a Web page without having to go through all the pages in between.

To bring up the history list, press **Ctrl** + **H** from the keyboard, or click on **Communicator** from the menu bar and select **History** from that menu.

Figure 2.4 illustrates a portion of a sample history list. You can select and highlight any item by using the up or down arrow on the keyboard or by using the mouse. Once you've highlighted the location you want, double-click on the highlighted item. If you click on the right mouse button, a menu pops up that allows you to go directly to the Web page or to add the name and URL of the highlighted item to the bookmark list. You will want to add the name of a Web page (and its URL) to the bookmark list when you want to be able to return to it in another session on the WWW. As you can see from Figure 2.4, there's lots of information in the history list about the sites visited through Navigator.

Figure 2.4—History List

Keeping Track—The Bookmark List

The bookmark list is a collection of hyperlinks to Web pages that you want to save from session to session. They could be your favorite sites, ones you find useful, or ones you've looked at briefly but want to return to in the future (particularly good when you're starting to research a topic). Each item on the bookmark list is a Web page title, and each entry is a hyperlink. The browser includes a program to let you manage and arrange the list.

To use the bookmark list to go from the current Web page to another, first view the list onscreen by clicking on the **Bookmarks** icon in the location toolbar and move the mouse over the entries. When you've highlighted the one you want, click with the left mouse button.

Another way to bring up the list is to select **Bookmarks** from the **Communicator** menu in the menu bar. Pressing Ctrl + **B** from the keyboard produces the list in editing mode. In that mode, you can not only highlight and select an item but also manipulate the entries on the list. Figure 2.5 shows a portion of a bookmark list with folders.

Figure 2.5—Portion of a Bookmark List

Getting Help

There are several ways to get help with using Netscape Navigator. Online help is available while you're using Netscape. There is a list of frequently asked questions (FAQ) with answers about using Netscape. Several Usenet newsgroups are dedicated to discussions about using a WWW browser.

Online Help

To receive online help while using Netscape Navigator, click on **Help** on the menu bar. This pulls down a menu from which you can select one of several types of information, including **Help Contents**. You can also activate this option by pressing the function key F1. Online help starts in a separate window. It contains information that you may need while using Navigator or other parts of Communicator. Another useful item is Product Information and Support. Clicking on that takes you to a Web page supported by Netscape Communications. That Web page has many useful links for getting answers for your questions about using Netscape products.

Frequently Asked Questions (FAQ)

Frequently asked questions or *FAQ* is a traditional way to collect common questions and provide answers on the Internet. As you browse the Internet, you'll see FAQs on all sorts of topics. Netscape maintains several FAQs about its products. You can access them by choosing **Help** in the menu bar and **Product Information and Support** from the pulldown menu or by explicitly opening a location using the URL.

You'll find the *World Wide Web FAQ* very useful. It's available in English and other languages at several sites on the WWW. You should pick the one closest to you. The primary site is *Boutell.com, Inc.*, **http://www.boutell.com/faq/**.

Usenet Newsgroups

There are several (at least 15) Usenet newsgroups that host discussions about the WWW, and each maintains its own FAQ. A list of Usenet newsgroups about the WWW is available through the World Wide Web FAQ mentioned above.

One direct link to the list of newsgroups is **http://www.boutell .com/faq/ngroups.htm**. You ought to check this URL because it has the names and descriptions of the groups, and it's likely to contain new ones as they're created.

You may want to read the following Usenet newsgroups:

❋ **comp.infosystems.www.browsers.ms-windows**
   For discussion of Web browsers used with Microsoft Windows and NT operating systems.

❋ **comp.infosystems.www.announce**
   Used to announce new Web pages.

Now we'll take a break from our detailed description of how to use a Web browser, and we'll go through an activity. The activity provides practice with using commands to browse a section of the WWW.

✳ Tip

Remember that the Web is always changing and that your results may differ from those shown here. Don't let this confuse you. The activities are meant to teach you fundamental skills. These skills don't change, even though the number of results obtained or the actual screens may look very different.

Activity 2.1   Using a Search Engine

Overview

In this activity, we'll search for information on the World Wide Web. We'll start by using a **search engine**, a program or service designed to search for information available through the WWW, to help us find resources about a specific topic. A search engine is a collection of software programs that collect information from the Web, index it, and put it in a database so it can be searched. A search engine also contains tools for searching the database; that's the part we'll use most of the time.

We type keywords or a phrase into a search form on a Web page, possibly set some options, and then click on a **Submit** button on the Web page. In what is usually a short time, we will see matching entries from the database—usually 10 per page. Each of the results contains a hyperlink to the entry, as well as a brief excerpt from the resource. All the results are ranked according to relevance or how closely they match the query.

Most of the search engines have indexed millions of Web pages, so it's likely that you'll get more results than you can check. The key to successful searching is to make your search phrase or keywords as precise as possible. We'll discuss ways of doing that in much more detail in Chapters 5 and 6.

Clicking on the icon **Search** in the command toolbar brings up a list of several search engines. Those and others are listed in Appendix B and throughout this text.

The topic for the search is Chinese art, specifically painting. Why that topic? Well, it's always nice to look at, try to understand, and learn about art, and we'll be able to use the topic to demonstrate some ways to use a search engine and move around the Web from page to page ("surfing"). We'll also go over using the online help from the search engine to make our search more precise.

When you try this activity, you're likely to see some differences in the results, because new resources are always being added to the search engine's database. Concentrate on the steps to take. You'll use the same techniques for other topics.

The search engine we'll use for this activity is AltaVista. It's very popular, has a large database of Web pages (more than thirty million), and gets high ratings in the popular and computer press. We'll use the keywords *Chinese art painting* to start, since that phrase describes the topic both generally (Chinese art) and specifically (painting). We'll go directly to the Web page for AltaVista by typing in its URL and typing the keywords for the search. After we see the first list of results, we'll look at the online help available through AltaVista to make the search more precise. Then we'll look at some of the results by following some of the hyperlinks.

Here are the steps we'll follow:

1. Start the browser.
2. Go to the home page for AltaVista.
3. Type in the keywords and start the search.
4. Read the online help.
5. Modify the search phrase to get more precise results.
6. Follow some of the hyperlinks returned by AltaVista.
7. End the session.

While you're going through the steps in this activity, practice using the **Back** and **Forward** icons. If you click on **Forward** as many times as you click on **Back**, you won't lose your place.

Details

1   Start the browser.

✱*Do It!* Double-click on the Netscape icon. Look for an icon that looks like one of the following:

Netscape   Netscape
Communicator   Communicator

2   Go to the home page for AltaVista.

✱*Do It!* Click on the location field, type **http://www.altavista.digital.com**, and press ⌈**Enter**⌋.

When you start your Web browser, your home page will appear on the screen. We're going to access AltaVista by typing its URL in the location field, as shown in Figure 2.6.

Figure 2.6—Opening Location to AltaVista by Typing Its URL

Soon after you press **Enter**, the search page for AltaVista ought to appear in the browser window, as shown in Figure 2.7.

3   Type in the keywords and start the search.

☀Do It! Type *Chinese art painting* in the search field and click on
search as shown in Figure 2.7.

To start the search, you type a word or phrase in the search field, then
click on the button labeled **search**. Figure 2.7 shows the keywords typed
into the box. In Chapters 5 and 6, we'll explain several of the features in
such search engines as AltaVista, but it's worth noting that there are
hyperlinks on this page to get help, go to a page where you can use
advanced techniques, or refine your search keywords. We'll stick with a
simple search for this activity.

Figure 2.7—Search Page for AltaVista with Keywords

After you click on **search**, the search engine returns a list of hyperlinks
to resources that contain information containing one or more of the
words in the search phrase. A portion of that page is shown in Figure 2.8. You see that the search engine found nearly half a million items!
They are arranged in order so that those which may be most relevant
are listed first. There are 10 on this page. We don't show it here, but if
you move to the end of the page (use the down arrow keys, press **PgDn**,
or use the vertical scroll bar), there's a link you can select to go to the
next 10 items.

The figure contains the following callouts:

497,600 matches!

Hyperlinks to resources found by AltaVista

Use the scroll bar to move to the end of this page where you ask for the next 10 items

Figure 2.8—Portion of First Page of Search Results

To see how we can make the search more precise, we'll read the online help. That will give us some tips about using AltaVista and obtaining better results.

4 Read the online help.

Do It! Click on the hyperlink labeled **Help** at the top of the Web page.

Figure 2.7 shows the location of the hyperlink labeled **Help**. Click on it to get some tips for using the search engine and for making the search more precise. The goal is to obtain more appropriate results. Figure 2.9 shows a portion of AltaVista's help page for simple searches.

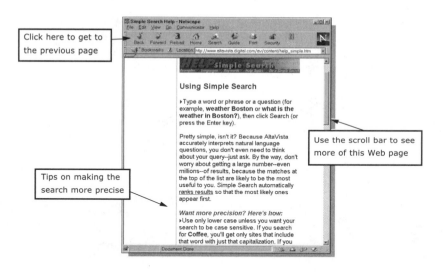

Click here to get to the previous page

Use the scroll bar to see more of this Web page

Tips on making the search more precise

Figure 2.9—AltaVista's Help for Simple Searches

Reading the text, we find several useful pieces of information:

- ❋ We can require a match for phrases, not just individual words, by including a phrase in quotes.

- ❋ The search is case-sensitive (*Chinese* gives different results from *chinese*).

- ❋ We may require certain words or phrases by putting a **+** in front of them. We can prohibit certain words by putting a **–** in front.

We're interested in Chinese art, specifically painting, so we'll modify the search by using the phrase *Chinese art* and by requiring the term *painting*. Looking through our initial results, we see that some are from sites that give us the opportunity to buy some of the art. This time we're just looking, so we'll exclude the term *buy*. With more searching experience, we'd learn that colleges and universities commonly put course listings or course descriptions on the Web. To bypass those for now, we'll exclude the term *courses*. We'll use the following:

"Chinese art" +painting -buy -courses

The AltaVista search page includes a hyperlink labeled *refine* that we could also use to modify the search phrase. When we click on **refine**, we find terms that AltaVista supplies. These words are synonyms and antonyms of those in the search phrase. Which to use? You can see that sometimes it's better to use **refine** if we need help coming up with terms. If those terms don't apply to our needs or if we think of our own terms, then we don't need to use **refine**.

5   Modify the search phrase to get more precise results.

We'll go back to the previous page so that we can enter our new search terms and get more precise results.

✳Do It! Click on the **Back** button in the toolbar.

✳Do It! Click on the search field, modify the search terms to **"Chinese art" +painting -buy -courses** and then click on the **search** button.

To replace the search terms, you can click on the field pane to the right of the last word, backspace over the terms, and type new terms. You can also use the left and right arrow keys to add characters or to delete them from the search terms.

Figure 2.10 shows a portion of the previous page with the new search terms typed in.

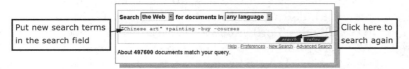

Figure 2.10—AltaVista Search Form with Modified Search Phrase

6   Follow some of the hyperlinks returned by AltaVista.

Figure 2.11 shows the first few results of the search. We reduced the number from nearly half a million to about sixty-six hundred. That's still lots to consider, but the first few have a good chance of being ones we'd like to see. You can access the items listed by clicking on the hyperlink. For each item, there's a brief description that you can use as a guide to help you decide whether to follow the link. For now we'll follow the hyperlink for **China the Beautiful**, as it looks the most promising. (If that one isn't listed, pick another that you think is appropriate.)

Chapter 2

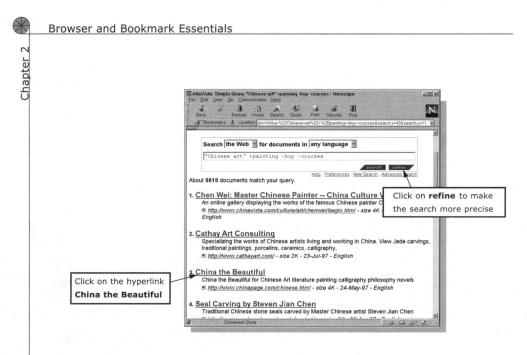

Click on **refine** to make the search more precise

Click on the hyperlink **China the Beautiful**

Figure 2.11—First Few Results of Modified AltaVista Search

Do It! Click on the hyperlink **China the Beautiful**.

Figure 2.12 shows the Web page "China the Beautiful." It has links to lots of topics related to Chinese art and Chinese literature. We see that there are links called **Paintings Gallery** and **Links to Museums and Art Galleries**. Further down the page there's a link called **Paintings**. We'll follow this one first; you're free to follow any you'd like. Before we follow any links, why don't we set a bookmark for this Web page?

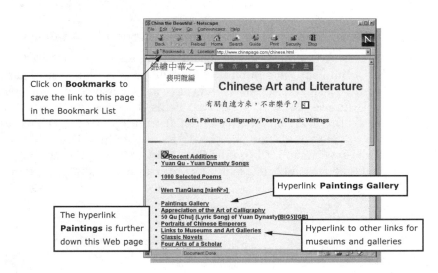

Click on **Bookmarks** to save the link to this page in the Bookmark List

Hyperlink **Paintings Gallery**

The hyperlink **Paintings** is further down this Web page

Hyperlink to other links for museums and galleries

Figure 2.12—"China the Beautiful" Web Page

Do It! Click on **Bookmarks** on the location toolbar and then select **Add Bookmark**.

An alternate way to add this page to the bookmark list is to use the keyboard shortcut **Ctrl** + **D**. With this added to the bookmark list we'll be able to come back to this site any time we'd like without having to go through the search. Now on to explore the other hyperlinks.

Do It! Use the scroll bar to move to the portion of the page that includes the link **Paintings**. Click on the hyperlink **Paintings**.

Clicking on the hyperlink **Paintings** brings up a list of links, as shown in Figure 2.13. Feel free to follow any of them to see images and, in some cases, to learn about the painters. You can use the **Back** button in the toolbar to return to this list.

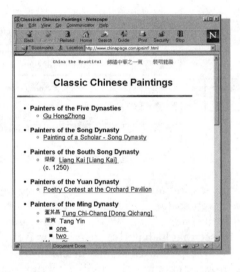

Figure 2.13—"Classic Chinese Paintings" Web Page

Now let's check out **Links to Museums and Art Galleries** on the Web page "China the Beautiful."

Do It! Click on the **Back** icon to return to the "China the Beautiful" Web page.

This takes us back to the Web page shown in Figure 2.12.

Do It! Click on the hyperlink **Links to Museums and Art Galleries**.

The Web page that comes up from the hyperlink **Links to Museums and Art Galleries** has several links to museums and art galleries around the world, and we could easily spend an hour or more looking at the exhibits. Browse a little, but don't get lost or forget whatever else you need to do today. We'll take a look at the bottom of the Web page (see Figure 2.14) to see if it says who is responsible for all these fine Web pages and to see if there are other links to follow.

❋Do It! Use the scroll bar or the **PgDn** key to get to the bottom of the Web page.

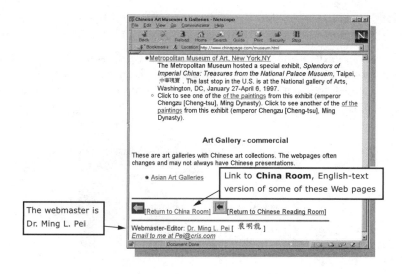

Figure 2.14—Bottom of "Chinese Art Museums & Galleries" Web Page

The information at the bottom of the page says that Dr. Ming L. Pei is the site webmaster. That means he's responsible for maintaining the pages at this Web site. If we click on his name, we can read more about him and see that he has also created this Web site. You may have noticed that the Web pages we looked at contained some Chinese characters. Some browsers are not able to display those characters. An all English-language version of these pages is available if you click on the hyperlink **The China Room**. We'll leave that for you to explore.

There are still lots of links we may want to follow, and we can do that by using the **Back** button in the command toolbar to return to the AltaVista page with the search results. We've also added one item to the bookmark list, and we can go directly to that page by clicking on **Bookmarks** in the location toolbar and selecting it from the list of bookmarks. There are still lots of items you may want to explore. Feel free to do so. Just remember, there may be other things going on in your life or work right now that need attention!

7   End the session.

You knew when we started that this had to end sometime. Now's the time. (You can, however, keep the Web browser open so that you're ready for the next activity.)

✳*Do It!* Click on **File** on the menu bar and select **Exit** from the menu.

That's it!

In this activity, we used a search engine to find hyperlinks to Web pages about Chinese art, specifically painting. After using the online help, we used search terms to make the search more precise. When you look at some of these Web pages, you may want to make the search even more specific. Perhaps you're interested in looking at the work and finding information about a specific painter, style of painting, or location. You can do that by modifying the search phrase or coming up with a new one.

Saving, Printing, and Mailing Items from the WWW

Suppose you're working on the WWW and you come across a document, data, program, picture, sound or video clip, or anything you'd like to save. Or maybe you want to email one of those items to someone else or get a printed copy of it. A Web browser comes with tools and commands to let you do these things. Commands are available through the pulldown menu under **File** in the menu bar, through some of the icons in the command toolbar, and through keyboard shortcuts.

Remember, just because something is available on the WWW doesn't necessarily mean you may make a copy of it. In many cases, the material—text, images, sound—can't be used for commercial purposes without written permission.

Saving Web Pages in a File

You can save any Web page in a file on your computer. When a page is saved, you get the text portion along with the HTML code for the page. Images, audio, and other types of elements in the page are not included because these things exist in files other than the one that holds the text you see on the screen. You may want to save a Web page in a file on your computer so you can access it in the future without connecting to the Internet. If the Web page has frames, click on the frame you want to save before following these steps.

To save a page, click on **File** in the menu bar and select **Save As** from the menu. The keyboard shortcut is [Ctrl] + **S**. A dialog box opens in which you confirm or give the name of the file to hold the page.

By default, a page is saved in source format, which means that it includes the text along with the HTML commands or tags used to create the page. It's really useful to see how others have used HTML to create and make Web pages when you're thinking about translating your designs for Web pages into HTML. To save only the text without HTML, you need to be sure the file name ends with **.txt** and that the file type selected is Plain Text. Figure 2.15 shows this.

Chapter 2

Add .txt to the name of the file and select **Plain Text** as the file type

Figure 2.15—Dialog Box with Options Set to Save Text Only

Saving Items on a Web Page into a File

Almost anything that has a hyperlink to it can be saved in a file. You can save items after you receive them—like saving a Web page to a file once the page is on the screen—or you can save them without seeing or hearing them beforehand. All the items are saved as files. Often, you're able to tell the type of information in a file by looking at the extension of the file name, such as **.doc** for a Microsoft Word file, **.gif** for an image, or **.wav** for an audio file. Saving a file from the Internet is called *downloading* the file.

To save whatever is on the other end of a hyperlink without viewing it first, move the mouse pointer to the hyperlink and click the *right* mouse button. When a menu pops up, select **Save Link As**. Another way to do this is to move the mouse pointer over the hyperlink, to hold down the **Shift** key, and to click the (left) mouse button.

The link can point to anything on the WWW—another Web page, a document in special format (such as a document prepared with a word processor or spreadsheet), an image, a compressed archive of files, a video file, an audio file, or even other possibilities. (Who knows what you'll find on the WWW?)

You can save an image in the browser window to a file by moving the mouse pointer over the image, clicking the *right* mouse button, and selecting **Save Image As** from the menu.

Whenever you save a file from the Internet, either directly or through a hyperlink, there's a possibility that the file will contain a computer virus or other software that may damage or erase your files. After you save a file, check it with antivirus software, which is a program that checks a file for a virus. A good source for information about computer viruses is *Computer Viruses and Security*, **http://galaxy.tradewave.com/galaxy/Engineering-and-Technology/Computer-Technology/Security.html**, by David Hull.

Printing a Web Page

You can print whatever you see in your browser window with a printer that's connected to your computer. When a Web page is printed, everything you see in the window—text, graphics, images—is passed on to the printer.

Giving the command to print brings up a dialog box in which you can select the printer, determine the number of copies, and indicate which pages of the Web page you want to print. The phrase *pages of the Web page* may seem strange, but remember that a Web page isn't a physical page. A Web page may contain only text, but it may also be in multimedia form. The Web page, in fact, exists only in electronic form. You can preview the printing by picking the preview option. This will give you an idea of the printed Web page's physical layout.

Mailing a Web Page

The text on a Web page can be mailed to any Internet address. Mailing a page means sending only the text on the page or sending the source. The *source* is the text, as well as all the HTML statements that specify hyperlinks, control the page format, and identify the source of the images and graphics on a page. In this sense, mailing a Web page is similar to saving a Web page in a file.

To mail a Web page, click on **File** in the menu bar and select **Mail Document**. A window pops up in which you indicate where you want to send the email, the subject, and anything else you'd like to write or include. The URL for the current Web page is automatically included in the message. You can send the page (either text or source) as an ***attachment*** to the email, or you can send it quoted (as text) in the body of the message. If you find something on a page that you want to share with someone else, it might be appropriate to mail them the URL. If they don't have access to a WWW browser, then it would be better to attach or quote the Web page. If you "quote" or copy the Web page text in the body of your message, you can edit the text and send only a portion of the page.

Using a Web Browser with Local Files

You can use a Web browser to view files on a disk on your computer. You don't need the Internet to access these files, called *local files*. It's really convenient to use your Web browser to look at local files—sometimes easier than opening another application or program to view a file. Once you view a file with the Web browser, you can work with it just like any Web page, including printing it or sending it by email. This is also a convenient way to check Web pages while they're being developed.

The local file has to be one with which your browser can work. You can't expect it to display a spreadsheet file without a program that lets you work with spreadsheets. On the other hand, you can expect it to work well with a text file or HTML file. The browser will let you view graphics or images if they're stored in GIF (file names end with **.gif**) or JPEG (file names ends with **.jpg**) formats.

These types of files work well, because your browser is already configured to work with such file types. For other types of files, you may have to set some *helper applications* in the preferences section of your browser. When you want to view a file, the browser starts a program called a *viewer* that lets you look at the file's contents. For example, if it's a text file, it's displayed in the window just as it appears. If it's a GIF, then the browser starts a viewer that lets you look at images. If it's an HTML file, the browser displays it by following all the HTML commands. If there is no viewer for your file, Netscape lets you know and gives you a chance to name a viewer for the file. A viewer is more than a program that lets you look at a file. It can also be a program that lets you hear the sound encoded in an audio file.

To view a local file, choose **File** from the menu bar and then select **Open Page**. This will bring up a dialog box, as shown in Figure 2.3. When that happens, you can type in the file name. Alternately, you can browse through your files. Click on **Choose File** until you find the one you'd like to view. That opens another dialog box titled **Open**. You can look for files of a specific type or all files by making a choice in the item labeled **Files of type...**

If the browser can work either directly or through a helper application, it will. If not, a dialog box will appear that lets you associate a helper application with files of that type. If you know the helper application you want to use, fill it in. If not, you may have to ask someone else for assistance.

Here are some places to check on the WWW for helper applications:

✸ Helper Applications. Netscape Communications Corporation, Inc., Mountain View, CA, **http://home.netscape .com/assist/helper_apps/windows_helpers.html**

✸ Learning to Use—Helper Applications. Team Web, University of Texas, Austin, TX., **http://wwwhost.cc.utexas .edu/learn/use/helper.html**

✸ WWW Browsers, MIME and Helper Applications, Doug Tower,University of California. San Diego, CA., **http:// ssdc.ucsd.edu/dt/helpers.html**

Using Bookmarks to Keep Track of Resources

You can save links to interesting and useful Web pages by adding hyperlinks to your bookmark list. The bookmark list is the name Netscape gives to the collection of hyperlinks you've saved; each one is like a bookmark into the World Wide Web. Whenever you're using the browser, you can call up your bookmarks and follow any of the links. You'll want to keep adding bookmarks to Web pages as you collect sources for research. Netscape and other Web browsers give you the tools to add, delete, annotate, and rename the bookmarks. You can also arrange them into folders, list them various ways, keep different files of bookmarks, and otherwise manage the collection. We will now go over some of the essential bookmark operations, and you'll see that sometimes there is more than one way to perform each one.

Add a Bookmark

Adding a bookmark means placing the Web page on the bookmark list. The phrase *bookmark a Web page* also means the same thing. Here are various ways to add a bookmark:

❋ Use the keyboard shortcut **Ctrl** + **D**.

❋ Click the *right* mouse button when the mouse pointer is on the Web page, frame, or hyperlink, and select **Add Bookmark**.

❋ Click on the Bookmarks icon in the location toolbar and select **Add Bookmark** from the menu.

❋ Drag and Drop: Move the mouse pointer to the Page Proxy icon in the location bar and hold down the left mouse button. Without letting go of the mouse button, drag the icon to the Bookmarks icon. A menu appears. Drag the Page Proxy icon to **Add Bookmark** on the menu and let go of the mouse button. The Web page is added to whatever folder is set to hold new bookmarks. To add a bookmark to any folder, drag the Page Proxy icon to the Bookmarks icon as before and choose **File Bookmarks** from the menu. That brings up a list of the folders in the bookmark list. After you drag the icon to a folder, "drop" it.

Display the Bookmark List

For the next few things we'll mention, you need to display the bookmark list either in a separate window or as a menu.

To display the bookmark list in a separate window, do one of the following:

❋ Use the keyboard shortcut **Ctrl** + **B**.

❋ Click on the Bookmarks icon in the location bar and select **Edit Bookmarks** from the menu. This displays the the bookmark list as a menu. You can use the mouse to display a folder or select an item in the list.

Jump to an Item in the Bookmark List

Jumping to an item means going directly to the Web page that the item represents. First, display the bookmark list, then move the mouse to the bookmark you want to use and click on it. If the bookmarks are arranged in folders or categories, select a category and then a bookmark.

Delete an Item from the Bookmark List

There will be times that you'll want to remove an entry from the bookmark list. To do that, display the bookmark list in a separate window, and click on the item to delete. Once you select an item in this way, you can delete it by doing one of the following:

❋ Press the **Delete** key.

❋ Press **Ctrl** + **X**.

❋ Click on **Edit** in the menu bar of the bookmark window and select **Cut** or **Delete**.

Search the Bookmark List

If there are many entries in the bookmark list, you may want to search the list for an entry. First, open the bookmark list in a separate window. Click on **Edit** and then select **Find**. (You can also use the keyboard shortcut **Ctrl** + **F**.) When a dialog box appears, type the word or phrase and click on the button labeled **OK**.

The bookmark list has many features that not everybody uses. You'll learn how to take advantage of them after gaining experience and feeling comfortable with the bookmark list. We'll go over a few features in the next activity.

Activity 2.2   Working with the Bookmark List

Overview

In this activity, we'll add items to the bookmark list. Then, we'll create a folder or category and add some items to it. Several other things can be done with the bookmark list and its entries, but to conserve space we won't demonstrate all of them here. When the bookmark list is displayed in its own window (see Figure 2.5), the commands for working with the list are all available through the window's menu bar. Here are a few things you can do from the pulldown menus:

❋ Insert a new bookmark, new folder, or new separator.

❋ Import a bookmark file.

❋ Save the current bookmark list to a file from the **File** menu.

❋ Cut, copy, paste, delete, or find items in the list.

❋ Access **Properties** from the **Edit** menu.

❋ Sort the bookmarks.

❋ Set the selected folder as the personal toolbar.

❋ Set the selected folder that will be used to hold new bookmarks.

❋ Select **Update Bookmarks** from the **View** menu to have Netscape see whether any of the bookmarks have changed since they were last visited.

In this activity, you'll see several different windows without a clear connection of how you get from one to the other. That's intentional. We want to concentrate on setting and using bookmarks. The windows that appear here could have come from one session or several sessions.

Details

Suppose you've started your Web browser in the same way as in previous activities and you're browsing the home page for the World Wide Web Virtual Library. A URL for that site is **http://vlib.stanford.edu/ Overview.html**. You'll want to add this page to your bookmark list so you can return to it in the future without having to type in the URL or remember the path you took to get there.

✻Do It! Press **Ctrl** + **D** to add the current Web page to the bookmark list.

Suppose that while you're browsing the Virtual Library, you select the category "Archaeology," and then you come upon the Web page "ArchNet: Museums and Research Facilities," **http://spirit.lib.uconn .edu/ArchNet/Museums/Museums.html**, as shown in Figure 2.16.

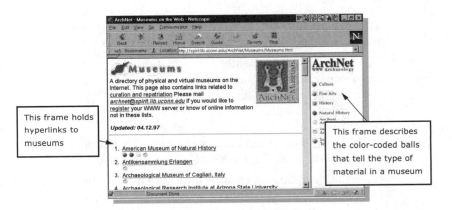

Figure 2.16—ArchNet: Museums and Research Facilities

From here, you visit several museums on the list and add some to the bookmark list. If the bookmark list was empty when we started or had no folders, then the bookmarks are added one after the other. If folders already exist, the new bookmarks are added to the folder that's labeled with a graphic image indicating it is the "new bookmarks" folder. For now, we'll assume that there weren't any folders in the bookmark list.

✻Do It! To view the bookmark list, use the keyboard shortcut **Ctrl** + **B**.

We discussed other ways of viewing the bookmark list in the section before this activity. You may want to try one of those instead.

Figure 2.17 shows the current bookmark list.

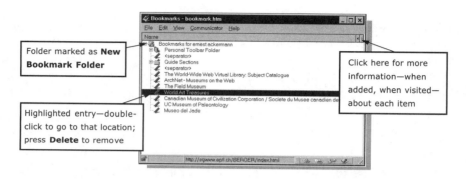

Folder marked as **New Bookmark Folder**

Click here for more information—when added, when visited— about each item

Highlighted entry—double-click to go to that location; press **Delete** to remove

Figure 2.17—Bookmark List

Clicking once on an entry highlights it. To jump to the location specified by the item, double-click on it.

To delete or remove an entry from the bookmark list, highlight it and press the **Delete** key or select **Cut** from the pulldown menu under **Edit**.

To change the name or other information about a bookmark item, select **Properties** from the pulldown menu under **View**. Select or highlight several entries by highlighting one and holding down the **Ctrl** key as you click on others. You can delete a group in the same way as you delete one item. To sort the entries in alphabetical order, highlight a group and choose one of the sort options—**By Name**, **By Location**, **By Created On**, or **By last visited**—from the menu under **View**.

Close the bookmark window by pressing **Ctrl** + **W** or clicking on the in the upper-right corner. The window can stay open while you're doing other things on your computer or on the Internet.

You can add more items any other time you're browsing or working with information on the World Wide Web. At some point, you may want to arrange your bookmarks into categories. Starting with the bookmark list shown in Figure 2.17, we'll add one folder titled **Museums** and put all the museum sites in that folder. Once the bookmark window is open, do the following steps to create a folder:

Do It! Click on **File** in the menu bar and select **New Folder**.

Clicking on **New Folder** brings up the window shown in Figure 2.18, except that the first pane is called **New Folder** and the second larger one is empty.

Do It! Click on the top frame and type **Museums**. Click on the bottom frame and type **Interesting Museums on the World Wide Web**. Click **OK** when you're finished.

Figure 2.18 shows the new folder window with all the information entered. Netscape automatically fills in the date on which this new piece of data was added.

Fill in these; they can be changed at any time

Figure 2.18—Bookmark Properties Window for a Folder

After you click **OK**, the folder is added to the bookmark list as shown in Figure 2.19.

Figure 2.19—Bookmark List with Newly Added Folder "Museums"

You can insert each of the hyperlinks or entries that represent a museum into the new folder in the same way, by using the "drag and drop" technique we mentioned earlier. Here are the instructions to move the item "The Field Museum of Natural History" into the folder.

※Do It! Click on **The Field Museum of Natural History** and hold down the left mouse button. Drag the highlighted entry to the folder called **Museums** and release the button.

Another way to move an item to a folder is to highlight the item, select **Cut** from the **Edit** menu, highlight the folder, and select **Paste** from the **Edit** menu.

After all the entries for museums are placed in the folder, the bookmark list will look as shown in Figure 2.20.

Chapter 2

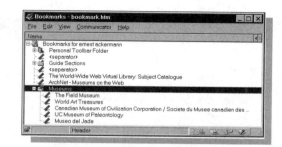

Figure 2.20—Bookmark List Showing Entries in the Folder "Museums"

As we said earlier, there are other things you can do with the bookmark list. Here are some things you may want to try:

- ❋ Double-click on the open folder to close it so that only the folder name appears in the list.
- ❋ Double-click again to open the folder.
- ❋ Move items that aren't in the folder to the bottom of the list in the same way that you added items to the folder.
- ❋ Sort the items in the list by highlighting more than one and choosing one of the sort or list options from the **View** menu.

_____ End of Activity 2.2 _____

Activity 2.2 showed how to arrange bookmarks into a folder. Once you start collecting bookmarks, it's a good idea to think about organizing them. You'll also want to think about deleting or discarding bookmarks when you don't need them anymore.

Summary

A Web browser is used to access the information and resources on the World Wide Web. Whenever you start the browser or access a hyperlink, the browser—which is a computer program—sends a request to have a file transferred to it. The browser then interprets the information in the file so that it can be viewed in the browser's window, or in some cases, viewed through another program. For example, if a hyperlink points to a text file, then the file is displayed in the window as ordinary text. If the hyperlink points to a document written in Hypertext Markup Language (HTML), then it's displayed by the browser. If the file is a sound file or an animation, then a program different from the browser is started so the file can be heard or seen. Most of the facilities and capabilities are built into the browser, but in some cases, your computer needs to be equipped with special equipment or programs. A good example of this is when a hyperlink points to a sound file. Your computer needs to have a sound card, speakers, and the software to play the sounds.

Starting a Web browser usually means first activating your connection to the Internet and then clicking on an icon or command to start Netscape Navigator. If the cost of using the Internet depends on how much time is spent being connected, then be sure to terminate the Internet connection when the Web session is over.

The commands you use to work with the Web browser are available through the menu bar, the toolbars (command toolbar, location toolbar, personal toolbar), and the keyboard. These features, along with the scroll bars, stay the same, regardless of what you're viewing or working with on the World Wide Web. The menu bar is a collection of pulldown menus that you can use for almost every operation or command. The **Help** menu lets you select one of several ways to teach yourself about Netscape, including an online manual. The command toolbar has a number of icons that give quick access to some of the commands in the pulldown menu. The **Search** icon displays a list of search services. Several commands are also available as keyboard shortcuts, meaning that you can type them directly on the keyboard instead of using a mouse. The location toolbar gives quick access to URLs and Web sites saved in the bookmark list or in the location field.

The browser lets you access, retrieve, work with, and enjoy the information and resources that make up the World Wide Web. To coin a phrase, the browser is your window to the Web.

Once a page is in the browser's window, you can move around the page using the keyboard, scroll bars, or mouse. You can search for words in the page. Move the mouse to a hyperlink (the pointer turns to a hand) and click on it to follow it. A URL can be typed in the location bar, or you can select a command or icon to open a location. In any of these cases, the browser will follow the URL you've typed or represent the hyperlink to view another Web page.

The browser keeps track of the sites you've visited during recent sessions. It does this so that you can backtrack and return to sites during a session. The history list holds records of and links to all the sites that you have visited recently. You can collect a set of hyperlinks in a list called the bookmark list. These will be available from one session to the next. The browser contains commands to let you maintain and manage your bookmark list.

Provided you're not breaking copyright laws or conventions, you can save information found on the World Wide Web into a file, print it, or mail it to an Internet address. You can also use the browser to view local files. When you're developing your own Web pages, you may want to use this method to test them before making them available to anyone on the Internet.

Selected Terms Introduced in This Chapter

attachment	content area
bookmark list	downloading

frames

frequently asked questions
  (FAQ)

helper applications

history list

menu bar

plug-ins

Point-to-Point-Protocol
  (PPP)

scroll bars

search engine

Serial Line Internet Protocol
  (SLIP)

status line

toolbars

Exercises and Projects

As you work through these exercises and projects, you'll practice using your Web browser and have the opportunity to visit several different Web sites. You're likely to find sites you'd like to come back to—in those cases, add them to your bookmark list!

1. Take some time to get familiar with the way your browser is set up to print Web pages. Start your browser and be sure a Web page is displayed in the content area. What happens when you click on the icon labeled **Print** in the toolbar or select **Print** from the **File** pulldown menu in the menu bar? Where is the Web page printed? Are there any special instructions you have to follow to get a printed copy of the current Web page? If you encounter problems, be sure your printer is turned on and connected to your computer. If you still have problems, contact a local expert.

2. Use your browser to view the Web page "About the World Wide Web," **http://www.w3.org/www**.

   a. Follow the link to the World Wide Web Virtual Library. (Another way to reach the site is to open the location **http://vlib.stanford.edu/Overview.html**.) Go to the section labeled **Broadcasters**. What are the names of five television and radio broadcasters, each from a different country? Follow the links to the Web sites you listed and write a brief description about what you find at each site.

   b. Go back to "About the World Wide Web." Follow the link labeled "CERN." (This may take a little while.) What did you find there? What is CERN?

3. This exercise involves the online help provided through your browser.

   a. Click on **Help** in the menu bar, and select **About Communicator**. What's displayed? Does it tell you which version of Netscape you're using? Which version of Netscape are you using?

   b. Click on **Help** in the menu bar and select **Help Contents**. What's displayed? Click on **Browsing the Web** in the frame on the right. Then click on **Links and URLs** in the frame on the left. Read the section that comes up. What is one thing you learned by reading it that you didn't know before?

c. With the **Help** window still open, click on **Index** and type **pop-up menu** in the search box. What appears? Read the section of the help index about pop-up menus. What did you learn?

4. Go to the AltaVista search engine **http://www.altavista.digital.com**, as we did in Activity 2.1. Using the search engine, find two or more Web pages that give a definition or good explanation for each of the following terms or phrases:

   ❋ Tai Chi
   ❋ Whistling tree frog
   ❋ Hertzsprung-Russell diagram
   ❋ Line-item veto
   ❋ Kerrville Folk Festival

5. Let's try another search engine. This time, use Infoseek with URL **http://www.infoseek.com**. Read the online help from Infoseek before you start the search. If you find a site you'd like to revisit, bookmark it. Find reliable information on each of the following topics:

   ❋ Italian Renaissance painting
   ❋ Italian Renaissance music
   ❋ Rock and Roll Hall of Fame
   ❋ Afro-Caribbean music
   ❋ Michael Jordan's scoring records
   ❋ Passenger car crash test results

6. For this exercise, we'll use another search engine, HotBot, **http://www.hotbot.com**.

   a. Go to the home page for HotBot and read the section "Getting Started" in the online help on the Web page. List their guidelines for smart searching, or print a copy.

   b. Using the tips and information you picked up in Part a of this exercise, find information about the following:

      ❋ Home drinking water quality
      ❋ Mahalia Jackson
      ❋ Chemical weapons ban treaty
      ❋ Alternative health care products
      ❋ Affirmative action and quotas
      ❋ Digital cash

   c. Now that you've had experience with three search engines, do you prefer one to the other? Please explain.

7. Lots of colleges and universities make information available on the Web. They include information about their academic programs, activities, costs, and other information.

   a. Go to the home page for Mary Washington College, **http://www.mwc.edu**. Click on the hyperlink labeled **Admissions**, and then click on **Information on Campus Visits**. That takes you to a Web page with directions to the college. Print out a copy and see if you can mail a copy of the directions to a friend.

   b. Now go to the home page for a college or university that's located near to where you live. If directions to the school are available on the Web, check the directions to see that they are accurate. If directions aren't available, find directions to another college or university. When you have the directions, print them out.

8. Go to the home page for the World Wide Web Virtual Library, **http://vlib.stanford.edu/Overview.html**. Follow the link labeled **Electronic Journals**.

   a. Before you start searching, click on the hyperlink **Search** (not the button labeled **Search**). The hyperlink takes you to a page that gives instructions on using the search tool for the electronic journals. Read the instructions on the page. What do they mean by a "wildcard" search? Suppose you use the term *economics* as the search word. Will there be a search only for those journals with the word *economics* in their title? Explain. Finally, suppose you wanted to find electronic publications about banking, finance, or both topics. What search words would you use?

   b. Using the search capabilities, find hyperlinks to electronic publications in an area that interests you. (Some examples are sports, international banking, multicultural, and multimedia games.) Visit the Web sites of at least three publications you've found this way. Which are they, what are their URLs, and what's available on those Web pages?

9. We listed three sources of information about using helper applications in this chapter. Visit all the sites with your Web browser and bookmark each one. Now create a bookmark folder named **Help on Helpers** and put the three bookmarks into that folder.

10. The Web page "Editor & Publisher's Database Directory Of The World's Online Newspapers," **http://www.mediainfo.com/ephome/npaper/nphtm/online.htm**, has lists of newspapers on the Web. Follow links to five different newspapers from at least three different continents. Bookmark each and create a bookmark folder named **Newspapers**. Move the bookmarks for the individual newspapers into that folder.

Using the
World Wide Web
for Research

The World Wide Web has revolutionized the way we do research. Instead of spending hours combing library indexes and catalogs, making endless telephone calls, or traveling to far-off places, with a few clicks of the mouse you can find an enormous amount of information on virtually any subject. The World Wide Web can answer quick reference questions such as "What is the exchange rate for the Japanese yen?" or "What is the population of Egypt?" It can also help you research deeper subjects such as recycling or congressional campaign contributions in the last election.

In the course of this chapter, you'll see how to find answers to these research and reference questions. We'll provide you with an introduction to research skills on the World Wide Web so that you can begin to go out and find whatever interests you. In later chapters, we will cover research skills in more detail.

The sections in this chapter are as follows:
* Browsing the World Wide Web: Using Directories
* Finding Information Gems in Virtual Libraries
* Searching the World Wide Web: Using Search Engines
* Using Several Search Engines Simultaneously: Meta-search Tools

You will learn the difference between *browsing* and *keyword search-ing* the WWW, and you will see examples that focus on each method. You'll discover when it is better to use a *directory* or *subject catalog* (topical lists of selected WWW resources, hierarchically arranged) and when it makes sense to start with a *search engine* (a tool that provides keyword searching ability of all known WWW resources). We will also cover the advantage of using virtual libraries, directories that contain only selected WWW resources. We will discuss employing several search engines simultaneously by using *meta-search tools*. We'll introduce you to a couple of different search engines and take you through the steps of using them.

If you know different tactics for finding information on the WWW, your searches will be more successful. We'll provide activities in this chapter that will give you practice in browsing and keyword searching. Once you learn how to use the WWW to its fullest potential, you will be amazed at what you can locate in a short period of time.

Let's start researching!

Browsing the World Wide Web: Using Directories

There are two basic ways to find information on the World Wide Web: You can browse directories by subject, or you can search by keyword in search engines. In this section, we'll focus on browsing directories; we'll cover keyword searching in search engines later in the chapter. While search engine databases are created by computer programs, directories are created and maintained by people. Directories don't cover the entire Web. In fact, directories are very small collections of resources, com-pared with the huge databases that search engines employ.

Browsing directories can be a very effective way to find the resources you need, especially if you need general information on a subject, such as recycling. If you are at the beginning of your research, or if you are searching for an overview of the topic at hand, it may also be helpful to use a directory. Many of the major search tools contain a directory and a search engine. Using these you can try both methods in one service. The directory part of the search engine is usually a subset of the entire database, and the sites listed in a directory are often evaluated, summa-rized, and given ratings. Some directories provide rudimentary search interfaces as well. Here are the most well-known directories on the World Wide Web:

* Excite Channels (Web sites)
  http://www.excite.com
* Galaxy
  http://galaxy.einet.net
* Infoseek
  http://www.infoseek.com

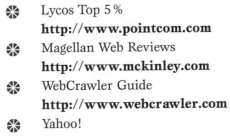

❋   Lycos Top 5 %
  http://www.pointcom.com

❋   Magellan Web Reviews
  http://www.mckinley.com

❋   WebCrawler Guide
  http://www.webcrawler.com

❋   Yahoo!
  http://www.yahoo.com

Directories, or subject catalogs, are topical lists of selected Web resources that are arranged in a hierarchical way. By *hierarchical*, we mean that the ***subject categories*** are arranged from broadest to most specific. For example, the following is a ***hierarchy***:

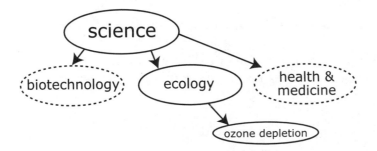

In this example, *Ecology* is a subcategory of *Science*, and *Ozone Depletion* is a subcategory of *Ecology*.

In a hypertext environment, such as the World Wide Web, browsing from one subject to a more detailed part of that subject is quite simple. We click on **Science**, which is the ***top-level category*** or heading, and the computer screen fills with a list of subject categories that are narrower than Science. This might include, for example, *Biotechnology*, or *Health and Medicine*, or, in our case, *Ecology*.

When we click on **Ecology**, the screen fills with even more subject categories, and we choose the subject we want, which is *Ozone Depletion*. In this case, the hierarchy ends here. After we choose **Ozone Depletion**, the screen fills in with a list of Web pages that we can now choose by clicking on their titles. This process is referred to as a ***structured browse***.

Some hierarchies have several levels, whereas others have only two. It depends on the directory you are using and the subject you are researching. None of the major directories use the same subject categories. In one directory, the term may be *Environment*; in another, the term may be *Ecology*.

In Chapter 1, we browsed Yahoo!, one of the most comprehensive directories on the World Wide Web. (We'll do more in Yahoo! in Chapter 4, "Directories and Virtual Libraries.") To illustrate the process of browsing in a detailed way, let's try an activity that will take you through a sample research problem in a different directory. We'll show you how easy it is to move from a broad subject category to a more specific one. We'll illustrate why browsing for information using directories can be a very satisfying way to do research on the WWW. In this activity, as in all the activities in the book, we'll give you a numbered list of each of the steps to follow and include the results you would have seen at the time this book was written.

✴ Tip

Remember that the Web is always changing and that your results may differ from those shown here. Don't let this confuse you. The activities are meant to teach you fundamental skills. These skills don't change, even though the number of results obtained or the actual screens may look very different.

Activity 3.1   Using a Directory to Browse for Information

Overview

In this activity, we'll access the search tool Excite, **http://www.excite .com**, and use its directory to find resources on recycling. Excite is a search tool that includes a search engine and a directory. You can access the directory by using the top-level subject headings that appear in Channels, Excite's interface. *Channels* are collections of Web resources arranged by subject, with a channel bringing together different types of resources, including listings of Web sites, news reports, TV listings, Web tours, and chat rooms.

We'll focus on the "Web Sites" section of Excite. Many of the resources included in "Web Sites" are reviewed by a subject specialist and given quality ratings. "Web Sites" is a subset of the Excite database. At the time of this writing, "Web Sites" has 140,000 Web pages in its directory. Excite's search engine, however, has more than fifty million Web pages in its database! After we locate some interesting information on recycling by browsing Excite's "Web Sites," we'll show you how to bookmark one of the useful resources we find.

We'll follow these steps:
1. Start the Web browser.
2. Go to the home page for Excite.
3. Browse the "Web Sites" portion of Channels.
4. Bookmark it!
5. End the session.

Don't forget to practice using the **Back** and **Forward** buttons to avoid losing your place.

Details

1   Start the Web browser.

Do It! Double-click on the **Netscape** icon.

2   Go to the home page for Excite.

Do It! Point to the location field and click the (left) mouse button.

The URL of the current Web page will change color. Now you can type in the URL for Excite.

Do It! Type **http://www.excite.com** in the location field and press **Enter**.

3   Browse the "Web Sites" portion of Channels.

Take a look at the list of subjects in Channels, as shown in Figure 3.1.

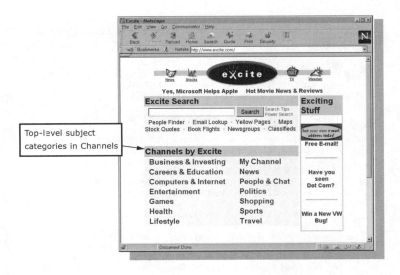

Figure 3.1—Channels by Excite

To access any of the resources in Channels, you need to click on a top-level category. This will bring to your screen all kinds of resources available in that subject area. Since the subject we're looking for is *recycling*, we need to find a subject category that would be related to this. A logical choice is **Health**. Follow these steps:

Do It! Click on **Health**.

After the screen fills, scroll down (use the down arrow key or the vertical scroll bar) until more detailed subject categories, or *subcategories*, appear on the left side of the screen. These subcategories will be listed under **Web Sites**.

❋*Do It!* Click on **Environment**, which is a subcategory of **Science**.

❋*Do It!* Click on **Conservation & Ecology**.

After the screen fills, look at the first several resources listed. Note that these have symbols next to them. These symbols mean that these Web pages are rated and reviewed by Excite subject specialists. Scroll down the list of these rated resources until you find **Recycler's World**. This resource is full of information about recycling. (If you don't find this resource, try to locate another one that covers recycling.)

❋*Do It!* Click on **Recycler's World**, as shown in Figure 3.2.

Take a look at it and follow a few hyperlinks. Click on the **Back** button in the menu toolbar if you want to return to the page before. If you go back to the resource list again, note that after the rated and reviewed resources, there are several more Web pages that you can choose from as well.

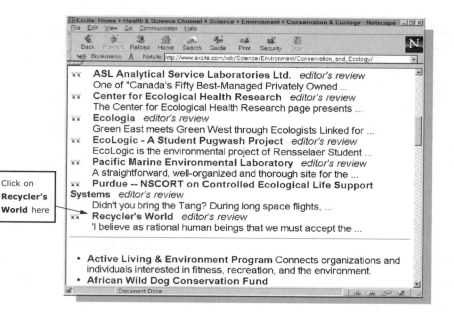

Figure 3.2—Results from Browsing for Recycling Information

4 Bookmark it!

After you've found this great site, you may want to return to it again someday, so let's put it in your bookmark list.

❋*Do It!* Simply click on **Bookmarks** in the location toolbar and select **Add Bookmark**.

The title of the URL is automatically added to your bookmark list.

5   End the session.

You can end the session now, or you can stay online to do the next activity.

✳Do It! To end the session now, click on **File** in the menu bar and select **Exit** from the pulldown menu.

✳Tip

Several times throughout this book we'll be asking you to make bookmarks to save the URL locations of valuable Web pages. You'll need to know how to delete bookmarks, especially if you're using a public computer. Follow these steps:

✳ Click on **Bookmarks** (which is located on the Location toolbar in Netscape).

✳ Select **Edit Bookmarks**.

✳ Highlight the bookmark you want to delete by pointing to it.

✳ Click on **Edit** and drag the pointer to **Delete** and let go, or press the Delete key.

This should delete the bookmark. See Activity 2.2 for more information about bookmarks.

✳

_____ End of Activity 3.1 _____

In this activity, we looked for information about recycling by browsing a directory. In Excite's "Web Sites" portion of Channels, we clicked on **Health** first, then **Environment** from the "Web Sites" list, and finally, **Conservation & Ecology** to take us to our desired location. There, we found a list of several Web pages focusing on ecological topics. Each directory on the World Wide Web will approach a subject differently. For example, in Magellan, **http://www.mckinley.com**, most of the Web pages about recycling would be found using a completely different subject hierarchy. In Magellan, the hierarchy looks like this:

life & style → environment → sustainable practices & communities → recycling

Browsing Versus Searching a Directory

It may be helpful to think of browsing a directory on the Web as similar to going through subjects in a card catalog. You may find exactly what you are looking for by browsing through many pages or cards filled with information, but then again, you may not. You may miss some related information, because your subject may appear in many different categories. For example, information on recycling appears in the "Conservation & Ecology" category in Excite's "Web Sites," but there may have been information on this in the **Waste/Toxics** category as well.

Browsing a directory requires that you think categorically about the subject you are researching. You have to be careful about the direction in which you are going when you do a structured browse. Many directories have simple keyword-searching ability for just this reason. Keyword searching was created to help people find information without having to know ahead of time the category in which the information lies. Keyword searching helps us find Web information more quickly, just as computerized library catalogs have helped us find books more quickly.

If you don't want to take the time to browse categories in a directory, you may want to search the directory by keyword. Or you can do both. It is a good idea to use different tactics when looking for something on the Web. Keep in mind, however, that when you search most directories by keyword, you will find Web pages that have the word or words that you are searching for in the titles, annotations, or URLs, not the Web pages themselves. In the next section, which focuses on virtual libraries, we'll explain how to search a directory using keywords.

Finding Information Gems in Virtual Libraries

Virtual libraries are directories that contain collections of resources that librarians or cybrarians have carefully chosen and organized in a logical way. The resources you find in a virtual library have been selected and placed there for their excellence and usefulness. The Web pages included are usually evaluated by someone knowledgeable in that field. Typically, virtual libraries provide an organizational hierarchy with subject categories to facilitate browsing. Most include query interfaces in order to perform simple searches. Virtual libraries are great places to begin your research.

Here are several of the best-known virtual libraries on the Web:

* �֎ Argus Clearinghouse
  http://www.clearinghouse.net
* ✖ Internet Public Library
  http://www.ipl.org
* ✖ Librarians' Index to the Internet
  http://sunsite.berkeley.edu/InternetIndex

❋ World Wide Web Virtual Library
http://vlib.stanford.edu/Overview.html

The main difference between virtual libraries and the directories we discussed earlier in the chapter is that virtual libraries are much smaller, because the resources included are selected very carefully. The people who organize virtual libraries are usually on the lookout for three major types of information: ***subject guides***, ***reference works***, and ***specialized databases***.

Subject Guides

A *subject guide* is a Web resource devoted to including hyperlinks to most, if not all, Web pages on a particular subject. For example, a resource devoted to listing Web pages on environmental ethics is a subject guide (see Figure 3.3).

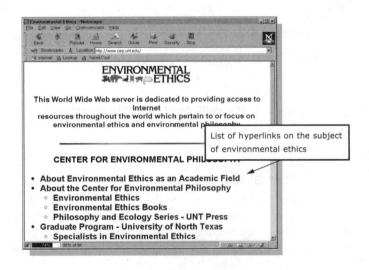

Figure 3.3—Subject Guide on Environmental Ethics

Reference Works

The other common type of resource collected by virtual libraries is a reference work. A *reference work* is a full text document with self-contained information. In other words, it doesn't necessarily contain hyperlinks to other resources.

A reference work on the World Wide Web is very similar to its print counterpart. A dictionary on the Web would look very much like a dictionary on the reference shelf. The only difference is that it would allow you to move around the document using hyperlinks instead of turning pages and looking in the index for related topics. There are encyclopedias, handbooks, dictionaries, directories, and many other types of reference works on the World Wide Web. Virtual libraries are also interested in including these types of works in their directories. Figure 3.4 pictures a reference work—the U.S. Postal Service's Zip Code Lookup and Address Information.

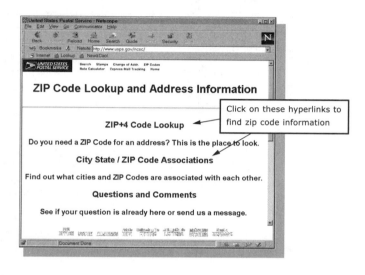

Figure 3.4—U.S. Postal Service's Zip Code Lookup and Address Information

Specialized Databases

Virtual libraries can be useful for finding *specialized databases* as well. A specialized database is an index that catalogs certain material, such as patent information, medical journal article citations, company financial data, court decisions, and so forth. Specialized databases can usually be searched by keyword. We'll discuss them in detail in Chapter 7.

Now that you know what types of information are collected in virtual libraries, we'll show you how to find these information gems. Let's do an activity to illustrate how useful virtual libraries can be for your research.

Activity 3.2   Finding Resources in a Virtual Library

Overview

In the beginning of this chapter, we mentioned several research and reference questions to which the World Wide Web can provide answers. One of those questions was "What is the population of Egypt?" We will find the answer to this question by using the Internet Public Library (IPL), a virtual library maintained by librarians at the University of Michigan.

The IPL is organized much like a traditional library. It has a reference section, a youth section, and many others. If you can't find what you're looking for, you can submit the question to a real librarian who will email the answer back to you. You can browse the IPL or search its contents. Browsing is the easiest way to find information, however, because the search tool doesn't search the contents of the resources, only the titles of the resources and annotations attached to them.

In this activity, we'll first browse the IPL by subject. Because we're trying to find an answer to a reference question, we'll open the Reference Collection. Then we'll go to the "Geography" section, as the population of Egypt would likely be found in a geographic resource. We'll also open a reference work and look for the statistic we want by using the Find in Page option in Netscape Navigator. After this, we'll show how to perform a keyword search in order to demonstrate the difference between searching and browsing in the IPL. We'll follow these steps:

1. Go to the home page for the Internet Public Library.
2. Open the Reference Collection.
3. Browse the Reference Collection.
4. Open *The World Factbook*.
5. Find the population of Egypt.
6. Search the Reference Collection.
7. Browse the results of the search.
8. End the session.

You'll see how quickly we can find not only the population of Egypt, but also other current information about that country. Let's get started!

Details

1   Go to the home page for the Internet Public Library. (We're assuming your Web browser is already started.)

✳*Do It!* Use the mouse to point to the location field and click the (left) mouse button.

The URL of the current Web page will change color. Now you can type in the URL for the Internet Public Library.

✳*Do It!* Type **www.ipl.org** in the location field and press **Enter**.

2   Open the Reference Collection.

✳*Do It!* First, click on **Reference** under the **Collections** heading.

Your screen will fill with a picture of a traditional library, complete with a reference librarian sitting at a desk, as shown in Figure 3.5.

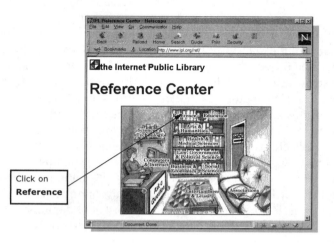

Figure 3.5—The Internet Public Library Reference Center

✳*Do It!* Click on **Reference** on the Reference Center page as shown in Figure 3.5.

3   Browse the Reference Collection.

After your screen fills, move down the list of subdivisions in the "Reference" section.

✳*Do It!* Click on **Geography**.

Why geography? This is the most logical subcategory to look under to find information on population. After your screen fills, scroll down the list to find the most appropriate source that would contain the answer to this question. By reading the annotations attached to the reference sources, we determine that *The World Factbook 1996* would be a good choice, because it provides "quick facts on countries of the world." *The World Factbook*, authored and published by the U.S. Central Intelligence Agency, is updated annually. It's also available in printed form.

4   Open *The World Factbook*.

✳*Do It!* Click on *The World Factbook 1996*.

Your screen will fill with a map of the world. As Egypt is in Africa, you need to open that area.

✳*Do It!* Click on the **Africa** box.

Now you'll be asked to click on the first letter of the country's name.

✳*Do It!* Click on **E**.

✳*Do It!* Click on **Egypt**.

Your screen should look like the one pictured in Figure 3.6.

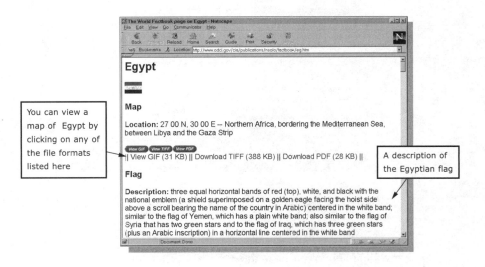

You can view a map of Egypt by clicking on any of the file formats listed here

A description of the Egyptian flag

Figure 3.6—Egypt in The World Factbook

5   Find the population of Egypt.

You could scroll down through the chapter on Egypt until you found population and other demographic statistics in the "People" section. Or you could follow these steps to find the population more quickly:

✳*Do It!* Point your mouse to **Edit** in the Netscape menu bar and choose **Find in Page**.

✳*Do It!* Type **population** in the pane next to **Find what**.

✳*Do It!* Click on **Find Next**.

✳*Do It!* Click on **Find Next** again.

This command will take you right to the statistic you want, as shown in Figure 3.7.

Population
of Egypt

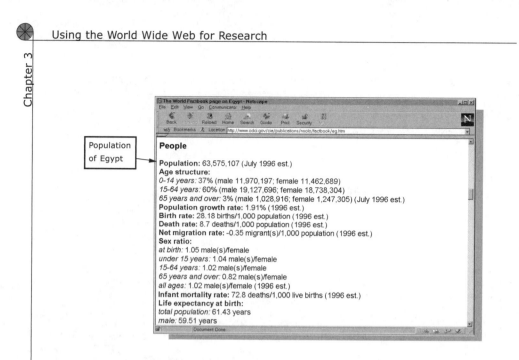

Figure 3.7—Demographic Information for Egypt from The World Factbook

6   Search the Reference Collection.

Now we'll show you how to search the Internet Public Library. We're going to type in the word **Egypt** first.

Do It! Click on the **Back** icon in the Netscape toolbar at the top of your screen until you are at the page that lists the resources in "Geography."

At the bottom of the page, there is a form that you can use to do a search. You'll be searching only those Web pages in the IPL's Reference Collection.

Do It! Type in the word **Egypt** in the form provided. Click **Search**.

The search tool responds with some Web pages, but none of them is *The World Factbook*.

Do It! Highlight Egypt and try typing in **populations**, as shown in Figure 3.8. Click **Search**.

We may be tempted to type in *population* (without an *s* at the end), but if we go back and look at the annotation for *The World Factbook*, we notice that the word used is *populations*, not *population*.

Click on **Search**

Type populations here

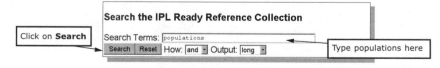

Figure 3.8—Searching the Reference Collection

7   Browse the results of the search.

The search tool responds with a collection of URLs that may be useful. Move down the list until you notice *The World Factbook*.

8   End the session.

You can end the session now, or you can stay online to do the next activity.

✳Do It! To end the session now, click on **File** in the menu bar and select **Exit** from the menu.

_____ End of Activity 3.2 _____

You can see from the preceding example that sometimes it is better to browse than to search a directory or virtual library. The search tool in the Internet Public Library doesn't find words that are in the body of the Web pages. The words indexed are in the Web pages' titles, their URLs, and their annotations. Because the word *Egypt* didn't appear in the title, URL, or annotation of *The World Factbook*, the search tool didn't locate it. We also pointed out that if we had typed *population* instead of *populations*, we wouldn't have had *The World Factbook* in the list of results.

Directories can be useful if you have a broad subject and aren't sure how to narrow down the search. They are also helpful if you want to get a general idea about the resources out there that will help you focus your topic. By browsing a directory in the first activity, we quickly found Web pages that focused on recycling.

Virtual libraries are especially useful as starting points for research on a particular topic or as places to go for answers to quick reference questions. But if you want to zero in quickly on Web pages that are specifically related to your topic, or if your topic is multifaceted or extremely detailed, or if you are sure about the keywords you are going to use, a search engine is what you need. In the following sections, we'll explore search engines and give a brief overview of the most common keyword search features.

Searching the World Wide Web: Using Search Engines

Search engines are tools that use computer programs called **spiders** and **robots** to gather information automatically on the Internet. With this information, they create a database.

Spiders are computer programs that go out on the Internet and locate hyperlinks that are available to the public, such as WWW and **Gopher** documents. These spiders, or robots, as they are commonly called, load these resources in a database, which you can then search by using a search engine. These spider, or robot, programs were created because the number of Internet documents has increased so rapidly that people can't keep up with indexing them manually. Each of the major search engines attempts to do the same thing—namely, index the entire Web—so they handle a huge amount of data.

There are advantages to computer-generated databases. They are frequently updated, give access to very large collections, and provide the most comprehensive search results. If you are looking for a specific concept or phrase, a search engine is the best place to start. And you would be smart to look in more than one, because each engine gives different results.

Here are the major search engines:

❋	AltaVista	**http://www.altavista.digital.com**
❋	Excite	**http://www.excite.com***
❋	HotBot	**http://www.hotbot.com***
❋	Infoseek	**http://www.infoseek.com***
❋	Lycos	**http://www.lycos.com***
❋	Open Text	**http://index.opentext.net**
❋	WebCrawler	**http://www.webcrawler.com***

*Denotes that the search engine has a browsable directory.

❋ Tip

Finding databases on the World Wide Web.

If you want to look for other databases on the World Wide Web, or want to keep up-to-date with the new ones that have been added, there are two excellent places to go:

All-in-One Search Page   **http://www.albany.net/allinone**

The Internet Sleuth   **http://www.isleuth.com**

Both of these sites provide access to many search engines and are usually referred to as *meta-search tools*, or more specifically, **all-in-one search tools**. We'll discuss these and similar services later in the chapter.

Search Engine Similarities

All of the major search engines are similar in that you enter keywords, phrases, or proper names in a *search form*. After you click on **search**, **submit**, **seek**, or some other command button, the database returns a collection of hyperlinks to your screen.

The database usually lists them according to their *relevance* to the keyword(s) you typed in, from most to least relevant. Search engines determine relevance in different ways. Generally, they base this determination on how many times the search terms appear in the document.

All search engines have online help to acquaint you with their search options. Two common search options that most search engines support are ***Boolean searching*** and ***phrase searching***. We will briefly discuss these two options below. Then, in Chapter 5, "Search Strategies for Search Engines," we will cover these and other search options, which are available on many (but not all) search engines, including **relevancy ranking**, **field searching**, **truncation searching**, and **proximity searching**.

Boolean Operators

The Boolean operators are AND, OR, and NOT.

❋ The use of AND placed between keywords in your ***search expression*** will narrow the search results.

For example, *hiking AND camping* would narrow your search so that you would receive only those sites that have both the words *hiking* and *camping* in them.

❋ Placing an OR between keywords broadens your search results. For example, *hiking OR camping* would retrieve those sites that have either the word *hiking* or the word *camping* in them.

hiking AND camping   *hiking OR camping*

❋ The NOT operator will also narrow the search.

For example, *hiking NOT camping* would narrow your search so you would get all hiking, but not camping.

hiking NOT camping

❋ In some search engines, if nothing is typed between two words, you can assume an OR is between them. This is what we'd refer to as a default setting.

In order to override this setting, you'd either have to type AND between the words or put a **+** before both words.

Phrase Searching

❋ Searching by phrase guarantees that the words you type in will appear adjacent to each other, in the order you typed them.

❋ Let's say you are searching for information on global warming. If you typed in the two words *global warming* separated by a space, the system you're using may assume that you are in effect saying *global AND warming*, or in some cases (depending on the search engine), *global OR warming*. Your search results would not be very precise, because the words *global* and *warming* could appear separately from each other throughout the document.

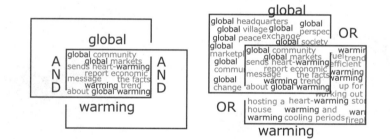

global AND warming; global OR warming

❋ Most search engines support phrase searching, requiring the use of double quotation marks around the phrase. We would type "global warming" in our example.

Search Engine Differences

The major search engines differ in the following ways:

❋ Size of the index.

❋ Search options (many search engines support the same options but require you to use different **syntax** in order to initiate them).

❋ Speed.

❋ Update frequency.

❋ Relevance of the search results.

❋ Overall ease of use.

It is important to know these differences, because in order to do an exhaustive search of the World Wide Web, you must be familiar with the different search tools. You cannot rely on a single search engine to satisfy every query.

At this point it may be helpful to do a couple of activities to illustrate how search engines work. The first activity will focus on Boolean searching, and the second on phrase searching.

Activity 3.3   Using Boolean Search Operators

Overview

Let's try to find Web pages on recycling plastic products. We found some general information on recycling in Activity 3.1 by searching the hierarchical directory of Excite Channels "Web Sites." This time we'll use a search engine to find more specific information, specifically about the recycling of plastics.

We'll use the search engine WebCrawler, which was one of the first to appear on the Web. To start, we will type in the keywords we want the Web pages to include. We'll examine the results and then check the help screen to find out how WebCrawler handles advanced search options. Then we'll do the search again using Boolean operators. We'll note how our search results were narrowed in size and how the contents of the pages were more relevant.

We'll follow these steps:

1. Go to the home page for WebCrawler.
2. Type in keywords and start the search.
3. Examine the search results.
4. Consult search help.
5. Modify the search by typing in a new search expression.
6. Examine the results.
7. End the session.

Ready? Let's start the engine!

Details

1   **Go to the home page for WebCrawler. (We're assuming your Web browser is already started.)**

Do It! Use the mouse to point to the location field and click the (left) mouse button.

The URL of the current Web page will change color. Now you can type in the URL for WebCrawler.

Do It! Type **http://www.webcrawler.com** in the location field and press **Enter**.

2   **Type in keywords and start the search.**

✷*Do It!* Type the keywords **recycling plastic products** in the search form next to **Search**.

✷*Do It!* Now click on the **Search** button. Figure 3.9 shows the keywords typed in.

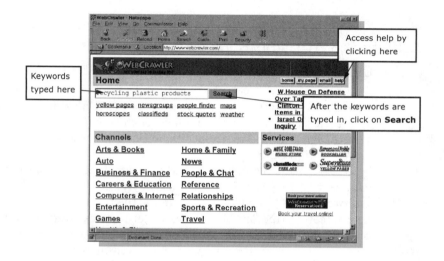

Figure 3.9—WebCrawler Home Page with Keywords Typed In

3   Examine the search results.

Notice the large number of hyperlinks retrieved by WebCrawler. They are listed according to their relevance to the search query, from most relevant to least relevant. After scrolling down and checking out some of the Web pages retrieved by this search, we start to think of other possibilities. What if there are some perfect hyperlinks out there that use the word *plastics* instead of *plastic*? How would we construct a search so we would get Web pages that included the words *recycling* and *products* and *plastics* or *plastic*? We're identifying the need to use Boolean operators, and we need to know whether WebCrawler supports Boolean searching. We hope that by using Boolean operators, we'll retrieve not only more relevant results but also fewer results. We could most easily find out whether WebCrawler supports Boolean searching by accessing its online help.

4   Consult search help.

Do It! Click on the **help** button on the left side of the screen, as shown in Figure 3.9.

A partial list of the search help topics appears in Figure 3.10.

Do It! Click on **Advanced Searching**, as shown in Figure 3.10.

Select **Advanced Searching**

Figure 3.10—Help Topics in WebCrawler

We discover that WebCrawler does support Boolean searching. We can use AND, OR, and NOT. Farther down on the "Advanced Searching" page, we also learn that if there are ANDs and ORs in one search statement, then parentheses must be used to guarantee good search results.

Do It! Click on the **WebCrawler** icon at the top left of the screen.

You should now be back on the WebCrawler home page.

5   Modify the search by typing in a new search expression.

Do It! Type **recycling and products and (plastic or plastics)**, as shown in Figure 3.11.

This search expression will retrieve hyperlinks to those sites that have the words *recycling* AND *products* (must have both words) AND *plastic* OR *plastics* (must have either one).

Do It! Click on **Search**.

Figure 3.11—Boolean Searching in WebCrawler

6   Examine the results.

Take a few minutes and explore the first Web pages retrieved. Notice that we received significantly fewer results by using the Boolean search operators.

Do It! To read the summaries or annotations of the Web pages, click on **summaries**, as shown in Figure 3.11.

Figure 3.12 shows the results with summaries, or annotations, attached. Note that you can also click on **Similar Pages** at the end of each annotation. This will lead you to other pages that are related to this particular page.

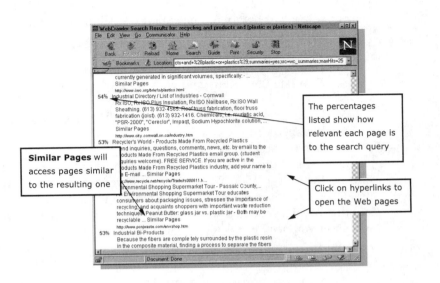

Figure 3.12—Hyperlinks to Recycling Plastics Information in WebCrawler

7   End the session.

Wasn't that easy? Let's end this session and do another activity. You can stay online and continue to the next activity or end this session now.

❋Do It! To disconnect, click on **File** in the menu bar and select **Exit** from the menu.

End of Activity 3.3

In the last activity, we illustrated the importance of looking at a search engine's online help screen. This caused us to type in the search expression that gave us the most precise and relevant results. In the following activity, we'll use another search engine to show the phrase-searching feature. At the beginning of the chapter, we mentioned that the World Wide Web can help us find the answer to the question "What is the exchange rate of the Japanese yen?" We're going to look for that answer now by using the search engine Infoseek, **www.infoseek.com**. Infoseek is one of the more popular search engines. It also includes a browsable directory.

Activity 3.4   Using Phrase Searching to Find Information

Overview

In this activity, we will open Infoseek and look at the online help before we begin searching. We will type in the phrase *currency exchange rates* using the syntax that is particular to Infoseek, and we will examine the results. We'll have you bookmark the best site we find so that you can start building your own reference library. We'll follow these steps:

1. Go to the home page for Infoseek.
2. Read the help screens in Infoseek.
3. Use the search form provided and type in a search expression.
4. Examine the results and click on a hyperlink that appears to have the information you need.
5. Find the currency exchange rate for the Japanese yen.
6. Bookmark it!
7. End the session.

Once you see how easy it is to find an answer to a reference question on the World Wide Web, you may never want to comb through newspapers or journals again. And after you make a bookmark to the site that provides the answer, you'll be able to flip to the information whenever you need it in a few seconds. Let's go find it!

Details

1   Go to the home page for Infoseek. (We assume your browser is already open.)

✳*DoIt!* Use the mouse to point to the location field and click the (left) mouse button.

The URL of the current Web page will change color. Now you can type in the URL for Infoseek.

✳*DoIt!* Type **http://www.infoseek.com** in the location field and press **Enter**.

2   Read the help screens in Infoseek.

✳*DoIt!* Click on **Tips**, as shown in Figure 3.13.

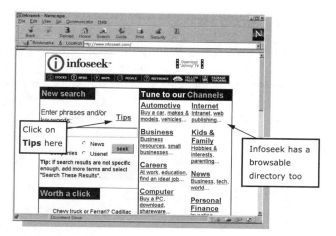

Figure 3.13—Infoseek Home Page

✷*Do It!* After your screen fills, click on **Quick Reference**.

Your screen should look like the one in Figure 3.14.

Notice that in Infoseek, you must place quotation marks before the first word and after the last word in the phrase you are searching for. This will ensure that the words in the phrase appear together.

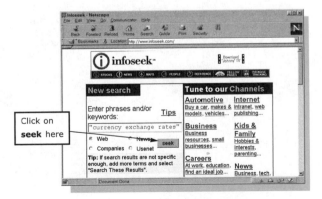

Figure 3.14—Infoseek Help

3   Use the search form provided and type in a search expression.

✷*Do It!* Scroll up to the top of the page and click on **Infoseek**.

✷*Do It!* Type the phrase **"currency exchange rates"** in the search form provided and click on **seek**, as shown in Figure 3.15.

Figure 3.15—Phrase Searching in Infoseek

4   Examine the results and click on a hyperlink that appears to have the information you need.

The first page or two of results should contain the most relevant resources. Find a resource in your hit list that most likely would have the information you are seeking. In this activity, we'll click on a Web page entitled "Currency Exchange Rates...Sonnet Financial's Daily Currency Rates as provided by Reuters." If you find it, click on it. If not, click on another Web page title that you think will help you find the information.

❋Do It! Click on **Currency Exchange Rates**, as shown in Figure 3.16.

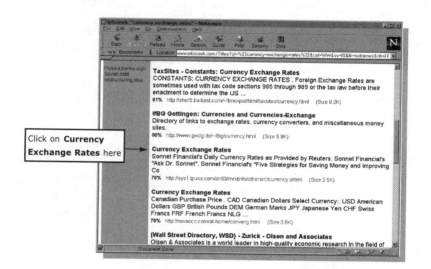

Figure 3.16—Hyperlinks to Foreign Exchange Rate Information

5   Find the currency exchange rate for the Japanese yen.

Your screen should look like the one pictured in Figure 3.17.

Figure 3.17—Currency Exchange Information Page

✳Do It! Click on the first hyperlink, **Sonnet Financial's Daily Currency Rates as Provided by Reuters**, as shown in Figure 3.17.

Figure 3.18—Currency Exchange Information for Various Countries

Figure 3.18 shows a list of many foreign currencies, with their quoted rates to the U.S. dollar. Note that the Japanese yen is listed with a buy and sell rate.

6   Bookmark it!

After finding this informative Web page, you may want to locate it again quickly, so let's put it in your bookmark list.

Do It! Point your mouse to **Bookmarks** in the location toolbar and click, as shown in Figure 3.18.

Do It! Point your mouse to **Add Bookmark** and click.

The URL's title is automatically added to your bookmark list. You can check the list to see that this happened.

Do It! Click on **Bookmark** again and see that the title of the location is there.

You can access this page later simply by clicking on it.

7   End the session.

Now that we've explored another dimension of searching the World Wide Web, it's time either to disconnect or to go to the next activity and cover new topics.

Do It! Click on **File** in the menu bar and select **Exit** from the menu.

If you're not using your own computer, you may want to delete your bookmarks at this time.

—————————————— End of Activity 3.4 ——————————————

In this activity, we focused on the phrase-searching feature. Most search engines support this feature. You can see how important it is. Imagine if we were only able to search for currency exchange rates without specifying that the three words appear next to each other in that order. We might get pages that had the word *currency* in the first paragraph and the other two words in the last paragraph, with no relationship between the words. In Chapter 5, we'll discuss this and other search features such as this in more detail.

In the next section, we'll talk about using meta-search tools. These resources allow you to use several search engine databases from the same Web site, or to do so simultaneously.

Using Several Search Engines Simultaneously: Meta-search Tools

We have mentioned the importance of looking in more than one search engine when trying to find relevant Web pages. Each search engine varies in size, indexing structure, update frequency, and search options. It can be confusing and time consuming to do your search in several databases, especially if you have to keep track of all of their differences.

To solve some of these problems, database providers have come up with meta-search tools. If meta-search tools allow you to use several search engines simultaneously, they are often called **parallel search** *tools* or *unified search interfaces*. Instead of building their own data-bases, meta-search tools use the major search engines and directories that already exist on the Internet and provide the user with search forms or interfaces for submitting queries to these search tools. Simply by submitting a query, the meta-search tool collects the most relevant sites in each database and sends them to the screen. Some sites merely list World Wide Web search tools with their search forms so you can search one at a time. These are called *all-in-one search tools*. Here are the most popular meta-search tools:

❋ All-in-One Search Page
  http://www.albany.net/allinone

❋ Internet Sleuth
  http://www.isleuth.com

❋ MetaCrawler
  http://metacrawler.com

❋ Search.Com
  http://www.search.com

❋ SavvySearch
  http://www.cs.colostate.edu/~dreiling/
  smartform.html

The All-in-One Search Page is a service that provides an alphabeti-cal list of Web search engines and directories, along with their search forms. Some of the search forms include the option of advanced search-ing, but some do not. Others offer the option of requesting the number of hits you want returned to you. See an example of the All-in-One Search Page in Figure 3.19.

Figure 3.19—All-in-One Search Page

95

The All-in-One Search Page is a good site for you to find out what different search engines and directories are on the Internet. It's not the best place to learn about the different search tools, because help screens are not included, and not all the options are listed on the search interface form. You may not be able to extract the most relevant sites using All-in-One, because you won't be aware of the best search methods for each database. If, however, you are very familiar with a particular search engine's capabilities, All-in-One would be a good site to have in your bookmark list.

The Internet Sleuth allows you to search one database at a time or several at once. Like the All-in-One Search Page, the other meta-search tools listed won't allow you to use each individual search engine's capabilities to their fullest, because you will be using a search interface to search several databases at once. For this reason, simple searches work best.

It can be interesting to do a search in one of these meta-search tools and to notice what different hyperlinks the various search engines return to you. What is most relevant in one database is not considered as relevant in another. The following example will illustrate how a meta-search tool performs a search in several databases at once. We'll discover how and when these tools can be useful.

Activity 3.5   Using a Meta-search Tool to Find Information

Overview

We'll be using SavvySearch, a meta-search tool that includes not only the major Web search indexes and directories, but also indexes of Usenet news, people, entertainment, and other topics. SavvySearch, like All-in-One, is available in multiple languages.

In this activity, we'll try to find information on campaign contributions to congressional candidates in the last national election. We want to keep the search simple, because we will be searching several databases at once, and meta-search engines have difficulty performing complicated searches in more than one database at a time. We will be typing in the words **congressional campaign contributions**.

We will take the following steps:
1. Go to the home page for SavvySearch.
2. Type the search expression in the search form.
3. Follow some of the hyperlinks returned by the databases.
4. Bookmark it!
5. End the session.

Let's find out how to use SavvySearch!

Details

1   Go to the home page for SavvySearch.

✳*Do It!* Use the mouse to point to the location field and click the (left) mouse button.

The URL of the current Web page will change color. Now you can type in the URL for SavvySearch.

✳*Do It!* Type **http://www.cs.colostate.edu/~ dreiling/ smartform.html** in the location field and press **⌷Enter⌷**.

2 Type the search expression in the search form.

SavvySearch supports Boolean searching by providing a pulldown menu under "Query options" and next to "Search for documents containing," as shown in Figure 3.20. The options are as follows: **all query terms (AND)**, **all query terms as a phrase**, and **any query term (OR)**. We want all of the words to appear in the Web pages that are returned to us, but the words do not necessarily have to be in a phrase, so make sure **all query terms** is selected. After you select a Boolean operator and type your search terms, SavvySearch will use the search expression you typed in and will search three databases at a time.

✳*Do It!* Type **congressional campaign contributions** in the search form provided.

✳*Do It!* Choose **all query terms** from the pulldown menu located under "Query options."

✳*Do It!* Click on **SavvySearch** to start your search.

Figure 3.20—SavvySearch with Search Expression Typed In

3 Follow some of the hyperlinks returned by the databases.

After you submit your search expression to SavvySearch, results from three databases will come back and fill your screen. In our case, the three databases are Lycos, Yahoo!, and Infoseek. You may find that three different databases are searched when you do this activity. Look at the results that the services found for you. Notice that the Web pages that Lycos brought to your screen aren't the same ones that the other services generated. This proves that the search services have different ways of determining the relevance of documents that search tools find.

Figure 3.21 shows a portion of the search results. After looking at the results, we decide that the most promising one is first on the Yahoo! list. Although this resource has no title, the annotation describes the page as including political and campaign resources and the CAPWEB guide to the U.S. Congress. If you don't see this resource on your list of results, try to find another Web page that includes congressional campaign information and open it.

✵Do It! Click on the first result in the Yahoo! list, as shown in Figure 3.21.

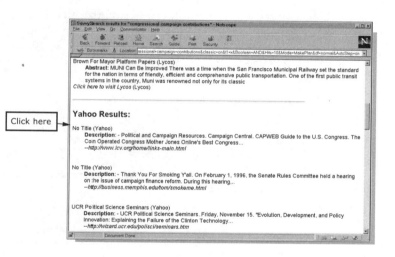

Figure 3.21—Partial Results from SavvySearch

If you scroll down through this page with the heading "Political and Campaign Resources," you'll discover many hyperlinks that will take you to information about different aspects of political campaigns. Take a look at the hyperlinks. Several of them may provide useful information. We'll try opening one of them to see what we can learn about congressional campaign contributions. **Vote Smart Web Project** looks promising. If you don't see **Vote Smart Web Project**, click on another hyperlink that looks useful.

✵Do It! Click on **Vote Smart Web Project**, as shown in Figure 3.22.

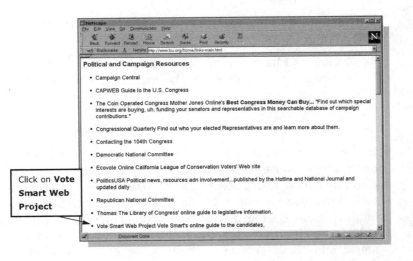

Click on **Vote Smart Web Project**

Figure 3.22—Political and Campaign Resources Page

Take a look at this Web page to see what types of information it can provide. If you click on **Candidates and Elected Officials**, you'll find lots of information about campaign finances, including detailed break-downs of contributions for elected officials and candidates.

4   Bookmark it!

Once you've found this great source of information, you don't want to lose track of it. Let's make a bookmark of the site so you can access it easily in the future.

Click on **Bookmarks** in the location toolbar. Point your mouse to **Add Bookmark** and click.

The title of the URL has now been added to your bookmark list.

After you've looked through the initial search results that SavvySearch returned, you could then ask the service to search more databases. They are listed at the bottom of the results screen, as shown in Figure 3.23. At this point, feel free to see what the other search engines have to offer, or go back to the earlier results (by clicking on the Back icon in the toolbar) and check out other Web pages that look interesting. Note that you can also search through Usenet archives by clicking on the category that has Deja News in it.

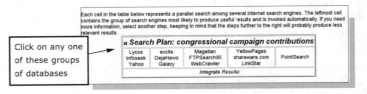

Click on any one of these groups of databases

Figure 3.23—SavvySearch Expanded Search Capability

5   End the session.

When you've finished exploring SavvySearch, you'll want to disconnect from Netscape.

✳*Do It!* Click on **File** in the menu bar and select **Exit** from the menu. If you like, you can delete the bookmarks you've made.

That's all there is to it!

_____ End of Activity 3.5 _____

In this activity, we used SavvySearch. Meta-search tools such as this one can save you time because you can use several search engine or directory databases at once. The major drawback of using meta-search tools is that you can't use the individual databases to their fullest capabilities because the tool has to search more than one database at a time using a search query mechanism that will satisfy all of them. For example, Infoseek doesn't support full Boolean searching, whereas Excite does. In a meta-search tool, the search interface would need to be able to search both databases, so it may not support a feature that one has and the other doesn't have.

Summary

The World Wide Web is an immense collection of valuable information generated by such organizations as universities, corporations, hospitals, associations, and government agencies. Most countries and several languages are represented on the Web. In addition to this, hundreds of thousands of individuals, such as scholars, students, doctors, librarians, teachers, and virtually anyone who wants to contribute to this vast accumulation of resources, are adding their home pages to the Web every day, all over the world.

Finding information on the World Wide Web is becoming easier all the time. There are two basic ways to accomplish it: either you can browse or search directories, or you can search by keyword in search engines. Browsing directories can be a very effective way to find the resources you need, especially if you're sure of the general information you're seeking. Directories index neither all of the pages in the World Wide Web nor all of the words that appear in the Web pages they catalog, however, so if you need specific information, a search engine is the tool you'll want to use. Search engine databases aim to cover the entire Web, and most of them index every word in each Web page.

To illustrate the difference, let's say we wanted to find information on a multifaceted topic, like the regulation of food safety. We may find something about it by browsing in a directory, but we'd have to be sure of the category that included it. Would we look under science, health, or government? We could search the directory using the keywords *food*, *safety*, and *government*, but if these words didn't appear in the categories, Web page titles, or annotations, there would be no results. In a search engine database, by contrast, all we need to do is type *"food safety"* (as a phrase) and *government* in a search form. The search engine will then scan its database, which includes the full text of Web pages from the entire Web, and will return the pages that match the search expression.

A directory would be more likely used if we were looking for general information, for example, resources on the AIDS virus. Directories depend on human beings to create and maintain their collections, with virtual libraries being the most dependent on people. Virtual libraries are the best directories to go to for subject guides and reference works. Virtual libraries are similar to traditional libraries, in that the cybrarians who manage them select and catalog the Web pages that are included in their directories, much as librarians select and catalog materials that are included in their libraries.

Selected Terms Introduced in This Chapter

all-in-one search tools
Boolean searching
browsing
directory
Gopher
hierarchy
keyword searching
meta-search tools
parallel search tools
phrase searching
reference work
relevance
robots
search engine

search expression
search form
specialized databases
spiders
structured browse
subcategory
subject catalog
subject category
subject guides
syntax
top-level category
unified search interfaces
virtual libraries

Exercises and Projects

1. Using Excite Channels, **http://www.excite.com**, find a list of AIDS/HIV resources by browsing. Find the three most relevant sites and make a note of their URLs.
2. Using Yahoo!, **http://www.yahoo.com**, find a list of upcoming film festivals by browsing and searching. Compare the results found from each mode. Did you get more results by browsing or by searching?
3. Using the Argus Clearinghouse, **http://www.clearinghouse.net**, find a subject guide on Celtic music. When was the subject guide updated?
4. Using Excite, **http://www.excite.com**, search for information on Nelson Mandela. Make sure you read the "Advanced Search Methods" section (click on **Search Tips** first) on how to search for proper names.

5. Find three Web pages, including one critical review, that discuss the classic 1941 movie *Citizen Kane* by using Infoseek, **http://www.infoseek.com**. How did you formulate the search request?

6. Use the meta-search tool Internet Sleuth, **http://www.isleuth .com**, to find the U.S. Government Manual. Access it and search for information on the Central Intelligence Agency. Make sure you read the search tips. How did you type in the search request? There are two choices for viewing the text. You may select TXT or PDF. The PDF (Portable Document Format) option is available only if you have Adobe Acrobat installed on your computer.

7. Using WebCrawler, **http://www.webcrawler.com**, look for the home page of Mary Washington College. First, search for it by typing in Mary Washington College. Note how many results were returned. Try it again by putting quotation marks around the phrase. How were the results affected? Why?

8. Using the Librarians' Index to the Internet, **http://sunsite .berkeley.edu/internetindex**, look for the "Blue Book" for automobiles. Try to find it by typing in keywords or by browsing the subject categories. How did you find it? Which way was easier?

9. Using the Librarians' Index to the Internet, **http://sunsite .berkeley.edu/internetindex**, find and connect to the International Lyrics Server. Search for lyrics to songs by the Cranberries. How many albums by this group were listed? Print or write down the lyrics to "Zombie."

10. Browse Yahoo!, **http://www.yahoo.com**, for a list of homebrewers' organizations. Write down the top-level category and all the subcategories you clicked on to reach the list.

4
Chapter

Directories and Virtual Libraries

In Chapter 3, "Using the World Wide Web for Research," we introduced different ways to investigate topics using the World Wide Web. One of the ways to find information is to browse directories. Directories, or subject catalogs, are especially useful for those with such general questions like "What resources does the World Wide Web have on vegetarianism?" and "What kind of information is available on mathematical sciences?" Directories can also help you find the best resources on a particular topic. For example, they would help with the questions "What are the best sites out there on the topic of Thai cooking?" and "What are the most useful career resources on the Web?"

Virtual libraries are the most specialized of all the directories. They are therefore the best places to find sites that collect Internet resources on a particular topic. For example, if you wanted all the Web sites that focus on the Middle East and North Africa, a virtual library would be a good start. In the last chapter, we covered a virtual library—the Internet Public Library. In this chapter, we'll look at another one and show how to use it.

In Chapter 3, we also browsed the directory in Excite's Channels for information on recycling. In this chapter, we'll cover directories in more detail by discussing features that are common to all directories and by showing how directories can differ from one another. We also will walk you through several activities to show you how best to use directories on the World Wide Web.

The sections in this chapter are as follows:
* Characteristics of Directories
* Browsing and Searching Directories
* Three Major Directories and How to Use Them
* Virtual Libraries: Directories with a Difference

Major Directories on the World Wide Web

❋ Excite Channels (Web Sites)

   http://www.excite.com

❋ Galaxy

   http://galaxy.einet.net

❋ Infoseek

   http://www.infoseek.com

❋ Lycos Top 5 %

   http://www.pointcom.com

❋ Magellan Web Reviews

   http://www.mckinley.com

❋ WebCrawler Guide

   http://www.webcrawler.com

❋ Yahoo!

   http://www.yahoo.com

Characteristics of Directories

Directories are topical lists of Internet resources arranged in a hierarchical way. Although they are meant to be browsed by subject, directories can also be searched by keyword. They differ from search engines in one major way—the human element involved in collecting and maintaining the information. Directories are created and maintained by people, whereas search engines rely on spiders or robots to scour the Internet for links. There are a number of differences between directories. One way to determine directories' particular characteristics is to ask the following questions about each of them:

❋ Who selects the included Web resources—directory administrators or people in the Internet community?

❋ Who categorizes the Web pages and sites—the people who submit them or directory administrators?

❋ How are the results displayed—alphabetically, by relevance, or by type of Web page?

❋ Are the resources rated? Are they annotated? Are they reviewed?

Each directory differs from others mainly in the level of quality control involved in its management. For example, some directory managers have very little control over their collections, relying on Web page submitters to provide annotations and decisions about where their resource should be placed in the directory's hierarchy. Other directory managers are much more selective not only about which resources they include, but also about where in the subject hierarchy the pages will be located.

Some directory editors write detailed **_annotations_** of the pages. These annotations can be evaluative, descriptive, or both. Annotations are Web page descriptions that either the Web page submitter or the directory editor attaches to the Web pages. Many annotated directories also rate Web resources using criteria that vary from one directory to another.

There are also directories that are made up of the most popular Web pages found by programs that count how many pages have hyperlinks to these sites. Web pages that are popular may be very different from ones that are rated as excellent.

Of all the directories, virtual libraries rely most on human beings in selecting and controlling the resources included in their collections. Virtual libraries are organized in a way that tames the Internet's chaotic nature and thus attempts to create a more traditional "library-like" setting in which to do research.

The human element involved in creating and maintaining directories creates both advantages and disadvantages for the user. Some of the inherent strengths of directories can be weaknesses, and vice versa. We'll examine some of these strengths and weaknesses here.

Strengths

The major advantages of using directories are as follows:

* Directories contain fewer resources than search engine databases.

* Many directories rate, annotate, or categorize chosen resources.

* Directories increase the probability of retrieving relevant results.

Because directories rely on people to select, maintain, and update their resource lists, they contain fewer resources than search engine databases. This can be a plus, especially when you are looking for information on a general topic. It's a lot easier and less time-consuming to go through a list of 50 or so Web pages than to sort through the thousands of pages that a search engine may present. In addition, many directories rate, annotate, analyze, evaluate, and categorize the resources included, which helps you find resources of the highest quality.

Although we'll discuss the evaluation of Internet resources in detail later in the book, now is a good time to bring up the issue of quality control and filtering of WWW sites. With thousands of resources appearing on the Web each day, it is important that there are people working to determine which sites and Web pages on the World Wide Web have the highest quality. For example, if we want to find some of the best Web pages for the mathematical sciences, we could try Magellan's directory. Magellan's Web Reviews is an annotated directory that also selects the best sites and rates them using a four-star system. Figure 4.1

shows the results from choosing the top-level category **Science**, then clicking on **Mathematics**, and then on **Resources**. You can browse through the list of annotated and rated resources until you find one or more that may be useful to you.

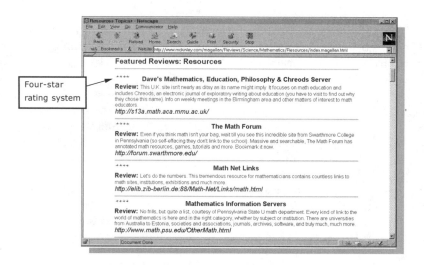

Four-star rating system

Figure 4.1—Rated/Annotated Sites in Math Sciences: Magellan Web Reviews

Weaknesses

There are three major disadvantages inherent in World Wide Web directories. They are as follows:

* Arbitrary hierarchical arrangements.
* Infrequent updates.
* Subjectivity of rating and annotating resources.

One of the major disadvantages of using some directories is that the hierarchical arrangements may be arbitrary. For example, let's say we are looking for information on vegetarianism. We want to start by finding a few sites. We decide to use Yahoo!, one of the best-known directories on the Web.

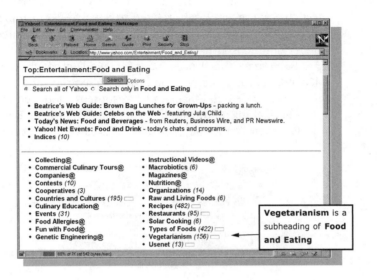

Figure 4.2—Vegetarianism in Yahoo! Directory

Note in Figure 4.2 that **vegetarianism** is located under the subcategory or subheading **Food and Eating**, which is located under the top-level category **Entertainment**. The people who organized this directory chose this hierarchy. Another directory might place **Vegetarianism** under the top-level category **Health**. The ability to search Yahoo! and most other directories by keyword solves this problem of arbitrary hierarchical arrangements.

Another drawback is that selecting, rating, and categorizing Web pages take a lot of time, so directories tend to be less up-to-date than search engine databases, which are constantly updated by computer programs that automatically gather new Web pages.

The third disadvantage inherent in directories is also an advantage—the resources are chosen by people who subjectively decide which ones are best. What seems a good resource to one person may not to the next. This is why it is important for the directory management to have well-stated criteria for selecting and rating resources.

Browsing and Searching Directories

There are two ways to find information in directories. You can browse by subject or search by keyword. These will be discussed in the following section.

Browsing

Browsing a directory is not difficult. You simply click on a subject category that you think will contain the subject you are seeking. This will take you to another level in the hierarchy, where you will choose another subject from the list of subjects that appear on your computer screen. You then examine the choices that are returned to you and select the one most closely related to your research topic. You continue this process until your screen fills with a list of resources that you can then examine to find the information you need.

Sometimes this process has two layers; other times it has several. It depends on the directory and how detailed the subject is. For example, if we were to search Magellan for resources about economics, we would start by clicking on the top-level category **Business**. **Economics & Statistics** is one of the subjects under this category, as noted in Figure 4.3.

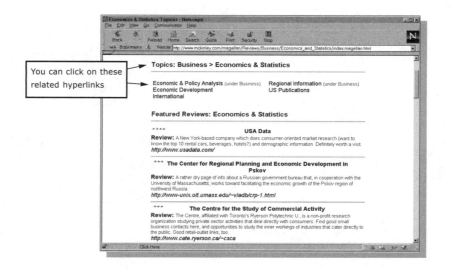

Figure 4.3—Topical Hierarchy in Magellan Web Reviews: Economics & Statistics

Now, let's try to find economics resources in Yahoo! The top-level category we need to click on is **Social Science**. Figure 4.4 shows that **Economics** is a subcategory of Social Science. Several subcategories under **Economics** cover specific aspects of the subject.

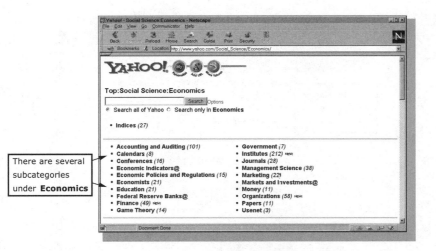

There are several subcategories under **Economics**

Figure 4.4—Economics Resources in Yahoo!

✳ Tip

If you don't find any resources on the topic you are looking for while browsing, you can use the **Back** icon 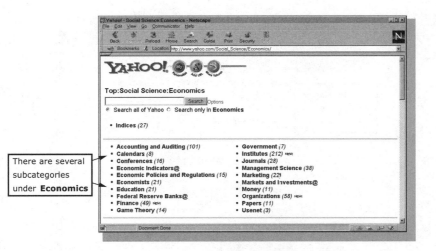 on your browser to return to another level. There, you can try a different subject heading that may lead you to successful results.

Searching

By now, you can probably see the advantage of being able to search a directory. It may be difficult to determine where in a directory's hierarchy a particular subject will be found. Searching a directory is not the same as searching the Web using a search engine. The primary difference is that when you search a directory, you have access to only those resources that are included in the directory, not the entire Web. Also, in some directories (such as Yahoo!), you do not search the full text of Web pages; you search only the words in the URLs (Uniform Resource Locators), the titles of the Web pages, and annotations (if they exist).

Let's take the example of the topic of vegetarianism that we explored earlier in the chapter. If you recall, Yahoo! places vegetarianism under entertainment in its hierarchical arrangement. Let's now find Web pages in Yahoo! about vegetarianism by doing a search. Figure 4.5 shows the keyword entered.

Figure 4.5—Keyword Search in Yahoo!

After we click on **Search**, the screen fills with the search results. Such a list of results is often referred to as a *hit list*. Note in Figure 4.6 that Yahoo! delivers category matches and site matches. *Category matches* are categories or headings with the word *vegetarianism* in the category field. *Site matches* are sites with the word *vegetarianism* in the titles of the Web sites, pages, or annotations.

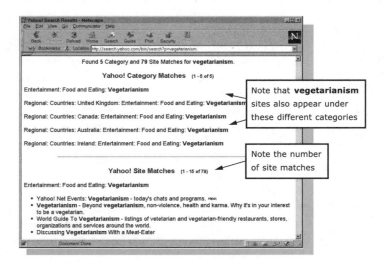

Figure 4.6—Yahoo! Directory Search Results

Note the advantage of searching versus browsing in this example. This search produced sites on the subject of vegetarianism that are under different categories in the directory.

Three Major Directories and How to Use Them

In this section, we will discuss a few well-known directories, pointing out their differences, similarities, and special features by doing some hands-on activities with them. The three directories we'll be using are Yahoo!, Magellan's Web Reviews, and WebCrawler Guide.

❋ Tip

Remember that the Web is always changing and that your results may differ from those shown here. Don't let this confuse you. The activities are meant to teach you fundamental skills. These skills don't change, even though the number of results obtained or the actual screens may look very different.

Activity 4.1   Yahoo!

Overview

Yahoo!, **http://www.yahoo.com**, is the most comprehensive directory on the World Wide Web. Yahoo! relies on Web page submitters to annotate and categorize the resources that are included, so some sites have a brief descriptive note, and some do not. Yahoo! strives to be extensive; consequently, there is no filtering of resources. You can browse Yahoo! or search it by keyword. Results in Yahoo! are listed in order of relevance to the search topic. If your search in Yahoo! brings up zero results, the search engine AltaVista will automatically perform your search for you.

In the following activity, we'll browse for information in Yahoo!, and then we'll search for the same information using the search query interface that Yahoo! provides. We'll be looking for information on Thai cooking by following these steps:

1. Go to the home page for Yahoo!
2. Browse Yahoo! for information on Thai cooking.
3. Search Yahoo! for information on Thai cooking.
4. Search AltaVista using the same search expression.
5. Bookmark it!
6. End the session.

Details

1   Go to the home page for Yahoo!

We're assuming your browser is already started.

❋ Do It! Use the mouse to point to the location field and click the mouse button.

The URL of the current Web page will change color. Now you can type in the URL for Yahoo!

✳*Do It!* Type **http://www.yahoo.com**, and press Enter .

2   Browse Yahoo! for information on Thai cooking.

✳*Do It!* Click on **Entertainment**, which is one of the top-level categories on Yahoo!'s list, as shown in Figure 4.7. We know that in Yahoo!, food-related sites are found under this category.

Figure 4.7—Top-level Category List in Yahoo!

✳*Do It!* Click on **Food and Eating** from the list of subheadings.

✳*Do It!* After the screen fills, click on the category **Countries and Cultures**, as shown in Figure 4.8.

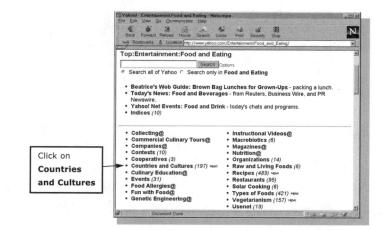

Figure 4.8—Subcategories of Food and Eating in Yahoo!

❋*Do It!* After the screen fills, scroll down until you find the word **Thai**. Click on it.

Look at the screen, which has filled with Web resources devoted to Thai cooking. You can click on the Web page titles to explore the delights of Thai cuisine. Many of these locations include recipes, complete with colorful pictures of the prepared foods. The main hierarchy for Thai cooking is "Entertainment: Food and Eating: Countries and Cultures: Thai." Notice the category "Companies@" in Figure 4.9. If you click on this, Yahoo! will take you to related sites on Thai cooking that appear in the "Companies" category. Figure 4.13 shows some of the Web sites that appear in the "Companies" category.

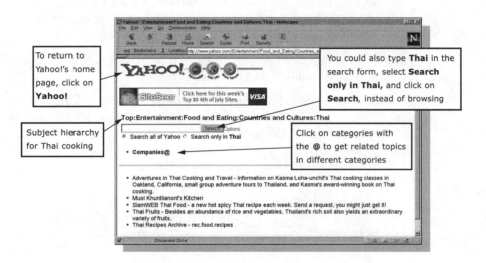

Figure 4.9—Results of Browsing Yahoo! for Thai Cooking Web Pages

3   Search Yahoo! for information on Thai cooking.

Keyword searching in Yahoo! is simple. You can save time by doing a keyword search. You should keep your search terms broad, however, because Yahoo! doesn't search the words in the bodies of Web pages.

❋*Do It!* Return to Yahoo!'s home page by clicking **Yahoo!**, as shown in Figure 4.9.

❋*Do It!* To discover what the search options are for Yahoo!, click on **Options** next to the search form. See Figure 4.10.

Figure 4.10—How to Find Search Options in Yahoo!

Take a look at the "Search Options" page in Yahoo! (as shown in Figure 4.11). We are searching for information on Thai cooking. Think of other words that might appear for this subject, for example *Thailand*, *cookbook*, or *cook*. If you click on **Advanced Search Syntax**, as shown in Figure 4.11, you'll learn that Yahoo! allows you to search for different endings to words by placing an asterisk at the end of the word's root. If we wanted to find the word *Thailand* as well as *Thai*, we could append an asterisk (*) to the root *Thai*. We could also append an asterisk to the word *cook* to find *cook*, *cookbook*, *cookery*, or *cooking*. The ability to search for different endings to root words is called ***truncation***.

Do It! On the "Search Options" page, point your cursor to the circle next to the method that reads **Matches on all words (AND)** and click. Next, point your cursor to the circle next to **Web Sites** and click.

Do It! Type in the pane next to the **Search** button the search expression **Thai* cook***, and press **Enter**.

This search will retrieve all of the words in the titles, URLs, or annotations of Web sites that match any derivation of the root *Thai* and all of the words that match derivations of the root *cook*. The search won't find the Yahoo! categories that match these words, only the sites. It will return the sites added in the past three years.

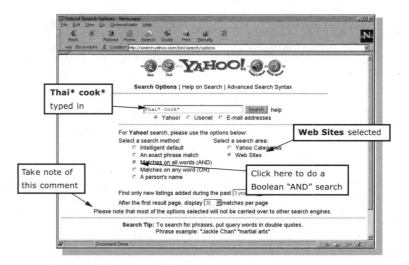

Figure 4.11—Yahoo! Search Options—Search Expression "Thai cook*" Entered*

Note that the resources found are from different Yahoo! categories, as shown in Figure 4.12. Some of them are from the "Business and Economy" top-level category. The results are listed in order of relevance to the search topic.

Figure 4.12—Yahoo! Search Results

4   Search AltaVista using the same search expression.

The sites that Yahoo! retrieved for us may be all we need, but let's say that after we read the short descriptions, we want to see what the entire World Wide Web has on this topic. Before we do this, however, note the comment at the bottom of the picture in Figure 4.11. It reads "Please note that most of the options selected will not be carried over to other search engines." This means that this search won't necessarily be performed the same way in another search tool.

✴*Do It!* Click on the place where the words **AltaVista Web Pages** appear.

Automatically, the AltaVista search engine searches the entire Web for the search expression *Thai* cook**. The results are listed by relevance, as shown in Figure 4.13.

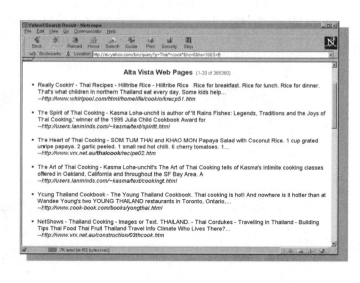

Figure 4.13—Results of the Search Request "Thai* cook*" in AltaVista

As you can see, the AltaVista search engine found thousands of sites on this topic. This search engine uses a database that covers most of the World Wide Web, whereas Yahoo! covers only a small portion of it. AltaVista also searches through every word in every page on the Web, whereas the Yahoo! search capability is limited to URL titles, category or Web site titles, and descriptions. Plus, we don't know if the Boolean AND operator was used in AltaVista as we had it set up to be used in Yahoo! Perhaps the words were connected by OR, which would give much larger results.

5   Bookmark it!

✳*Do It!* Scroll down the list of sites found in AltaVista until you come to **Young Thailand Cookbook**, as shown in Figure 4.14.

If you can't find this Web page on your list of results, choose another one. Explore the site and then place a link to it in your bookmark list.

✳*Do It!* Click on **Bookmarks** in the location toolbar. Point your mouse to **Add Bookmark** and click. Automatically, the title of the URL is added to your bookmark list. You can access this Web site at a later date by clicking on the title in your list.

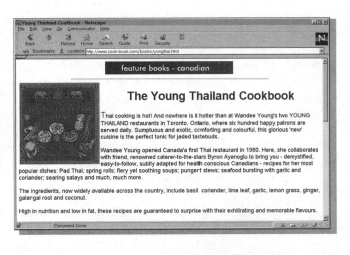

Figure 4.14—"The Young Thailand Cookbook"

6   End the session.

You've learned a lot about Yahoo! Now it's time to discover the features of other directories. You can either end the session or continue to the next activity.

✳️*Do It!* To end the session now, click on **File** on the menu bar and select **Exit** from the menu.

End of Activity 4.1

In Activity 4.1, we saw the difference between browsing Yahoo!'s subject categories for a topic and performing a keyword search. A keyword search in Yahoo! looks for words that are in the URLs, the subject categories, and the titles of the Web pages. You can search AltaVista from Yahoo!, but to use AltaVista's search capabilities to the fullest, you should search directly from AltaVista's home page. We'll show you how to do this in Chapter 5, "Search Strategies for Search Engines."

Activity 4.2   Magellan Web Reviews

Overview

Magellan annotates, reviews, and rates most sites that are included in its directory, Web Reviews. This directory is a subset of Magellan's database, which is searchable by a search engine. Web Reviews has about sixty thousand Web pages, whereas the full database has about fifty million Web pages. Of the thousands of sites submitted each day, Magellan's editorial team selects the sites to be included or reviewed. Web Reviews also has Green Light sites; these sites have been evaluated as to their suitability for all audiences, not just mature ones.

Like Yahoo!, Magellan's Web Reviews can be browsed as well as searched. Results are presented according to how relevant they are to the search topic. In this activity, we will browse and search by keyword using Magellan. We can browse Magellan's categories the same way we browsed Yahoo!'s categories in the last activity. Magellan has a partnership with the Excite search engine, which allows you to search Excite directly from the Web Reviews search results page, in the same way we searched AltaVista from the Yahoo! search results page. As we mentioned earlier in the chapter, Magellan uses a four-star rating system for each of the sites rated. In this activity, we'll browse and search by keyword for the same subject that we searched for in Yahoo!—Thai cooking.

We'll follow these steps:

1. Go to the home page for Magellan.
2. Browse Magellan's Web Reviews for Web pages on Thai cooking.
3. Read the search tips.
4. Search Magellan's Web Reviews for Web pages on Thai cooking.
5. Search Magellan's entire database for Web pages on Thai cooking.
6. End the session.

Details

1   Go to the home page for Magellan.

❋Do It! Use the mouse to point to the location field and click.

The URL of the current Web page will change color. Now you can type the URL for Magellan.

❋Do It! Type **http://www.mckinley.com**, and press Enter.

2   Browse Magellan's Web Reviews for Web pages on Thai cooking.

❋Do It! From the Magellan home page, click on **Life & Style**.

❋Do It! From the subcategories listed, click on **Food & Drink**.

❋Do It! Now click on **Cooking & Recipes**.

❋Do It! Click on **Recipes**.

❋Do It! Click on **Recipes Around The World**.

Your screen should look similar to the one in Figure 4.15. The most logical category to click on now is **Asian**.

❋Do It! Click on **Asian**, as shown in Figure 4.15.

Figure 4.15—Browsing in Magellan's Web Reviews

None of the resources listed is specifically about Thai cooking or recipes. One of them may mention Thai cooking, but we want to find some Web pages that focus specifically on Thai food. Searching the directory by keyword may give us more results. Perhaps there are some resources in different categories. Before we do a search, it's a good idea to read the search tips.

3   Read the search tips.

✳*Do It!* Click on **Search Tips and Help,** as shown in Figure 4.16.

Figure 4.16—Partial Results of Browsing Magellan's Web Reviews

There are several help categories. Read through them all. Some of the things we learn include the following:

✳   Magellan uses a device called *concept searching*, which automatically searches for synonyms of the keywords you enter.

❇ Magellan supports Boolean searching, but AND, OR, and NOT have to be in capital letters when used.

❇ You can limit your search to reviewed resources only, or to Green Light sites, or you can search the entire Web.

❇ Magellan is case-sensitive, so you must capitalize the first letter of a proper noun.

4   Search Magellan's Web Reviews for Web pages on Thai cooking.

After you've finished browsing the help screens, click on the **Back** button to return to the page you started with: **Search Tips and Help**. At the top of the screen is a search form, as shown in Figure 4.17. We want to search the reviewed sites only.

❇*Do It!* Click on **Reviewed Sites Only**.

❇*Do It!* Type **Thai AND cooking** in the search form.

❇*Do It!* Click on **search**, as shown in Figure 4.17.

Figure 4.17—Search Query Entered in Magellan

By typing in the search expression this way, we have essentially said that we want the words *Thai* and *cooking* to appear somewhere in the directory's Web pages. Unlike Yahoo!, Magellan's Web Reviews searches not only the words in the titles, URLs, and annotations, but also all the words in the pages. In this search, we are searching the entire directory, and we are asking for all sites that match the keywords to be returned. See Figure 4.18 for the results of this search.

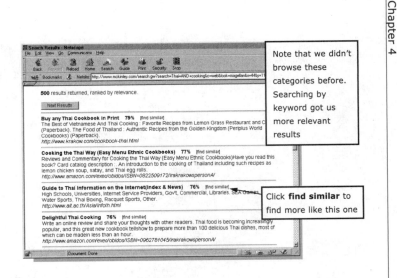

Figure 4.18—Results of Search "Thai AND cooking" in Magellan's Web Reviews

The results of the above search are listed in order of relevance to the search topic. This means that the first Web site is the most relevant. You could click on **find similar** next to a Web page that interests you, if you wanted to see other pages like it.

5 Search Magellan's entire database for Web pages on Thai cooking.

What if we wanted to see what Magellan's entire database, and not just the resources in its directory, has on the topic of Thai cooking? We can do this quite easily.

Do It! Scroll up to the top of the screen. Near the search query box, click on **The Entire Web**.

Do It! Click **search**.

The results of this search partially appear in Figure 4.19. Notice how the number of results increased dramatically.

Figure 4.19—Search Results—Magellan's Database for "Thai AND Cooking"

6   End the session.

You can either end the session now or continue to the next activity.

 To end the session now, click on **File** on the menu bar and select **Exit** from the menu.

_____ End of Activity 4.2 _____

In Activity 4.2, we started searching for information on Thai cooking by browsing a directory, Magellan's Web Reviews. The browse didn't turn up anything worthwhile, so we searched the directory, hoping to find some Web pages that weren't in the categories we browsed. We then expanded our search to the entire Web by using Magellan's search engine. Although the number of search results increased greatly, the smaller set of reviewed documents found by the directory search might have been all we needed. The main purpose of the activity was to show the different ways to manipulate a combination search engine-directory database to obtain as much information as possible. In Activity 4.3, we'll explore a different directory—the WebCrawler Guide.

Activity 4.3   The WebCrawler Guide

Overview

The WebCrawler Guide is a selective directory of some five thousand or so of the "best" resources available on the Web. It is part of the WebCrawler search engine. WebCrawler has an editing team to review every single resource included in the Guide. You can start to explore the

Guide by clicking on any of the 15 channels that appear on WebCrawler's home page. WebCrawler's Channels are categories that include several types of resources on a particular subject, including news, chat groups, specialized databases, and the Guide.

In this activity, we'll browse the Guide's subject categories to find information on what the outlook is like for certain careers in the near future. We'll open the WebCrawler Guide, determine which subject categories to click on, and eventually find some reviewed resources that will give us this information. We'll also view one of the resources found.

We'll follow these steps:

1. Go to the home page for WebCrawler.
2. Open the Careers & Education Channel.
3. Open the Career Resources category from the WebCrawler Guide.
4. Access the Occupational Outlook Handbook.
5. End the session.

Details

1   Go to the home page for WebCrawler.

🔆Do It! Click on the location field, type **http://www.webcrawler .com/**, and press **Enter**.

Figure 4.20 shows what the WebCrawler home page looks like. It may not look like this on your computer screen. Don't be alarmed—this is perfectly normal, because the Web is always changing.

Figure 4.20—WebCrawler's Home Page

2   Open the Careers & Education Channel.

Do It! Click on the channel entitled **Careers & Education**, as shown in Figure 4.20.

Figure 4.21 shows the Careers & Education channel. Note that there are career services, including job listings databases along the right side of the screen. The guide is located on the left side.

Click on **Career Resources** here

Career services are listed here

Figure 4.21—Careers & Education Channel in WebCrawler

3   Open the "Career Resources" category from the WebCrawler Guide.

Do It! Click on the hyperlink entitled **Career Resources**, as shown in Figure 4.21.

4   Access the Occupational Outlook Handbook.

Your screen will fill with a list of hyperlinks that have career information, as shown in Figure 4.22. Each one of the titles includes a review of the resource listed. Let's select one of the titles to see a review.

Do It! Click on **Occupational Outlook Handbook**, as shown in Figure 4.22.

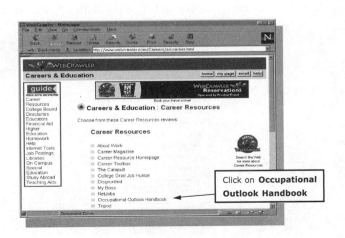

Figure 4.22—Career Resources in WebCrawler

Figure 4.23 shows the review that the WebCrawler editing staff wrote about this resource. The review tells us who published this work (the U.S. Department of Labor) and other important things about it, including that the document is searchable by keyword. Note that if you wanted the WebCrawler search engine to go out and search its database for similar Web pages, you could just click on the WebCrawler icon located on the right side of the screen.

To view the actual handbook, you'll need to click on its hyperlink from the review page.

❋Do It! Click on **Occupational Outlook Handbook**, as shown in Figure 4.23.

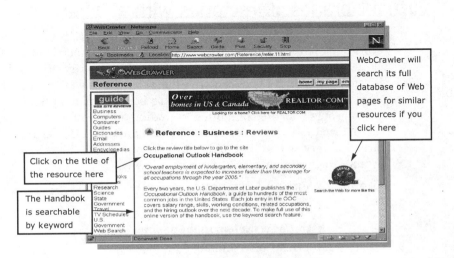

Figure 4.23—WebCrawler's Review of the Occupational Handbook

Part of the first page of this document appears in Figure 4.24.

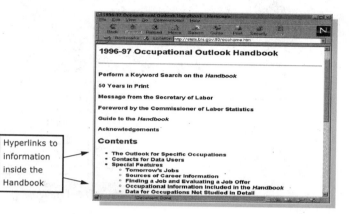

Hyperlinks to information inside the Handbook

Figure 4.24—Department of Labor's 1996–97 Occupational Outlook Handbook

4   End the session.

You can either end the session now or continue to the next activity.

Do It! To end the session now, click on **File** on the menu bar and select **Exit** from the menu.

_____ End of Activity 4.3

In Activity 4.3, we saw how helpful a selective, annotated directory can be. By using the WebCrawler guide, we were able to zero in quickly on a few good resources that cover the topic of careers.

Virtual Libraries: Directories with a Difference

Virtual libraries are directories with resources that librarians or cybrarians have organized in a logical way. In Chapter 3, we looked closely at a virtual library—the Internet Public Library. Virtual libraries are often referred to as ***annotated directories*** as well. It is helpful to think of these specialized directories as being similar to libraries, because people who are committed to finding the very best resources on the Internet have carefully selected and maintained the resources in a virtual library. These people usually rate or analyze the resources and arrange them so they will be found easily.

The Major Virtual Libraries

* Argus Clearinghouse
   http://www.clearinghouse.net
* Internet Public Library
   http://www.ipl.org

  �֍ Librarians' Index to the Internet
     http://sunsite.berkeley.edu/InternetIndex

  ✖ World Wide Web Virtual Library
     http://vlib.stanford.edu.Overview.html

As we discussed in Chapter 3, there are three major types of resources that virtual libraries are most apt to contain: **subject guides**, **reference works**, and **specialized databases**. Subject guides are Web resources that include hyperlinks to sites on that particular subject. Reference works are full-text documents, such as dictionaries, encyclopedias, almanacs, and so forth. Specialized databases are searchable indexes that catalog certain types of material, such as journal article citations, financial data, and so forth.

It may be helpful to do an activity in a virtual library to show you how to obtain a subject guide. We will be using the Argus Clearinghouse for this activity.

Activity 4.4   The Argus Clearinghouse

Overview

Let's say you are interested in doing research on the Middle East. Unsure of which particular issue or country you are interested in researching, you would like to see a subject guide to the World Wide Web on the subject of the Middle East. A virtual library would be an excellent place to begin this search. Since the Argus Clearinghouse is a virtual library, let's start there.

The Argus Clearinghouse (formerly Clearinghouse for Subject-Oriented Internet Resource Guides) is a virtual library provided by Argus Associates. The resources included in the Argus Clearinghouse cover most subject areas. Subject specialists from all over the world write the subject guides, and subject specialists on the Argus staff rate and analyze each guide. You can browse and perform keyword searches in the Argus Clearinghouse. In this activity, we will illustrate how to browse the directory.

Let's explore the Argus Clearinghouse by following these steps:

1. Open the Argus Clearinghouse.
2. Browse for subject guides on the Middle East.
3. Search for a Middle East subject guide.
4. End the session.

If you find a subject guide on the topic you are researching, it can save you a lot of time and energy by helping you navigate the Web's vast sea of information. Let's see what we find on the Middle East.

Details

1   Open the Argus Clearinghouse.

Do It! Use the mouse to point to the location field and click.

The URL of the current Web page will change color. Now you can type in the URL for the Argus Clearinghouse.

Do It! Type **http://www.clearinghouse.net** and press ⏎Enter⏎.

See the *Argus Clearinghouse* home page in Figure 4.25.

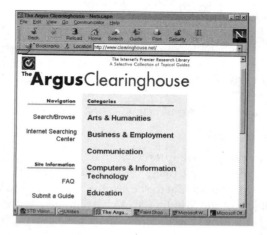

Figure 4.25—Top-level Subject Categories in the Argus Clearinghouse

2   Browse for subject guides on the Middle East.

Do It! Click on the top-level subject category **Places & Peoples**.

Wait until the screen fills with a list of subcategories.

Do It! Click on **Asia**.

There will be more subjects listed.

Do It! Click on **Middle East**.

Your screen should now look like the one in Figure 4.26.

Figure 4.26—List of Subject Guides on the Middle East in Argus Clearinghouse

Do It! Click on **The Middle East–North Africa Internet Resource Guide**, as shown in Figure 4.26.

The screen will fill with information that the Argus Clearinghouse provides, as shown in Figure 4.27. The Web page cites the guide's author, the organization with which he is affiliated, and ways to contact him. The clearinghouse also gives information about the rating system, the keywords attached to the guide, and the date when the guide was last checked for currency and accuracy. See Figure 4.27. You can now go to the subject guide by clicking on its URL.

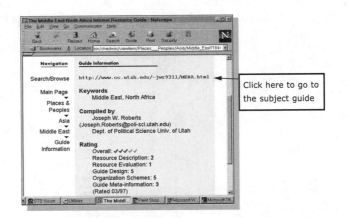

Figure 4.27—Information Page—Middle East-North Africa Resource Guide

⁕*Do It!* Click on the URL for the Middle East–North Africa Internet Resource Guide.

The Middle East–North Africa Internet Resource Guide functions as a directory to Internet resources dealing with all aspects of that region. It is an excellent place to begin a research project on the Middle East.

3 Search for a Middle East subject guide.

⁕*Do It!* Click on the **Back** button to return to the Argus Clearinghouse.

⁕*Do It!* Click on **Search/Browse** under the "Navigation" section.

A search form will appear. We want to find a subject guide on the Middle East, so we enter that topic into the form.

⁕*Do It!* Type **Middle East** in the search form, and then click on **submit search**, as shown in Figure 4.28.

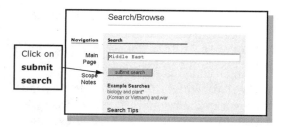

Figure 4.28—Searching the Argus Clearinghouse for "Middle East"

The results of this search partially appear in Figure 4.29. We picked up one more subject guide by searching the guide rather than by browsing. This means that there was one guide that wasn't in the Middle East subject category. Can you determine which one it is?

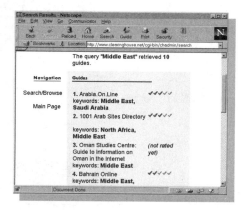

Figure 4.29—Results of Searching the Argus Clearinghouse for "Middle East"

4   End the session.

Since we are at the end of the chapter, you might want to disconnect.

✳*Do It!* Click on **File** on the menu bar and select **Exit** from the menu.

_____ End of Activity 4.4 _____

With the Argus Clearinghouse's search capability, we picked up one relevant subject guide that the structured browse didn't produce. This is another example of how keyword searching can enhance results. In Activity 4.4, we could easily see the difference between a virtual library and a Web directory such as Yahoo! A virtual library such as the Argus Clearinghouse is very selective about the Web resources that are included and the way they are rated. Keep in mind that virtual libraries are very small collections of Web resources, so they may not always have what you need.

Summary

Directories are topical lists of Internet resources, arranged hierarchically to facilitate browsing by subject. Most directories have a search capability, which can help you avoid occasionally becoming lost in arbitrary subject categories. Directories depend on the work of individuals who collect, categorize, maintain, and, in many cases, evaluate Web sites to make it easier for people to find what they are looking for. Directories vary in how they are organized, whether or not sites are evaluated, and if they are, which criteria are used.

Because the Web sites included in directories rely on people for their selection and maintenance, they are necessarily much smaller than the databases that search engine spiders or robots create. This difference can be an asset in some cases and a detriment in others. When you are looking for a "few good sites" to start with, a directory can save you time, especially if your subject is broad and you're at the beginning of your research. Search engines are not meant to give you a few sites. They exist to bring everything to your screen that is on the World Wide Web and that fits your search expression. Search engines are best for finding very specific information or for researching multifaceted topics.

Virtual libraries are directories maintained by librarians, or cybrarians, who select materials for the directory based on their excellence and value to the Internet public, much as librarians in a traditional library do. Virtual libraries are the best places to find subject guides. These guides are usually maintained by people who are knowledgeable about the subjects covered.

It is a good idea to know how to use the different directories we covered in this chapter and to explore others. Keep one or two of your favorites in your bookmark list so you can find them quickly.

Selected Terms Introduced in This Chapter

annotated directories
annotations
hit list
reference works

specialized databases
subject guides
truncation

Exercises and Projects

The following exercises require the browsing and searching skills covered in Chapter 4. They will transfer to any directory, even if it wasn't covered in the chapter.

1. Go to Yahoo!, **http://www.yahoo.com**. Using Yahoo!'s browsing and searching capabilities, find information on the ethical, legal, and social issues of the Human Genome Project. Which way was easier and why?

2. Go to the Argus Clearinghouse, **http://www.clearinghouse .net**, and find some subject guides on the subject of immigration. First, try to find them by browsing through the subject categories. Take note of the URLs you find. Then, perform a keyword search in the Argus Clearinghouse, using *immigration* as the keyword. Describe the differences in the subject guides you found using both methods. Which was the best method to use?

3. Find the full text of St. Augustine's *Confessions* in Latin. Try to find it in the WebCrawler Guide, **http://www.webcrawler .com**, and in Infoseek's directory, **http://www.infoseek.com**. Write down the steps you took to find it in each of the directories.

4. Open the WWW Virtual Library, **http://vlib.stanford.edu/ Overview.html**.
   a. Click on **Category Subtree**.
   b. Find a subject guide on "Soils and Subtrates."
   c. Open this Web page and find out who publishes it. In what country is the organization located? Take a look at the URL for this Web page. How can you tell from the URL the country in which it's located?

5. Using Yahoo!, **http://www.yahoo.com**, find the entire text of William Shakespeare's *Hamlet*. Describe the steps it took for you to find it.

6. Find the reference book *Bartlett's Familiar Quotations* in three different directories. Cite the directories you used. Write down the steps you went through in each directory to find it.

7. Open Magellan, **http://www.mckinley.com**, and do a test to decide which Boolean operator is assumed between two keywords if none is specified. In order to do this test, you'll have to do the following:

a. Type two keywords in the search form and click on **search**.
b. Write down the number of hits from this search.
c. Type the two terms separated by an **AND**.
d. Write down the number of hits from this search.
e. Type the same two terms separated by an **OR**.
f. Write down the number of hits from this search.
g. Compare the number of results found in Step b with the number of results in Steps d and f.

What can you conclude from this exercise?

8. Find two popular Web pages on the subjects of massage and stress therapy. *Hint:* You'll need to use *Lycos Top 5%*, **http://www.pointcom.com**. How did you go about finding these Web pages? Write down the steps you took to find them and the URLs of the pages you found.

9. Go to the Argus Clearinghouse, **http://www.clearinghouse.net**, and find two subject guides that focus on mysticism. Using the Argus Clearinghouse subject categories, find them by browsing by subject. Write down the subject categories in the hierarchy you used.

10. Someone has told you about a Web site called *The Perseus Project*. Try to find it by going to the Librarians' Index to the Internet, **http://sunsite.berkeley.edu/internetindex**. You can find it by doing a keyword search or by browsing the subject or category headings. Once you find it, write down a few things about it: the URL, the person who created and maintains the site, and the scope of the information.

5
Chapter

Search Strategies for
Search Engines

In Chapter 3, "Using the World Wide Web for Research," we introduced keyword searching in search engine databases. In this chapter, we'll cover searching these databases in detail. Why is it so important to learn how to search these databases? Search engines are the most powerful search tools on the World Wide Web, with the most popular being those that access the largest databases. Most of the major search engines claim to index the entire World Wide Web. Many also index Usenet newsgroups, FTP, and Gopher sites. None of the search engines is exactly alike. Some are better for certain kinds of information than others. Maybe you've tried a few search engines and have found that some engines retrieve too many documents that aren't at all what you wanted. Perhaps at other times they don't retrieve enough information. This chapter should clear up some ambiguities you may have about why some searches work well and others don't.

This chapter will include the following sections:
* Search Engine Databases
* Search Features Common to Most Search Engines
* Output Features Common to Most Search Engines
* A Basic Search Strategy: The 10 Steps

The Major Search Engine Databases on the World Wide Web

❈	AltaVista	**http://www.altavista.digital.com**
❈	Excite	**http://www.excite.com***
❈	HotBot	**http://www.hotbot.com***
❈	Infoseek	**http://www.infoseek.com***
❈	Lycos	**http://www.lycos.com***
❈	Open Text	**http://index.opentext.net**
❈	WebCrawler	**http://webcrawler.com***

*Denotes that the search engine also has a directory.

Search Engine Databases

Knowing how search engine databases are indexed can help you select the most appropriate tool for your research needs, retrieve the most relevant information, and understand why results vary from one database to another.

Indexing

In Chapter 4, we discussed directories and how human beings control their contents. In directories, site managers and cybrarians assign keywords to Web pages. They describe the Web page with a few words. This *keyword indexing* enables you to find that page if any of the words you type in match the words used to describe the page.

How a Spider Works—Searching the Internet for New Documents

In search engines, a computer program, called a spider or robot, gathers new documents from the World Wide Web. The program retrieves hyperlinks that are attached to these documents, loads them into a database, and indexes them using a formula that differs from database to database. The search engine then searches the database according to the request you enter. Although robots have many different ways of collecting information from Web pages, the major search engines all claim to index the entire text of each Web document in their databases. This is called *full-text indexing*. All of the major search engines are full-text databases.

Some robot programs are intuitive; they know which words are important to the meaning of the entire Web page, and some of them can find synonyms to the words and add them to the index. Some full-text databases, such as Excite, use a robot that enables them to search on concepts, as well as on the search query words. In some search engines, the robot skips over words that appear often, such as prepositions and articles. These common words are called *stop words*.

Some search engines allow Web page submitters to attach *meta-tags* to their pages. Meta-tags are keywords that describe the page but may not appear on the page. They appear only in the HTML source document. Meta-tags allow Web pages that don't have a lot of text in them to come up in a keyword search.

When to Use Search Engine Databases

Search engines are the best tools to use when you are looking for very specific information or when your research topic has many facets. We saw in Chapter 4 that directories are helpful when you are looking for general and single-faceted topics. Usually when you need information on a very detailed or multifaceted subject, however, a search engine will give you not only more information, but also the most precise and up-to-date information possible. Even though most of the major search engine databases attempt to index the entire Web, each one has a different way of determining which pages are most relevant to your search request. In one database, a relevant document may be fiftieth on the list; in another database, the document may be first. In order to retrieve the most relevant documents, you should become familiar with many search engines and their features.

Search Features Common to Most Search Engines

It's important to understand the different search features before you begin using a search engine for research. The reason for this is that each search engine has its own way of interpreting and manipulating search expressions. In addition, many search engines have *default settings* that you may need to override if you want to obtain the most precise results. Because a search can bring up so many words, it is very easy to have a lot of hits with few that are relevant to your query. This is called *low precision/high recall*. You may be satisfied with having very precise search results with a small set returned. This is defined as *high precision/low recall*. Ideally, using the search expression you enter, the search engine would retrieve all of the relevant documents you need. This would be described as *high precision/high recall*.

Search engines support many search features, though not all engines support each one. If they do support certain features, they may use different *syntax* in expressing the feature. Before you use any of these search features, you need to check the search engines' help pages to see how the feature is expressed, if it is supported at all. We will now list the most common search features and explain how each feature is used.

Boolean Operators

We discussed Boolean operators briefly in Chapter 3. Knowing how to apply Boolean operators in search expressions is extremely important. The diagrams show the different operators and how they are used.

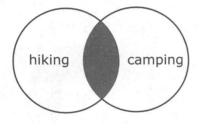

hiking AND camping

Use an AND between search terms when you need to narrow your search. The AND indicates that only those Web pages having both words in them will be retrieved. Some search engines automatically assume an AND relationship between two words if you don't type AND between them. This would be a default setting of the search engine.

hiking OR camping

An OR between search terms will make your resulting set larger. When you use OR, Web pages that have either term will be retrieved. Many search engines automatically place an OR between two words if there is nothing typed between them. This would be a default setting of the search engine.

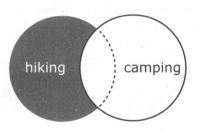

hiking NOT camping

The NOT operator is used when a term needs to be excluded. In this example, Web pages with both *hiking* and *camping* in them would not be retrieved. Some search engines require an AND in front of the NOT. In this case, the expression would be written like this: hiking AND NOT camping.

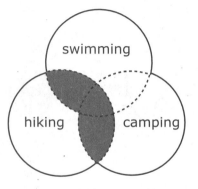

hiking AND (camping OR swimming)

This example shows **nested Boolean logic**. Use this logic when you need to include ANDs and ORs in one search statement. For example, say that there is a term that must appear in your results. You want to search for this term along with a concept that you can describe with synonyms. To do this, you would need to tell the search engine to find records with two or more synonyms and then to combine this result with the first term. In the example above, the parentheses indicate that *camping* or *swimming* will be processed first, and that this result will be combined with *hiking*. If the parentheses were not there, the search engine would perform the search from left to right. All pages with both the words *hiking* and *camping* would be found first, and then all pages with the word *swimming* would be included. This would give you an unacceptable result, so you must be careful when using nested Boolean logic.

Implied Boolean Operators

Implied Boolean operators, or pseudo-Boolean operators, are short-cuts to typing AND and NOT. In most search engines that support this feature, you would type " + " before a word or phrase that must appear in the document and "-" before a word or phrase that must not appear in a document.

Phrase Searching

A *phrase* is a string of words that must appear next to each other. *Global warming* is a phrase, as is *chronic fatigue syndrome*. Use phrase-searching capability when the words you are searching for must appear next to each other and must appear in the order in which you typed them. Most search engines require double quotation marks to differentiate a phrase from words searched by themselves. The two phrases mentioned above would be expressed like this: "global warming" and "chronic fatigue syndrome." Phrase searching is one of the most helpful search features, as it increases the chance that your search will have relevant results.

Proximity Searching

Proximity operators are words such as *near* or *within*. For example, you are trying to find information on the effects of chlorofluorocarbons on global warming. You might want to retrieve results that have the word *chlorofluorocarbons* very close to the phrase *global warming*. By placing the word *near* between the two segments of the search expression, you would achieve more relevant results than if the words appeared in the same document but were perhaps pages apart. This is called ***proximity searching***.

Truncation

Truncation is the process of looking for multiple forms of a word. Some search engines refer to truncation as *stemming*. For example, if you were researching postmodern art, you might want to retrieve all the records that had the root word *postmodern*, as well as *postmodernist* and *postmodernism*. Most search engines support truncation by allowing you to place an asterisk (*) at the end of the root word. You would need to see the help screen in the search engine you are using to find out which symbol is used. For example, in this case we would type **postmodern***. Some search engines automatically truncate words. In those databases, you would type **postmodern** and be assured that all the endings would also be retrieved. In these cases, truncation would be a default setting of the search engines. If you didn't want your search expression to be truncated, you would need to override the default feature. You would find out how to do this by reading the search engine's help screens.

Wildcards

Using ***wildcards*** allows you to search for words that have most of the word in common, except for maybe a letter or two. For example, we might want to search for both *woman* and *women*. Instead of typing

woman or **women**, we could place a wildcard character (most often an asterisk) to replace the fourth letter. It would look like this: **wom*n**.

Field Searching

Web pages can be broken down into many parts. These parts, or *fields*, include titles, URLs, text, summaries or annotations (if present), text, and so forth. (See Figure 5.1.) *Field searching* is the ability to limit your search to certain fields. This ability to search by field can increase the relevance of the retrieved records.

Figure 5.1—The Parts of a Web Page

Case Sensitivity

Case sensitivity is an important feature, especially if you are looking for proper names. Some search engines recognize capitalization, but some do not. If a search engine does recognize capitals, it can lead to a much more precise search, especially if you're looking for proper names such as Sting, the Who, or Brad Pitt. If the search engine you are using doesn't recognize capitals, just think of the results you'd get by entering **sting** in the search query box.

Concept Searching

Concept searching occurs when a search engine automatically searches for Web pages that have similar terms to the ones you entered in the search query box. Excite supports this feature.

Limiting by Date

Some search engines allow you to search the Web for pages that were added to the database between certain dates. In *limiting by date*, you can find only the pages that were entered in the past month, in the past year, or in a particular year.

Output Features Common to Most Search Engines

The way a search engine displays results can help you decide which search engine to use. The following features are common to many engines, but as we saw earlier with the search features, the engines all have different ways of determining and showing these features.

Relevancy Ranking

Most search engines measure each Web page's relevance to your search query and arrange the search results from the most relevant to the least relevant. This is called *relevancy ranking*. Each search engine has its own algorithm for determining relevance, but it usually involves counting how many times the words in your query appear in the Web pages. In some search engines, a document is considered more relevant if the words appear in certain fields, for example, the title or summary field. In other search engines, relevance is determined by the number of times the keyword appears in a Web page divided by the total number of words in the page. This gives a percentage, and the page with the largest percentage appears first on the list.

Annotations or Summaries

Some search engines include short descriptive paragraphs of each Web page they return to you. These annotations, or summaries, can help you decide whether or not to open a Web page, especially if there is no title for the Web page or if the title doesn't describe the page in detail.

Results Per Page

In some search engines, the *results per page* option allows you to choose how many results you want listed per page. This can be a time saver, because it sometimes takes a while to go from page to page as you look through results.

Sorting Results

Some services allow you to choose how you want your results sorted—by relevance, URL, location, organization, and so forth. This feature is known as *sorting*.

Duplicate Detection

It is not unusual to retrieve several instances of the same Web page in your results. Some search engines detect these duplicates and remove them. In meta-search engines or unified search interfaces, *duplicate detection* is a common feature.

Modification of Search Results

Some search engines will insert a copy of your search request on the first page of your results to make it easier for you to modify the query if you so desire. With others, you may be required to return to the original search form before making this *modification of search results*. Some search engines allow you to search only the results of an earlier search, which can be extremely helpful.

Meta-tag Support

Some search engines acknowledge keywords that a Web page author has placed in the meta-tag field in the HTML source document. This means that a document may be retrieved by a keyword search, but that the search expression may not appear in the document.

A Basic Search Strategy: The 10 Steps

The following list provides a guideline for you to follow in formulating search requests, viewing search results, and modifying search results. These procedures can be followed for virtually any search request, from the simplest to the most complicated. For some search requests, you may not want or need to go through a formal search strategy. If you want to save time in the long run, however, it's a good idea to follow a strategy, especially when you're new to a particular search engine. A basic search strategy can help you get used to each search engine's features and how they are expressed in the search query. Following the 10 steps will also ensure good results if your search is multifaceted and you want to get the most relevant results.

The 10 steps are as follows:

1. Identify the important concepts of your search.
2. Choose the keywords that describe these concepts.
3. Determine whether there are synonyms, related terms, or other variations of the keywords that should be included.
4. Determine which search features may apply, including truncation, proximity operators, Boolean operators, and so forth.
5. Choose a search engine.
6. Read the search instructions on the search engine's home page. Look for sections entitled "help," "advanced search," "frequently asked questions," and so forth.
7. Create a search expression using syntax that is appropriate for the search engine.
8. View the results. How many hits were returned? Were the results relevant to your query?
9. Modify your search if needed. Go back to Steps 2 through 4 and revise your query accordingly.
10. Try the same search in a different search engine, following Steps 5 through 9 above.

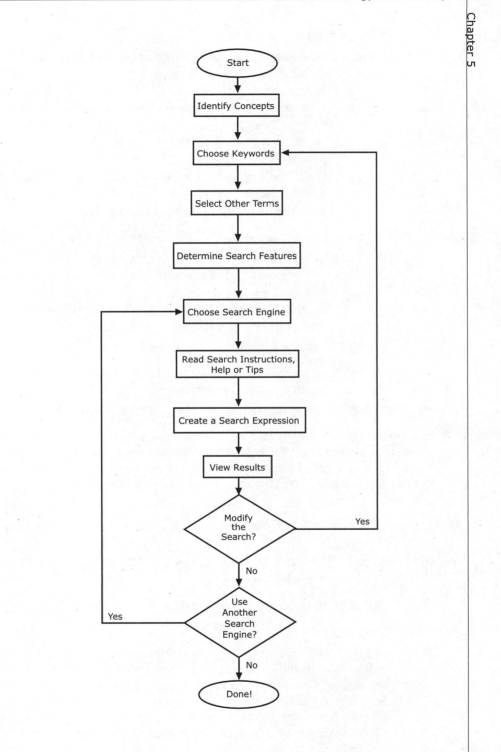

Search Tips

If you feel that your search has yielded too few Web pages (low recall), there are several things to consider:

❋ Perhaps the search expression was too specific; go back and remove some terms that are connected by ANDs.

❋ Perhaps there are more terms to use. Think of more synonyms to OR together. Try truncating more words if possible.

❋ Check spelling and syntax (a forgotten quotation mark or a missing parentheses).

❋ Read the instructions on the help pages again.

If your search has given you too many results and many are unrelated to your topic (high recall/low precision), consider the following:

❋ Narrow your search to specific fields, if possible.

❋ Use more specific terms; for example, instead of cancer, use the specific type of cancer in which you're interested.

❋ Add additional terms with AND or NOT.

❋ Remove some synonyms if possible.

In order to explain these concepts in the most practical way, we'll do an activity in two full-text databases.

❋ Tip

Remember that the Web is always changing and that your results may differ from those shown here. Don't let this confuse you. The activities are meant to teach you fundamental skills. These skills don't change, even though the number of results obtained or the actual screens may look very different.

Activity 5.1 Search Strategies in AltaVista and Open Text

Performing a Search in AltaVista

Overview

In this activity, we are going to search for resources on a multifaceted topic. We want to find World Wide Web documents that focus on how self-esteem relates to young girls' likelihood of developing eating disorders. There has been a lot of research in the past 10 years about how changes in modern life have hurt teenage girls' development, and we'd like to see if any of this research has been published on the Web.

Following the steps of the basic search strategy, we need to examine the facts of our search, choosing the appropriate keywords and determining which search features apply. Then, we'll go to the search engine and read the search instructions. We'll explore AltaVista first. Then, we'll perform the same search (using the appropriate syntax) in Open Text. Let's see how these two search engines handle this multifaceted topic.

Details

1   Identify the important concepts of your search.

The most important concepts of this search are the development of eating disorders in adolescent girls and the way this is related to their lack of self-esteem.

2   Choose the keywords that describe these concepts.

The main terms or keywords include the following: teenage girls, self-esteem, and eating disorders.

3   Determine whether there are synonyms, related terms, or other variations of the keywords that should be included.

For teenage: adolescent, adolescence.

For eating disorders: anorexia nervosa, bulimia.

For self-esteem: self-respect.

4   Determine which search features may apply, including truncation, proximity operators, Boolean operators, and so forth.

When developing a search expression, keep in mind that you place **OR** between synonyms and **AND** between the different concepts, or facets, of the search topic. If you write down all the synonyms you choose, it may help with the construction of the final search phraseology. Table 5.1 shows the three major concepts, or facets, of the search topic with their synonyms, connected with the appropriate Boolean operators. Keep in mind there can be different ways to express the same idea. For example, for the facet teenage girls, you could say **"teenage girls" or "adolescen* girls"** instead of **(teenage or adolescen*) and girls**. Note that by using the truncated word **adolescen**, we would retrieve the words *adolescent* and *adolescence*. Before you get online, take a few minutes to determine whether you have used all the search features that you possibly can. It can save you a lot of time in the long run.

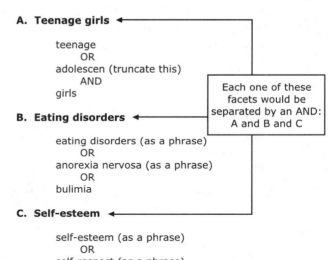

A. Teenage girls

teenage
OR
adolescen (truncate this)
AND
girls

Each one of these facets would be separated by an AND: A and B and C

B. Eating disorders

eating disorders (as a phrase)
OR
anorexia nervosa (as a phrase)
OR
bulimia

C. Self-esteem

self-esteem (as a phrase)
OR
self-respect (as a phrase)

Table 5.1—Formulation of the Search Strategy

5   Choose a search engine.

In this activity, we are going to search AltaVista first. This search engine supports full Boolean searching, which is a search feature we need for this topic. AltaVista's advanced search mode has a large search form, which makes it easier to type in a lengthy search expression.

✳*Do It!* Click on the location field, type **http://www.altavista.digital .com**, and press **Enter**.

6   Read the search instructions on the search engine's home page. Look for sections entitled "Help," "Advanced Search," "Frequently Asked Questions," and so forth.

AltaVista has two search modes: simple and advanced. The simple search mode only supports implied, or pseudo-Boolean, searching. This means that you could perform an AND and NOT search by typing a + before the word if it has to appear in each of the results, and a – before words that you don't want in the results. Since our topic involves many ORs, we will need to do an advanced search.

When you open AltaVista, you will see the simple search form. You will need to go to the advanced search section. Then you will want to look at the search instructions for its advanced search capability.

✳*Do It!* Click on the **Advanced Search** hyperlink.

Your screen will fill with the advanced search form.

✸*Do It!* Click on the **Help** hyperlink.

See Figure 5.2 for some parts of the search help information.

Figure 5.2—Help for Advanced Searches in AltaVista

After reading the extensive help screens in AltaVista, you can start determining how to construct your search expression. In addition to reviewing how to combine Boolean operators with phrases and parentheses, you'll need to find out how AltaVista truncates words. You'll also need to read the section on ranking. This is a crucial part of AltaVista's advanced search mode. You must type words in this section that you want to have in the first documents returned to you. If you don't, the results will be listed in any order, and the first documents may not be as relevant as the last documents returned.

7   Create a search expression using syntax that is appropriate for the search engine.

Now that you've read the search help, it's time to formulate the search expression. It will help to write it out before you type it in the search form. Here is a possible way to express this search:

(teenage or adolescen*) and girls and ("eating disorders" or "anorexia nervosa" or bulimia) and ("self-esteem" or "self-respect")

Keep in mind that you can always modify your search later. Let's try entering it in AltaVista's advanced search form.

✸*Do It!* Click on the **Back** icon to return to the advanced search form.

❋*Do It!* Enter the search expression in the form provided, as shown in Figure 5.3.

❋*Do It!* In the **Ranking** field, type in the phrase **"eating disorders"** as shown in Figure 5.3.

Make sure all of the quotation marks are present and that you've closed all of the parentheses properly. Check your spelling and determine whether you have ANDs and ORs in the proper places.

❋*Do It!* Click on **search**.

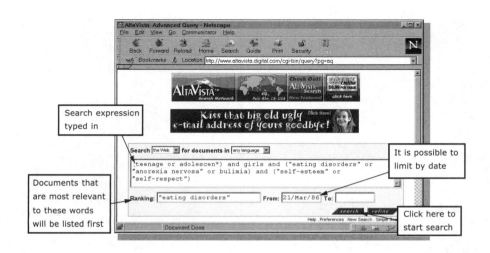

Search expression typed in

It is possible to limit by date

Documents that are most relevant to these words will be listed first

Click here to start search

Figure 5.3—Advanced Search in AltaVista with Search Expression Entered

8 View the results. How many hits were returned? Were the results relevant to your query?

Note the number of hits this search has returned to your screen. Look at a few of the titles. Do they appear to be relevant? Figure 5.4 shows the first few. Because the Web is always changing, the results shown may not be the same ones that you retrieve.

❋*Do It!* Click on the title of the first result on the list.

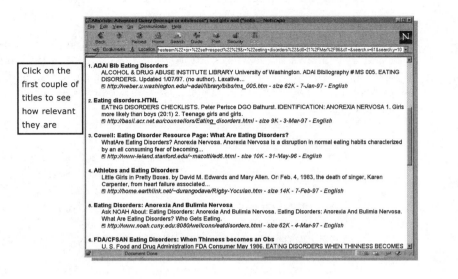

Click on the first couple of titles to see how relevant they are

Figure 5.4—Results of AltaVista Search

Examine the first page that appears on your screen. Is the information relevant to the search query? Scroll down to the bottom of the page and click on **next** to see the next page of results, as shown in Figure 5.5. Look through the results on this page to determine whether they seem relevant.

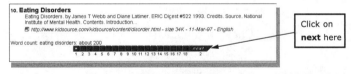

Click on **next** here

Figure 5.5—Navigating Search Results in AltaVista

9   Modify your search if needed. Go back to Steps 2 through 4 and revise your query accordingly.

The results seem relevant, and the number of hits is an adequate set with which to work. You may, however, want to limit the results by date. You could do this by going back to the search query screen and typing a date in the space provided, as shown in Figure 5.4.

10   Try the same search in a different search engine, following Steps 5 through 9 above.

Since our topic is multifaceted and requires a powerful search engine, we'll do the same search in Open Text.

Performing the Same Search in Open Text

Overview

Open Text is a full-text index of Web pages, FTP sites, and Gopher sites. Open Text allows Boolean searching, field searching, and proximity operators in an easy-to-use interface. Using the same concepts and keywords that we employed in AltaVista, we will see how Open Text performs our search.

We'll follow these steps, which correspond to Steps 6 through 9 of the basic search strategy:

1. Read the search instructions on the search engine's home page. Look for sections entitled "Help," "Advanced Search," "Frequently Asked Questions," and so forth.
2. Create a search expression using syntax that is appropriate for the search engine.
3. View the results. How many hits were returned? Were the results relevant to your query?
4. Modify your search if needed. Go back and revise your query accordingly.
5. End the session.

Details

1   **Read the search instructions on the search engine's home page. Look for sections entitled "Help," "Advanced Search," "Frequently Asked Questions," and so forth.**

First we need to open Open Text.

✳*Do It!* Click on the location field, type **http://index.opentext.net**, and press **Enter**.

✳*Do It!* Click on **Help** on Open Text's home page.

✳*Do It!* Click on **Search Tips**.

Your screen should look like the one in Figure 5.6.

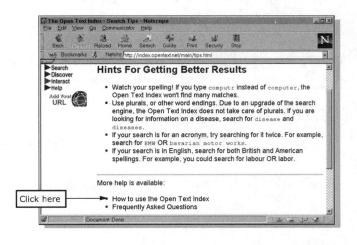

Figure 5.6—Open Text Help

✳**Do It!** Click on **How to use the Open Text Index**, as shown in Figure 5.6.

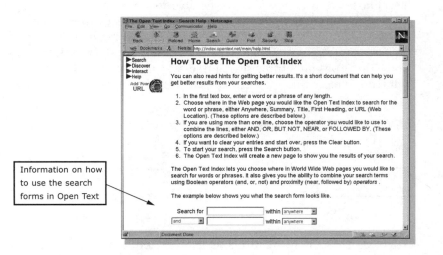

Figure 5.7—More Open Text Help

Open Text, like AltaVista, has two search modes: simple and power search. The simple search mode allows for terms or phrases to be typed in, but full Boolean searching is not supported. Since our topic requires advanced Boolean logic, we want to do a power search.

The power search screen in Open Text looks much different than the advanced search query screen in AltaVista. Open Text supports field searching in a straightforward way, and the text boxes make it simple to perform Boolean searches, as shown in Figure 5.7.

Details about the order of operations are shown in Figure 5.8.

Details about the
order of operations

Things to keep in mind when using the search engine

- Operators are applied in the order they appear. For example, if the first line's *Search for* field contains donkey and its operator is OR, and the second line has horse and BUT NOT, and the third line has mule, your results will include all the Web pages that contain donkey and all pages containing horse, but with all the pages containing mule excluded.
- Remember that the Open Text Index ignores case and some punctuation.

Figure 5.8—Search Tips in Open Text Power Search

2   Create a search expression, using syntax that is appro-
     priate for the search engine.

✳*Do It!* After checking out the help pages, go to the power search page
     by scrolling to the bottom of the screen and finding a hyperlink
     for **Power Search**.

✳*Do It!* Now click on **Power Search**.

Now you are ready to start searching your topic in Open Text. We know
that Open Text supports phrase searching and Boolean searching, so
we won't need to change our concepts. What is going to be different
from AltaVista is that we don't need to type quotation marks around
the phrases we use. Nor will we be able to use nested Boolean logic
properly, because there is no way to insert parentheses around the ORs
we enter. Because Open Text supports field searching in an uncompli-
cated way, we might want to try some of our terms only in certain fields.
Open Text gives only three search lines at first. Our search expression
will require more lines. Open Text has provided a way to increase the
lines.

✳*Do It!* Click on **More lines** on the power search page, as shown in
     Figure 5.9.

Click on **More lines**
here before you begin

Figure 5.9—Open Text Power Search Page

After you click on **More lines**, Open Text presents two more lines.
Let's begin typing the search terms. The completed search query appears in Figure 5.10.

✳*Do It!* Type **teenage** on the first line. Click on the pulldown menu
     next to **within** and choose **summary**. This will limit the results
     so that teenage will only occur in the summary fields of the
     Web pages.

✳*Do It!* On the next line, click on the pulldown menu on the left and
     choose **or**. On the line next to it, type **adolescen*** and choose
     summary from the field search pulldown menu on the right.

✳*Do It!* On the next line, leave the pulldown menu on **and**. Then type **girls** in the space provided. Choose **summary** for the field here as well.

✳*Do It!* Now move to the next line, and as before, leave the pulldown menu on **and**. Type **eating disorders** in the space provided. Choose **anywhere** on the right so that all fields will be searched.

✳*Do It!* On the next pulldown menu, choose **or**. Type the phrase **anorexia nervosa** in the search term space, and leave **anywhere** in the field-searching pulldown menu.

Figure 5.10—Open Text Power Search with Search Terms Entered

✳*Do It!* Click on **Search**.

3 **View the results. How many hits were returned? Were the results relevant to your query?**

Look at the results of the search query, as shown in Figure 5.11. Your results may be different. We need to add more synonyms and the remaining facet of our search topic.

Chapter 5

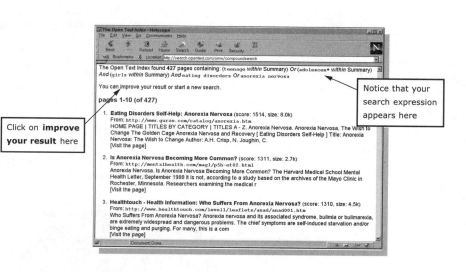

Figure 5.11—Search Results from the First Search Query in Open Text

4   Modify your search if needed. Go back and revise your query accordingly.

Do It! Click on **improve your result**.

Open Text gives one more search form with two accompanying pulldown menus.

Do It! In the new pulldown menu provided, choose **Or**. Then type **bulimia** in the search term box. The right-hand box should remain set at **Anywhere**. Your screen will look like the one in Figure 5.12.

Do It! Click on **Search**.

Refine your result by combining it with a new search		
Search for:	Search Clear	
teenage	Within: Summary	Or
adolescen*	Within: Summary	And
girls	Within: Summary	And
eating disorders	Within: Anywhere	Or
anorexia nervosa	Within: Anywhere	Or
bulimia	Within: Anywhere	

Figure 5.12—Open Text Power Search with Revised Search Term Entered

Since the last term added was connected to the other terms with an *or*, the results have increased. The use of *or* broadens search results, as shown in Figure 5.13.

Open Text gives 10 results per page

The Open Text Index found **858** pages containing: (teenage *within* Summary) *Or* (adolescen* *within* Summary) *And* (girls *within* Summary) *And* eating disorders *Or* anorexia nervosa *Or* bulimia

You can improve your result or start a new search.

Note search strategy

pages 1-10 (of 858)

1. **Eating Disorders Self-Help: Anorexia Nervosa** (score: 1514, size: 8.0k)
From: http://www.gurze.com/catalog/anorexia.htm
HOME PAGE | TITLES BY CATEGORY | TITLES A - Z. Anorexia Nervosa. Anorexia Nervosa, The Wish to Change The Golden Cage Anorexia Nervosa and Recovery [Eating Disorders Self-Help] Title: Anorexia Nervosa: The Wish to Change Author: A.H. Crisp, N. Joughin, C.
[Visit the page]

Figure 5.13—Results of Modified Search Expression in Open Text

We can now modify our results even more by adding the third facet of the search topic—self-esteem.

✳️*Do It!* Click on **improve your result**.

✳️*Do It!* In the additional space provided, type **self-esteem**. Leave the new Boolean operator set on **And**. Keep the search capability set on **Anywhere**. See Figure 5.14.

✳️*Do It!* Click on **Search**.

Refine your result by combining it with a new search

Search for: search   Clear

teenage	Within:	Summary	Or
adolescen*	Within:	Summary	And
girls	Within:	Summary	And
eating disorders	Within:	Anywhere	Or
anorexia nervosa	Within:	Anywhere	Or
bulimia	Within:	Anywhere	And
self-esteem	Within:	Anywhere	

Figure 5.14—More Terms Added to Search Expression in Open Text

As Figure 5.15 shows adding this final facet to the search narrowed the results considerably. Most of the results are extremely relevant to the topic. Look at some of the Web pages retrieved. You could modify the results again if you wished.

The Open Text Index found **115** pages containing: (teenage *within* Summary) *Or* (adolescen* *within* Summary) *And* (girls *within* Summary) *And* eating disorders *Or* anorexia nervosa *Or* bulimia *And* self-esteem

You can improve your result or start a new search.

pages 1-10 (of 115)

1. **ANRED - Anorexia Nervosa and Related Eating Disorders, Inc.** (score: 1121, size: 34.8k)
From: http://www.diane.com/anred.html
Post Office Box 5102 Eugene, OR 97405. USA http://www.anred.org. Please note: The information offered in this site is NOT intended as medical or psychological advice or treatment. If you have questions or concerns about yourself or someone you care about, p
[Visit the page]

Figure 5.15—Final Results in Open Text

Keep in mind that if we added **self-respect** to the search query by OR-ing it with **self-esteem**, our results would not be accurate. Since Open Text doesn't support nested Boolean searching, all the records with the phrase **self-respect** would be added to the previous results, which is not what we would want.

5   End the session.

You can end the session now or continue to the next activity.

✳*Do It!* To end the session now, click on **File** on the menu bar, and select **Exit** from the menu.

_____ End of Activity 5.1 _____

As we saw in this activity, AltaVista and Open Text handle multifaceted search queries differently. In some ways, the AltaVista search form makes it easier to perform a search, because it is large and because you can type in a long search expression with ease (if you have read the search help carefully). On the other hand, Open Text provides "text boxes" for field searching. This makes searches easy for those who want to limit keywords to certain fields or those who find it difficult to use Boolean operators.

There are pros and cons to using any of the search engines. Sometimes it comes down to which service you are more comfortable with using. In the following two activities, we'll be searching for the same topic in two very different databases: Infoseek and MetaCrawler. Infoseek is a full-text search engine database, whereas MetaCrawler is a meta-search tool, which allows you to search several search engines simultaneously. In performing searches in each of these indexes, we will follow the steps laid out in the basic search strategy.

Activity 5.2   Search Strategies in Infoseek

Overview

We'll be searching for the same information that we did in Activity 5.1—how self-esteem relates to teenage girls' likelihood of developing eating disorders. In Activity 5.1, we have already done Steps 1 through 4 of the basic search strategy, so we'll now do the following steps, which correspond to Steps 5 through 10 of the strategy:

1. Choose a search engine.
2. Read the search instructions on the search engine's home page. Look for sections entitled "Help," "Advanced Search," "Frequently Asked Questions," and so forth.
3. Create a search expression using syntax that is appropriate for the search engine.
4. View the results. How many hits were returned? Were the results relevant to your query?
5. Modify your search if needed. Go back and revise your query accordingly.
6. Try the same search in a different search engine.
7. End the session.

Details

1   Choose a search engine.

We'll be searching Infoseek, another popular search engine. Infoseek doesn't support Boolean searching as AltaVista and Open Text do, but it does allow for the use of implied Boolean operators—the + and the –. These operators represent the Boolean AND and NOT, but there is no OR capability in Infoseek. This makes it difficult to search for synonyms. Infoseek does allow you to search the results of another search, which is one way around this limitation. Let's go to Infoseek and see how it handles our topic.

Do It! Click on the location field, type **http://www.infoseek.com**, and press **Enter**.

View the Infoseek home page, as shown in Figure 5.16.

Figure 5.16—Infoseek Home Page

2   Read the search instructions on the search engine's home page. Look for sections entitled "Help," "Advanced Search," "Frequently Asked Questions," and so forth.

Do It! Click on **Tips**, as shown in Figure 5.16.

Do It! Now click on **Quick reference**.

You can read through the tips if you like.

The "Quick Reference to Syntax" page appears in Figure 5.17. From reading the search tips, we determine the following:

❋   Infoseek supports phrase searching by requiring quotes to be placed around words that must be together or by placing hyphens between adjacent words.

✳ A **+** should be placed in front of a word or phrase that must be present in the Web pages found.

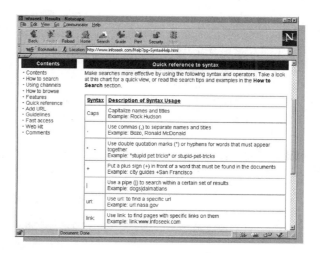

Figure 5.17—Search Help in Infoseek

3 Create a search expression, using syntax that is appropriate for the search engine.

Since full Boolean searching isn't supported, it's better to not type in too many words or phrases at this point. If we typed in **+ "anorexia nervosa" + bulimia + "self-esteem"** in addition to the two phrases below, we would be requiring that *all* phrases and words appear in the Web pages, which might give us too few results. It's best to start out with fewer terms at first and to see what results we obtain. We can always modify our results later.

✳*Do It!* Click on **Home** at the top of the page.

✳*Do It!* Type **+ "teenage girls" + "eating disorders"**, and click on **seek** as shown in Figure 5.18.

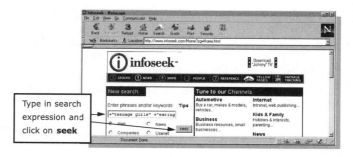

Figure 5.18—Search Expression Entered in Infoseek

4   View the results. How many hits were returned? Were the results relevant to your query?

This search retrieved some very relevant hits. A few of these results appear in Figure 5.19. Don't be surprised if you obtain different results.

Figure 5.19—Results of Search in Infoseek with Added Keyword Phrase

5   Modify your search if needed. Go back and revise your query accordingly.

Infoseek allows you to search only the results of a search. Let's say that of the documents that the search retrieved, you want to know which ones have the phrase "self-esteem" in them. All that is required is to type **+ "self-esteem"** in the search form provided and to indicate that only these results should be searched. Let's do that now.

Do It! In the search form provided, type **+ "self-esteem"**, as shown in Figure 5.19.

Do It! Click on **Search These Results**.

Figure 5.20 shows the results of this modification. Remember that you may have different results, because the Web is always changing.

Chapter 5

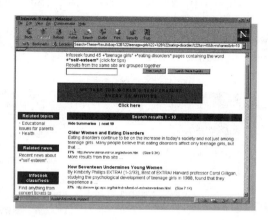

Figure 5.20—Results of Modifying the Original Search in Infoseek

6   Try the same search in a different search engine.

Next we're going to try the same search in MetaCrawler in Activity 5.3.

7   End the session.

You can exit the Internet now or go on to the next activity.

❄️*Do It!* To exit now, click on **File** on the menu bar, and select **Exit** from the menu.

_____ End of Activity 5.2 _____

Infoseek proved to be an effective search engine. We obtained fewer results than in AltaVista or Open Text, because there is no OR capability in Infoseek. The use of the Boolean OR expands results, whereas the use of AND or + narrows results.

Activity 5.3   Search Strategies in MetaCrawler

Overview

In this activity, we'll look for information on the same topic in MetaCrawler. As stated before, MetaCrawler is a meta-search tool. Also known as parallel-search tools or unified search interfaces, meta-search tools don't create their own indexes. They merely provide a search interface so that you can use several search engines and directories at the same time with one search expression. Currently, MetaCrawler searches five different databases: AltaVista, Excite, Lycos, WebCrawler, and Yahoo! Meta-search tools can be very useful for single-word subjects but unreliable for multiterm, multifaceted searches, such as the one we have been using in this chapter. Let's see how MetaCrawler handles our topic. We will be following Steps 5 through 10 of the basic search strategy, as we did in Activity 5.2.

Details

1   Choose a search engine.

Let's open MetaCrawler.

✳️*Do It!* Click on the location field, type in the URL for MetaCrawler, **http://www.metacrawler .com**, and press **Enter**.

Your screen should look like the picture in Figure 5.21.

Figure 5.21—MetaCrawler Home Page

2   Read the search instructions on the search engine's home page. Look for sections entitled "Help," "Advanced Search," "Frequently Asked Questions," and so forth.

In order to find out how to use MetaCrawler, read its documentation.

✳️*Do It!* Click on **FAQ** on the left side of the screen, as shown in Figure 5.21.

✳️*Do It!* Scroll down and click on the hyperlink **How can I refine MetaCrawler searches?**

Here you will notice that MetaCrawler uses implied Boolean operators (+ and –) and that phrase searching, using double quotation marks, is a supported feature. See Figure 5.22.

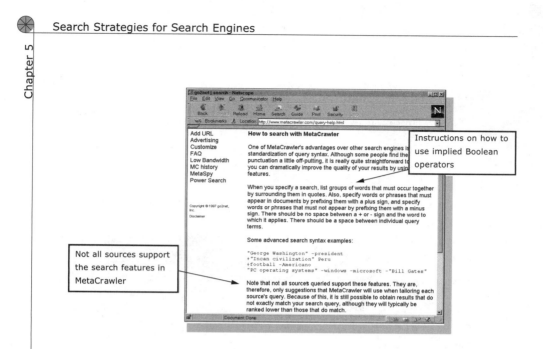

Figure 5.22—MetaCrawler Documentation

3   Create a search expression using syntax that is appro-
     priate for the search engine.

First, we need to find MetaCrawler's search form.

Do It! Scroll to the bottom of the "FAQ" page.

Do It! Type the following search expression in the search form:

+ "teenage girls" + "eating disorders" + "self-esteem"

Do It! Click on **all**.

By using this search expression and choosing **all**, you are telling
MetaCrawler to find all the Web pages in which each of these three
phrases occur. The + in front of each phrase indicates that the phrase
must appear somewhere in the Web pages.

Do It! Click on **Search**.

This will initiate your search request. See Figure 5.23.

Figure 5.23—Submission of MetaCrawler Search Query

As MetaCrawler works to satisfy the search request, it will list on the
screen the different search tools it has searched so far, along with the
number of the results found in each one. You can't always rely on these

results, however. If MetaCrawler says there are zero results in a certain database, this doesn't necessarily mean that there are zero results. Sometimes the search query in MetaCrawler doesn't coincide with the search features supported in the individual databases. When the results appear, they are listed by relevance and not by the search engine or directory in which they were found. MetaCrawler should detect and weed out duplicates. Figure 5.24 depicts how the results will be listed. Remember that your results may differ from the ones shown here.

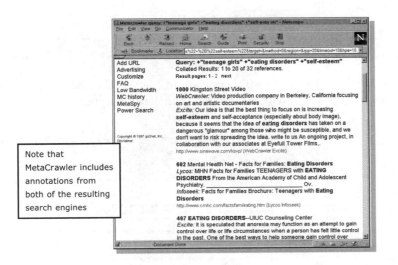

Note that MetaCrawler includes annotations from both of the resulting search engines

Figure 5.24—MetaCrawler Results

4   View the results. How many hits were returned? Were the results relevant to your query?

After looking through the results, we decide to modify our search to see if we can get more hits.

5   Modify your search if needed. Go back and revise your query accordingly.

Since MetaCrawler does not support nested Boolean searching, it may be unwise to add too many synonyms for the words we've already entered. We could add one more term, for example **bulimia**, and then change the search option to **any** instead of **all**. The danger would be that some of the results may not be as relevant as we would like. In effect, this would be the same as placing an OR between each word instead of an AND.

Let's modify our search by adding the extra keyword and changing the search options.

✳Do It! Scroll to the bottom of the page.

✳*Do It!* Place the cursor at the very beginning of the search query box and type **+ bulimia**. Make sure there is a space between bulimia and **+ "teenage girls"**.

✳*Do It!* Click next to **any**.

✳*Do It!* Click on **Search**.

The search query screen should look like the one in Figure 5.25.

+**bulimia** added;
any chosen

Figure 5.25—Modification of MetaCrawler Search

A partial list of the results appears in Figure 5.26. Notice how many more results resulted from changing the search options.

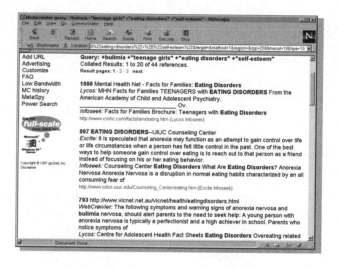

Figure 5.26—Results of Modifying Search in MetaCrawler

6   Try the same search in a different search engine.

If you like, you could try the same search in a different search engine on your own.

7   End the session.

✳*Do It!* Click on **File** on the menu bar, and select **Exit** from the menu.

End of Activity 5.3

In Activities 5.1, 5.2, and 5.3, we searched for information on the same topic in four different search engines. Each one had its own particular syntax and individual search and output features. We saw the importance of reading each search engine's documentation before going online. All of the search engines gave relevant results, but none of them gave the same results.

Summary

Search engines are tools that search databases. These search engines have been created by computer programs, commonly referred to as spiders or robots. These spiders go out onto the World Wide Web and put every single word of every Web page they find into a database. With the help of our search request, the search engine then searches this full-text database for us. Some databases are not full-text, but instead consist of selected words from Web documents.

In either case, each search engine accesses its database differently. Even though many search engine databases claim to cover the entire Web, the same search performed in more than one database never returns the same exact results. If you want to do a thorough search, you should become familiar with a few of the different search engines. Toward this end, it is important to understand the major search features, such as Boolean logic, phrase searching, truncation, and others before you get online. It is also necessary to read each search engine's documentation before you enter the search request in the query box. You may want to check the documentation often, since search engines are constantly changing their search and output features.

It can help to try your search in a meta-search tool if you're not overly concerned about obtaining precise and comprehensive results. That way, you can gather hits from several databases at once.

In this chapter, we introduced the basic search strategy, a 10-step procedure that can help you formulate search requests, submit them to search engines, and modify the results retrieved. We have focused on the major search engines on the World Wide Web, but there are several hundred smaller search engines on the Web that search smaller databases. We'll discuss these in some detail in Chapter 7, "Specialized Databases." In addition, there are other search engines that are not free to the public; they require passwords or subscription costs. Our intent in this chapter was to give you a foundation in searching any database, no matter whether it is large or small, fee-based or not. All of the steps in the basic search strategy apply to any database.

Selected Terms Introduced in This Chapter

case sensitivity	full-text indexing
concept searching	high precision/high recall
default settings	high precision/low recall
duplicate detection	implied Boolean operators
fields	keyword indexing
field searching	limiting by date

low precision/high recall
meta-tags
modification of search results
nested Boolean logic
proximity searching
relevancy ranking

results per page
sorting
stop words
syntax
wildcards

Exercises and Projects

1. Using the advanced search mode in AltaVista, **http://www .altavista.digital.com**, and Infoseek, **http://www.infoseek .com**, look for relevant resources on the following topics:

   * The writings of Jack London
   * Ebola virus
   * Chronic fatigue syndrome
   * Symptoms of decompression sickness

   Write down the first three Web pages retrieved by both search engines. Were any the same? Write down the search expression you used for each topic in every database. For each topic, list any problems you had and how many times you needed to modify the search request in each search engine.

2. Do an advanced search in AltaVista, **http://www.altavista .digital.com**, for resources on asteroids. How many Web pages were returned by your search? Narrow the results by clicking on **refine**. Mark two or three words that the system has selected, intending for you to browse. Now redo the search with the extra terms. What happened to the number of search results returned to your screen?

3. Find a current mission statement and recent annual report for Merck & Co. Perform the search in Open Text, **http://index .opentext.net**, and MetaCrawler, **http://www.metacrawler .com**. Write down the search expressions you used in each database to obtain the result.

4. Using AltaVista, **http://www.altavista.digital.com**, find the periodic table of elements. How many hyperlinks did you find? Compare two of the periodic tables you found. Which one was easier to use? Why?

5. In Open Text, **http://index.opentext.net**, use all of steps in the basic search strategy to perform a search on the following topic: "The problems encountered in deep sea diving." Give special consideration to finding possible synonyms and using truncation. Write down the steps you took. What problems, if any, did you encounter? Did you need to modify your search strategy? If so, how did you do this?

6. Using the advanced search mode in AltaVista, **http://www .altavista.digital.com**, search for information about Newt Gingrich. Find Web pages in which his name appears near the word *ethics*. Then limit your search to those Web pages that were entered into the database since October 1, 1996. How many search results did you obtain? Look at the first couple of pages. Do they appear to be relevant? Go into at least two Web pages and use Find in Page to do a search inside the Web page, looking for the words *Newt Gingrich*. Did the words appear in the documents? *Hint:* **Find in Page** is found under **Edit** in the menu bar.

7. Use MetaCrawler, **http://www.metacrawler.com**, to find information on baby boomers and social security. How many results did you obtain? Write down the first three Web page titles in the results list and their URLs. Write down the search expression you used.

8. Using the advanced search mode in AltaVista, **http://www .altavista.digital.com**, look for information on how mad cow disease causes Creutzfeldt-Jakob disease in humans. Keeping in mind that mad cow disease is also known as Bovine Spongiform Encephalopathy, incorporate this into your search in the correct way. Write down the search expression that you used and the total number of hits retrieved. Did the results appear to be relevant to your search request? Write down three of the most relevant titles with their URLs.

9. Open Lycos, **http://www.lycos.com**, and find information on whether there is an increasing number of youth gangs in cities in the United States. Try to determine whether there has been an increase in juvenile crime and violence in America, and if so, what the reasons are. Write out the search strategy, and explain how you entered the information in Lycos. Did you need to modify your search to obtain the most relevant results? If so, how did you modify it?

10. Using the advanced search mode in AltaVista, **http://www .altavista.digital.com**, find information on a new drug that has been developed by Glaxo-Wellcome (a pharmaceutical company) for AIDS and HIV. The drug is commonly referred to as 1592, or 1592U89. Write out the search expression you used. Open a Web page or two and find *1592* or *1592U89* somewhere in the document using the Find in Page function in Netscape. Now try to find similar information using Infoseek, **http:// www.infoseek.com**. Write out the search expression you used and the number of results received.

6
Chapter

Using Search Engines

In this chapter, we'll continue to focus on searching databases, employing the 10-step basic search strategy described and used in Chapter 5. We'll do several activities that showcase search and output features that we didn't cover in earlier chapters. To refresh your memory, we list the strategy here.

Basic Search Strategy: The 10 Steps
1. Identify the important concepts of your search.
2. Choose the keywords that describe these concepts.
3. Determine whether there are synonyms, related terms, or other variations of the keywords that should be included.
4. Determine which search features may apply, including truncation, proximity operators, Boolean operators, and so forth.
5. Choose a search engine.
6. Read the search instructions on the search engine's home page. Look for sections entitled "help," "advanced search," "frequently asked questions," and so forth.
7. Create a search expression using syntax that is appropriate for the search engine.
8. View the results. How many hits were returned? Were the results relevant to your query?
9. Modify your search if needed. Go back to Steps 2 through 4 and revise your query accordingly.
10. Try the same search in a different search engine, following Steps 5 through 9 above.

We'll refer to the steps in the strategy as we go through each activity.

❋ Tip

Remember that the Web is always changing and that your results may differ from those shown here. Don't let this confuse you. The activities are meant to teach you fundamental skills. These skills don't change, even though the number of results obtained or the actual screens may look very different.

Activity 6.1   Search Strategies in HotBot

Overview

In the first activity, we will look for recent information (that is, within the last six months) on the Shining Path, a revolutionary group in Peru. Before we get online, we will follow Steps 1 through 5 of the basic search strategy as we formulate the main ideas of our search.

❋ Steps 1 and 2: The important concepts and keywords are *Shining Path* and *Peru.*

❋ Step 3: Since the Shining Path is a revolutionary movement in Peru, we'll want to include the phrase in Spanish, the primary language spoken in Peru. *Shining Path* in Spanish is *Sendero Luminoso.*

❋ Step 4: Since we don't want pages that have information about *Tupac Amaru*, another revolutionary group in Peru, we'll need to use the Boolean NOT operator. We'll also need to search with the phrases *Shining Path* and *Sendero Luminoso*, if possible.

❋ Step 5: We'll choose HotBot, **http://www.hotbot.com**, a full-text database that is good for very specific searches because it supports full Boolean searching and has the capability to limit searches by date.

Now we're ready to go online and search HotBot. We'll follow these steps, which closely correspond to Steps 6 through 9 of the basic search strategy:

1. Go to the home page for HotBot.
2. Read the search instructions on HotBot's home page (Step 6).
3. Create a search expression using syntax appropriate for HotBot (Step 7).
4. View the results (Step 8).
5. Using the **Find in Page** function, search a Web page for the keywords *Shining Path* or *Sendero Luminoso* (Step 8).
6. Modify the search by limiting it to educational sites only, and view the results (Step 9).
7. End the session.

Details

1   Go to the home page for HotBot.

Do It! Click on the location field, type **http://www.hotbot.com**, and press **Enter**.

2   Read the search instructions on HotBot's home page.

Do It! Click on **Help** as shown in Figure 6.1.

Figure 6.1—HotBot Home Page

Your screen will fill with the help directory. While the "Getting Started" section has some basic information, the "Frequently Asked Questions" section is more comprehensive, so we'll look there.

Do It! Click on **Frequently Asked Questions**.

This will take you to a page entitled "HotBot Frequently Asked Questions."

Do It! Scroll down the page until you find "FAQ Categories."

Do It! Click on **Advanced search features**, as shown in Figure 6.2.

Click on **Advanced search features** here

Figure 6.2—FAQ Categories in HotBot

A list of frequently asked questions about HotBot's search features appears, as shown in Figure 6.3.

Click on the first question

Figure 6.3—Search Features in HotBot

✳*Do It!* Click on the first question.

The first question and answer appear in the window. You can go through all the questions that HotBot answers about its search features.

After reading through all the frequently asked questions and answers, we can conclude that HotBot:

✳ supports phrase searching by offering the option *the exact phrase* in the pulldown menu or by enclosing the phrase in quotation marks.

❀ supports Boolean searching by choosing words from the pulldown menus, or by typing **and**, **or**, and **not**.

❀ supports nested Boolean logic.

❀ ignores the case in most searches.

3 Create a search expression using syntax appropriate for HotBot.

You may want to review the section called "Search Features Common to Most Search Engines" in Chapter 5 before working on this step.

❀ Because we want pages that match the phrase *Shining Path* or *Sendero Luminoso*, and that match the word **Peru** but not the phrase *Tupac Amaru*, we need to use nested Boolean logic. This means that we will use parentheses around the two phrases to separate the OR expression from the NOT, and parentheses around all three phrases to separate them from the word *Peru*. It would look like this: **((Shining Path or Sendero Luminoso) not Tupac Amaru) and Peru.** (*Note:* Since we are formulating a Boolean expression for this search, we need to use Boolean operators to exclude terms.)

❀ Since HotBot is not case-sensitive, there is no need to capitalize proper nouns.

❀ HotBot supports phrase searching, so we will need to put quotation marks around the phrases. Now the search expression will look like this: **(("shining path" or "sendero luminoso") not "tupac amaru") and peru.**

❀ To search only those pages entered in the last six months, we need to choose from the options under **Date**.

❀*Do It!* Scroll down to the bottom of the FAQ page. Click on the **BACK TO SEARCH** button in the lower-left corner.

You will now be at HotBot's home page.

❀*Do It!* Choose "**Boolean phrase**" from the pulldown menu next to **Look for**.

❀*Do It!* In the next line, type the following: **(("shining path" or "sendero luminoso") not "tupac amaru") and peru.**

❀*Do It!* Point to and click on the box next to **Date**. Click on the pulldown menu and select **in the last 6 months**.

Your screen should now look like the one pictured in Figure 6.4.

❀*Do It!* Click on **SEARCH**.

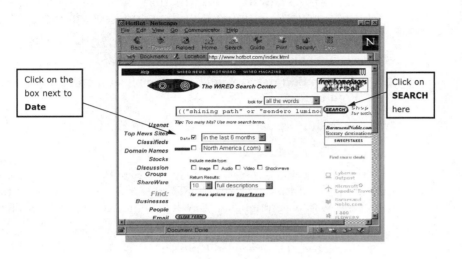

Click on the box next to **Date**

Click on **SEARCH** here

Figure 6.4—Search Request Entered

4   View the results.

The results of this search partially appear in Figure 6.5.

❋ *Do It!* Click on a Web page that looks interesting and that does not have the search expression's keywords in the title or annotation.

This site is ranked 99% relevant to the search query

The date listed is the date the Web page was added to the database

Figure 6.5—Partial List of Results in HotBot

To go directly to the portion of a page that mentions the keyword(s) you searched for, you can use the Find in Page function. To demonstrate how this works, you'll need to click on a Web page that doesn't have the search expression's keywords in the title or annotation. The reason for this is that you don't want to select a page that may have the keyword(s) only in the title or annotation.

5   Using the **Find in Page** function, search a Web page for the keywords *shining path* or *sendero luminoso*.

Once you are in a Web page that looks interesting, try to find the words *shining path* in the page, as shown in Figure 6.6.

Do It! Click on **Edit** in the menu bar at the top of the screen. Choose **Find in Page**.

Do It! Type **shining path** in the pane next to **Find what**.

Do It! Click on **Find Next**.

Did you find the phrase *shining path*? If not, try to find the phrase *sendero luminoso*. One of these phrases should appear in the Web page. If they don't, the Web page publisher may have entered one or both of the phrases as meta-tags.

Do It! To remove the embedded **Find** screen, click on **Cancel**.

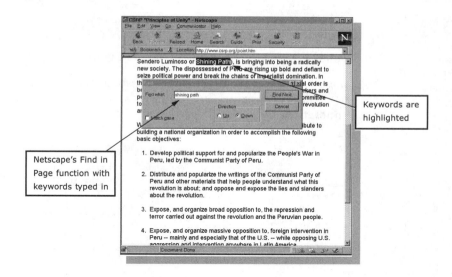

Netscape's Find in Page function with keywords typed in

Keywords are highlighted

Figure 6.6—Using the Find in Page Option to Locate Keywords in Web Pages

6   Modify the search by limiting it to educational sites only, and view the results.

Do It! Click on the **Back** button in the toolbar to return the results.

Do It! Scroll up to the top of the list.

Do It! Click on **REVISE SEARCH**.

You will return to the original search query screen.

Do It! Click on the box next to **Continent**.

❊*Do It!* Click on the pulldown menu and choose **North America (.edu)** from the list.

❊*Do It!* Click on **SEARCH**.

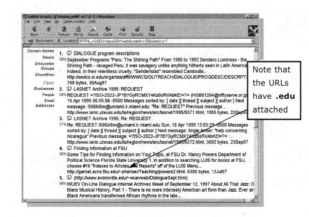

Figure 6.7—Limiting a Search to Educational Web Pages in HotBot

Modifying your search results by location in this way will return only those Web pages that have URLs ending in **.edu**, which means that they will come from North American educational sites, as shown in Figure 6.8. This doesn't mean that every Web page is going to be authored by a university or college department, however. Many of them will be home pages of students and other people associated with academic institutions. Using this limiting device is just one way to help you narrow results.

Figure 6.8—HotBot Results—Web Pages Originating from Educational Sites

7   End the session.

You can end the session now or stay online to do the next activity.

✳*Do It!* To end the session now, click on **File** on the menu bar and select **Exit** from the menu.

_____ End of Activity 6.1 _____

HotBot proved to be a good index to search for the topic we chose. It supports nested Boolean logic, phrase searching, and limiting by date. In the next activity, we'll use AltaVista to search for the same topic. AltaVista is one of the largest full-text databases, as is HotBot. It is also a good search engine to use when looking for specific information. We showcased AltaVista's advanced search mode in Activity 5.1. In this activity, we'll employ its simple search mode. This time, we won't focus on limiting by date as we did in HotBot. The simple search mode in AltaVista doesn't support date searching (although the advanced mode does). We'll demonstrate AltaVista's field-searching capability by limiting our results to those URLs that have a particular host name.

Activity 6.2   Search Strategies in AltaVista's Simple Search Mode

Overview

Since we already followed Steps 1 through 4 of the basic search strategy in Activity 6.1 by determining the keywords and search features (phrases, synonyms, Boolean logic, and so forth), and since we chose the search engine (Step 5), we can proceed to Steps 6 through 9. We will take the following steps in this activity:

1. Go to the home page for AltaVista.
2. Read the instructions for AltaVista's simple search mode (Step 6).
3. Create a search expression using syntax appropriate for AltaVista's simple search mode (Step 7).
4. View the results (Step 8).
5. Modify the search by limiting it to Web pages with csrp.org in the host name portion of the URLs, and then view the results (Step 9).
6. End the session.

Details

1   Go to the home page for AltaVista.

✳*Do It!* Click on the location field, type **http://www.altavista.digital .com**, and press Enter.

2   Read the instructions for AltaVista's simple search mode.

✳*Do It!* Click on **Help** on AltaVista's home page, as shown in Figure 6.9.

Click on
Help here

Figure 6.9—AltaVista Home Page

A partial list of the help topics available appears in Figure 6.10. AltaVista gives examples of the particular search features it supports.

Implied Boolean searching is supported

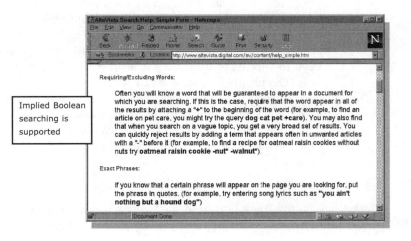

Figure 6.10—Help for Simple Searches in AltaVista

After reading the search help screens, we determine that AltaVista
✳   supports phrase searching by requiring the user to enclose the words in quotation marks.

❋ uses implied Boolean operators (+ and –), and not full Boolean logic (AND, OR, NOT).

❋ is case-sensitive, so it recognizes capitalization. (In other words, if you don't capitalize the first letters in proper nouns, it will find matches for the words in lowercase and uppercase. If you use capital letters, however, an exact match will occur.)

3 **Create a search expression, using syntax appropriate for AltaVista's simple search mode.**

You may want to review the section called "Search Features Common to Most Search Engines" in Chapter 5 before working on this step.

❋ We want *Shining Path, Sendero Luminoso, Tupac Amaru,* and *Peru* searched as proper nouns, so we'll capitalize the first letters of these words.

❋ Since we are searching with the phrases *Shining Path, Sendero Luminoso,* and *Tupac Amaru,* we need to put quotation marks around them.

❋ Full Boolean logic is not supported, so we'll need to use implied Boolean logic. The phrase **Shining Path** *must* appear in the Web pages, so we'll put a + in front of this phrase. We may want **Sendero Luminoso** to appear as well, but it's not absolutely necessary, so we'll enter this without a + in front of it. Since there is no way in the simple search mode to place an OR between keywords or phrases, this is the best we can do. We also want the word **Peru** to appear, so we'll place a + in front of this word, as well. The phrase **Tupac Amaru** *must not* appear, so we need to place a – in front of this phrase. In essence, we are telling the search engine to return to our screen those Web pages that must have *Shining Path,* may have *Sendero Luminoso,* must have *Peru,* and must not have *Tupac Amaru* in them.

Now we're ready to type in the search expression.

❋*Do It!* Click on the **Back** button in the toolbar, or click on the **AltaVista Search Network** icon at the top of the page.

❋*Do It!* Type the following in the search form provided:

+ **"Shining Path" "Sendero Luminoso"** + **Peru** – **"Tupac Amaru"**.

The search query is shown typed in Figure 6.11.

Figure 6.11—AltaVista Search Query Entered Using Implied Boolean Operators

❋Do It! Click on **search**, as shown in Figure 6.11.

4   View the results.

❋Do It! The results appear in Figure 6.12. Scroll down the list of results until you find a Web page entitled **CSRP: Mumia Abu-Jamal on the Revolution in Peru**. Click on this title.

This Web page is published by an organization called the Committee to Support the Revolution in Peru (CSRP). It is important to find out who publishes Web pages so you can determine how objective or subjective the information is.

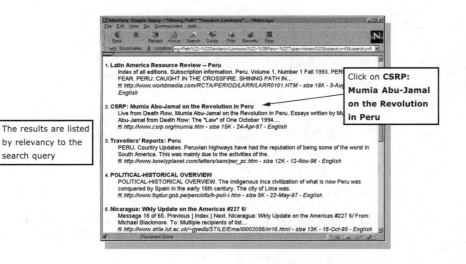

Figure 6.12—Results of AltaVista Search

179

5   Modify the search by limiting it to Web pages with **csrp.org** in the host name portion of the URLs, and then view the results.

AltaVista supports field searching. You'll need to refer back to the online help to find out how to do this.

✳*Do It!* Return to the search results page by clicking **Back**.

✳*Do It!* Click on **Help** at the top of the page.

✳*Do It!* Scroll down until you see a table entitled "Special Functions for Web Searches."

Figure 6.13 shows the portion of the help screen in AltaVista that describes how to constrain or limit searches by field. Note that you can search by host name. What this means is that you can search by the name of the organization, company, or educational facility by limiting your search to just those URLs with the name you are seeking. In our example, we want to examine the results for those Web pages that the CSRP has published. The CSRP is the host, and it is an organization. We know this by the **.org** in CSRP's URL.

Figure 6.13—Field Searching Explained in AltaVista

To limit the results to just those Web pages that have **csrp.org** in the host name portion of the URL, we will first need to return to our original search query.

✳*Do It!* Click on **Back** twice in the toolbar at the top of the screen.

✳*Do It!* Place your cursor at the end of the search expression (after "Tupac Amaru"), press the spacebar, and type **host:csrp.org**.

✳*Do It!* Click on **search**.

View the results that appear on your screen after this modification. All of the Web pages returned should have **csrp.org** in the host name portion of their URLs, as shown in Figure 6.14.

*Figure 6.14—Limiting Search to URLs with **csrp.org***

6   End the session.

You can end the session now or stay online to do the next activity.

✳*Do It!* To end the session now, click on **File** on the menu bar and select **Exit** from the menu.

End of Activity 6.2

In Activities 6.1 and 6.2, we focused on finding general information on a fairly obscure topic, the Shining Path. We discussed how to narrow results by excluding words that we didn't want in the search results, by limiting results by date, and by limiting the results to certain URLs. In the next section, we'll concentrate on searching for specific items, such as information about writers and their works, quotations, or specific lines of poetry.

Using Search Engines for Specific Information

When looking for specific information, you can use the basic search strategy, but you can employ it a bit more loosely than when you develop multifaceted searches. You'll need to prepare your search strategy before you get online by deciding whether there are name variations to include and determining what search features to employ, such as phrase searching, Boolean operators, and so forth. Choosing a database will be as important as it ever was; you'll want a database that supports features that will help you find the most precise results.

Full-text search engine databases (AltaVista, HotBot, Excite, Infoseek, and so forth) are the best places to go for specific information because most every word in every page is indexed. In the following activity, we'll show you how to use search engines to find very specific information, such as proper names and quotations. When looking for information about a person, a quotation, or a line of poetry, it is essential to be exact when you type in the search request. If you are looking for a name, you also must include the different ways it might appear in the index you're searching. When you look for a quotation or line of text, it is again very important to know most of the major words in the phrase and to spell them correctly. The following activity is an excellent example of both of these types of searches.

Activity 6.3 Finding Specific Information in Excite

Overview

We're going to search Excite, **http://www.excite.com**. In Chapter 3, we discussed a directory called Excite Channels Web Sites. Excite's search engine covers the entire Web. Excite is large and powerful and is mostly full-text, in that it ignores certain words, such as articles and prepositions. Excite supports concept searching; that is, the search engine automatically searches for synonyms of the words you enter. For example, if you asked for *teenager,* it might return results with the word *adolescent* as well.

In this activity, we are going to do a couple of different searches, one on a person's name and the other on a line of poetry. First, we'll search Excite's database for information, and hopefully for a bibliography, of the works of the writer Saki. Before going online, we have done our homework and have learned that Saki is also known as H.H. Munro, Hector Munro, or Hector H. Munro. After we do that search, we'll look for the poem with the line "Till human voices wake us, and we drown."

We'll follow these steps:

1. Go to the home page for Excite.
2. Read the search tips.
3. Formulate and enter the search expression.
4. View the results and access a Web page.
5. Search for the line of poetry "Till human voices wake us, and we drown."
6. View the results and access *The Love Song of J. Alfred Prufrock.*
7. End the session.

Details

1 Go to the home page for Excite.

✳*Do It!* Click on the location field, type **http://www.excite.com**, and press Enter.

2   Read the search tips.

Do It! On Excite's home page, click **Search Tips**, as shown in Figure 6.15.

Figure 6.15—Excite's Home Page

The list of help topics in Excite appears in Figure 6.16. It's a good idea to read the help information thoroughly.

Figure 6.16—Help Screen in Excite

Do It! Click on the first help topic, **What is Excite Search?** Read through all of the help topics.

After reading the help topics, we determine that Excite

- ✳ uses a program that performs searches by concept. This means that synonyms of the keywords you type in are automatically searched and retrieved.
- ✳ supports concept searching only when you use implied Boolean operators.
- ✳ supports full Boolean searching. AND, OR, and NOT must be in all capital letters.
- ✳ does not support concept searching when full Boolean searching is used.
- ✳ supports phrase searching by requiring that the phrase be enclosed in quotation marks.
- ✳ is case-insensitive, so there is no need to capitalize.
- ✳ supports nested Boolean searching if you place parentheses around the words that are connected by AND or OR.

3   Formulate and enter the search expression.

Now we're ready to formulate the search expression by applying Excite's search features to our search question. We'll consider the following parameters:

- ✳ To retrieve all of Saki's names, we'll enter the different names connected by OR. This means that *any* of Saki's names may be retrieved.
- ✳ The name Saki and the variant names can all start with lowercase letters.
- ✳ The names with more than one word must be placed in parentheses, because the words must appear next to each other as phrases.
- ✳ There are two facets to our search—the writer's name and his works. Because both of these facets will be connected by an AND, and because both have synonyms that will be OR'd together, we need parentheses around each facet.

✳*Do It!* Click on the Excite logo in the upper-left corner to return to Excite's home page.

✳*Do It!* In the search form provided, type the following search expression:

(saki OR "hector munro" OR "h.h. munro" OR "hector h. munro") AND (writings OR bibliography).

✳*Do It!* Click on **Search**.

4   View the results and access a Web page.

A partial listing of the search results appears in Figure 6.17.

✻*Do It!* Click on the first Web page to appear on the list, **H. H. Munro, Saki**. If this title is not in your list of results, choose a similar title.

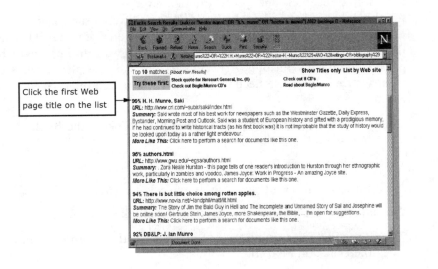

Click the first Web page title on the list

Figure 6.17—Results of Search for Saki's Writings or Bibliography

After your screen fills, scroll down the page until you see the hyperlink **A bibliography of Saki's works.**

✻*Do It!* Click on **A bibliography of Saki's works.**

The beginning of the bibliography appears in Figure 6.18.

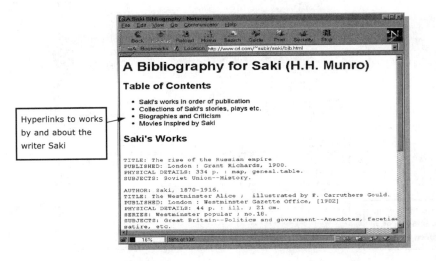

Hyperlinks to works by and about the writer Saki

Figure 6.18—First Page of "A Bibliography for Saki (H.H. Munro)"

5 Search for the line of poetry "Till human voices wake us, and we drown."

In looking for a line of poetry or a quotation, we want all of the words to be found together, not spread throughout a document, so the rules for phrase searching will apply. In Excite, small words such as prepositions and articles are not indexed, but the search engine will still locate the major words in a string. In this activity, we want to know which poem contains this line of poetry. Let's try typing in the phrase and see what we find. First, we need to return to the search query screen in Excite.

Do It! From the "Saki Bibliography" Web page, click on the **Back** button on the toolbar.

You should now be in Excite.

Do It! Click on the Excite icon in the upper-left corner.

You should be at Excite's home page with a blank search form.

Do It! Type in **"Till human voices wake us and we drown"**, and then click on **Search**.

6 View the results and access "The Love Song of J. Alfred Prufrock."

A partial list of the results of this search appears in Figure 6.19. Several sites are listed. Scroll down until you find **The Love Song of J. Alfred Prufrock**.

Do It! Click on the title **The Love Song of J. Alfred Prufrock**, as shown in Figure 6.19.

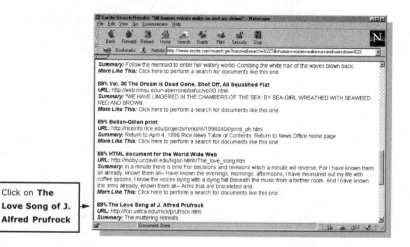

Click on **The Love Song of J. Alfred Prufrock**

Figure 6.19—Results of Search for Line of Poetry

Figure 6.20 shows the beginning of the poem that should include the line of poetry you're seeking.

Figure 6.20—The Love Song of J. Alfred Prufrock

To find the line, "Till human voices wake us, and we drown," we can use the Find in Page function.

✳*Do It!* Click on **Edit** in the menu bar. Choose **Find in Page**.

✳*Do It!* Type the words **human voices** in the search form next to **Find what**, as shown n Figure 6.21.

Figure 6.21—"What the Thunder Said" Web Site

7   End the session.

✳*Do It!* To end the session, click on **File** on the menu bar and select **Exit** from the menu.

End of Activity 6.3

Activity 6.3 focused on finding specific information in search engines. Note that even though the topics were not multifaceted, you still benefited from using the search strategy discussed earlier in the chapter. Before you type a search expression, if you think of possible synonyms and phrases for even the simplest search topics, it can save you time and produce relevant results quickly.

Summary

This chapter continued Chapter 5's discussion of ways to use search engines' power to their fullest. Formulating search expressions before you get online and keeping in mind the possible search features available to you are both of utmost importance. After you choose a search engine, you need to translate your search expression into the appropriate syntax for that search engine.

This chapter introduced several ways to search, including using implied Boolean operators and full Boolean capabilities, and limiting results by date and by certain parts of the URL. The examples showed how to search for specific information, including lines of poetry and titles of works. We also reviewed the Find in Page feature, which helps you locate search terms in the documents your search query returns.

Exercises and Projects

1. Find Web pages using AltaVista, **http://www.altavista.digital .com** (simple search mode), on total quality management. Modify your search to include only those pages published by the IBM Corporation. How many Web pages on total quality management did you find? How many were published by the IBM Corporation? Write down the search expressions you used.

2. Using Excite, **http://www.excite.com**, HotBot, **http://www .hotbot.com**, and AltaVista, **http://www.altavista .digital.com**, find the following two quotations: "Time flies like an arrow," and "Fruit flies like a banana." These quotes are usually found next to each other. Write out the search expressions used. Can you find the person to whom these quotes have been attributed?

3. Find Web pages on the effects of chlorofluorocarbons, or CFCs, on the ozone layer and on global warming. Use Excite, **http:// www.excite.com**, and HotBot, **http://www.hotbot.com**, formulating the search expression so that you are using the nested Boolean search feature, not implied Boolean operators.

4. Using HotBot, **http://www.hotbot.com**, try to find lists of job openings for college or university teaching positions in foreign countries, limiting your results to the past year. Write out the search expression you used.

5. Find some information on air bag safety and children. Go to Infoseek, **http://www.infoseek.com**. Type in **air bags** as a phrase and click **seek**. How many results did you get? Now go

to the bottom of the screen. Making sure that the **Search these results** option is selected, narrow your search results by using another keyword. How many results do you have now? Modify your search again by adding another keyword, and write down the number of results you retrieved from this final modification.

6. Use AltaVista's simple search mode, **http://www.altavista .digital.com**, to find information on heart disease. Type in **+ "heart disease"** and begin the search. After the results appear, click on **refine**. Choose at least two keywords from the list of words that appear by selecting **require** from the pulldown menu alongside each term. Resubmit your search and compare these results to the results from the first search. Which search features does the **refine** feature emulate? Why would you need to be careful about not choosing too many words, especially synonyms, to include in the search expression?

7. Using Excite, **http://www.excite.com**, look for information on Edgar Rice Burroughs and Tarzan. Formulate two search expressions, one with implied Boolean operators and the other with full Boolean operators. Compare the number of results found with both expressions. Why is there a discrepancy between the results? You may need to read the search tips in order to answer this question.

8. Go to HotBot, **http://www.hotbot.com**, and search for Web pages on the presence of Pepsi or Coca-Cola in foreign countries. Read the help information provided by HotBot. Do you need to use Boolean operators? Phrase searching? Write the search expression you used.

9. You want to find out what cities have bid to be the host of the 2004 Olympics. Try searching for this answer using Infoseek, **http://www.infoseek.com**, and Lycos, **http://www.lycos .com**. What search expression did you use? Which search engine returned the most relevant results on the first try? Why do you think the most relevant results were in this search engine and not the other one?

10. You are looking for a picture of St. Catherine's Monastery, located in the Sinai Peninsula of Egypt. Try to find it in any of the major search engines. In which search engine(s) did you find it? Write down the name of the search engine in which you found it and the search expression you used. Try to find some information about the monastery. What famous mountain is located there?

7
Chapter

Specialized Databases

New databases containing public information or material not proprietary in nature frequently appear on the World Wide Web. These databases, many of which are maintained by government agencies and nonprofit organizations, can quickly provide you with a wealth of information that formerly was difficult or time-consuming to obtain.

Specialized databases are indexes that can be searched, much like the search engines explored in Chapters 5 and 6. The main difference is that specialized databases are collections on particular subjects, such as medical journal article abstracts and citations, company financial data, United States Supreme Court decisions, census data, patents, and so forth. You can find information in specialized databases that you often would not locate by using a global WWW search engine. If you know there is a specialized database on the subject you are researching, using that database can save you time and give you reliable, up-to-date information.

We covered subject guides in Chapters 3 and 4. The difference between a subject guide and a specialized database is that subject guides are collections of URLs in a particular area (many times these URLs are hyperlinks to specialized databases), whereas a specialized database contains the actual data or information you are seeking. Some specialized databases do contain hyperlinks to other specialized databases, however, if the two databases have related topics. One of the databases covered in this chapter has this feature.

This chapter will discuss such databases and will include the following sections:
* Overview of Specialized Databases
* How to Find Free Specialized Databases
* Using Specialized Databases

Overview of Specialized Databases

Bibliographic and Full-text Databases

In this chapter, we'll show you two major types of databases: bibliographic and full-text. A ***bibliographic database*** is a list of citations that describes and identifies titles, dates, authors, and other parts of written works. It doesn't contain the full text of the articles themselves. A ***full-text database***, on the other hand, includes the entire text of the indexed work. A full-text database can contain financial, scientific, or other types of data. The major difference between a bibliographic and full-text database is that the bibliographic database describes the entity, whether it be an article, a book, a work of art, or any other product, whereas the full-text database includes a description and the work itself.

Proprietary and Free Databases

There are hundreds of ***proprietary*** or ***commercial databases*** on the World Wide Web, but these are available only if you or your organization has purchased access to them. For example, FirstSearch, DIALOG, STN, and Lexis-Nexis all provide proprietary databases.

Proprietary databases have certain value-added features that databases in the public domain do not have. Here are some examples of that enhanced content:

- ❋ Proprietary databases are likely to include extra information that helps the researcher. For example, most of the databases in FirstSearch (the Online Computer Library Center's (OCLC) proprietary database system) have links to library holdings. This means that if you find an article or book in a database provided by FirstSearch, such as Medline, you can immediately find out which libraries own the material. Even though Medline is available free to the public from the National Library of Medicine, you might prefer to use the FirstSearch version if you want to know who has the listed journal articles.

- ❋ Proprietary databases also allow you to download information easily. For instance, some of these databases include financial information that is commonly free to the public, but they charge for the use of their databases because they have made it much easier for the user to download the information to a spreadsheet program.

- ❋ Proprietary databases often index material that others do not. The information is distinguished by its uniqueness, its historical value, or its competitive value (for example, private company financial information).

    ❋   Proprietary database systems are more responsible to their users. Because they charge money, they are more apt to provide training and other user support, such as distributing newsletters that update their services.

Accessing Fee-based Databases

If you would like to have a list of the proprietary databases on the market, you might access "FACSNET: Directory of Databases," **http://www .facsnet.org/report_tools/CAR/cardirec.htm**, a Web page published by the Poynter Institute for Media Studies. The people there have compiled a list of online databases that charge fees.

    Remember, you can always ask a reference librarian at your local library about accessing proprietary databases. The library may have several databases on CD-ROM, or may have purchased access to databases via the Internet.

    The specialized databases covered in this chapter are all free and open to anyone.

How to Find Free Specialized Databases

Sometimes you'll stumble across specialized databases while doing a keyword search in a search engine. A database might pop up in the search results without your actually looking for it. Occasionally, a Web page will have a hyperlink to a database, or a friend or colleague will tell you about a particular site.

    There is a more precise way to find them, but even this is not always foolproof. Virtual libraries, meta-search tools that include lists of databases, and directories are often the best sources to use when looking for specialized databases. If a specialized database isn't listed in one of these types of resources, you may find a database listed in a subject guide. It's important to keep in mind that if you don't find what you're looking for in one resource, that doesn't mean it doesn't exist. You may find it in another resource. The following tools are the most helpful in listing specialized databases and subject guides:

    ❋   Internet Public Library (IPL) Reference Center, **http:// www.ipl.org/ref**, is a virtual library that provides a good starting point for finding reference works, subject guides, and specialized databases.

    ❋   Internet Sleuth, **http://www.isleuth.com**, is a meta-search tool. In other words, it is a collection of databases, with each database having a hyperlink and a search form attached. You can also search up to six databases simultaneously in the Sleuth.

- ❋ Librarians' Index to the Internet, **http:// sunsite.berkeley.edu/internetindex**, is another virtual library. It is a searchable and browsable collection of Web resources, including subject guides and specialized databases, which librarians select and annotate.

- ❋ Yahoo!, **http://www.yahoo.com**, is one of the most popular and comprehensive directories on the World Wide Web. It is a good place to find subject guides (Yahoo! calls them *indices*) and specialized databases.

❋ Tip

A good way to keep up with new search tools, especially specialized databases, is to subscribe to the Scout Report. For information on how to subscribe to this valuable weekly publication, send email to **listserv@cs.wisc .edu** Type **info scout-report** in the body of the message. You can also visit the Web page, **http://www.scout.cs.wisc.edu/scout/report**, which provides the same list of new resources on the Web and includes hyperlinks to the reviewed titles. It also includes all of the previous Scout Reports.

Using Specialized Databases

Just as search engines do, specialized databases support different search features. Most of these databases support many of the same search features covered in Chapters 5 and 6, such as Boolean searching, truncation, and phrase searching. Many databases have search instruction pages, just as the major search engines do.

In this chapter, we'll be doing three activities that will familiarize you with some of the most useful types of databases on the World Wide Web. We've chosen databases from three subject areas: medicine, business, and law. We selected these three areas because the Web has become an excellent medium for research in these three fields. Much of the useful information needed for research in these fields is in the public domain. We'll search first for medical information. While you move through the activities, you may want to review the search features and the 10-step basic search strategy introduced in Chapter 5.

❋ Tip

Remember that the Web is always changing and that your results may differ from those shown here. Don't let this confuse you. The activities are meant to teach you fundamental skills. These skills don't change, even though the number of results obtained or the actual screens may look very different.

Searching for Medical Information

The World Wide Web is becoming an excellent source for health and medical information. Medical centers and physicians create home pages that discuss specific aspects of health care, and you can find these pages by doing searches in the major search engines. Medical reference books are also appearing on the Web. For example, the entire *Merck Manual of Diagnosis and Therapy*, **http://www.merck.com**, a well-known medical diagnostic handbook, is now online. You can also find citations to medical journal articles on the Web.

In the first activity, we'll look for a specialized database to help us find journal articles on a medical topic. In the example, we'll use the Librarians' Index to the Internet to help us find a hyperlink to Medline, which is a bibliographic database devoted to medical journal literature. There are several ways to find hyperlinks to Medline providers on the Web. Keep in mind that we are showing you only *one* way to do it.

Activity 7.1   Searching Medline

Overview

We are doing research on Creutzfeldt-Jakob disease. This is the human disease that has been linked to eating beef from cows with bovine spongiform encephalopathy (BSE), commonly referred to as *mad cow disease*. We need to find recent articles from medical journals that would update our general knowledge of Creutzfeldt-Jakob disease, focusing on the connections between it and BSE.

We know that the National Library of Medicine publishes a database called *Medline*, and we've heard that it may be available on the Web for free. How can we find it? Let's try the Librarians' Index to the Internet. After we find it, we'll access Medline, search it, and view the results. We will take the following steps:

1. Go to the home page for the Librarians' Index to the Internet.
2. From the list of health and medicine resources, find and open **HealthGate Medline Search**.
3. Look at basic search help.
4. Type in search terms and retrieve results.
5. Choose citations from the list of results.
6. Display full records of selected citations.
7. End the session.

Details

1   **Go to the home page for the "Librarians' Index to the Internet."**

⊛*Do It!* Click on the location field, type **http://sunsite.berkeley.edu/ internetindex**, and then press **Enter**.

Click on **Health, Medicine** from the Librarians' Index to the Internet home page, as shown in Figure 7.1.

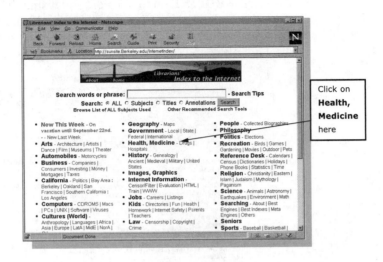

Figure 7.1—Home Page for Librarians' Index to the Internet

2   From the list of health and medicine resources, find and open **HealthGate Medline Search**.

❋*Do It!* Click on **HealthGate Medline Search**, as shown in Figure 7.2.

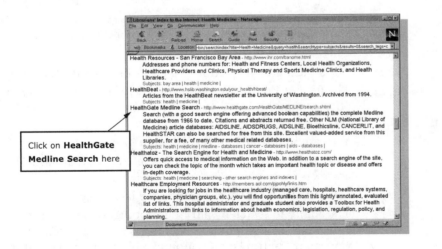

Figure 7.2—Health and Medicine Resources—Librarians' Index to the Internet

3   Look at basic search help.

HealthGate's searchable databases are listed as shown in Figure 7.3. If you selected **MEDLINE** on this screen, you would find out that *Medline* contains journal article references dating back to 1966. Produced by the National Library of Medicine, *Medline* is the premier database for medical literature and can provide answers to many research questions.

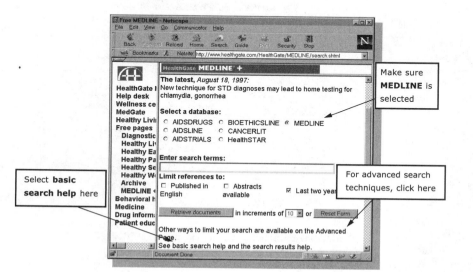

Make sure **MEDLINE** is selected

Select **basic search help** here

For advanced search techniques, click here

Figure 7.3—HealthGate Medline

✻*Do It!* Click on **basic search help** at the bottom of the HealthGate search query page, as shown in Figure 7.3.

By reading the basic search help information, we discover the following:

❋   The default Boolean operator used between terms is *and*. If other operators are necessary, you must use the advanced search page.

❋   You can limit results to English only.

❋   You can limit your search to those references that have abstracts only.

❋   You can also limit your search to the last two years only.

❋   The ability to search by phrase is not mentioned. You can either assume that phrase searching is not supported, or you can try putting quotes around a phrase to find out if it is a feature.

❋ The advanced search mode allows you to limit your search to particular fields, such as individual journal titles, article types (for example, review articles and clinical trials), certain years, and many other specifications. For this activity, we'll confine our search to the basic search mode.

4 Type in search terms and retrieve results.

Now we're ready to do our search.

❋Do It From the basic search help screen, click the **HealthGate Medline** icon at the top of the page.

You should return to the basic search screen.

❋Do It Type **Creutzfeldt-Jakob disease and bovine spongiform encephalopathy** in the search form.

❋Do It Select **Published in English** under **Limit references to**.

Your screen should look like the one in Figure 7.4. The default date limit is the last two years. If you want to search farther back than that, simply click on the box to remove the check. In this activity, we'll leave the date at the default. We're ready to submit the search request.

❋Do It Click on **Retrieve documents**.

❋ Tip

When you select **Retrieve Documents**, a dialog box titled **Security Information** may pop up. It serves as a warning to let you know that, when you're working with the type of form used by Medline, the information you're submitting is being transferred through the Internet in an insecure manner. You can click on the **Continue** button to transmit the information or you can click on the **Cancel** button to stop the transaction. To go through the rest of the activity click on **Continue**. If you don't want a dialog box like this to come up in the future, click on the check box **Show This Alert Next Time**; that will turn off this type of warning. Netscape's security features are discussed in Chapter 2. To learn more about them, review that chapter or click on **Security** in the toolbar.

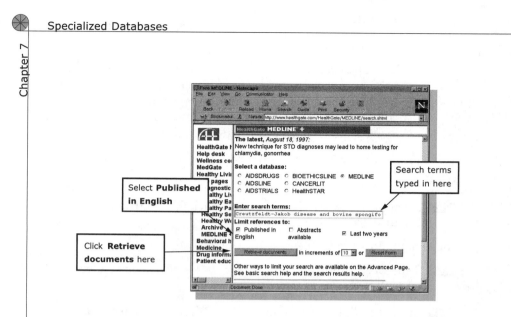

Select **Published in English**

Search terms typed in here

Click **Retrieve documents** here

Figure 7.4—Medline Search Query Entered

A partial list of the results appears in Figure 7.5. The results list brief citations that include the author, article title, abbreviated journal title, date, and an indication of whether an abstract is available.

5   Choose citations from the list of results.

If you want to see the full record, you can click on the hyperlink. If you'd like to see more than one record at a time, click on the boxes next to the citations you wish to see.

✱*Do It!* Click the box next to the article **Ironside, JW: Review: Creutzfeldt-Jakob disease**, as shown in Figure 7.5.

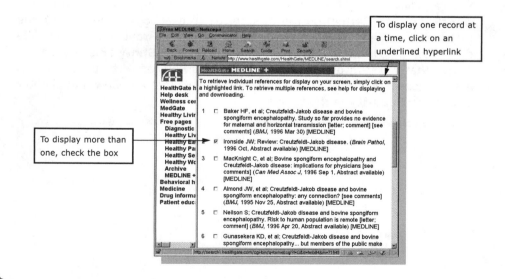

To display one record at a time, click on an underlined hyperlink

To display more than one, check the box

Figure 7.5—Partial List of Search Results in Medline

✽*Do It!* Select two other citations that appear to be relevant.

6 Display full records of selected citations.

✽*Do It!* Scroll down to the end of the page and click on **Retrieve Selected References**, as pictured in Figure 7.6.

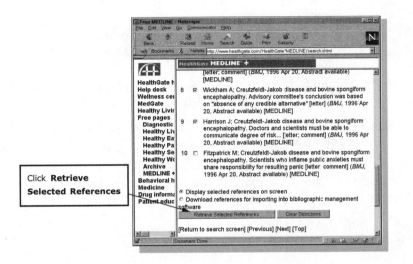

Figure 7.6—Selecting Multiple Records at Once in Medline

Look at the portion of the first record that appears in Figure 7.7.

✽*Do It!* Scroll through the complete record.

Note the detailed information that the abstract provides.

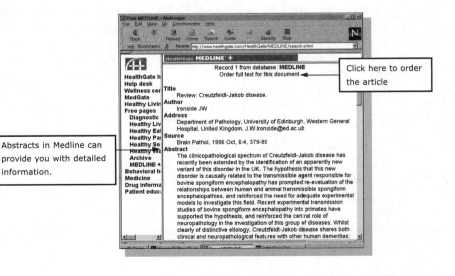

Figure 7.7—Medline Record with Abstract

Let's say you wanted a copy of this article, which appears in the journal *Brain Pathology*. You could go about this in several ways:

- ✳ Find out if your local public or academic library carries this journal. If so, copy the article there.

- ✳ Call your local hospital and find out if it owns the journal and if the public is allowed to photocopy articles from its library.

- ✳ Initiate an interlibrary loan request from your library if the journal is not available from the previously mentioned sources.

- ✳ If all these measures fail, you can request a copy of this article from HealthGate *Medline*.

✳◁Do It▷ To order a copy of the article, click on **Order full text for this document**, as shown in Figure 7.7.

HealthGate Medline allows you to have the article sent by regular mail, fax, rush fax, courier, or rush delivery. You can use a major credit card to pay for it.

7 End the session.

You can end the session now or stay online for the next activity.

✳◁Do It▷ To end the session now, click on **File** on the menu bar and select **Exit** from the menu.

_____ End of Activity 7.1 _____

Medline is available on the World Wide Web through several providers. In our example, we chose HealthGate as the interface because it is user-friendly and doesn't require registration. Some database providers require you to register with them by filling out a form, usually including your email address and job title. In addition to requiring registration, some Medline providers charge a fee to use the database.

Medline can provide you with the most up-to-date medical research information available anywhere. This example barely touches the surface of the searching possibilities in this database. Whether you're researching an illness or gathering information for a biology paper, Medline is an invaluable resource.

Searching for Business Information

The World Wide Web has become a useful place to conduct business research. Most companies use their home pages as marketing or communication tools. These home pages may include annual reports, press releases, and biographies of the people in top-level management. The home pages may also include information about the company products and services, including catalogs.

If you want to find a company's home page but don't know the URL, you can often guess it by typing the company's name with **http://www.** at the beginning and **.com** at the end. For example, if you were looking for the home page for Sears, Roebuck, and Company, you could try typing **http://www.sears.com**. This is the correct URL for Sears, Roebuck, and Company. You could also use a search engine to look for the company's name, limiting the results to URLs (see Chapter 6) that include **sears.com**.

If you want to do industry research, you can use business-related subject guides. These contain hyperlinks to businesses within the particular industry that interests you. You can easily find subject guides in virtual libraries and major directories.

You can also find business directories on the Web by using one of the virtual libraries or meta-search tools listed at the beginning of the chapter. Keep in mind that companies that provide the most financial information on the Web are usually publicly traded. Public companies are required to provide very detailed financial information to the U.S. government, whereas privately held companies are not. If a private company is listed in a nonproprietary (open-to-the-public) database, some financial information will be available, but not nearly as much as if it were a public company.

Activity 7.2   Searching Hoover's Online

Overview

In this activity, we'll show you how to locate and use a business database. The database, Hoover's Online, is a full-text service that has financial and industry information, plus links to United States Securities and Exchange Commission (SEC) filings and other databases. Parts of Hoover's Online are available to subscribers only. We'll focus on the parts that are open to the general user. You can find the largest public and private U.S. companies in Hoover's, but the financial information given for the privately held companies is much less extensive. We'll show you how to use the Internet Sleuth, a meta-search tool, to locate Hoover's. We'll follow these steps:

1. Go to the home page for the Internet Sleuth.
2. Find the list of business databases.
3. Open Hoover's Online.
4. Perform a search on a company name.
5. Go into the EDGAR Online database
6. Search for companies by location and industry.
7. End the session.

Details

1 Go to the home page for the Internet Sleuth.

Do It! Click on the location field, type **http://www.isleuth.com**, and press **Enter**.

Your screen should look like the one in Figure 7.8.

Figure 7.8—The Internet Sleuth Home Page

2 Find the list of business databases.

Do It! Click on **Business**, as shown in Figure 7.8.

Do It! Click on **Market Research**, as shown in Figure 7.9.

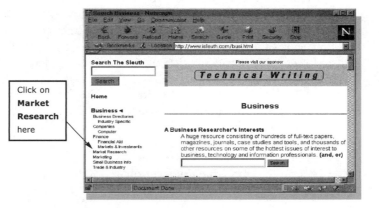

Figure 7.9—Business Resources in the Internet Sleuth

3   Open Hoover's Online.

Do It! Scroll down the list of business directories until you come to **Hoover's Online** and click on it, as shown in Figure 7.10.

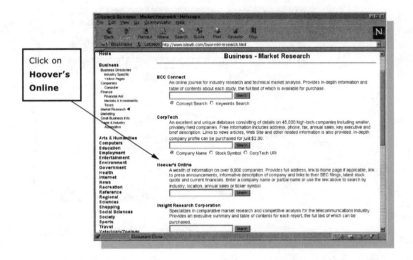

Click on **Hoover's Online**

Figure 7.10—Link to Hoover's Online in the Internet Sleuth

Note that the Internet Sleuth allows you to search Hoover's from its directory. In order to take full advantage of a database's capabilities, it's sometimes a good idea to go directly to the database and search it from there.

Hoover's Online home page is shown in Figure 7.11.

4   Perform a search on a company name.

Let's try to find information about Netscape Communications Corporation.

Do It! Type **netscape** in the search form under "Company Name," as shown in Figure 7.11.

Do It! Click on **Find.**

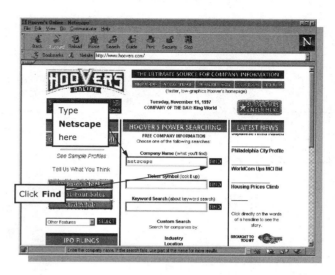

Figure 7.11—Hoover's Online Home Page

Figure 7.12 shows part of the company information that is provided by Hoover's. It is called a company capsule. The company profiles and financials sections have information that's available to subscribers only. The capsule provides a brief descriptive paragraph about the company and includes the address, names of directors, links to quarterly financial information, and more.

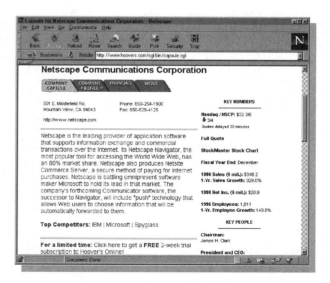

Figure 7.12—Company Capsule for Netscape Communications Corporation

If you scroll down this page, you'll find hyperlinks to full-text articles about Netscape Communications Corporation, as shown in Figure 7.13.

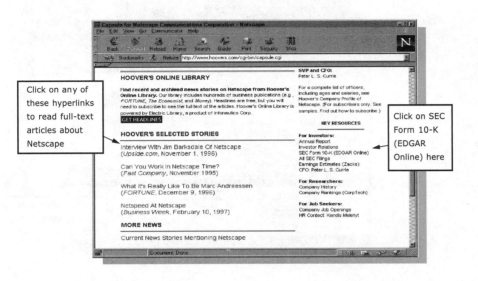

Figure 7.13—More Information About Netscape Communications Corporation

5   Go into the EDGAR Online database.

The SEC requires public companies to make an annual financial disclosure, called a *10–K report*. To obtain Netscape's 10–K, look for **SEC Form 10-K (EDGAR Online)**, as shown in Figure 7.13. You may need to scroll through the page. If Netscape were a privately held company, there would be no link to EDGAR, because private companies aren't required to report their financial information to the government.

Do It! Click on **SEC Form 10-K (EDGAR Online)**.

You are now in the EDGAR Online database, which is in partnership with Hoover's Online. You'll see a list of filing dates, a list of form types, and the name of the company—in this case, Netscape Communications Corporation. We're looking for the 10-K or 10-Q form.

This page contains a link for a 10-K report. Let's open it.

Do It! Click on the **NETSCAPE COMMUNICATIONS CORP**. hyperlink next to the 10-K filed on March 28, 1997, as shown in Figure 7.14.

Figure 7.14—EDGAR Online Database

A portion of this report appears in Figure 7.15.

Netscape's Annual Report for 1996

Figure 7.15—Form 10-K for Netscape Communications Corporation

✱Do It! Click on the **Back** button on the Netscape toolbar to return to EDGAR.

✱Do It! Scroll down to the bottom of the page and click on **Return to Hoovers**.

You should now be back at the *Hoover's Online* home page.

6   Search for companies by location and industry.

Hoover's Online offers a unique service that allows you to search for companies in a certain industry or in a particular state or metropolitan area. Once you locate the names of the companies, you can follow Hoover's links to the companies' home pages and other information about them. We'll do a brief exercise using this service.

Scroll down on the *Hoover's Online* home page until you see "Custom Search – Search for companies by: Industry, Location, Annual sales, Company type." The full service is for subscribers only but non-subscribers can try part of it for free.

🟊*Do It!* Click on **free**, as shown in Figure 7.16.

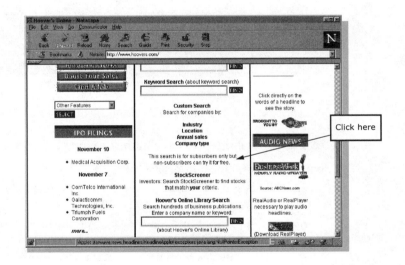

Figure 7.16—Accessing Industry Information from Hoover's Online Home Page

Your screen should look like the one in Figure 7.17.

Figure 7.17—Information on Searching by Industry in Hoover's Online

Do It! Click on **guidelines** to obtain searching information.

Some of the guidelines inform us of the following:

❋ This service allows you to select multiple values from the pulldown menus.

❋ If you search by annual sales, you must not use any nonnumerical characters or you won't receive any results.

❋ The capsules have links to other Web sources that provide you with further information about the company.

❋ Hoover's company profiles are not available to non-subscribers.

In our example, we'll look for automobile manufacturers in Michigan.

Do It! Click **Back** to return to the previous page.

Do It! Scroll down until you find the section called "SEARCH BY LOCATION."

Do It! Choose **Michigan** from the **OR State/Province** scrolling list, as shown in Figure 7.18.

Do It! Scroll down the page until you come to **SEARCH BY INDUS-TRY**. Choose **Automotive manufacturing** from the scrolling list, as shown in Figure 7.18.

Choose **Michigan** from the pulldown menu

Automotive **manufacturing** selected

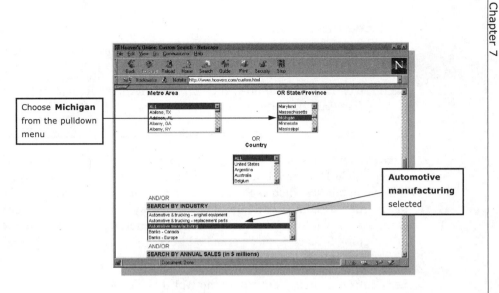

Figure 7.18—Searching For Companies by Industry in Hoover's Online

✴️*Do It!* Scroll down and click on **Find**.

The results appear in Figure 7.19. Note that in the **Links** column you can click on **WebSite** to go to that company's home page or click on **Capsule** to obtain other company information. You cannot use the **Profile** hyperlink unless you have a subscription to Hoover's.

You can click on these hyperlinks for more information

Company Name	State	Industry Description	Links				
Chrysler Corporation	MI	Automotive manufacturing	Capsule	Profile	Financials	WebSite	JobSite
Ford Motor Company	MI	Automotive manufacturing	Capsule	Profile	Financials	WebSite	JobSite
General Automotive Corporation	MI	Automotive manufacturing	Capsule				
General Motors Corporation	MI	Automotive manufacturing	Capsule	Profile	Financials	WebSite	JobSite
Volkswagen of America, Inc.	MI	Automotive manufacturing	Capsule			WebSite	

Figure 7.19—Search Results—Michigan Automotive Manufacturing Companies

7   End the session.

You can end the session now or stay online and proceed to the next activity.

✳*Do It!* To end the session now, click on **File** on the menu bar and select **Exit** from the menu.

───────────────── End of Activity 7.2 ─────────────────

Hoover's Online is an example of a combination full-text database and subject guide. Hoover's provides financial information and links to other full-text databases, such as EDGAR, and it has hyperlinks to other Web pages, such as company home pages. You may want to use Hoover's Online when you're job hunting, doing a research report on industries, or searching for a company's email address.

Searching for Legal Information

Legal information is plentiful on the World Wide Web. The U.S. federal government has put much of its legal documentation up on the Web. For example, the *United States Code* (the text of current public laws enacted by Congress), the *Federal Register* (the daily report of new laws passed by government agencies) and the *United States Code of Federal Regulations* (the *Federal Register* codified by subject) are all on the Web in searchable form. A growing number of states publish their statutes or laws in collections similar to the *United States Code;* these are also available.

In addition to statutes or laws, court opinions from all jurisdictions are appearing on the World Wide Web. In this activity, we'll show how easy it is to get a full-text copy of a United States Supreme Court opinion.

Activity 7.3   Searching for United States Supreme Court Opinions

Overview

In this activity, we'll show how to obtain a copy of the Supreme Court opinion from the famous 1954 case Brown v. Board of Education. To find the database that indexes United States Supreme Court opinions, we'll use Yahoo! We could probably find this database by using the other resources listed at the beginning of the chapter as well. This activity will follow these steps:

1. Go to the home page for Yahoo!
2. Browse Yahoo!'s directory for databases on United States Supreme Court decisions.
3. Select **FindLaw: Supreme Court Opinions**.
4. Search **FindLaw** for **Brown v. Board of Education**.
5. Display the full text of the court opinion.
6. End the session.

Details

1   Go to the home page for Yahoo!

(Do It!) Click on the location field, type **http://www.yahoo.com**, and press **Enter**.

2   Browse Yahoo!'s directory for databases on United States Supreme Court decisions.

(Do It!) From Yahoo!'s top-level subject categories or headings, click on **Law**, a subheading of **Government**.

(Do It!) From the list of subject categories that appear, click on **Judiciary and Supreme Court@**.

(Do It!) From this list of subject headings, click on **Supreme Court**.

(Do It!) Click on **Court Decisions**.

Your screen should look like the one in Figure 7.20.

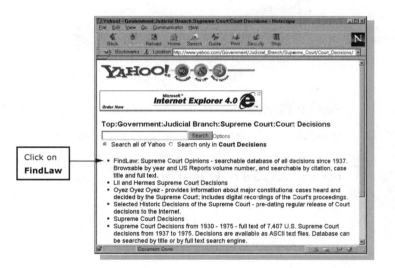

Click on
FindLaw

Figure 7.20—Results—Browsing Yahoo! for a Supreme Court Decisions Database

3   Select FindLaw: Supreme Court Opinions.

(Do It!) Click on **FindLaw: Supreme Court Opinions**, as shown in Figure 7.20.

Note that there are a few other databases that index full-text versions of United States Supreme Court decisions, but at the time of this writing, FindLaw appears to be the only one that indexes recent opinions.

Your screen should look like the one pictured in Figure 7.21. Note that FindLaw has a search help link (**options** next to the **Search FindLaw** button). If you wanted to search FindLaw by keyword, you'd be wise to look at the help pages. Because FindLaw has a "Party Name Search" category, we won't need to do a keyword search in the entire database.

Figure 7.21—FindLaw: Supreme Court Opinions Page

4   Search FindLaw for "Brown v. Board of Education."

Do It! Scroll down the page until you come to "Party Name Search."

Do It! In the box under "Party Name Search," type the following: **Brown v. Board of Education**.

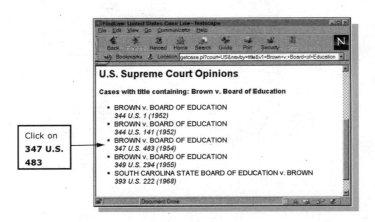

Figure 7.22—Party Names Entered

✳Do It! Click on **Search**.

Your screen should look like the one in Figure 7.22.

FindLaw has returned a few citations that match our search request. We are interested in the 1954 case.

5   Display the full text of the court opinion.

✳Do It! As shown in Figure 7.23, click on **BROWN v. BOARD OF EDUCATION 347 U.S. 483 (1954)**.

Figure 7.23—Results of Search for Brown v. Board of Education

The full text of the court opinion partially appears in Figure 7.24.

Click here to get a list of cases that have cited this case

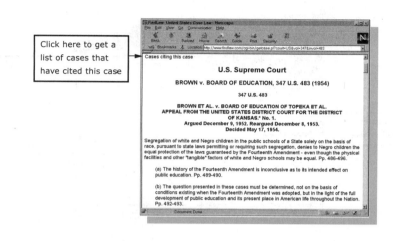

Figure 7.24—Full-Text Opinion of Brown v. Board of Education

Moving from a court opinion to a related court opinion is very simple in a hypertext environment. Throughout the court opinion, you'll find links to related cases, as Figure 7.25 illustrates. Click on the hyperlink and you'll be taken to the full text of these related cases. Keep in mind, however, that the creators of FindLaw have not indexed all court opinions. They are in the process of adding more until they have the entire collection online. Even though there is a link to an opinion, the text of the opinion may not have been added to the database yet.

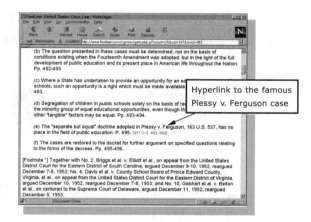

Hyperlink to the famous Plessy v. Ferguson case

Figure 7.25—Hyperlinks to Related Court Opinions

6   End the session.

To end the session, click on **File** on the menu bar and select **Exit** from the menu.

In addition to providing the full text of United States Supreme Court opinions, FindLaw, **http://www.findlaw.com**, provides the full text of the United States Constitution, along with links to cited Supreme Court cases. The *United States Code* and the *Code of Federal Regulations* are also available through FindLaw. It has links to state law resources, as well as law school information. You can see the advantage of linking all of these resources in one database, as it's easy to read related material in a hypertext environment.

Summary

Specialized databases are searchable collections on particular subjects. The U.S. government and nonprofit organizations maintain many of the free, nonproprietary databases on the Web, but commercial databases are also starting to appear with greater frequency. The difference between a specialized database and a subject guide is that a subject guide is a collection of URLs in a particular subject area, whereas a database contains the actual data or information you are seeking. Many databases provide hyperlinks that take you from one related field to another. Some databases have hyperlinks to other specialized databases or related URLs as well.

You can easily find specialized databases by accessing virtual libraries or meta-search tools, such as the Internet Sleuth. Specialized databases are also found in subject guides. These databases are like search engines, in that they all support different search features. Most databases have search instruction pages that you should read before you start searching. This chapter focused on databases in the fields of medicine, business, and law. We chose these topics because the World Wide Web has become an excellent medium for research in these fields.

Selected Terms Introduced in This Chapter

bibliographic database
commercial database
full-text database

proprietary database
specialized database

Exercises and Projects

1. Search HealthGate Medline, **http://www.healthgate.com**, for articles on the Ebola virus. Limit your search to review articles that have abstracts and that are published in English. You'll need to do this search from the advanced page. How many articles did you find? Write down three of the most interesting titles.

2. Using Hoover's Online, **http://hoovers.com**, look for companies in Arizona that are in the electrical components–semiconductor industry. How many companies matched your search query? How many of the companies have a Web site? Write down the names of two of the companies listed, along with their addresses.

3. Using the Internet Sleuth, **http://www.isleuth.com**, find a directory of lawyers and law firms in the United States. What is the name and URL of the database you found? Connect to this database and search for attorneys or law firms in Cincinnati, Ohio, specializing in bankruptcy cases. How many firms or attorneys did you find? List at least three, including their addresses.

4. Go to the Librarians' Index to the Internet, **http://sunsite .berkeley.edu/internetindex**. Find the IBM Patent Server. Explain the steps you took to locate it. Look for patents granted since 1995 on the subject of graphical user interfaces. How many patents did you find? Write down the numbers of three patents you found.

5. Use Yahoo!, **http://www.yahoo.com**, to find the *Internet Movie Database*. Explain the procedure you followed to locate this database. Once you have accessed it, find out who played Boo Radley in the 1962 film *To Kill a Mockingbird*.

6. Using the Internet Sleuth, **http://www.isleuth.com**, find the Vietnam Veterans Memorial Wall database. Describe how you found it. Search the database for names of people from your hometown or state that appear on the wall. Did you find any? If so, write down two names.

7. Go to the Internet Public Library, **http://www.ipl.org**, and look for Peterson's Education Center. How did you find it? Look for a brief description of Oberlin College. Oberlin has a unique history that makes it stand out from the rest of the four-year colleges in the United States. What is the significance of Oberlin's student acceptance policy?

8. Can you name the top 10 home run hitters? Go to the specialized database *Total Baseball*, **http://www.totalbaseball.com**, and select the hyperlink **Batting** under the "Records" category. While you're there, look through the players' biographies for information about Al Lopez. What's his connection with the Cleveland Indians and the Chicago White Sox? In which year did he have the most home runs of his career? In which year did he have his best batting average?

9. Go to the specialized database Travelocity's Destinations and Interests, **http://ps.worldview.travelocity.com**, and use the search form to get information about jazz festivals. List three that will take place in the U.S. within the next year. For each, list a phone number to call for information and the cost of tickets (if that information is available). Do the same for three jazz festivals in countries on continents other than North America.

10. Go to the Internet Sleuth, **http://www.isleuth.com**. What specialized databases are listed there that deal with baseball? While you are using the Internet Sleuth, search the directory of databases to find a list of specialized databases for another sport or some other topic related to recreation.

Chapter 8

Searching Library Catalogs

In this chapter, we will discover the wealth of information to be found in library catalogs. Numerous types of libraries exist in the world, and every one has a catalog of its holdings. In addition to the large national libraries (such as the Library of Congress), academic libraries (such as the Harvard University Library), and public libraries (such as the New York Public Library), there are thousands of special libraries that are part of larger organizations, corporations, and government agencies. Most of the libraries in all these categories, in the United States and in foreign countries, are rapidly making their catalogs accessible to the public through the Internet. Because of the World Wide Web's graphical interface and its hypertext environment, it is easy for people to access and use these catalogs.

This chapter will give you several ways to find library catalogs on the World Wide Web and provide you with pointers on how to use them most effectively.

It will include the following sections:
* Overview of the Development of Online Catalogs
* Characteristics of Online Library Catalogs
* Ways to Find Library Catalogs

want to request through interlibrary loan through the library you're affiliated with. There may also be situations where you want to search a *special collection* that is part of a larger library or a *special library* that collects information on a narrow subject and catalogs its holdings in greater detail than a larger library. There are several other reasons why you may need to search another library's catalog sometime. This chapter will give you several ways to find library catalogs on the World Wide Web and provide you with pointers on how to use them most effectively.

Characteristics of Online Library Catalogs

Library online catalogs provide more than library holdings information for books and journals.
By using online library catalogs, you can learn a good deal of information. You can determine whether a book is checked out and which books and articles have been placed on reserve. Library catalogs can tell you the different names periodicals have had in the past.

Each library catalog vendor offers different features.
Each time you search another library's catalog, you'll see different search features, because libraries don't all use the same software for their online catalogs. Each library chooses a *vendor*, or software company, to organize its records in that vendor's style. The catalogs' various search features are similar to those of search engines, which we discussed in Chapter 5.

Library catalogs are different from search engines.
Unlike Internet search engines, library catalogs do not usually index each word in every work that the library holds. Instead, they index the records of the library's collection.

Each record in a library catalog can be searched by field.
Each record in a library catalog has specific fields that are searchable. For example, subject headings, titles, authors, and so forth are fields. Some catalogs allow you to search by keyword. When you perform a keyword search, you are searching for words that appear anywhere in the records.

Full-text cataloging is possible.

More and more academic libraries are cataloging the full-text version of journals to which they have access via proprietary databases. For example, Project Muse is a collection of full-text journals published by Johns Hopkins University. If an academic library has purchased Project Muse, it may create a link from its OPAC to the full-text journal. If you are searching the library catalog remotely, you would probably not be allowed access to the full-text journals, because you would not be an authorized user of the service.

Special library collections can be searched.

You can use catalogs to search for materials in specialized libraries. You might want to search a special collection that is part of a larger library, or a *special library* that collects information on a narrow subject and catalogs its holdings in greater detail than a larger library. You may also wish to search for a *digital collection*. Many libraries have developed digital collections of such archival materials as photographs, records, manuscripts, and maps. You can find a few of these digital collections at the *LIBCAT* site, **http://www.metronet.lib.mn.us:80/lc/lc1.html**, which we will visit in Activity 8.2. From the main page, click on **World Wide Web**. Scroll down until you find "Sampler: Exhibits and Image Archives."

In any of these situations, if you find a useful holding in a remote library, you can obtain that resource through interlibrary loan from your local library. It is also becoming easier for you to email records to yourself when you do searches in Web-based catalogs. Despite this ease of use, you might be looking for ways to save time when doing searches in library catalogs. Like search engines, library catalogs have faster response times in the early morning. It may also save time to search several libraries' catalogs at once. Some regions have set up multilibrary consortia, which will have a catalog that contains the holdings of all the libraries in the group. You can find regional library consortia by looking in Libweb, **http://sunsite.berkeley.edu/libweb**.

Ways to Find Library Catalogs

The following sites are the most useful for finding library catalogs on the Web.

Libweb at Berkeley   http://sunsite.berkeley.edu/libweb

Use Libweb to find all types of libraries. Some require you to use Telnet, and others allow you to use your Web browser. Be aware that the library catalogs for some of the libraries listed here are unavailable for remote use, especially those of foreign libraries. In some cases, the library's home page is all that is included.

LIBCAT   http://www.metronet.lib.mn.us:80/lc/lc1.html

LIBCAT gives lots of information on searching library catalogs—Telnet and Web-based alike. Look here to find a list of special collections and the names of libraries in which they are located.

webCATS   http://library.usask.ca/hywebcat

webCATS is for finding only Web-based library catalogs. You can also use it to search for libraries by vendor; that search would locate only library catalogs using the type of catalog software with which you are familiar.

We'll demonstrate how to find three different types of library catalogs and search them. In the first activity, we'll go to a national catalog, the Library of Congress. The second activity will take us to Brandeis University's library catalog. Finally, in the third activity, we'll search the special library catalog of the World Bank and IMF Libraries.

❈ Tip

Remember that the Web is always changing and that your results may differ from those shown here. Don't let this confuse you. The activities are meant to teach you fundamental skills. These skills don't change, even though the number of results obtained or the actual screens may look very different.

❈

Activity 8.1   Using Libweb to Find a National Catalog

Overview

In this activity, we are going to search the national catalog of the United States—the Library of Congress. We will be searching for books about the Berlin Wall. If you want to find out almost everything that's been published on a certain topic, it's a good idea to start either with a large university library or the Library of Congress. To help us connect to the OPAC, we will go to Libweb, a service available through the University of California at Berkeley. We'll follow these steps:

1. Go to the home page for Libweb.
2. Select **The Library of Congress**.
3. Find the online catalogs and select a mode of searching.
4. Search for books on the Berlin Wall.
5. Print the list of records.
6. End the session.

Details

1   Go to the home page for Libweb.

❈ Do It! Point to the location field and click. Type **http://sunsite .berkeley.edu/libweb** and press ⌷Enter⌷.

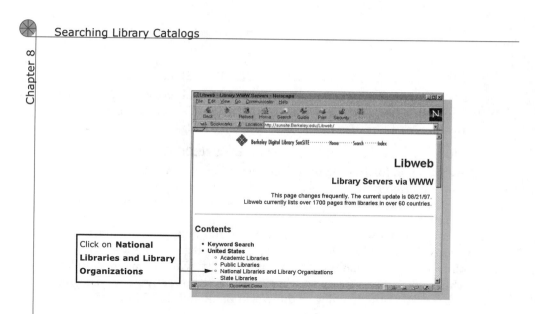

Click on **National Libraries and Library Organizations**

Figure 8.1—Using Libweb to Find Academic Library Catalogs

2   Select **The Library of Congress**.

Do It! Click on the hyperlink **National Libraries and Library Organizations**, as shown in Figure 8.1.

Your screen will fill with an alphabetical list of library names.

Do It! Scroll down until you see **Library of Congress**. Click on its hyperlink.

This will take you to The Library of Congress home page, as shown in Figure 8.2.

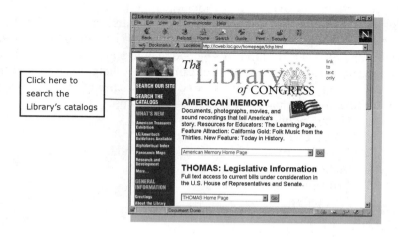

Click here to search the Library's catalogs

Figure 8.2—Home Page of the Library of Congress

3   Find the online catalogs and select a mode of searching.

❋*Do It!* Click on **SEARCH THE CATALOGS**, as shown in Figure 8.2.

Your screen should look very much like the one in Figure 8.3.

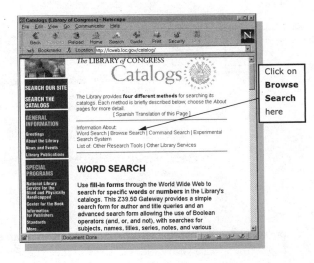

Figure 8.3—Library of Congress Catalogs

Since we are searching for a subject, we will select the **Browse Search** mode.

❋*Do It!* Click on **Browse Search**.

Your screen will look like the one in Figure 8.4. It supplies information about how to use Browse Search.

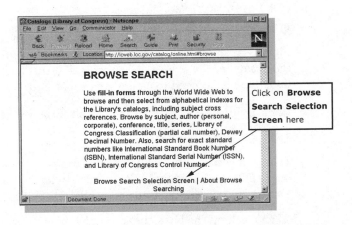

Figure 8.4—Information about Browse Search

❋*Do It!* Click on **Browse Search Selection Screen**, as shown in Figure 8.4. The screen that comes up will look like the one in Figure 8.5.

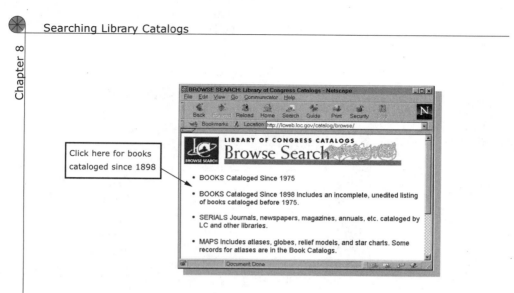

Click here for books cataloged since 1898

Figure 8.5—Browse Search Selection Screen

We can search for books cataloged since 1975, or we can search for books cataloged since 1898. Keep in mind that these are books *cataloged* since these years, not *published* since these years. Because we want a record of everything the library has on the topic of the Berlin Wall, we'll choose **BOOKS Cataloged Since 1898**, just to be on the safe side.

❋*Do It!* Click on **BOOKS Cataloged Since 1898**, as shown in Figure 8.5.

Your screen will fill with the types of searches you can perform in the catalog.

❋*Do It!* Click on **Subject**.

4   Search for books on the Berlin Wall.

Figure 8.6 shows the search query screen. Note the examples listed at the bottom of the screen. We can see that this catalog is not case-sensitive; there is no need to capitalize proper nouns.

❋*Do It!* Enter **berlin wall** in the search form provided.

❋*Do It!* Click on **Browse**.

The catalog has returned a list of ***Library of Congress subject headings (LCSH)*** that include the words *Berlin Wall*. (See Figure 8.7.) Select the records you want to see by clicking on the box next to each one.

❋*Do It!* Click on the boxes next to the subject headings that contain the words **Berlin Wall** (note that the capitalization of *wall* is inconsistent—click on both upper- and lowercase versions).

❋*Do It!* Click on the button next to **Full format**. This will allow your records to be displayed with full information about each book.

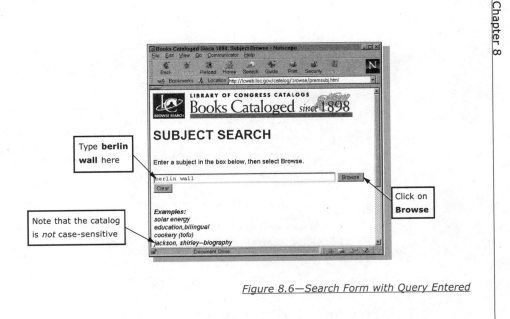

Type **berlin wall** here

Click on **Browse**

Note that the catalog is *not* case-sensitive

Figure 8.6—Search Form with Query Entered

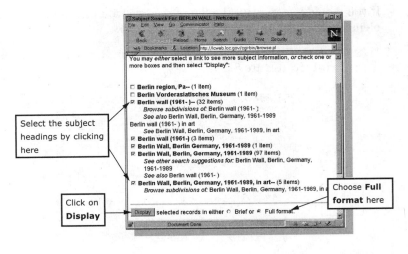

Select the subject headings by clicking here

Choose **Full format** here

Click on **Display**

Figure 8.7—Subject Headings with the Words "Berlin Wall"

❋*Do It!* Click on **Display**.

One of the records is displayed in Figure 8.8.

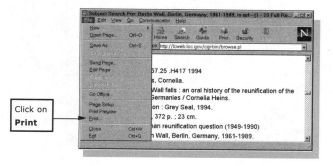

Figure 8.8—One Result of Subject Search

5   Print the list of records.

If you would like to print the list of records, you can use the pulldown menu commands under **File**.

✸*Do It!* Click on **File**. From the pulldown menu that appears, choose **Print**. See Figure 8.9.

Figure 8.9—How to Print Search Results

You will now be prompted to choose the pages you want to print, as shown in Figure 8.10. The default option is **All**. For this exercise, we don't want to print all of the pages.

✸*Do It!* Click on the button next to **Pages**. Make sure the number **1** is in the first box. This will print only the first page.

✸*Do It!* Click on **OK**.

Choose
Pages

Click on **OK**

Figure 8.10—Print Screen

You could also download the records to a disk by choosing **Save As** from the **File** pulldown menu and inserting a disk in the A: drive of your computer. You would name your file "A:file-name," and the list of records would be downloaded to the disk.

6   End the session.

You can either end the session now, or you can stay online and continue to the next activity.

✳*Do It!* To end the session now, click on **File** on the menu bar and select **Exit** from the menu.

_____ End of Activity 8.1 _____

This activity showed how easy it is to search a Web-based library catalog. Searching a large library such as the Library of Congress can be a very good way to start finding materials on your topic. After doing such a search, you can try to obtain the items by requesting an interlibrary loan through your own library. The interlibrary loan office will find the materials for you and let you check them out for a period of time. Because the Library of Congress doesn't loan out its materials, the interlibrary loan personnel at your library will try to find the materials at a library that does lend materials. The availability of nonbook items, such as films, videos, and microform will depend on the individual libraries that hold the items. Some lend nonbook items and some do not.

Activity 8.2   Using LIBCAT to Find Special Collections

Overview

If you are doing research on a particular subject and want to gather virtually everything ever written on that subject, and in any format, a special collection can help you immeasurably. Many academic and public libraries across the country (and the world) maintain special collections on a myriad of subjects. Usually, items in a special collection do not circulate, so visitors can always find what they want on the library shelves. In addition to books, special collections may contain original letters, documents, sound recordings, audiotapes, and so forth. Special collections may also catalog privately published books and individual articles from obscure journals that may not be in libraries near you.

In this activity, we want to find books written in Spanish by the Spanish writer Felipe Alaiz on the Spanish Civil War. We want to find out if there is a library somewhere in the United States with a special collection on the Spanish Civil War. Since *LIBCAT* has a list of special collections that are included in libraries in the United States, we'll start there. We'll follow these steps:

1. Go to the home page for *LIBCAT*.
2. Search the list of special collections for the Spanish Civil War.
3. Connect to Brandeis University's library catalog.
4. Search by the author's name, Felipe Alaiz.
5. Do a related-subject search.
6. End the session.

Details

1   Go to the home page for LIBCAT.

Do It! Click on the location field, type **http://www.metronet.lib .mn.us:80/lc/lc1.html**, and press Enter.

2   Search the list of special collections for the Spanish Civil War.

Do It! Click on **Special Collections via Online Library Catalogs**, as shown in Figure 8.11.

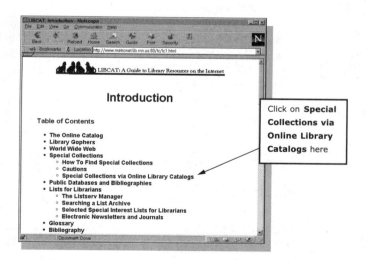

Figure 8.11—Introduction to LIBCAT

Your screen will fill with a list of special collections arranged in alphabetical order by the collection name. The libraries that house the special collections are listed next to the collection names.

✳Do It! Scroll down the list until you find "Spanish Civil War." Note that this special collection is located at Brandeis University, as shown in Figure 8.12.

Note that Brandeis University has a Spanish Civil War collection

Figure 8.12—Spanish Civil War Collection at Brandeis University

3   Connect to Brandeis University's library catalog.

Scroll down to the bottom of the list until you see the menu options under **METRONET**.

✳Do It! Click on **US Libraries**. See Figure 8.13.

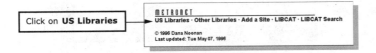

Click on **US Libraries**

METRONET
US Libraries · Other Libraries · Add a Site · LIBCAT · LIBCAT Search
© 1996 Dana Noonan
Last updated: Tue May 07, 1996

Figure 8.13—LIBCAT Options at the End of the Special Collections Page

You are now at the library catalog selection screen. You need to select the appropriate part of the alphabet for the library you want to search. Brandeis University would be found in the AB section.

✳Do It! Click on **AB** under "Table of Contents," as shown in Figure 8.14.

Click on **AB** here

Figure 8.14—Online Catalogs Listed in LIBCAT

You need to scroll down the list until you come to **Brandeis University**. You will see two entries for this school. One is the Web page for the university, and the other is its catalog.

✱*Do It!* Click on **Brandeis University (MA) WWW Catalog**, as shown in Figure 8.15.

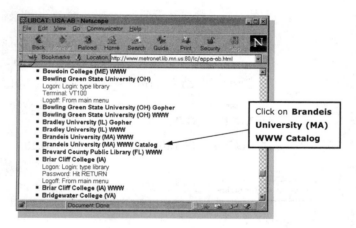

Click on **Brandeis University (MA) WWW Catalog**

Figure 8.15—Brandeis University on the LIBCAT List of Libraries

Now you are in LOUIS, Brandeis University's library catalog. As Figure 8.16 reflects, you can search by keywords, subject, title, author, call number, or in other ways. Help is also readily available.

4   Search by the author's name, Felipe Alaiz.

To begin an author search in LOUIS, you need to choose the **Search by Author** method.

✱*Do It!* Click on **Search by Author**, as shown in Figure 8.16.

Click on **Search by Author**

Help is available by clicking here

Figure 8.16—Brandeis University Library Catalog

✳Do It! In the search form provided, type in **alaiz, felipe**, as shown in Figure 8.17. Note in the instructions that LOUIS is not case-sensitive, so there is no reason to capitalize the author's name.

✳Do It! Choose **am Books only** ("am" is an abbreviated code that the catalog uses to describes the field "Books") from the pulldown menu below the search query box.

✳Do It! Choose **spa Spanish** from the "Language" pulldown menu.

✳Do It! Click on **Begin Author Search**.

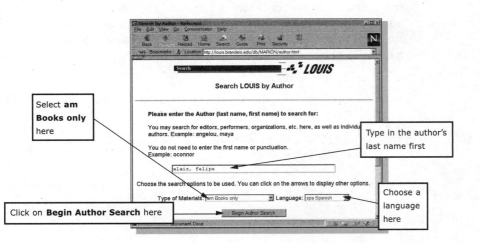

Select **am Books only** here

Type in the author's last name first

Click on **Begin Author Search** here

Choose a language here

Figure 8.17—Search Request Entered in LOUIS

5 Do a related-subject search.

Figure 8.18 shows the results of the search query. The catalog lists the author, title, and call number of each book retrieved.

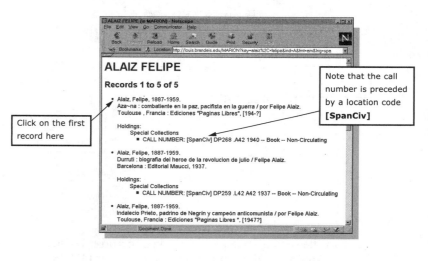

Figure 8.18—Results of Author Search

To see more descriptive information about the books, you'll need to click on the author-title record fields.

❋Do It Click on the first record on the list.

Clicking on a record will give you a detailed description of the book, as shown in Figure 8.19. (Note that the first record on your screen may not be the same one chosen in this example.) This book is about someone named Manuel Azaña. If you wanted to find out more about him, you could click on the first subject heading—his name. If you clicked on the subject heading **Spanish Civil War Collection**, you would obtain a list of all the items in this collection.

6 End the session.

You can either end the session now or you can continue on to the next activity.

❋Do It To end the session, click on **File** on the menu bar and select **Exit** from the menu.

End of Activity 8.2

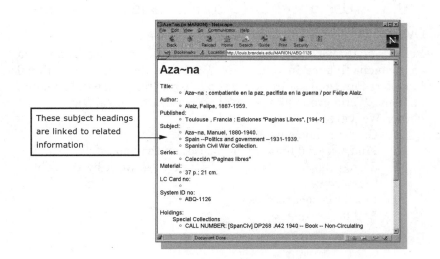

These subject headings are linked to related information

Figure 8.19—Full Description of the First Book Listed

Searching for items in a special collection proved to be quite simple. If this had been an actual research project, you would have been wise to print the search results. Then, you could have taken the citations with you when you traveled to the Brandeis library. You might also have checked to see if there were any items in the circulating collection at Brandeis that interested you. If so, you could have gone to your area library and submitted an interlibrary loan request for them.

In the following activity, we will search a special library catalog. Special libraries should not be confused with special collections. Special collections are materials that are part of a larger library, whereas special libraries are independent offices affiliated with organizations, such as associations, businesses, research institutes, and government agencies. Special libraries usually collect materials that are very pertinent to the type of business or research with which the parent organization concerns itself.

Special libraries frequently have much more detailed cataloging procedures than other libraries. For example, a university library catalog would rarely contain journal articles in its catalog. You would find only the title of the journal if it were in that library's collection. But special libraries will often catalog articles if they are specifically related to the parent organization's interests.

Some special libraries don't allow visitors. You'll need to read any stipulations about visitors in their home pages. Let's proceed to the next activity, in which we'll show you a special library catalog. Although Libweb and LIBCAT have links to special libraries, we'll use webCATS this time to start our search.

Activity 8.3   Using webCATS to Find Special Libraries

Overview

In this activity, we'll look for current information on privatization and government finance in Zimbabwe. We know that the International Monetary Fund and the World Bank publish a great deal of information on Third World economies, so we hope that either organization has a library. We will follow these steps:

1. Go to the home page for webCATS.
2. Find a special library that focuses on the topic.
3. Search the Joint Bank-Fund Library Network by the subject "Zimbabwe."
4. Email selected records.
5. End the session.

Details

1   **Go to the home page for webCATS.**

Do It! Click on the location field, type **http://library.usask.ca/ hywebcat**, and press **Enter**.

2   **Find a special library that focuses on the topic.**

Do It! Click on **Library-Type Index**, as shown in Figure 8.20. We need to click on this in order to see the list of libraries by type.

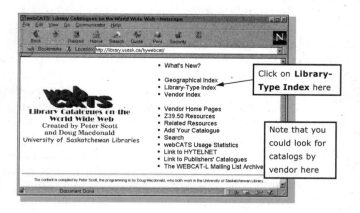

Figure 8.20—webCATS Home Page

Next, we need to select special libraries.

Do It! Click on **Special** in the "Library-Type Index," as shown in Figure 8.21.

Now your screen will fill with an alphabetical list of special libraries throughout the United States and the world.

Figure 8.21—Library-Type Index in webCATS

✳*Do It!* Scroll down the list until you come to **World Bank and IMF Libraries (New York)**, and then click on it, as shown in Figure 8.22.

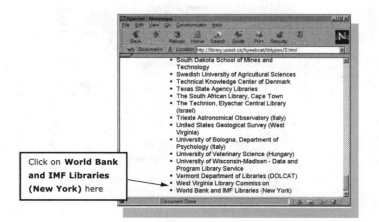

Figure 8.22—List of Special Libraries in webCATS

3   Search the Joint Bank-Fund Library Network by the subject "Zimbabwe."

The World Bank and IMF Libraries home page appears in Figure 8.23. It is officially named the *Joint Bank-Fund Library Network*. Before we search the library's catalog, let's find out some general information about the library, including a visitor policy, if available.

✳*Do It!* Click on **Outside Visitor Information**, as shown in Figure 8.23.

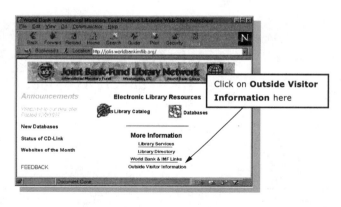

Figure 8.23—The World Bank and IMF Libraries Home Page

Your screen should appear like the one in Figure 8.24. There is a brief description of the library's catalog (named JOLIS for Joint Libraries Information System) as well as hyperlinks to other valuable information, including visitor access. If you want to learn about the features of the JOLIS catalog, you would click on "About JOLIS." To search the catalog, you'd access the "Search the JOLIS Library Catalog" hyperlink.

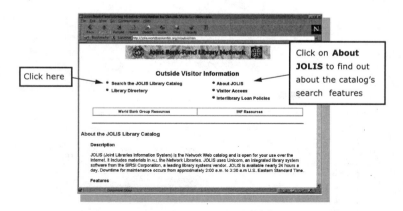

Figure 8.24—Information about the Joint Bank-Fund Library

✱*Do It!* Click on **Search the JOLIS Library Catalog**, as shown in Figure 8.24.

Your screen should look like the one in Figure 8.25.

✱*Do It!* Click on the box that contains the picture of the stack of books and that is labeled **Library Catalog**, as shown in Figure 8.25.

You have several search choices available, as Figure 8.26 shows.

Click here for the
library catalog

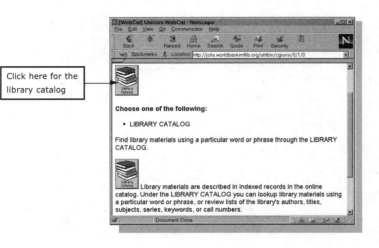

Figure 8.25—Accessing the Joint Bank-Fund Library Catalog

Click on **Subject**
here or here

Figure 8.26—Search Choices in the Joint Bank-Fund Library Catalog

❋*DoIt* Click on **Subject**.

The subject search form partially appears in Figure 8.27. We are looking for all types of information, including journal articles, on the topic
of Zimbabwe. We want to limit our information to resources published
within the past two years.

❋*DoIt* Enter **zimbabwe** in the search query box next to "subject."

❋*DoIt* Next to "pubyear," type in **1996–1997**.

❋*DoIt* From the pulldown menu next to "language," choose **ENGLISH**.

✳*Do It!* Click on the **Search Catalog** button to start the search.

Note that the catalog is not case-sensitive

You can choose the language you want here

Figure 8.27—Search for the Subject "Zimbabwe" in the JOLIS Catalog

Partial results of this search appear in Figure 8.28. If we want to see more descriptive information about each item, we must click on the **View** icon connected to each record. We are interested in looking at the title "A blacklist with a difference."

✳*Do It!* Click on the **View** icon next to the title "A blacklist with a difference."

Click here

Figure 8.28—Results of Subject Search

Figure 8.29 shows the complete catalog record for this item. Note that this is an article in a journal titled **BUSINESS AFRICA/ECONOMIST INTELLIGENCE UNIT**. We know it is a journal article because a volume number and page numbers appear in the citation.

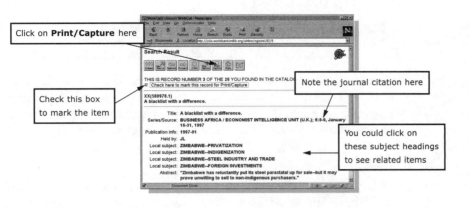

Click on **Print/Capture** here

Check this box
to mark the item

Note the journal citation here

You could click on
these subject headings
to see related items

Figure 8.29—Detailed Catalog Record of an Article

4 Email selected records.

The online catalog vendor that the Joint Bank-Fund Library uses makes it possible for the researcher to mark records for later printing or emailing. In this example, we will show you how to email a record to yourself.

✳*Do It!* Point at the box next to **Check here to mark this record for Print/Capture**, and click.

✳*Do It!* Click on the **Print/Capture** icon, as shown in Figure 8.29.

After you click on the **Print/Capture** icon, you will see a screen that looks much like the one in Figure 8.30.

✳*Do It!* Type your email address in the box next to **Email to**.

✳*Do It!* Click on the **Email** icon.

Keep in mind that only the *records* you captured will be sent to you, not the actual documents.

Figure 8.30—Search Results Capturing Screen

5   End the session.

✳Do It! Click on **File** on the menu bar and select **Exit** from the menu.

_____End of Activity 8.3_____

Activity 8.3 showed how easy it is to locate and search a special library's catalog. A special library focuses on a subject in greater detail than an academic or public library, which allows you to find small pieces of information cataloged individually, including journal articles.

Summary

Libraries around the world are making their library catalogs compatible with the World Wide Web. These graphical user interface (GUI) systems have made it easier for people to search library catalogs from remote sites. The Web makes it possible for a library to integrate text, graphics, and other media and to include hyperlinks to outside resources. Hundreds of libraries have yet to migrate to Web-based systems and still use Telnet programs to enable access. This chapter focused on Web-based systems.

There are many reasons why you may want to search a library catalog remotely. You may need to visit a library collection that might contain useful research information, and you want to be sure of what's there before you go. You may also want to do an exhaustive search of your subject to find bibliographic records that you could then request through interlibrary loan from your library. There are many types of libraries and certain types are better for some topics than for others. This chapter covered some of the major library catalog-finding services on the World Wide Web which make it easy to find the different types of libraries and their catalogs.

Selected Terms Introduced in This Chapter

Dewey decimal classification
    system
digital collections
graphical user interface (GUI)
Library of Congress
    classification system
Library of Congress subject
    headings (LCSH)

online catalog
online public access catalog
    (OPAC)
special collection
special library
Telnet
vendor

Exercises and Projects

1. Use LIBCAT, **http://www.metronet.lib.mn.us:80/lc/ lc1.html**, to locate a special collection on the Wright brothers. What library has the collection? Access the library's catalog. Search for papers, interviews, and the personal history of the Wright brothers. Also search for a couple of books about the

Wright brothers. Email at least two records to yourself. Write down the steps you took to access the library with this special collection.

2. Use webCATS, **http://library.usask.ca/hywebcat**, to help you find library catalogs organized by vendor. Search an academic library catalog that uses innovative interfaces and one that uses SIRSI. In each system, perform a search on an author with whom you are familiar. After your searches, decide which catalog system you liked the best. Were the search features the same or different in each? Explain.

3. Use Libweb, **http://sunsite.berkeley.edu/libweb**, to access the catalog of the National Library of Canada. Find a book by David Cameron titled *Nationalism, Self-Determination and the Quebec Question*. What is the call number? How many copies of the book does the library hold? Does the library have any other books by David Cameron? If so, record the titles of at least two of them.

4. Use LIBCAT, **http://www.metronet.lib.mn.us:80/lc/ lc1.html**, to find the Bowdoin College library's Web-based catalog. Try to find a biography of Sarah Orne Jewett, an author from Maine who wrote *The Country of the Pointed Firs*. Write down all the steps you took to find this biography. In what field did you search in the library catalog to find information about this writer?

5. Access the National Institutes of Health (NIH) Library by using webCATS, **http://library.usask.ca/hywebcat** (*Hint:* this is a medical library). Search the library's catalog for information on multiple myeloma. Find three books on the topic and write down the call numbers for each. Write down the library's hours and find out if the library allows visitors.

6. You are doing research on the history of coal mining in Wales. It makes sense to search a library catalog from the United Kingdom. Go to LIBCAT, **http://www.metronet.lib.mn.us:80/lc/ lc1.html**, and choose **Appendix C: Online Catalogs Outside the U.S.** From this list, choose **United Kingdom**. Now go to COPAC, a catalog that combines the university library catalogs of Cambridge, Edinburgh, Leeds, Glasgow, and Oxford. Find books written about the history of coal mining in Wales. In what field did you search? What subject terms did you use? How many books did you find?

7. Try to find the address and telephone number of the NIH Library. You may need to browse or search Yahoo!, **http:// www.yahoo.com**, to find the home page for the National Institutes of Health, which may give you this information.

8. Let's say you are doing research on modern Russian politics. You've found a useful citation to the journal *Russian Politics and Law*, but your local library doesn't subscribe to it.

Georgetown University is nearby and you want to search its library's catalog to see if it owns this journal. The year you need is 1993. Use Libweb, **http://sunsite.berkeley.edu/ libweb**, to search Georgetown's catalog for this journal. Does the library carry the journal? Do they own issues from 1993? Write down the steps you took to find this information.

9. You are doing research on the Battle of Wounded Knee, which occurred in 1890 in South Dakota. You want to find books on this topic and would prefer to search South Dakota library catalogs. Go to webCATS, **http://library.usask.ca/hywebcat**. Select **Consortia** from the **Library-Type Index** and scroll down until you find the **South Dakota Library Network**. Click on it. Now search for materials on Wounded Knee in all the libraries that are available. How did you formulate your search? How many results did you retrieve? Email the list to yourself. What are the advantages of searching a library consortia?

10. For this exercise, you'll search a library catalog using Telnet. Use Libweb, **http://sunsite.berkeley.edu/libweb**, to connect to the Ann Arbor (Michigan) Public Library catalog. The library's catalog will provide instructions on how to use the catalog. Search the catalog for information on the history of Ann Arbor. Write down the call numbers, authors, and titles of one book and one video recording. Note the call numbers. They look different from the call numbers in the other online catalogs we've seen. Can you guess what kind of classification system this library uses?

9
Chapter

FTP: Searching Archives, Downloading Files

The Internet was primarily created so that researchers could exchange ideas and share the results of their work. It stands to reason, then, that one of the basic Internet services would be to enable people to copy files from one computer to another on the Internet. *FTP*, which stands for File Transfer Protocol, is that basic Internet service. It dates back almost to the beginnings of the Internet, the early 1970s, and it's used to share information in any type of file. Most of these files are publicly available through what is called *anonymous FTP,* since no special password other than *anonymous* is needed to retrieve the files. A computer system that allows others to connect to it through anonymous FTP is called an anonymous FTP site or an *FTP archive*. The collection of files available at an anonymous FTP site is also called an FTP archive.

This chapter will focus on using FTP and FTP archives as two more facets of doing research on the Web and using Web browsers. There will also be a brief introduction to using an FTP client (an FTP program on your computer) to upload and download files without using a browser.

The chapter will have the following sections:
* Understanding the URL Format for FTP
* Downloading a File by Anonymous FTP
* Locating FTP Archives and Other Sites for Finding Software
* Downloading and Working with Files from Software Archives
* Using an FTP Client Program

Web browsers, the Web, and HTTP (Hypertext Transfer Protocol) all transfer files across the Internet. Hence, they allow the same sort of sharing. What is now the World Wide Web wouldn't have been possible without the notions associated with FTP and its use. In fact, one of the first search services available on the Internet (as of 1990) was designed to find files stored in FTP archives. Called Archie (short for *archive*, according to its originators), this service is still available. It works by indexing the titles of files from a database built from the entries in many FTP archives. This index, in turn, takes the form of a database. When a user supplies a search term, Archie displays the locations of matching files. When you think about it, you'll see that it works a lot like many of the search engines we've discussed in earlier chapters.

Do we still need to use FTP? Yes. FTP can be used to transfer any type of file. It's commonly used nowadays to distribute software throughout the Internet. Most of these software programs are available as **shareware**, which means that you retrieve (download) the program from an archive, use it, and purchase it if you find the program useful. FTP is an efficient way to transfer files when you know the exact name and location of the file—and that's all included in its URL. Using FTP, you can also transfer a file from your computer to another. This is called **uploading** a file. When you upload, you usually have to give a login name and password to the other computer system; it's not the same as anonymous FTP. This turns out to be a good way to work on one computer and transfer your work to another. Some people use this technique to update or create Web pages. They do their work on one computer and then transfer the files to a computer that acts as a Web server.

Understanding the URL Format for FTP

These days, much of the access to files by FTP is through a Web browser. As you know, that means you need to be familiar with the URL format for FTP. Here is the general form of a URL for anonymous FTP:

ftp://name-of-ftp-site/directory-name/file-name

Note the following features:

- The URL for anonymous FTP starts with **ftp://**.
- The name of the FTP site follows //.
- The directory name starts with the first single / and goes up to, but does not include, the last /.
- The name of the file follows the last /.
- All the slashes (/) go in the same direction and slant to the right.

Suppose a friend tells you, "I found this picture of Mars with great detail and colors. You can get it by anonymous FTP at the FTP site for the Jet Propulsion Laboratory, **ftp.jpl.nasa.gov**. You'll want to get the file **marglobe.gif**. It's in the directory **pub/images/browse**. There are also some animations at the same site in **pub/images/anim**." You'd like to view the image, and she's told you everything you need to retrieve it. The URL for that file is **ftp://ftp.jpl.nasa.gov/pub/images/browse/marglobe.gif**.

Matching this to the general form, we have the following:

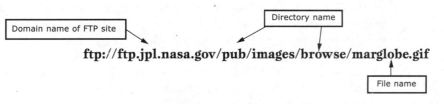

You can also use a URL to refer to a directory. For example, if you use the URL **ftp://ftp.jpl.nasa.gov/pub/images/browse**, the Web browser displays a list of all the files or subdirectories in the directory **/pub/images/browse**, as displayed in Figure 9.1. Each file or subdirectory is represented as a hyperlink, and you can view it by clicking on its name.

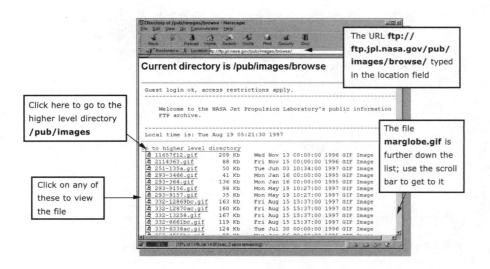

Figure 9.1—FTP Archive Displaying Directory Files

Downloading a File by Anonymous FTP

There are two ways to retrieve a file—that is, copy it from a remote site to the computer you're using.

Method 1: View the File First, and Then Save It Using the File Menu

If you type the file's URL or if you click on a hyperlink, the file will be transferred to the Web browser. This is useful if you want to view the file before you save it, but the file will be transferred to your computer first. If the browser is configured to display or play a file of that type, you'll see (and hear, if possible) the file's contents in the Web browser window. Some examples of files of this type are text files, Web pages that are text files with HTML commands, or GIF or JPEG image files.

The file may also be displayed in a window created by another program called a *helper application*. If there is no helper application installed to display the file, a message box pops up saying "No Viewer Configured for File Type." If the file is displayed in the browser window, select **Save As** from the **File** pulldown menu in the menu bar. This opens a **Save As** dialog box on the screen. Set the directory or folder name, and then click on the button labeled **Save**. If the file comes up in the window for another application, such as Microsoft Word, save it through the commands for that application. See the tip below to handle a file type that doesn't match any type that your browser can work with.

Method 2: Save the Hyperlink in a File Without Viewing It by Using the Right Mouse Button or Shift and Click

If a hyperlink to the file is present in the Web browser's window, you can save the hyperlink. To retrieve the file without viewing it, put the mouse pointer on the hyperlink and press the right mouse button. When a menu pops up, choose **Save Link As**. This opens a **Save As** dialog box on the screen. Set the directory or folder name, and then click on the **Save** button.

Another way to do this is to place the pointer on a hyperlink. Then hold down the Shift key, click on the hyperlink, and release the Shift key. This immediately opens a **Save As** dialog box. You can save it to the file you've specified on your computer.

❋ Tip

What to Do When "No Viewer Configured for File Type" Pops Up

The message "No Viewer Configured for File Type" means you've come across a file type that your browser doesn't know how to handle at the present time. Select the option that lets you **Save to Disk**. A **Save As** dialog box pops up, asking you to specify the folder in which you want to store the file. If you want to see or hear the file, then be sure you have any hardware and software you need to uncompress, display, or play the file after it has been transmitted. There are lots of variations and possibilities for the necessary equipment and programs, so we can't cover all of them here. But if you do have everything you need, you may want to configure the browser so that it knows what to do with files of that type in the future. In Netscape's online help, you can find instructions about informing Netscape about a particular

---

helper application. Click on **Preferences** on the **Edit** pulldown menu in the menu bar, select the **Applications** panel, and click on the **Help** button if you're using Netscape 4. If you're using Netscape 3, click on **Options** in the menu bar, select **General Preferences**, choose **Helpers**, and click on the **Help** button.

The following activity goes through the steps involved in downloading a file by anonymous FTP when using a Web browser.

Tip

Remember that the Web is always changing and that your results may differ from those shown here. Don't let this confuse you. The activities are meant to teach you fundamental skills. These skills don't change, even though the number of results obtained or the actual screens may look very different.

Activity 9.1   Retrieving a File by Anonymous FTP

Overview

In this activity, we'll retrieve the file that we mentioned previously, the one containing an image of Mars. We will retrieve the file using the two methods mentioned above to demonstrate how each is done.

Suppose the browser is already started and ready for use. First, using Method 1, we'll retrieve the file by typing the URL **ftp://ftp.jpl.nasa.gov/pub/images/browse/marglobe.gif**. Web browsers can display files of this type. The file will be displayed, but it won't be saved into a file that we can use again until we select **Save As** from the **File** pulldown menu in the menu bar and set the folder and file name for it. In this case, we will view the file's contents before saving it.

Then we'll save the same file by using Method 2. We'll enter the URL for the directory that contains the file **ftp://ftp.jpl.nasa.gov/pub/images/browse/**, find the file's hyperlink, and use the right mouse button to retrieve it. Retrieving a file this way is quicker, because the browser doesn't have to display it first.

Details

Method 1: View the File First

Type the file's URL in the location bar so that you can view the file.

Do It! Click on the location field, type **ftp://ftp.jpl.nasa.gov/pub/images/browse/marglobe.gif**, and press [Enter].

If the URL is correct and the image is still available, the browser will display the image of Mars.

You can now save this image in a file on your computer.

Do It! Click on **File** in the menu bar.

A menu pops up.

Do It! Select **Save As** from the menu.

A **Save As** dialog box appears, as shown in Figure 9.2.

The next step is to store the file in an appropriate folder or directory. You can save the file in the current folder. Alternately, you could select or create another folder to hold the image. Figure 9.2 shows the file being stored in a folder named **images**. Store the file wherever you'd like. It is a good idea to have one folder for all items of a similar type or a collection of files related to a project. That way it's easier for you to find the file the next time you want it.

Figure 9.2—Save As Dialog Box for Saving marglobe.gif

Once you have chosen an appropriate folder, you need to save the file.

Do It! Click on the button labeled **Save**.

Method 2: Save the Hyperlink in a File Without Viewing It

Go to the Web page with the hyperlink we want.

Do It! Click on the location field, type **ftp://ftp.jpl.nasa.gov/pub/images/browse/**, and press **Enter**.

This connects you by anonymous FTP to the archive server at **ftp.jpl.nasa.gov** and displays the listings of the directory **/pub/images/browse**, as shown in Figure 9.1.

Find the entry for **marglobe.gif**. There are several ways to do this. You could browse the listings by pressing the down arrow key **↓** or the **PgDn** key or by using the vertical scroll bar. A more direct way is to use **Find** to let the browser locate it.

Do It! Press **Ctrl** + **F**, or click on **Edit** in the menu bar, and select **Find in Page**. Type the name of the file to retrieve, and then click on the button labeled **Find Next**.

❋*Do It!* The browser will take you to the first occurrence of whatever you entered, if that string is in the text portion of the Web page. If there are several items that match, press **Ctrl** + **G** to find the next until you reach the hyperlink. Press **Cancel** on the **Find** dialog box to move it off the screen.

You'll eventually reach the portion of the listing that resembles what is shown in Figure 9.3.

Directory listing—here's the hyperlink we want

Figure 9.3—Directory Listing Showing Hyperlinks

The listing in Figure 9.3 contains an icon for each file. The icons here indicate that the files are images. This listing also contains the size of each file, the date it was last modified, and an annotation describing the file type.

You can now retrieve the file.

❋*Do It!* Move the cursor or mouse pointer to the name **marglobe.gif**. The cursor turns into a hand when it's sitting on a hyperlink. Press the right mouse button and select **Save Link As** from the menu.

❋*Do It!* A **Save As** dialog box appears, as shown in Figure 9.2. Select the proper folder or directory for the file and click on the button labeled **Save**. A box labeled **Saving Location** appears on the screen. That box keeps you updated about the progress of the transfer from the remote site to your computer.

Congratulations! You've successfully retrieved a file by anonymous FTP.

End of Activity 9.1

In Activity 9.1, we used a Web browser to retrieve a file through anonymous FTP. You go through the same steps to retrieve any type of file. In this case, because the image comes from NASA, it is available for your personal use. Before using it for any commercial purposes, be sure to obtain permission. You can retrieve files by anonymous FTP at no cost, but having retrieved a file doesn't give you the right to use it any way you'd like. The information in these files needs to be treated in the same way as information that's part of a book, newspaper, audio recording, or video recording.

Locating FTP Archives and Other Sites for Finding Software

In the previous activity, we used an FTP archive to retrieve a file. The archives are a collection of directories arranged according to some scheme. A common arrangement is for the top level to be arranged by the type of computer system (such as Mac, PC, and Unix) and for the levels below that to be ordered according to the type of software (such as games, utilities, and Internet). You start at the home or root directory and, by clicking on hyperlinks that represent folders or directories, you move to or browse through the archive. Once you've located the file you want, you can download it using one of the methods described in Activity 9.1.

There are several well-established and reliable FTP archives in the world. The following list is representative of the general purpose archives. The first has a search form available so you can find files in the archive. The second has a Web page interface that you use to go through the archives. The last is a more traditional type of listing; the items are well organized, but you have to find your own way.

* UIArchive, University of Illinois at Urbana-Champaign
  http://uiarchive.cso.uiuc.edu
* Wuarchive, Washington University in St. Louis
  http://ftp.wustl.edu
* Garbo archives, University of Vaasa, Finland
  ftp://garbo.uwasa.fi

Because millions of files are available through FTP, you can appreciate how difficult it is to find the name of a file and its archive without some automated search tool. In 1990, Peter Deutsch, Alan Emtage, and Bill Heelan at McGill University created a service named Archie and released it for public use. Archie is available with an interface specially designed for use with a Web browser. You enter the name or a portion of the name of the file you're looking for. Archie returns a collection of hyperlinks to files or directories that match the name used in the search box. For more information on using Archie, look at the home page for Archie's home, Bunyip Information Systems, **http://www.bunyip.com /products/archie**. Here's a list of a few Archie servers. Try one!

* Archie Search at Bunyip
  http://archie.bunyip.com/archie.html

❈ ArchiePlex Form at FUNet
**http://www.funet.fi/funet/archie/
archieplexform.html**

❈ FTP Search v 3.5
http://ftpsearch.ntnu.no/ftpsearch

Using Archie is all well and good, provided you know the name or a portion of the name of the file you're seeking. Sometimes you need to guess what the name might be. But it can still be difficult. A better approach is to arrange files in categories according to their function—such as sound files, desktop utilities, games, HTML editors, and so forth—and a description of each. If there is a way to search the collection by file names and descriptions, then we have a more useful service.

Several of these are available on the Web. We'll look at some in the next activities and in the exercises. Many of the files accessible through these sites are software, programs, or collections of programs and other files, which are distributed as shareware. The files are in either executable form (their names end with **.exe**) or compressed form (their names end with **.zip** or **.gz**). We explained these file types in Chapter 1, and we'll show you how to work with them in the next section. Here are a few sources on the Web that list FTP and software or shareware archives:

❈ FTP Software Search Engines
http://ds1.internic.net/tools/soft.html

❈ Librarians' Index to the Internet
http://sunsite.berkeley.edu/internetindex,
then select **Computers, Software**

❈ nerd's HEAVEN: The Software Directory Directory
http://boole.stanford.edu/nerdsheaven.html

❈ Wired Cybrarian: Technology: Software and Downloads
**http://www.wired.com/cybrarian/tech/
downloads.html**

❈ Yahoo! Top:Computers and Internet:software:shareware
**http://www.yahoo.com/computers_and_internet/
software/shareware**

Downloading and Working with Files from Software Archives

Several services on the Web act as archives and distributors of software in the form of shareware or *freeware* (software that may be used and distributed at no cost). Each service supplies links to the programs; when you click on the link, the software is transferred to your computer, essentially by FTP. In other words, you select the software you'd like, and you then use a Web browser to download it to your computer.

Shareware Often Comes in Packages

Most of the files in the archives are packages, or collections of related files. These are in packages because to install, run, and use a single program usually requires several files, such as program libraries, instructions for installing and registering the program, and online help files. When you retrieve these, you get all the files you need combined in one file, the package.

The files or packages are processed by a compression program, which reduces the total number of bytes necessary to represent the information in the package. Reducing the size of a file means it takes less time to download the file. Because of this compression, you must do two things to the package after you receive it: uncompress it and extract the individual files from the package.

Compressed files or packages have names that usually end in **.zip**. Two popular compression programs are PKZIP and WinZip (which are both shareware); these are also mentioned in Chapter 1. You will definitely want a copy of either of those utilities. As you might guess, they are both available in compressed format, as packages.

How can we extract the files necessary for those compression programs or similar packages? These and many other packages are in what is called a self-extracting archive. The package's file name ends in **.exe**. When you click on the name, it starts extracting its own components. For example, the software for the Netscape and Microsoft browsers is in that format.

This compressed format isn't used only with programs. Any single file or collection of files can be compressed and transmitted in that compressed format. In the course of writing this book, we used this technology. Because each chapter has so many images, the files were quite large. We put each chapter and the images into a single package and then compressed it using either PKZIP or WinZip. We used FTP to send the compressed packages to the publisher.

Downloading and Installing Software

Here are the steps involved in downloading and installing shareware or freeware programs and associated files:

- ❋ Find the program you want to retrieve in a software archive.

- ❋ Create a folder or directory to hold the program from the archive on your computer.

- ❋ Click on the hyperlink in the software archive to the program. As soon as you indicate where it should go using a **Save As** dialog box, it will be transferred to your computer.

- ❋ If the file name ends in **.exe**, then it's likely a self-extracting archive. Locate it using Windows Explorer and double-click on it. It will either install itself—follow the instructions—or it will extract its parts into the current directory.

* If the file name ends in **.zip**, then you have to use a program such as PKZIP or WinZip to extract the components. You usually select the folder or directory in which they will go.

* In either case, look for a file with a name similar to **Readme** or **Instructions** to see what steps you need to take to install the program or to work with the files in the package. In many cases, the extracted files need to go through some other processing by a program named **Setup** before they are ready to use.

* Be sure to check the program and associated files for computer viruses. Many of the archives check files for viruses before making them available to the public, but you ought to check them yourself.

Obtaining a Copy of PKZIP or WinZip

You can see from the above steps that you'll need a copy of PKZIP or WinZip, but you don't need both.

To get a copy of PKZIP, go to the home page for *PKWARE*, **http://www.pkware.com**. Spend a little time reading about PKZIP, the way it works, and file compression in general. Click on the hyperlink that takes you through the steps of downloading the software. Store it in a new folder only for PKZIP. Once it has finished downloading, there will be a new application (program) in the folder. Click on it and follow the instructions. It will install itself in a directory or folder. Once it's installed, go to that directory, using Windows Explorer, and read the file named **Readme**, which contains information about the files you've installed. The program's name is PKZIP; click on it when you need to use it.

To get a copy of WinZip, go to the home page for *WinZip* with URL **http://www.winzip.com**. Spend a little time reading about WinZip, how it works, and about the topic of file compression. Click on the hyperlink that takes you through the steps of downloading the software. Store it in a new folder only for WinZip. Once it's finished downloading there will be a new application (program) in the folder. Click on it and it will lead you through the steps of installing the program in a folder on your computer. The name of the program is WinZip; click on it when you need it.

Acquiring Antivirus Software

You will also want a program that checks files for computer viruses. Several are available, and you can get shareware versions to evaluate and determine which you like best. One, F-PROT, makes its software free to individuals; commercial customers or organizations must pay for using it. Here are three sites that offer shareware versions of their antivirus and virus protection software:

❋ F-PROT, Data Fellows
http://www.datafellows.com

❋ Norton AntiVirus, Symantec
http://www.symantec.com/avcenter

❋ VirusScan for Windows 95, McAfee
http://www.mcafee.com

If you don't have an antivirus program on your computer, visit one of the sites, download the most recent version, and install it. Any of the antivirus programs from the sites listed above come as compressed packages. After you download one of these, you'll need to use the software to uncompress and extract the files into a folder. Once you have done that, look for a file with a name such as **Readme** to get instructions on how to install the software. In many cases, you can install the programs on your system by clicking on an application or program in the folder named **Setup**. You follow the same steps for installing these programs as for almost any other software that you download.

Using Software Archives and FTP Search Services

In an earlier section of this chapter, we listed the URLs of some lists of software archives or sites in which you find software to download through FTP.

What You'll Find in the Archives

Software archives maintain their own collection of files, and FTP archives have hyperlinks to the files, which are usually stored at the Web site for the person or organization that markets the software. Both types include a search form so you can search the collection for files, and several also have reviews, descriptions, and links to the software arranged into categories so you can browse the items accessible through the archive.

The files are usually arranged in categories according to the type of software, such as games, Internet, utilities, and personal use. Sometimes they are also arranged according to the type of operating system they're designed for, such as MS-DOS, Windows 3.x, Windows 95/NT, or Macintosh.

Some archives are dedicated to programs for a particular operating system, and some only to Internet software. Two examples are **Windows95.com**, which specializes in software for Windows 95/NT systems, and **TUCOWS**, which has software to be used for working with the Internet. **ZDNet Software Library** is a good example of a full-featured software archive with extensive reviews of many of the items it lists.

Here's a list of a few archives:

General:

DOWNLOAD.COM	**http://www.download.com**
FILE MINE	**http://www.filemine.com**
FilePile	**http://www.filepile.com/nc/start**
SHAREWARE.COM	**http://www.shareware.com**
SNOOPIE File Search	**http://www.snoopie.com/query.html**
ZDNet Software Library	**http://www.hotfiles.com**

Specialized:

Stroud's Consummate Winsock Applications	**http://cws.internet.com**
TUCOWS	**http://tucows.phx.cox.com**
Windows95.com	**http://www.windows95.com**

Before You Download

We're going to demonstrate downloading and installing some software in Activity 9.2. Before you download software, you need to answer a few questions for yourself.

Is the program appropriate for my computer system?

Most of the software archives include a description of the system requirements for the software you'll download. Check that you have enough memory (RAM) to run the program (some require 16 megabytes to run properly) and that you have the correct operating system. Software that's developed for a Windows 95 or Windows NT system won't work properly if it's installed on a system running Windows 3.1 or on a Macintosh system.

Do I have enough storage space on my disk to hold the software?

Again, look at the system requirements to see that you have enough disk space to hold the new program along with your other software.

Do I meet the licensing requirements?

Most software is available as shareware to anyone, but some software is available only to educational or nonprofit institutions. The software will likely come with a licensing agreement; you'll need to read this and decide whether to consent to it.

Do I have permission to install the software?

If you're working on your home computer, then there's probably no problem. However, if you're working on a computer that's owned by your school or company—and probably being shared by others—check local policies to see whether you may install new software on the computer.

Do I have the software I need to install the software?

Check to see if you have the proper software, such as PKZIP or WinZip, to extract the parts of the package. Oftentimes, this will be stated in the description of the software. Also look at the name of the package. If it ends with **.zip**, then you'll need a program such as the one we've mentioned to install it.

Will the software have a detrimental impact on other software on my computer?

This isn't always easy to answer until the software is installed, in which case it may be too late. Read as much as you can about the software before installing it to see if it will have a detrimental impact on existing programs or system configuration. Be sure you can check it for viruses before installing it.

Will I be able to "uninstall" the program if things don't go well?

Most software nowadays comes with a program that makes it easy to remove the primary program and all associated files if and when you need to do this.

Now we'll go through some of the details involved in downloading and installing software from an archive.

Activity 9.2   Downloading and Installing Software from a Software Archive

Overview

We've been searching for and finding information on the Web throughout this book. In many instances, we've added some resources to our bookmark list. The list has grown and needs some organization and management. We know we can do this through our browser, but we're interested in seeing if there is some software that has better tools for organizing and managing our bookmark collection. In this activity, we'll go to one of the software archives, find something we'd like to try, check to see that it's appropriate to download and install, and then go through the steps necessary to install it. Here are the steps we'll follow:

1. Go to the home page for the ZDNet Software Library.
2. Search the library for software dealing with bookmarks.
3. Select software to download and check the system requirements.
4. Download the software.
5. Install the software.

Of course, we'll want to try the program at some point, but we won't show that here.

Details

We'll assume that the Web browser is started and displayed on the screen.

1 Go to the home page for the ZDNet Software Library.

⁕*Do It!* Click on the location field, type **http://www.hotfiles.com**, and press **Enter**.

The ZDNet Library is a large, well-organized, and well-maintained software archive. We use the URL for its home page, **http://www.hotfiles .com**, to access the software library or archive. The home page appears in Figure 9.4. We're going to search for software dealing with bookmarks in the next step. The term *bookmarks* is entered in the search form in Figure 9.4.

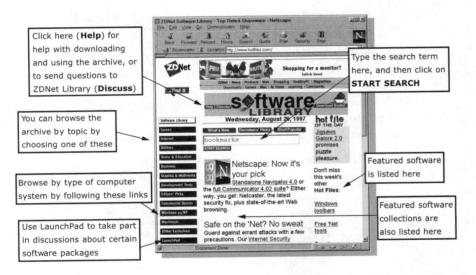

Figure 9.4—Home Page for ZDNet Software Library

We see from the home page that we can search or browse the archive either by type of software or by type of computer system. Several types of software and individual programs are listed. For example, when we retrieved this page, there was a hyperlink to a collection of software titled **Internet Security ToolKit**. We also see there's a **Help** hyperlink so we can learn more about downloading and using this archive. We know from using other search services that it's a good idea to click on **Help** and to do some reading before we continue.

⁕*Do It!* Click on the hyperlink **Help**.

This takes us to the help page for *ZDNet Software Library*. Read the section titled **Easy Download Guide**.

✳*Do It!* Click on the hyperlink **Easy Download Guide**.

We'll follow the steps listed there after we select the software to download. In the next step, we'll start searching for software that deals with bookmarks, but it's worth spending a little time to browse some of the categories.

2   Search the library for software dealing with bookmarks.

✳*Do It!* Go back to the home page for ZDNet Library.

✳*Do It!* Type **bookmarks** in the search box, and click on **START SEARCH**.

You can search for software by typing a keyword or phrase in the search box and clicking on the button labeled **START SEARCH**.

3   Select software to download and check the system requirements.

A portion of the Web page listing the search results appears in Figure 9.5. It's worth taking some time clicking on the hyperlinks for some of the packages to read the ZDNet Library review. In addition to a link to the review, we see the date the software was added to the archive, its rating, and the number of downloads (other folks retrieving the software) listed. To be specific we'll click on the hyperlink for **WebTabs v1.0**.

✳*Do It!* Click on the hyperlink for **WebTabs v1.0**.

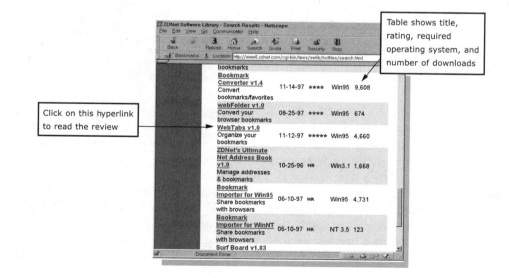

Figure 9.5—Web Page Showing Search Results

The Web page for WebTabs is shown in Figure 9.6. The entire Web page isn't shown there, but after reading all of it, we see that it is designed to run on a computer that uses a Windows 95 operating system and that in compressed form it takes up 2,303,081 bytes—roughly 2 megabytes. Once it's expanded, we can expect it to take up about twice as much space, and we need to decide if we have enough disk space to install it. If after reading the review we feel the software will be useful to us, it is appropriate for our computer, and we have enough space for it, then we can start downloading it.

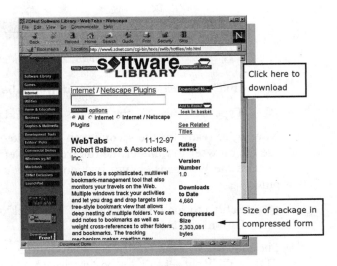

Figure 9.6—ZDNet Library Information about WebTabs

4   Download the software.

We're going to follow the steps in the ZDNet download guide.

First we'll create a folder to hold the package. We're using Windows 95 so we first activate Windows Explorer by clicking on the **Start** button, selecting **Programs**, and then choosing Windows Explorer.

We'll use Windows Explorer to display the contents of drive C:. Click on **File** in the menu bar, select **New**, and then click on **New Folder**.

The window you'll see appears in Figure 9.7. If you're using other software to manage your files, read the instructions in the download guide.

Figure 9.7—Creating a New Folder Using Windows Explorer

A new folder is created. We'll name it **WebTabs**.

✷Do It! Type **WebTabs** for the folder's name and press **Enter**.

Now we're ready for the second step in the download process. We can use the browser to transfer the file from ZDNet Library to our system. Be sure the Web page shown in Figure 9.6 is displayed on your computer.

✷Do It! Return to the browser window and click on the hyperlink **Download Now**.

The browser will attempt to transfer the file to your computer using FTP. You'll likely get a dialog box message such as "Unknown file type" or some other warning. In any case we click on a button that lets us save the file to disk. If you were using a browser other than Netscape, you might get a different message. You want to save the file to your disk. Click on a button that lets you do this. A **Save As** dialog box will appear.

✷Do It! Use the controls in the **Save As** dialog box to select the folder **WebTabs**, as has been done in Figure 9.8. Then click on **Save**.

Figure 9.8—Save As Dialog Box with WebTabs as the Selected Folder

A window titled "Saving Location" pops up on the screen to show the estimated time it will take to download the file and the progress of the download. Depending on the speed of your modem, how busy the server is at ZDNet, and current Internet traffic, it could take a few minutes or longer (up to an hour in extreme cases) to download the file. Figure 9.9

shows the **Saving Location** box. It shows that the download is about 50 percent finished. We can estimate that it will take about 20 to 30 minutes for the download.

Figure 9.9—Saving Location Window Showing the Progress of the Download

When that box closes, we're ready to install the software.

5   Install the software.

The downloaded file will be in the **WebTabs** folder we created on drive C:. To see what it looks like, use Windows Explorer to open the folder **WebTabs**.

✳Do It! Use Windows Explorer to open the folder **WebTabs**.

The listing indicates that the file is a compressed, or zip, file, as shown in Figure 9.10. It will appear this way if we've installed WinZip on our computer. If we had installed PKZIP instead, it would still be listed as a compressed file.

Double-click on the file icon to uncompress and extract the parts

We see the file is a compressed or "zip" file

Figure 9.10—View of the Downloaded File

✳Do It! Double-click on the **webtbs** icon.

Double-clicking on the icon starts WinZip. If WinZip was installed with the Wizard option, then the software will take us step-by-step through extracting the parts of the package and installing the software. If not, then click on **Extract** to extract and uncompress the files. In either case, extract all the files to this directory. Figure 9.11 shows the contents of the folder **WebTabs** after the files have been extracted (and we've pressed the key **F5** to refresh the folder display).

Double-click on **install** to read about installing the program

Double-click on either of these to read the **readme** file before installing the program

Double-click on **wtinstall** to start installing the program

Figure 9.11—View of WebTabs after Extracting Files

Before going any further, we'll read some of the documentation that comes with the software.

✳*Do It!* Double-click on the icon for **readme**.

Double-clicking on either icon labeled **readme** allows us to read the contents of that file. It describes some of the program's features and requirements.

✳*Do It!* Double-click on the icon for **install**.

Double-clicking on the **install** icon opens a brief document that tells us about the installation file, **wtinstall**. The document also says that an uninstall program will be available so that we can remove the program and all its parts when we want to do this. We might, for example, decide that we don't want to purchase the program after the shareware trial period ends—after 30 days, in this case.

Now we're ready to install the program so that we can use it. When we double-click on the **wtinstall** icon, a program will start to lead us through the installation process. We will take all the usual options as the installation or setup program proceeds.

✳*Do It!* Double-click on the icon for **wtinstall**.

A setup program starts. When it finishes, the WebTabs program will be installed in the folder **C:\Program Files\WebTabs**, and **WebTabs** will be added to our **Start** menu. It's instructive to use Windows Explorer to see what's in the folder **C:\Program Files\WebTabs**. You'll see the program, and you need to click on its icon to start it. You will also see a program or application named **Unwise**; double-click on its icon to remove WebTabs from the system.

One more thing: Now that we've installed WebTabs, we don't need the files in the folder **C:\WebTabs** anymore. It's safe to delete that folder at this point.

_____ End of Activity 9.2 _____

In Activity 9.2, we downloaded and installed a program from a software archive. The steps we followed were fairly typical, although the details can change, depending on the program downloaded and the software archive used. We installed the program by clicking on an icon labeled **wtinstall**. In most other cases, we'll click on an icon labeled **Setup** or **Install**.

Using an FTP Client Program

In the examples and activities discussed so far in this chapter, we have used FTP through the Web browser. That may be all you need to search for and retrieve information from the Web or Internet using FTP. Sometimes, though, you may want to use an FTP program that's separate from the browser. To use an FTP program this way, you'll still need an Internet connection from your computer. The program you run will download files from a server or upload files from your computer to a server. This is the sort of client/server interaction we discussed in Chapter 1. The FTP program you use acts as a client.

When you work with an FTP client to contact another computer (called the *server* or *host*), you'll need to have certain pieces of information. The following list explains what you must know.

You'll need the Internet *domain name* or address of the server, or host.

The client uses the domain name to contact the server. Earlier in the chapter, in the section "Understanding the URL Format for FTP," we pointed out the domain name portion of a URL that implies the use of FTP.

If you're going to be downloading software, you'll need a user name and a password on the host.

If you're using anonymous FTP, the user name is "anonymous" and the password is your email address. If you're going to download some files from your user account on the server system, you'll use your assigned user name and password.

If you're going to be uploading files to another computer, you'll need a user name and password on the host.

The user name and password enable you to upload files to a directory or folder that isn't necessarily available to the public.

Of course, you'll also need an FTP client for your computer. Several are available as shareware, but one in particular is highly recommended. It's WS_FTP, and it's free for personal use. To get a copy appropriate for your system, go to the *Junod Software* home page, **http://www.gabn .net/junodj**. John A. Junod has written and continues to maintain WS_FTP. Several very good guides to using WS_FTP are available on the Web. Here's a short list:

* Quick Reference Guide: Using Ws_FTP
  http://www.ckp.edu/technical/reference/wsftp.html
* WS FTP v4.5
  http://riceinfo.rice.edu/Computer/Facilities/Colleges/ PC/WSFTP/WSFTP.html
* Installing and Configuring WS_FTP
  http://usats.com/learn/ftp.shtml

We'll briefly go over how to use WS_FTP, but look at some of these guides for more help when you're ready.

First download and install the appropriate version of the software from Junod Software. Use the same techniques discussed in Activity 9.2.

Once the program is installed, start it by selecting it from the **Start** menu, clicking on an icon on your desktop, or clicking on an icon in a folder. Which one of these you choose depends on how it was installed. When it starts, a session profile pops onto the screen.

Figure 9.12 shows a session profile for connecting to a system with the host name (same as the domain name) **www.mwc.edu**. The user id or login name for this user is **ernie**. A password isn't typed in here; it will be typed in when the host system is contacted. If a password were saved with this profile, then anyone using the computer could access the files belonging to user **ernie** on **www.mwc.edu**. If this were to be an anonymous FTP session, then the box labeled **Anonymous** would be checked. You can select other servers with different profiles by clicking on the button to the right of the profile name.

Figure 9.12—Sample Session Profile for WS FTP

To contact the host, click on the button labeled **OK**. Acting as a client, WS_FTP attempts to contact the host system. Another window pops up that shows whether the host has been contacted. The user then has control over the transfer of files.

Figure 9.13 shows the window that appears when WS_FTP starts an FTP session with **www.mwc.edu**. The left column lists the files in the current folder of your computer, the client. The right column lists the files in the directory with which you've connected on the host computer.

You can choose a file to transfer by selecting it from the appropriate column. You'll see that there are scroll bars to let you scroll through the list of files and directories on both the client and host computers. In each column, the subdirectories of the current directory are listed in the upper panel and the files are listed in the lower panel.

Click on .. to go up one level in the directory structure

Use these buttons to change directories, create, or delete (remove) a directory

To upload a file, highlight it in this column and then click on the button labeled ➡

Controls for this session are here

Brief log of results listed here

Figure 9.13—Session Window for WS FTP

Suppose we want to **upload** the file named **chap1.zip** from the client computer—that's the computer your using—to the host. We highlight **chap1.zip** as shown in Figure 9.13 and click on the button labeled ➡. In doing so, we move the file from the client (listed on the left) to the host (listed on the right).

After we click on ➡, another dialog box called Transfer Status pops up showing information about the transfer of the file from one computer to another over the Internet. Figure 9.14 shows the window for the upload we've been discussing. The items shown include the total number of bytes to transfer, the number transferred so far, the rate of transfer, how much time has been spent so far, and the estimated remaining time. That window will stay on the screen until the transfer is complete. You can stop the transfer by clicking on the **Cancel** button.

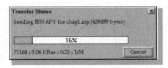

Figure 9.14—Transfer Status Window

To download a file, select the directory on the local system that will hold the file, highlight the name of the file in the list on the right, and click on ⬅.

WS_FTP is one example of an FTP client. It presents a graphical user interface for transferring files between a client and server. Other client programs have a strictly text-based interface. With those, you use a command *get*, as in **get etiquet.zip**, to download a file. You use the command *put*, as in **put chap1.zip**, to upload a file.

Summary

FTP stands for file transfer protocol. With FTP, you can share or copy files from one Internet site to another. Anonymous FTP is the term used when you copy a file from one computer to another without giving a login name or a password. Collections of files available by anonymous FTP are called anonymous FTP archives.

To retrieve a file by anonymous FTP through a Web browser, use a URL in the form **ftp://name-of-ftp-site/directory-name/file-name**. One example of such a URL would be **ftp://ftp.jpl.nasa.gov/pub/ images/browse/marglobe.gif**. To browse a directory, use a URL in the form **ftp://name-of-ftp-site/directory-name**. An example would be **ftp://ftp.jpl.nasa.gov/pub/images/browse**. If the URL is for a file, the Web browser will attempt to display the file. You can then save it into a file on your computer. If you give the URL for a directory, the files and subdirectories of that directory will be displayed as hyperlinks. Put the mouse pointer on the hyperlink and press the right mouse button. When a menu pops up, choose **Save Link As**. This opens a **Save As** dialog box on the screen. Set the directory or folder name, and then click on the **Save** button.

Literally trillions of bytes of information, programs, and resources are available by anonymous FTP. Archie, one of the first Internet search programs, is a tool specifically designed for searching anonymous FTP archives. When you supply a keyword, the names of the files, directories, and sites in the database are searched. Several other search services and software libraries search a database that holds descriptions and reviews of software available through anonymous FTP. Some of the software archives also have entries arranged by the type of program (for example, antivirus programs) or by the operating system (for example, Windows 95 or Macintosh).

Transferring a file from another computer to the computer you're using is called downloading. That's what you do when you retrieve a program from an FTP archive. Many of the programs depend on a number of auxiliary files to be run and used effectively, such as online help. These files are put together into a package, and the contents are compressed to allow for easier and faster storage and transfer.

After you retrieve one of these packages of software, you need to process it to extract the components. If the package name ends with **.exe**, then it's a self-extracting archive. Click on the name of the package, and it will unpack itself. If the name ends with **.zip**, you'll need to use a program, such as PKZIP or WinZip.

Once the files are extracted, you will run a program (application) to install the program. To be safe, you'll also want to scan the software for computer viruses before you install it. Look for a file with a name such as **Readme**, and read it before you install the program. It may help you decide whether the program is appropriate for you and your computer system. Finally, look for a program—often named **Setup** or **Install**—that you'll run to install the program.

An FTP client program is one that you run on your computer to exchange files with another computer that acts as the host, or server. This program is not usually part of the Web browser. To access another computer through FTP, you need to give the client program the Internet domain name for the host computer. That's the part of the URL that immediately follows **ftp://**. For example, in the URL **ftp://ftp.jpl.nasa .gov/pub/images/browse/marglobe.gif**, the domain name is **ftp.jpl.nasa.gov**. Once connected, you can upload files from your computer to the host or download files from the host to your computer. You can do either one by using a graphical interface provided by the client or by using the commands *put* and *get*.

Selected Terms Introduced in This Chapter

anonymous FTP	FTP archive
domain name	shareware
freeware	upload

Exercises and Projects

This set of exercises or projects is designed to give you practice using anonymous FTP. Along the way, you will see some of the resources available. In some exercises, you'll be asked to find the location, or URL, of similar files or resources. To do that, feel free to use any of the search services with which you're familiar.

1. Use your Web browser to retrieve the document whose URL is **ftp://cpsr.org/cpsr/privacy/privacy_international/ international_laws/un_charter.txt**.
    a. What is it about?
    b. What is the domain name of the site being contacted?
    c. What protocol is used to transfer the file? Explain.
    d. Find the same document at a Web site that uses a different protocol for transferring the file to your browser.

2. *Homophones* are words that sound the same but that are spelled differently. For example, *here* and *hear* are homophones. Can you think of a hundred more? A list of homophones is available by anonymous FTP at **ftp://crl.nmsu.edu/CLR/lexica/ homophones/homophones.txt**.
    a. Retrieve the list and browse through it. List a few homophones.
    b. What is the domain name here?
    c. Use the URL **ftp://crl.nmsu.edu/CLR** to find out the name and purpose of this anonymous FTP archive.
    d. Can you find another list of homophones on the Web? Give the URL.

3. Retrieve a copy of the Anonymous FTP Frequently Asked Questions (FAQ) List, **ftp://rtfm.mit.edu/pub/usenet-by-group/news.answers/ftp-list/faq**. Put it in your bookmark list.

   a. The FAQ contains an answer to this question: "What types of FTP information are available?" Write a summary of the answer.

   b. Give a brief synopsis of the copyright notice you see when you connect by anonymous FTP to the directory **/pub/usenet-by-group** at **rtfm.mit.edu**.

4. Internet standards documents are often stated in documents called Request for Comments (RFC).

   a. Retrieve the file **rfc1855.txt** from **ds.internic.net** in the directory **/rfc**. Start with the URL **ftp://ds.internic.net/rfc** and work from there.

   b. What does that document have to say about FTP? (*Hint:* Look in Section 4.1 of the RFC.)

5. Health care for pets too!

   a. Write down the steps necessary to retrieve the file named **health-care.Z** from the directory **/usenet/news.answers/dogs-faq** at **ftp.uu.net**.

   b. Retrieve the file. It is compressed. If you have a program that can uncompress it, use that now. You can get a version of it in uncompressed form from either **rtfm.mit.edu** in the directory **/pub/usenet-by-group/news.answers/dogs-faq**, from **ltp.univ-lyon.fr** in the directory **/pub/faq/dog-faq**, or from **mrcnext.cso.uiuc.edu** in the directory **/pub/faq/usenet-by-group/news.answers/dogs-faq**.

   c. There is a similar file about health care for cats. Can you find it?

6. The search tool at UI Archive lets you search for files in a number of FTP archives, including Garbo, SimTel, SunSite, and WinSite. Visit each of these. Then briefly describe the purpose of each archive and what you're likely to find at those sites.

7. Retrieve a copy of the file with the URL **ftp://nic.merit.edu/introducing.the.internet/answers.to.new.user.questions**. Using that file, write a one- or two-sentence answer to each of the following questions.

   a. What is the difference between the *Internet* and an *internet?*

   b. What is an advantage of the domain name system (DNS)?

   c. What is Archie?

   d. How is Archie different from FTP?

   e. What is Gopher?

8. Using any two of the Archie servers mentioned in the text, use the string "Africa" to request an Archie search with an exact match.
    a. Which server gave the most results?
    b. Which server gave the results that would be most useful to you?

9. Using any of the Archie servers mentioned in the book, do the following steps.
    a. Find at least one FTP archive that is different from the ones mentioned in Exercise 5 above but that has the file **health-care.Z**. Give the URL you used to retrieve the file.
    b. Find at least one FTP archive different from the ones mentioned in Exercise 5 above that has the file **health-care**. Give the URL you used to retrieve the file.

10. Using the images available through URL **ftp://ftp.jpl.nasa.gov/ pub/images/browse**, collect the URLs for images of all the planets in the solar system. Put them in one bookmark folder.

11. Do you know about Neko? Go to the software archive FilePile, **http://filepile.com/nc/start**. Search for a program that lets you experience Neko. What is Neko? What are the system requirements for using the program? Download and install it. Be sure to select your operating system as part of the search form on FilePile's home page.

12. Do you need an alarm while you're using your computer?
    a. Go to the software archive ZDNet Library, **http://www .hotfiles.com**/, and search for programs that act as alarm clocks. Choose one program to download, and explain why you made that choice. Download and install the program. Did it work as you anticipated it would? If you're not happy with it, remove it from your computer system.
    b. Go to the software archive File Mine, **http://www.filemine .com**, and search for an alarm clock program. Choose one program to download, and explain why you made that choice. Download and install the program. Did it work as you anticipated it would? If you're not happy with it, remove it from your computer system.
    c. Write a few sentences comparing the features of the two archives. Which do you prefer? Why?

13. Download and install the appropriate version of the software from Junod Software, **http://www.gabn.net/junodj**. Use the same techniques discussed in Activity 9.2. Using that program, download at least two of the files, from different sites, mentioned in the previous exercises. Do you see any advantage to using an FTP client rather than a Web browser for accessing FTP archives? Any disadvantages? Explain.

Finding Email Addresses, Phone Numbers, and Maps

Your Web browser and some of the services on the World Wide Web make it relatively easy to find email addresses and phone numbers for people, businesses, and government agencies. Finding a phone number or street address without using the Web involves searching through the appropriate phone book(s), dialing 411 for Information, and paying charges for the service. Alternately, it would mean searching the CD-ROMs that list phone numbers and addresses.

Using the Web to find an address or phone number is usually much more direct. Through the Web browser, you search a large collection of data. Using the browser this way demonstrates some of the advantages of using a computer and an electronic database to search for information. The search is based on fields or portions of a form you complete. After you give the necessary information and click on a button, millions of entries in the database are searched to give results matching your request. You can select the results you want to use.

This chapter includes two activities. In one, you will find information about an individual. In the other, you will use a service to obtain information (including maps and driving directions) about a business or government agency.

This chapter will include the following sections:
- Advantages and Disadvantages of Using These Services
- Issues of Ethics and Privacy
- Lists of White Pages Web Services

There are several services for finding information about people or businesses, and their Web sites are relatively easy to locate. One way is to open the Web page for the Netscape guide to finding people; its URL is **http://guide.netscape.com/guide/people.html**. If you're using Netscape 4, you can get to it by clicking with the right mouse button on **Guide** in the command toolbar and selecting **People** from the menu. The browser returns a window similar to the one shown in Figure 10.1. (It features one of the services listed on the left side.) Because these services are used to look up addresses and phone numbers, they're often called *people finders* or ***white page services***.

Figure 10.1—Netscape "People" Web Page

If you try more than one service, you'll notice that they are similar. They all search their databases using the information you enter into fields in a form. Each field holds a specific type of information that matches entries in the database. For example, typing **El Paso** in the field labeled **Last Name** isn't likely to help you find information about an address in El Paso. The database will instead be searched for people whose last name is El Paso. This type of searching, which is based on the entries or values of specific predefined categories, is called ***field searching***.

Advantages and Disadvantages of Using These Services

The white page services give you fast access to very large databases of email addresses, phone numbers, street addresses, and other information. Some services also provide maps, driving directions, and information about businesses in a specific area. Here are several good reasons to use these services:

- ❋ You met people at a conference, business meeting, or another situation, and you want to get in touch with them again.

- ❋ You wonder which of your old or current friends have email and what their addresses might be.

- ❋ You're applying for a job or interviewing at a company, so you want the company address, a map of the surrounding area, information about the community in which it's located, and directions by car.

You use your Web browser to access these services and information. That means you can use the tools and techniques you have already acquired and don't need to learn how to work with an entirely new program or interface to the database. Also, you can use the browser to save, print, or email your search results if you want to take them with you. As you can see, there are many advantages to using such services.

The main disadvantage is that many times, you can't find the information you'd like for an individual. The overwhelming majority of entries in these databases are related to businesses. Listings for individuals appear when people register (give information about themselves) in these directories. Individual listings also come from addresses people use when they post an article on Usenet or from membership or mailing lists that are often related to computers. It is impossible to find a directory of everyone with access to the Internet—there's no central control of registry service for Internet users, and no single agency could keep pace with the increasing numbers of people using the Internet and World Wide Web. Sometimes you can only find information for folks who use computers and the Internet, or information that may be out-of-date or inaccurate. On the other hand, these services may be the only means of finding someone's email address quickly. The surest way, if you can do it, is to ask people directly for their email addresses!

Now we'll show you how to use one of the white pages services to find an email address, street address, and phone number.

❋ Tip

Remember that the Web is always changing and that your results may differ from those shown here. Don't let this confuse you. The activities are meant to teach you fundamental skills. These skills don't change, even though the number of results obtained or the actual screens may look very different.

Activity 10.1   Finding an Individual's Email Address, Phone Number, and Mailing Address

Overview

In this activity, we'll use the Web service Four11 to search for an individual's email address, specifically that of Ernest Ackermann. We'll also follow a link that would give us his phone number. You could follow the steps we go through here to search for anyone's email address, phone number, or mailing address. The details may be different if you're using something other than Four11, but the steps will almost be the same. Here are the steps we'll take:

1. Go to the home page for Four11.
2. Fill in the form.
3. Activate the search and note the results.
4. Search for a phone number and note the results.

Details

We assume you've started Netscape or another browser.

1   Go to the home page for Four11.

✳ *Do It!* Click on the location field, type **http://www.four11.com**, and press **Enter**.

The home page for Four11, with the information necessary for our search, appears in Figure 10.2. We've noted a number of features or options. Take a few moments to see what's available at this Web site. Click on the hyperlink **Help/FAQ** to learn more about using the service, and don't be shy about trying interesting links. Note that there are links to other types of directories. There is also a link that allows you to register or add information about yourself.

✳ **Tip**

Remember that anyone on the Web can access this information, so don't include information that you wouldn't feel comfortable or safe sharing with any stranger browsing through this database.

✳

Before we move on, note that Four11 has a clear link to its acceptable use policy. This policy addresses issues about commercial use of the database information, privacy, and the accuracy of the information users provide.

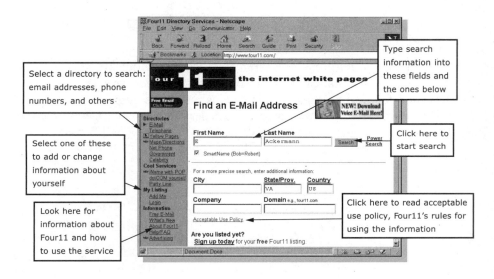

Figure 10.2—Home Page for Four11

2 Fill in the form.

Figure 10.2 shows information entered into some but not all of the fields. When you use Four11, you can fill in as few or as many fields as you wish. Filling in more fields makes your search more specific and restricted. If we fill in only the **State** field, we get too many responses (more than five thousand, in this case!). Regardless of how many records are found, Four11 lists no more than one hundred.

✳*Do It!* On the *Four11* home page, type **E** into the **First Name** field, **Ackermann** into the **Last Name** field, **VA** in the **State** field, and **US** in the **Country** field. Note that **Ackermann** ends with *two* n's.

You probably noticed that we only put an initial in the "First Name" field. Four11 treats entries in the name fields as being the beginnings of names; if you enter *Johns* as a last name, you will also receive results for *Johnson*. We'll receive information about all the people in Virginia who are listed in the Four11 database if their first names start with *E* and if their last names start with *Ackermann*.

3 Activate the search and note the results.

✳*Do It!* Click on the button labeled **Search**.

Clicking on the **Search** button sends the search request to Four11 for processing. Within a few seconds, depending on how heavily the Internet is being used, the Four11 server sends another Web page to your browser. The new page has the search results. Figure 10.3 shows the results of our search.

Figure 10.3—Results of Search for Email Address

Figure 10.3 shows three entries with the first name **Ernest** and the last name **Ackermann**. Does this guy have three addresses, or are they addresses for different people? We can't tell from here, but we can use the domain name or email location information to help us choose. Since the Ackermann we're looking for works at Mary Washington College, we might try the **@mwc.edu** listing first. (Except for the possible waste of time, there's no harm in trying all of them.)

❋ Tip

Before following one of these links, you ought to know that our search criteria may not yield any results or may give too many results. If we don't get any results, we might want to make the search more general by not filling in so many fields. If we get too many results, then we need to make the search more specific, usually by providing more information in the fields. To change entries in the search fields, you click on the **Modify Search** button.

❋

❋Do It) Click on the link **ernest c ackermann**.

Clicking on the link **ernest c ackermann** brings up a Web page, shown in Figure 10.4. Relatively speaking, it gives a lot of information about Ackermann, including his email address, a link to his home page, and alternate email addresses. There's so much available on him because he registered with Four11 and supplied this information. Otherwise, the page would hold little more than his email address.

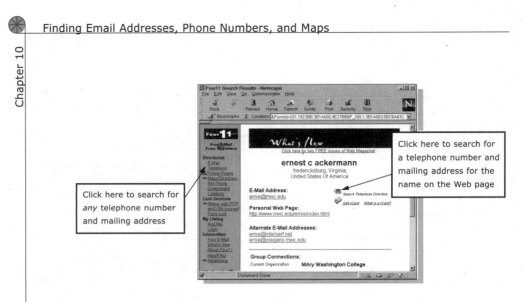

*Figure 10.4—Four11 Search Results for **ernest c ackermann***

4   Search for a phone number and note the results.

✱*Do It!* Click on the telephone icon to the left of **Search Telephone Directory**.

You click on the telephone icon to reach the Four11 Web page with the person's telephone and address information. That brings up a Web page with the person's name, along with city, state, and zip code information. The Web page for this example appears in Figure 10.5.

Figure 10.5—Four11 Web Page for U.S. Telephone Directory

To obtain complete address information, click on the name. Check the Four11 help page to see if this search service provides information only from U.S. phone books—a common practice. As with the email address search, several types of services may be listed.

End of Activity 10.1

In Activity 10.1, we looked for an individual's email and street address using Four11, one of many search services. Other services may be somewhat different, but they will be similar enough that you'll be able to use them.

Privacy and Ethical Issues

In Activity 10.1, you saw how easy it is to find an individual's email address, phone number, or mailing address. Services such as the one you used make it possible to search a centralized collection of millions of records in seconds. This capability raises a number of questions related to privacy and the ethical use of the information in such records. An example of such a question is this: Where does the information in these databases originate? Most of the services obtain their information from public sources, such as published phone books and registration lists for online services. All services encourage individuals to register with them. If you register, you must provide information about yourself. In return, you gain access to some features not available to the general public. Some services only list information provided by registered users or by those who have supplied data on another voluntary basis.

What control does an individual have over the information in these databases? Much of it comes from public sources, such as phone books, so accuracy and issues of whether a listing appears at all sometimes need to be addressed at the source of the information. You can request that you not be listed in such services. Most of the online white pages services make it relatively easy for you to do that. The problem is that you have to send an email request or fill out a form for *each* service. There's no way to ask that information about yourself be hidden or removed from every service.

Can users perform so-called reverse searches? For example, can they type in a phone number and find the name and address of the person with that number? This feature isn't available in most services, but it is available in some. Using this capability would help someone identify a person based on the phone number. Services in which the user pays a fee for searching often permit these reverse searches. These include CD-ROM-based databases that give full access to phone book information.

Questions related to ethical use of the information almost all deal with using the information for online junk mail—mass mailings related to commercial activity. Such unsolicited email (usually advertising something or soliciting money) is called **spam**. Phone listings in online databases could also be used to generate lists for commercial calls for telemarketing.

Most of the services on the Web include a policy statement saying that the information they provide isn't to be used for commercial purposes, but the services don't police the people searching their databases.

In their statements, they only promise to respond to complaints from others. It's really up to individuals to protect their privacy and to demand ethical behavior on the Web and Internet.

Before registering for one of these services, you need to read policies about how your personal information will be used. You can usually find such policies by clicking on hyperlinks labeled **Help**, **About**, **Acceptable Use Policy**, or **FAQ** from the service's Web page. Here are two examples of policy statements:

❋ BigFoot Privacy List FAQ
http://www.bigfoot.com/Policy/policy.htm

❋ Four11 Acceptable Use Policy
http://www.four11.com/cgi-bin/Four11Main?Aup

Some services make it more difficult than others to obtain a long list of email addresses or phone numbers. As we saw in Activity 10.1, Four11 doesn't give direct access to a list, but the service we'll use in Activity 10.2—InfoSpace—does provide this access. Mailing addresses and phone numbers are available in other forms, such as commercial (but not very expensive) CD-ROM-based products. Anyone interested in large-scale mailings or telemarketing would probably use those products to procure lists of phone numbers or addresses.

The questions raised by the use of this technology are typical of what we need to be aware of and concerned about as more information becomes readily available through the use of computers, networks, and other technologies. There are lots of advantages to using these tools, but we need to think about, and act on, the ramifications of making this type of information so easily accessible.

Activity 10.2   Search for a Business Address, a Phone Number, a Map, and Driving Directions

Overview

In this activity, you will find information about a specific business. You will use techniques that you can later apply when finding the same types of information about other organizations or government agencies.

Suppose you've got a job interview scheduled with Netscape Communications Corporation in Mountain View, California. You'd like to know the address and phone number of the office, and it would help to have a map of the area. It would also be nice to know a little about the community. No problem! We'll go to the InfoSpace Web site, find its business section, and search for Netscape's address and phone number. Once you have that information, you'll use InfoSpace's hyperlinks to find the following things: a map showing the business's location, the names and types of businesses in the area, some background information about the city, and even driving directions!

You'll follow these steps:
1. Go to the home page for the InfoSpace Web site.
2. Follow the hyperlink to the business phone directories.
3. Search for the business's address and phone number.
4. Follow hyperlinks for more information.

You follow the same steps to get information about any business.

Details

We assume your Web browser is already started.

1   Go to the home page for the InfoSpace Web site.

✳*Do It!* Click on the location field, type **http://www.infospace.com**, and press **Enter**.

A portion of the InfoSpace home page appears in Figure 10.6. It has links to different types of information. These include telephone directories and lists of email addresses for individuals, businesses, and the government at city, county, state, and federal levels; lists of Web pages, fax numbers, and toll-free phone numbers for businesses; directories for businesses and other information about localities; and "yellow pages" for the United States and Canada.

Figure 10.6—Portion of InfoSpace Home Page

2   Follow the hyperlink to the business phone directories.

✳*Do It!* Click on the hyperlink **Businesses by Name** in the **Yellow Pages** section.

Figure 10.6 shows where to click. A few seconds after you click on this hyperlink, another Web page will be displayed. There, in the three fields of a search form, you will type the name and address (if you know it) of the business for which you're seeking information. Figure 10.7 shows the completed search form. It isn't necessary to fill in all of the fields, but the less information you give here, the more general the search will be and the more items it will return. InfoSpace returns at most a hundred items, and they're listed 10 per page. InfoSpace sometimes changes the forms and Web page to access information; for this reason, what you see may not look exactly as its shown here, but you'll be able to find your way.

3   Search for the business's address and phone number.

With the hyperlinks in Figure 10.7, you can also search for businesses by category and by proximity to an address. You can get directions to a business as well.

✱Do It! Complete the form by typing **Netscape Communications** in the field labeled **Business Name** and **Mountain View** in the field labeled **City**. Select **California** from the list of states.

*Figure 10.7—InfoSpace Search Form for **Business by Name***

✱Do It! Click on the button labeled **Find**.

Clicking on **Find** sends your information to the database. The results appear shortly and are shown in Figure 10.8.

Figure 10.8—Search Results from InfoSpace

4   Follow hyperlinks for more information.

To save space here, we won't show what happens if you follow all the possible links. You ought to try it for yourself. Look in the "Exercises and Projects" section at the end of the chapter to find a list of suggestions for exploring the information available this way.

❋*Do It!* Click on the hyperlink labeled **Map**.

This hyperlink brings up a map of the region. The Web page holding the map has controls, so you can zoom in or zoom out for more or less detail about the region. In some cases, you'll want to print the map to take with you on your travels.

❋*Do It!* Click on the hyperlink labeled **Directions**.

This hyperlink brings up a Web page in which you give a starting address. The address you've selected is used as the destination address. Click on one more hyperlink to obtain detailed driving directions. You may want to print these or email them to someone else (yourself too!).

❋*Do It!* Click on the hyperlink labeled **Find Near Address**.

This hyperlink brings up a Web page that you can use as a yellow pages guide to the city or region near the address.

❋*Do It!* Click on the hyperlink labeled **City Guide**.

This hyperlink takes you to a Web page with a search form. There, you type in the name of a city, state, and maybe a zip code. Once you have completed the search form, click on the button labeled **Find**.

Do It! Enter **Mountain View** and **California** into the search form, and click on the hyperlink labeled **Find**.

This hyperlink brings up a Web page similar to the one in Figure 10.9. It contains links to local weather, businesses, and other resources.

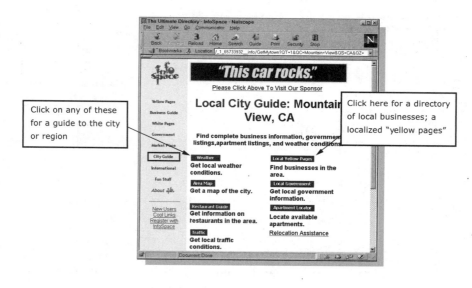

Figure 10.9—Links to Local Information in InfoSpace

<hr>

End of Activity 10.2

In Activity 10.2, you used search forms provided by InfoSpace to obtain information about a business. You'd go through similar steps and have many of the same options (for example, seeing a map and getting driving directions) if you used InfoSpace to find the address of an individual or government agency. You could also click on the hyperlink labeled **Government** in Figure 10.6 to obtain information about government agencies, services, offices, and officials. Figure 10.10 shows the result of clicking on this hyperlink. You can get information about government at the national, state, and local levels, and you can also get information about embassies in Washington, D.C.

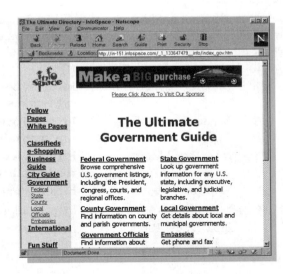

Figure 10.10—InfoSpace Government Information Web Page

Keeping Current: White Pages and Map Web Services

In this chapter we've featured some white pages services and saw in Activity 10.2 a way to find a map of an area. Some links to Web pages that list white pages services and map services are given here.

Lists of White Pages Web Services

Several Web pages contain lists of the white pages services discussed in this chapter. To see what new features these services offer, you need to check these sites occasionally. Here's a selected list of resources to keep you current on the topic of white pages services:

- ❈ Flip's Search Resources
  http://aa.net/ ~ flip/search.html

- ❈ Netscape—Guide: People
  http://guide.netscape.com/guide/people/people.html

- ❈ People Search: Looking for Someone?
  http://home.sprynet.com/sprynet/ kenkirk/people1.htm

- ❈ Search.Com, Email Addresses
  http://www.search.com

- ❈ Yahoo!—Reference: White Pages
  http://www.yahoo.com/Reference/White_Pages

Map Services

In Activity 10.2 we used InfoSpace to find a map of the area surrounding an address. There are several map services on the Web. To see what new features these services offer, you need to check these sites occasionally. Here's a selected list of resources:

❈	DeLorme CyberRouter	**http://www.delorme.com/ cybermaps/cyberrouter.htm**
❈	Excite Travel: Maps	**http://city.net/indexes/ top_maps.dcg**
❈	Lycos Road Maps	**http://www.lycos.com/ roadmap.html**
❈	MapQuest	**http://www.mapquest.com**
❈	Yahoo! Maps	**http://maps.yahoo.com/yahoo**
❈	Zip2 Yellow Pages	**http://www.zip2.com**

Try one the next time you need a map or driving directions.

Summary

Several services that let you search for email addresses, phone numbers, mailing addresses, and other information about individuals and businesses are available on the World Wide Web. The services are available as Web pages, so you use your browser for searching them. They provide electronic access to the white pages (and in some cases the yellow and blue pages) of a phone book. The difference here is that you can also search for email addresses. Plus, instead of searching an individual phone book, you can search a very large collection of phone books.

Although various services provide different features, you use them all in about the same way. In each case, you complete a form by entering names, addresses, or other information in fields. Then, you click on a button on the Web page. The information you have supplied is passed to the service, and its database is searched based on the entries in the fields. For example, the entry in the "Last Name" field is matched with the last names in the database. This is an example of field searching. Once the results are displayed, you select the relevant information from a list. Some services have separate directories for individuals, people, and government. Some provide maps, while others give different features. As more people use these tools, we're likely to see more similarities between the services.

The advantages of using these tools are that we can search millions of records in a matter of seconds. We use our Web browser to do it, which means that we don't necessarily have to learn a new interface to the data or new techniques to work with results. We can save, print, or email the results in the same way as with any other Web page.

The disadvantages are that the available information may not be up-to-date or complete. Plus, having rapid access to this type of information raises questions about privacy and the ethical use of this information. Most services have a hyperlink from their home pages that takes you to a policy statement regarding these issues. You need to be aware of your rights and responsibilities when you register with or use these services. Also, be sure not to give these services information that wouldn't be safe to share with a complete stranger. Putting information on these services is like tacking it up on thousands of bulletin boards throughout the world.

Several Web sites list hyperlinks to these white pages services, or "people finders" as they're sometimes called. You can access some of the major lists by clicking on the **People** directory button in the Netscape browser, going to **www.search.com**, and going to the address book sections. You could also look in the "Reference" section of Yahoo!

Selected Terms Introduced in This Chapter

field searching

spam

white pages services

Exercises and Projects

1. Using Four11, **http://www.four11.com**, as shown in Activity 10.1, find the email address and mailing address for the publisher of this book.

2. Using Four11, **http://www.four11.com**, as shown in Activity 10.1, search for the email address and phone number of the people listed below. Try each category to see whether these people are in the Four11 databases.

   a. Yourself.

   b. A friend you haven't seen in a long time.

   c. Your instructor or supervisor.

   d. A current friend, classmate, or coworker.

   e. The president of the United States or the Speaker of the House of Representatives.

3. Try the previous exercise with a white pages service other than Four11. To find some others, use the URL **http://guide.netscape.com/guide/people.html**. Compare your results. Which gave more complete and accurate results? Which do you prefer to use?

4. Using any of the white pages services, look up email addresses of people with the same last name as yours. See what results you get when you

   a. put no restrictions on the search.

   b. restrict the search to your country.

   c. restrict the search to your state.

   d. restrict the search to your city.

5. Read the privacy or policy statement for two services on the Netscape people page. Compare the two. Which is more practical? Which more strongly protects an individual's privacy? Which of the two makes a stronger commitment to ensuring the appropriate use of the information it provides?

6. Look at the policies and procedures for the service BigFoot. Is it possible for an individual to remove an entry from a database? How is that done? What's to prevent one person from removing or altering the information stored about another? Investigate the same issues for the service InfoSpace.

7. For any white pages service, find answers to the privacy questions raised above. Where does the service get its information for its database? What control does an individual have over the information in the database? Does it permit reverse searches?

8. Go to the home page for the InfoSpace Web site, **http://www .infospace.com**, as we did in Activity 10.2.
    a. Find the address and phone number for Radio City Music Hall in New York City.
    b. Using the facilities at InfoSpace, print a map that shows where to find Radio City Music Hall, and obtain driving directions from your location to Radio City Music Hall.
    c. Repeat Parts a and b for the Wells Fargo Bank in San Francisco.
    d. Repeat Parts a and b for Franklin, Beedle & Associates in Wilsonville, Oregon.

9. Using the InfoSpace Web site as in Activity 10.2, find the following:
    a. The address and phone number for your school or business.
    b. The names of businesses in your town that provide commercial printing services.
    c. The names of all the businesses dealing with computer hardware within a one-mile radius of 1301 College Street, Fredericksburg, Virginia.

10. Some of the white pages services have specific links to government information. Compare the government information offerings of two services; for example, Four11 and InfoSpace. Which has more complete and accurate information? Which do you prefer?

11. Some of the services have information only about people in the United States. Others have information (such as email addresses, phone numbers, and business addresses) for other countries as well. Find at least two services that offer international service. Compare them for completeness, accuracy, and ease of use.

Searching Email Discussion Group Archives and Usenet Newsgroup Archives

Email and Usenet news are two popular uses of the Internet. In fact, email is *the* most popular, and both show some of the unique features of communication on the Internet. With no difference in effort, one person can send a message to one or thousands of people, and one person can receive information on a topic or an answer to a question from anywhere on the Internet. People have been using email since the beginning of the Internet, and those with common interests have formed email *discussion groups*—also called *interest groups, mailing lists,* or *listservs*—based on specific topics. *Usenet,* which originated independently of the Internet, is a system for exchanging messages called *articles* arranged according to specific categories called *newsgroups*. The articles or messages are passed from one system to another, not as email between individuals. Group discussions take place as individuals compose and post messages, answer questions, and respond to other people's statements.

In this chapter, we'll concentrate on finding discussion groups and newsgroups that deal with specific topics and determining the resources available through the group. We'll also cover ways of searching archives of Usenet articles. We will give a brief overview of how to access and use the two forms of group discussion—email discussion groups and Usenet newsgroups. There are some differences in the methods and tools you use to work with each. The last section of the chapter covers an important topic: proper etiquette or behavior in a discussion group or newsgroup.

The chapter will include the following sections:
* Email Discussion Groups
* Usenet Newsgroups
* Etiquette in a Discussion Group or a Usenet Newsgroup

To get more detailed information on using discussion groups and newsgroups, see Chapters 4 and 5 in *Learning to Use the World Wide Web* by Ernest Ackermann, and the Web pages accompanying those chapters at http://www.mwc.edu/ernie/Lrn-web04.html and http://www.mwc.edu/ernie/Lrn-web05.html.

Both email discussion groups and Usenet newsgroups allow for group communication. The primary difference is that you must first subscribe to or join an email discussion group, whereas anyone with a *newsreader*—such as the one included with Netscape—can browse and interact with a newsgroup. Both email discussion groups and Usenet newsgroups give you valuable resources when searching for information on specific topics or seeking answers to questions. Here are a few reasons that these resources are so helpful:

- ❋ The group itself. The articles or messages posted to discussion groups and newsgroups are sometimes read by thousands or millions of people throughout the world. Replying to messages, giving help, and supplying accurate information when possible are part of Internet culture. Although it's unreasonable to expect group members to do your research for you, the group can be very helpful.

- ❋ The discussions—the messages or articles—are often archived and can be searched and retrieved.

- ❋ The thousands of frequently asked questions (FAQs) and periodic postings on a specific topic are usually compiled and updated by volunteers.

Email Discussion Groups

Email discussion groups are made up of people anywhere on the Internet who agree to communicate about a certain topic using email. The group named "Herbs," for example, supports discussions about the use of herbs and spices in cooking. Anyone can join or subscribe to the list. Discussions are usually on the main topic, but messages on other topics are usually tolerated or redirected to other groups. Each message sent to the group's address is routed, virtually immediately, through email to all group members. In this section we'll cover the details of working with discussion groups. We'll use the term *discussion group* or *list* to refer to any of these types of groups. Some of the topics we'll cover are:

- ❋ Essential Information about Discussion Groups
- ❋ Ways to Join, Contribute to, and Leave a List
- ❋ Ways to Find and Retrieve a Group's Archives
- ❋ Ways to Locate Discussion Groups about Specific Topics
- ❋ Sources of Information about Discussion Groups on the Internet

Essential Information about Discussion Groups

It's All Done by Email
Email is the medium for all communication in a discussion group. Using email, a person makes a request to join, or *subscribe* to, a group. That person then shares in the group discussions. Any message sent to the group is broadcast via email to all group members; these discussions are public. There is an exception, however; some groups are moderated, in which case a message sent to the group is first routed to the *moderator*. Some groups are very large, with thousands of subscribers. Some are very diverse, with members throughout the world. An active group generates several email messages per day.

You Decide How Much You Want to Participate
Being a member of a discussion group means that you can join in discussions, ask questions, help others with questions, make announcements related to the group, or just see what others are talking about. You'll find members with all levels of experience. You don't have to respond to every message; you can simply read or even ignore some of the discussions. It's usually a good idea just to read messages when you first join a group, so you can get an idea of the discussion's general tone and level. Some folks use the term *lurking* to describe this act of observing discussions. Lurking is just fine; it may be exactly what you want.

When Everything Goes Well, the Group or List Is Managed by Software
Most of the management of a list—tasks such as adding new members or subscribers and removing members who choose to leave (or *unsubscribe* from) a list—is handled automatically by software. A program runs on the computer that serves as the host system for the list. The software maintains the files associated with the list and responds to commands from the membership. As a member of a list, you usually can retrieve archives of past discussions or obtain a list of the current members. These requests for service are handled by commands you send to an email address, called the *administrative address*, which passes the command on to the software managing the list. Because these requests are satisfied automatically by a computer program, the requests need to be in a specific form that the software can understand.

Know the Difference between the Group or List Address and the Administrative Address
When you're a member of a list, you need to know two addresses, and you need to know when to use them.

1. The address of the group, sometimes called the *list address* or *group address*, is what you'll use to communicate with the group. When you send email to this address, the mail is delivered to all group members.

2. The address you use to request services or to give commands to the software managing the list is sometimes called the administrative address. With this address, you can subscribe, unsubscribe, receive several messages as one email as a digest, retrieve a list of members, request archives, and so on. This is the same address you use to join the list.

It's easy to make a mistake and confuse the two addresses. If you send a request to the wrong address, a member of the list will usually remind you of the correct address. If you send a message that's passed on to the managing software but was meant for the members of the list, you'll usually get a reply back indicating that the message wasn't in the proper form.

Each Group Has a Name

The name of a discussion group is usually part of the group address. Here are some examples:

- One list about noncommercial aspects of photography is called photo-l. The list address is **photo-l@csuohio.edu**.

- One list used for announcing new or changed Web sites and other resources is *net-happenings*. Messages are submitted to the moderator who then passes them onto the group. The messages are labeled with a category such as "BOOK," "COMP," "K12," or "SOFT." *Net-happenings* is a service of Internet Scout Project in the Computer Sciences Department at the University of Wisconsin-Madison and the list moderator, Gleason Sackman. The list address is **net-happenings@cs.wisc.edu**.

- One of several lists used for practicing working with a discussion group is called test-listproc. The list address is **test-listproc@listproc.mwc.edu**.

Remember: Never Send a Message to Join (Subscribe) or Leave (Unsubscribe) a Discussion Group or List Address

Use the administrative address for these. Below, we'll point out some ways of finding the names and administrative address for a list.

Getting Help and a List of All Commands

Send the simple message

help

to the administrative address. You'll receive by email a list of all the commands you can use with the list. This works for any type of software managing a list. Some lists also provide a reference card (via email) that explains all the commands. If the managing software is Listserv, send the command

info refcard

to the administrative address of any system that supports Listserv.

Ways to Join, Contribute to, and Leave a List

Several different types of software are used to manage a mailing list. The most common ones are Listproc, Listserv, and Majordomo. Most of the commands are the same for the different types of lists. We'll work with one type, Listproc, and use the list test-listproc. This list was set up for people to learn about using a discussion group, so feel free to practice with it.

Here is the information you'll need about this list:

List Name: test-listproc
Administrative Address: **listproc@listproc.mwc.edu**
List Address: **test-listproc@listproc.mwc.edu**

To Join a Discussion Group or Mailing List, Send Email to the Group's Administrative Address

The body of the message should contain only *subscribe,* the list name, and your full name. Using the example, you would send email to **listproc@listproc.mwc.edu** with the following message:

> **subscribe test-listproc *your-full-name***

For example: **subscribe test-listproc chris athana**

What Happens Next?

If you've used the proper address and the list still exists, you ought to receive a response from the software managing the list within a few minutes, hours, or maybe a day or two. The response will either say that you've succeeded in subscribing or ask you to confirm your request to join. To confirm, you usually just have to reply *OK* in the body of the message. If the address isn't correct, you'll probably have your mail returned as undeliverable, or you'll get email saying that the list doesn't exist at the site. Look up the address once more and try again.

Let's assume you've succeeded in subscribing and that you've received email about the list. In most cases, you'll receive an email message welcoming you to the list. *Save the welcome message!* It usually contains important information about unsubscribing from the list and about other commands with which you can request services. It also tells you how to get more information. Once again, save that message! You'll probably need that message in the future.

To Leave, or Unsubscribe from, a Discussion Group or Mailing List, Send Email to the Group's Administrative Address

The body of the message should contain only *unsubscribe* and the list name. Using the example, send email with the message

> **unsubscribe test-listproc**

to **listproc@listproc.mwc.edu**. Some lists allow you to unsubscribe from or send a message to the list only from the same address you used to join or subscribe to the list. That is a strict policy; some users access the Internet from a network of systems, and they may not always be using a system with the same address. If you have problems sending or posting a message to a list, try posting a message from the address you used to subscribe to the list.

To Post a Message, Question, or Reply to the Group, Send Email to the List Address

Using the example, send email to **test-listproc@listproc.mwc.edu**.

One Other Address You May Need Is That of the List Owner or Moderator

You'll probably get that address with your "welcome to the group" email. Write to the owner or moderator when you have questions about the nature of the list, if you think something is wrong with the list, or if you want to volunteer to help the moderator. Send special requests or questions you can't resolve to the address of the list owner, administrator, or moderator.

Ways to Find and Retrieve a Group's Archives

Most discussion groups keep archives of the messages posted to the group. They sometimes contain useful information, so you'll want to know how to gain access to and retrieve files from the archives.

Searching the Archives by Topic

Many lists are *archived*, which means that collections of past messages are kept so that members can retrieve them. These are usually categorized only by date, so it may be difficult to search the archives for messages related to a specific subject. Some progress is being made in this area. The University of Buffalo, for example, provides a forms-based interface for searching the archives of the lists hosted there. Use the URL **http://listserv.acsu.buffalo.edu/archives** to try this service. Another site to try is *NetSpace Mailing List WWW Gateway* (LWGate), **http://www.netspace.org/cgi-bin/lwgate**. Some lists also keep FAQ collections about the topics discussed on the list and other files useful to the group members. To get a list of the names of the files in a group's archives, send email containing the command

index *list-name*

to the list's administrative address. Substitute the name of a specific list for *list-name*. For example, to get the archives for the list test-listproc, send the message

index test-listproc

to **listproc@listproc.mwc.edu**.

Retrieving a File from the Archives

The previous section described how to acquire a list of files. You can retrieve any of the files in the list's archives by sending a command to the administrative address. You might see something on the list you'd like to retrieve, or someone may tell you about a file in a list's archives. The precise commands you use may differ from one type of list to another. For specific instructions, send the command **help get** or **help send**.

You either use the command **get** or the command **send** to retrieve a file from an archive (depending on the type of software that manages the list). Include the list name and the file name. Table 11.1 lists the commands to use for each type of software, along with an example. Substitute the specific list name for *list-name* and the specific name of a file for *file-name*. Remember to send your commands to the administrative address for the list.

List Type:	Listproc
Command:	**get *list-name file-name***
Example:	**get photo-l photo-l.sep-25**

List Type:	Listserv
Command:	**get *file-name file-type list-name***
Example:	**get aou101 txt birdchat**

Note: Listserv software requires you to specify the type of file. This file type appears in the list of files in the archive.

List Type:	Majordomo
Command:	**get *list-name file-name***
Example:	**get f-costume topics**

Table 11.1—Retrieving a File

Ways to Locate Discussion Groups about Specific Topics

There are more than 70,000 email discussion groups, with more added each day. A group named new-list carries announcements of new lists. To join the list, send email to **listserv@listserv.nodak.edu** with the message

sub new-list *your-first-name your-last-name*

The number of discussion groups and the rate of increase make it almost impossible to keep current with the available groups. It's probably more important (and certainly more practical) for you to know how to find the names of lists that focus on a topic that interests you.

You're likely to hear about some lists from your correspondents on the Internet. You'll also see lists mentioned if you read Usenet news. To find lists by topic you can use one of the following services. When you use these services you type in a keyword or key phrase, and the software searches a database of list names, descriptions, and associated addresses. You'll get the information you need (list name, address for joining the list, address of the list, address of the list owner or moderator, etc.) for the appropriate lists.

❋ Catalist, **http://www.lsoft.com/lists/listref.html**, a catalog of listserv lists. Catalist allows you to search or browse the database of the more than 10,000 lists that use Listserv.

❋ Liszt: Searchable Directory of Email Discussion Groups, **http://www.liszt.com**.

❋ Publicly Available Mailing Lists, **http:/www.neosoft.com /internet/paml**. This Web page, which Stephanie de Silva maintains, has names, addresses, and information about lists available through the Internet.

❋ Reference.COM, **http://www.reference.com**. This Web site lets you search for discussion groups, Usenet newsgroups, and archives of selected discussion groups and newsgroups.

❋ The lists section of tile.net, **http://tile.net/lists**. Click on the hyperlink **Search** to search for lists. In this case, the search brings back all the information you need to join a list, along with hyperlinks that make it easy to subscribe.

In the next activity, you will practice using one of these services. When you use such services, you will type in a keyword or key phrase, and the software will search a database of list names, descriptions, and associated addresses. You'll obtain the information you need (list name, address for joining the list, address of the list, address of the list owner or moderator, and so forth) for the appropriate list.

❋Tip

Remember that the Web is always changing and that your results may differ from those shown here. Don't let this confuse you. The activities are meant to teach you fundamental skills. These skills don't change, even though the number of results obtained or the actual screens may look very different.

❋

Activity 11.1   Finding a Discussion Group

Overview

One of the most comprehensive collections of discussion groups that's been designed for searching through the Web is Liszt: Searchable Directory of Email Discussion Groups. The site is relatively easy to use and gives useful information about the discussion groups in its database. We can search by typing one or more keywords into a form. Liszt allows for Boolean expressions and has instructions clearly available through hyperlinks on the home page. A subject guide to selected discussion groups is also on the home page.

We'll follow these steps:

1. Go to the home page for Liszt.
2. Search for discussion groups dealing with business ethics.
3. Browse the results to learn about the discussion groups found and how to subscribe.

Details

We assume that the Web browser is already started and is available on the screen.

1   Go to the home page for Liszt.

⚡*Do It!* Click on the location field, type **http://www.liszt.com**, and press **Enter**.

Using this URL, we go to the home page for Liszt. A portion of it appears in Figure 11.1. Like other Web or Internet services, Liszt regularly improves or expands its service. The Web pages you see may be different from these, but they will be similar.

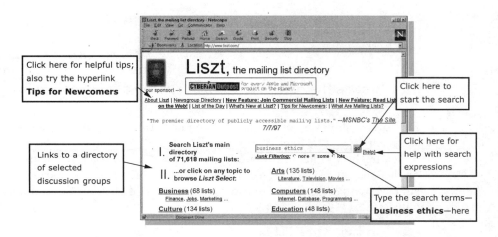

Figure 11.1—Liszt Home Page: Searchable Directory—Email Discussion Groups

2   Search for discussion groups dealing with business ethics.

Liszt's home page has a place next to the button labeled **go** for you to type keywords or a Boolean expression. You can also use an asterisk (*) in a word as a wildcard. Click on the hyperlink **help** for complete information about search expressions. Here, we'll type **business ethics**, as shown in Figure 11.1 and we'll click on **go**.

⚡*Do It!* Type **business ethics** in the form and click on the **go** button.

By default, Liszt searches its database for descriptions of discussion groups that contain *all* the terms. A portion of the Web page showing the search results appears in Figure 11.2. Your results may not be exactly the same as these.

Chapter 11

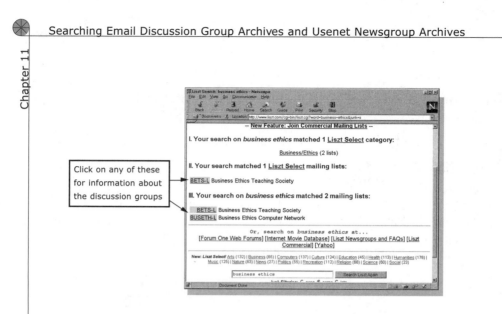

Figure 11.2—Search Results Using "business ethics"

Click on any of these for information about the discussion groups

3 Browse the results to learn about the discussion groups found and how to subscribe.

Figure 11.2 shows a portion of the Web page that holds the search results. Although this book does not reflect it, the results are color coded, indicating how much information is available. (The system is explained on the Web page.) Clicking on any of the results brings up an intermediate page with links for more information. We will click on the second one, **BUSETH-L**.

❋*Do It!* Click on **BUSETH-L**.

Figure 11.3 shows a portion of the page that appears.

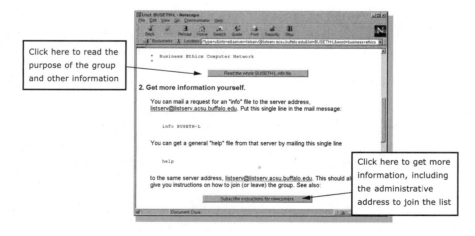

Click here to read the purpose of the group and other information

Click here to get more information, including the administrative address to join the list

Figure 11.3—Web Page about the Discussion Group BUSETH-L

Clicking on the button labeled **Read the whole BUSETH-L info file** brings up the same thing you would see if you sent a request for information to the administrative address. This information usually includes a statement of the list's purpose and the name and email of the person in charge of the list. Clicking on the button labeled **Subscribe instructions for newcomers** yields that information, including the administrative and list addresses for the discussion group.

Do It! Click on **Subscribe instructions for newcomers**.

Figure 11.4 shows a portion of the Web page that tells how to subscribe to the list. Read through the information on the Web page before subscribing to any list. There's more useful information further down the Web page.

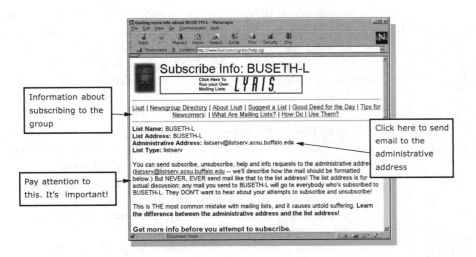

Figure 11.4—Information about Subscribing to the Discussion Group

You can join the list at this point by clicking on the hyperlink that represents the administrative address. When you have finished with this page, press the **Back** icon in the command toolbar to return to the list of discussion groups in Figure 11.2. Look at these lists, or search for more.

End of Activity 11.1

Activity 11.1 showed how to use Liszt to search for discussion groups based on a topic. For each group found, we could have retrieved information about the group and ways of subscribing. Liszt has discussion groups or mailing lists arranged into a subject directory. In addition, Liszt makes it possible to search for Usenet newsgroups. You can use the other search services mentioned in this chapter in a similar manner.

Sources of Information About
Discussion Groups on the Internet

For more information on discussion groups, you may want to consult the following Web resources.

❋ "How to Find an Interesting Mailing List," by Arno Wouters, identifies and describes several sources of lists and other information related to discussion groups and mailing lists. The document also contains some information about using Internet services to search for lists. The file containing the document is available by email and on the Web. To retrieve it by email, send the message

get new-list wouters f = mail

to **listserv@vm1.nodak.edu**. One URL to use when you retrieve it is **http://http2.sils.umich.edu/ ~ lou/wouters**.

❋ *Discussion Lists: Mailing List Manager Commands*, by James Milles, contains information about working with discussion lists, interest groups, and mailing lists. The file is available by email and on the Web. To retrieve it by email, send the message

get mailser cmd nettrain

to **listserv@listserv.acsu.buffalo.edu**. To retrieve it through your Web browser, use the URL **http://lawwww .cwru.edu/cwrulaw/facility/milles/mailser.html**.

❋ The directory entries at Yahoo! deal with mailing lists. If you use the URL **http://www.yahoo.com/text/ computers_and_internet/internet/mailing_lists** or otherwise go to the Yahoo! directory section "Top: Computers and Internet:Internet:Mailing Lists," it takes you to a collection of hyperlinks that give information about using discussion groups or mailing lists.

❋ *Email Discussion Groups/Lists—Resources,* **http://www .webcom.com/impulse/list.html**. This page has a summary of the basic commands for discussion groups and links to lots of other resources related to searching, finding, and using discussion groups or lists.

❋ *Internet Mailing Lists Guides and Resources,* **http://www .nlc-bnc.ca/ifla/I/training/listserv/lists.htm**. This comprehensive resource is maintained by the International Federation of Library Associations and Institutions.

Usenet Newsgroups

Another popular means of exchanging information is Usenet news. Sometimes it's called Netnews or just News. Usenet was originally created for people to share information on Unix computer systems. Now it's available to everyone through the Internet. You use Usenet news for the same reasons you use a discussion group—to exchange or read information about specific topics. Here are some ways in which Usenet news differs from discussion groups:

- With Usenet, you have access to many groups. Some sites carry hundreds or thousands of groups; others carry fewer groups or different ones, depending on the policies and procedures of that site.

- Messages to a group aren't exchanged between individuals using email; instead, messages are passed from one computer system to another.

- You use software called a newsreader to read and manage the news (articles) available through Usenet, instead of using your email program or sending commands to a remote site.

Usenet is similar to a bulletin board system (BBS), except that most bulletin boards are managed by one person and are run on one computer. With Usenet, there is no single person, group, or computer system in charge. All the computers and people that are part of Usenet support and manage it. Usenet is a community with its own generally agreed-upon code of etiquette. Involving thousands of computers, hundreds of thousands of messages, and millions of people, Usenet is very large. Once you become comfortable with Usenet news, you'll find that it helps you find answers to different types of questions, get help on a variety of topics, and keep up with what's happening in the world and on the Internet.

In addition to the articles in each newsgroup, many newsgroups have FAQs available. Volunteers maintain these collections of commonly asked questions. Several search engines give the option of searching archives of articles or postings to Usenet news. Later in this chapter, we'll take a detailed look at using one of those—Deja News.

We don't have space here to go into all of the details of using a newsreader and working with Usenet news. We will give enough information to get you started, but for more information, you ought to look at Chapter 5 of *Learning to Use the World Wide Web* by Ernest Ackermann or visit the Web page **http://www.mwc.edu/ernie/Lrn-web05.html**. Here's a list of the topics we'll cover in this section.

- Essential Information about Usenet News
- Organization of Usenet Articles

❋ FAQs

❋ Ways to Locate Newsgroups about Specific Topics

❋ Sources of Information about Usenet News on the Web

❋ Ways to Search Usenet Archives

Essential Information about Usenet News

It's not easy to define Usenet because it's so diverse. Instead, we'll try to describe how it works and how to work with it.

❋ Usenet is made up of computers and people that agree to exchange or pass on collections of files.

❋ Each file is called an article and belongs to one or more newsgroups. There are newsgroups on all sorts of topics. Some are specialized or technical groups, such as **comp.protocols.tcp-ip.domains** (topics related to Internet domain style names). Some deal with recreational activities, such as **rec.outdoors.fishing.saltwater** (topics dealing with saltwater fishing). One, **news.newusers.questions**, is dedicated to questions from new Usenet users.

❋ People at each site can read the articles, ignore them, save or print them, respond to them through email to their authors, or *post* their own articles. *Posting* means composing either an original article or a response to someone else's article, and then passing it on to Usenet.

❋ There are thousands of computers involved, and an estimated fifteen to thirty million people participate in Usenet news.

❋ In order to read or post articles, you need to use a program called a *newsreader*. A Web browser often has a newsreader included with it. Netscape Communicator, for example, includes a newsreader you access by selecting **Collabra Discussion Groups** from the pulldown menu **Communicator** in the menu bar. Communicator provides at least three other ways of getting there—if you want to use it, click on **Help** in the menu bar and check the appropriate sections of the online guide.

Organization of Usenet Articles

All articles belong to one or more newsgroups. Many newsgroups have a charter that states the newsgroup's purpose and the topics discussed within the group. An article is either a follow-up to another article or a new piece on a different topic. Posting an article to more than one newsgroup is called *cross-posting*.

Threads

There may be several articles on the same topic in a single newsgroup. If each of the articles has been posted as a follow-up to some original article, then the collection of these articles is called a *thread*. You'll probably want to have the articles arranged into threads. It really helps to have this sort of organization for a collection of articles in a particular group. You follow a thread by reading the articles one after the other.

Newsgroup Categories

Each newsgroup has a name that gives the topic or topics for the articles in the group. The groups are arranged or named according to a hierarchy. When you look at the name of a newsgroup, you'll see that it usually consists of several words or names separated by periods. The first part of the newsgroup name is the name of the top level of the hierarchy. As you move to the right, the names become more specific. Here is a nice long name: **rec.music.makers.guitar.acoustic**.

Starting on the left, **rec** is the name of a top-level group; it includes groups that deal with artistic activities, hobbies, or recreational activities. The next name, **music**, indicates that the group addresses topics related to music. The next, **makers**, tells you that this group is about performing or playing music, rather than reviewing music or collecting recordings, for instance. The last two names, **guitar** and **acoustic**, pretty much nail this down as dealing with discussions or other matters related to playing or performing acoustic guitars. To give you a feeling for this naming scheme, here are a few other groups in the **rec.music** hierarchy: **rec.music.makers.piano**, **rec.music.makers.percussion**, **rec.music.marketplace**, **rec.music.reggae**, **rec.music.reviews**.

There are more than 16,000 newsgroups and several major, top-level categories. We won't list the categories here. A complete list, *Master List of Newsgroup Hierarchies,* **http://home.magmacom.com/ ~leisen/master_list.html**, is maintained by Lewis S. Eisen.

What Is a Newsreader?

A newsreader is the interface between a user and the news itself. It allows you to go through the newsgroups one at a time. Once you've chosen a newsgroup, it allows you to deal with the articles it contains. The newsreader keeps track of the newsgroups you read regularly, as well as the articles you've read in each newsgroup.

Here, we'll talk about using the newsreader included with Netscape Navigator. There are a number of other newsreaders available. Three highly recommended ones are Free Agent, NewsXpress, and WinVN. To read about each of these, open the URLs **http://www.forteinc.com/ forte/agent/freagent.htm**, **http://www.malch.com/nxfaq.html**, and **http://www.ksc.nasa.gov/software/winvn/winvn.html**.

Starting the Newsreader. In Netscape Communicator, click on **Communicator** in the menu bar, and then select **Collabra Discussion**

Groups from the pulldown menu. (Check the online help from your browser for other ways to access Usenet news.) A window called the **Netscape Message Center** will open, listing your mailboxes and the name of the news server or servers. Click on the name of a news server to see a list of newsgroups. (If neither newsgroups nor a news server is listed, then you need to check that the entries in the Groups Server category in Preferences are set properly—that's covered below.) Then select a newsgroup. If you want one that isn't listed, you can subscribe to it by clicking on **File** in the menu bar and selecting **Subscribe to Discussion Groups**; these menus are available only in the Netscape Message Center window or the Netscape Discussion window. It may take some time—perhaps a few minutes—for the list of all newsgroups to be retrieved from the server. You'll see them in the newsgroup pane as documents and folders; the folders represent the categories in the Usenet hierarchy. Select the ones you'd like to look at regularly by clicking on the box to the right of a newsgroup's name. Once you select a group, a Netscape Discussion window pops up. It has two panes: one for the list of articles and the other to read a selected article. An example of that window is shown in Figure 11.5.

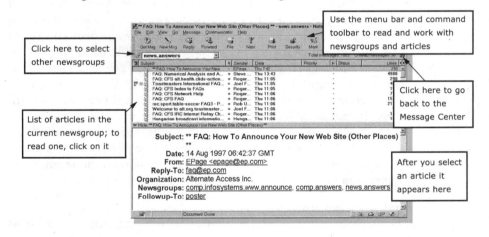

Figure 11.5—Sample Netscape Discussion Window—Newsgroup news.answers

Setting News Preferences. The computer you're using needs to contact a news server (sometimes called an NNTP server) to receive and interact with Usenet news. ***NNTP*** stands for ***Network News Transport Protocol***, the protocol used to exchange Usenet news. Your newsreader needs to have the Internet name or IP address of that computer. This may already be set on your computer, or you may have received instructions about how to do it. If you can read Usenet news, then you don't have to worry about this. Instructions for setting news preferences are first, click on **Edit** in the menu bar, then click on **Preferences**, select the category **Mail & Groups**, and finally select **Groups Server**. It's crucial that this is filled in correctly so you can work with

Usenet news. The pane just below **Discussion groups (news) server** must be filled in with the Internet domain name or IP address of a news server. The name or IP address that goes here depends on how your Internet services are provided. You should get this information from your Internet provider or someone in your organization. You probably won't have to change other entries in this panel.

Posting an Article. Posting an article means composing an article—a message, a question, a great discourse on some deep philosophical or extremely important political topic—and distributing it to a newsgroup. Usenet is a fairly open forum. There is no central control, and there are thousands of newsgroups on all sorts of topics. But some topics are not appropriate for some newsgroups. Before you post anything, read "A Primer on How to Work with the Usenet Community," **ftp://rtfm.mit .edu/pub/usenet/news.announce.newusers/A_Primer_on_How_to _Work_With_the_Usenet_Community**. You'll also find this posted in **news.announce.newusers**. When using Netscape News (Collabra), you post a new article to the current newsgroup by clicking on the icon labeled **New Msg** in the command toolbar. To post a follow-up to the current article, click on the icon labeled **Reply**.

FAQs

Many newsgroups have volunteers who put together and maintain a collection of common questions and answers. Most newsgroups have FAQs that are very informative and useful. You can find them posted either in the newsgroup for which the FAQ was created or posted to **news.answers**.

Be sure to consult the FAQ for information before you post a question to a newsgroup. It may be embarrassing for you if you post a question to a newsgroup and receive several replies (or follow-ups) letting you (and everyone else reading the newsgroup) know that you should read the FAQ before asking other questions. It could also be annoying to other group members to see questions that could be answered with a little research beforehand. Some places to look for FAQs (other than the newsgroup) are **ftp://rtfm.mit.edu/pub/usenet-by-group** and **http://www.cis.ohio-state.edu/hypertext/faq/usenet/top.html**.

Ways to Locate Newsgroups about Specific Topics

There are thousands of newsgroups. How can you find out which to read or which ones even exist? To find the groups your server carries, you select **Show All Newsgroups** from the pulldown menu **Options** in the menu bar of the news window.

There are several lists of newsgroups available through Usenet. Keep your eye on the newsgroups **news.answers**, **news.lists**, or **news.groups** so you can read or save these listings when they appear (usually monthly).

Some Web sites enable you to search for newsgroups. For the sites we'll mention, use the URL to bring up a Web page. On that page, enter a keyword or phrase, click on a button labeled **Search**, and then work with the results. In both cases, if a newsgroup is found, click on its name to read articles in the group. Whether that's successful depends on whether your news server is set up to receive that newsgroup. Here are the Web sites:

❋ Deja News, **http://www.dejanews.com**. Deja News was originally developed to read archives of news articles. It also allows keyword searching for newsgroups.

❋ Liszt of Newsgroups, **http://www.liszt.com/news**. The searching results in a list of newsgroups, each with a brief description.

❋ Reference.COM, **http://www.reference.com**. Searching here brings up a list of newsgroups. Clicking on a name gives a brief description of the groups and the average number of articles posted daily.

❋ tile.net/news, **http://tile.net/news**. Searching here brings up a list of newsgroups. Clicking on the name of a newsgroup takes you to a page that tells about the amount of articles posted daily and what percentage of Usenet sites carry the group. There's also a form that lets you search Lycos using newsgroup names as keywords.

Sources of Information about Usenet News on the Web

Some of the best information about Usenet is part of Usenet itself. There are several newsgroups that a beginning or infrequent user should browse. These newsgroups include information about Usenet, FAQ lists for Usenet and several newsgroups, and articles that will help you use Usenet. Here are the newsgroups:

news.announce.newgroups	This newsgroup has articles about forming and announcing new newsgroups. It's the place to obtain the lists of all newsgroups.
news.announce.newusers	This newsgroup has explanatory and important articles for new or infrequent Usenet users.
news.answers	This newsgroup is where periodic Usenet postings are put. The periodic postings are primarily FAQs. This is often the first place to look when you have a question.
news.newusers.questions	This newsgroup is dedicated to questions from new Usenet users. There is

no such thing as a "dumb question" here. You ought to browse this group to see if others have asked the same question that's been bothering you. Once you get some expertise in using Usenet, you'll want to check this group to see if you can help someone.

The articles you will want to read are posted in **news.announce .newusers**. Here's a list:

* A Primer on How to Work with the Usenet Community
* Answers to Frequently Asked Questions About Usenet
* Hints on Writing Style for Usenet
* How to Find the Right Place to Post (FAQ)
* Rules for Posting to Usenet
* Usenet Software: History and Sources
* Welcome to news.newusers.questions
* What Is Usenet?

Links to these articles and other resources about Usenet are available on several different Web pages. Here's a short list of some good general resources:

Chapter 5 Usenet—Reading and Writing the News
http://www.mwc.edu/ernie/Lrn-web05.html
Usenet Info Center Launch Pad
http://sunsite.unc.edu/usenet-i/home.html
news.newusers.questions
http://cs1.presby.edu/~jtbell/usenet

Ways to Search Usenet Archives

Several of the major search engines include options for searching Usenet news. Some of these are listed in Table 11.2.

Name	URL	Ways to Search Usenet Archives
AltaVista	**http://www.altavista. digital.com**	Select Search Usenet
Excite	**http://www.excite.com**	Select Where:Usenet Newsgroups, or Select Where:Usenet Classifieds
HotBot	**http://www.hotbot.com**	Select Search:Usenet News
Infoseek	**http://www.infoseek.com**	Select Usenet Newsgroups

Table 11.2—Search Engines that Have Options for Searching Usenet Archives

There are also a few search engines dedicated to searching archives of Usenet news. Here are two.

1. Deja News, **http://www.dejanews.com**. This was the first search engine devoted to Usenet. In addition to searching, it allows you to post articles, browse, and find newsgroups.

2. Reference.COM, **http://www.reference.com**. This allows searching for newsgroups and discussion groups. You browse and post to newsgroups only if you register (free) with Reference.COM.

Most of these keep archives of Usenet articles for six months to a year, so they're useful for finding information that's being discussed currently or relatively recently.

Now we'll do an activity in which we'll search for Usenet news articles using Deja News.

Activity 11.2 Searching Usenet News Using Deja News

Overview

To use Deja News to search for Usenet articles on a specific subject, we'll use a key phrase, and Deja News will report back a list of articles. We'll be able to read any of the articles, and we'll note the names of the newsgroups that hold the articles in case we want to read other articles in that group. We'll also see the email address of each article's author; this address is part of every article posted to Usenet. We could send email to the authors if we had questions or comments about what they wrote, thereby taking advantage of their expertise. In this activity, we'll also look at the features and options available to us when we use Deja News.

We'll search using the phrase *Appalachian banjo music.* Why? You've always been interested in music, and you like different types of music. Now you want to listen to and maybe play banjo tunes and music—specifically, Appalachian banjo music. We'll use Deja News to search Usenet news for recent articles on this topic. Here are the steps we'll follow:

1. Go to the home page for Deja News.
2. Search for articles using the phrase "Appalachian banjo music."
3. Browse the results.
4. Note the names of newsgroups and authors' email addresses.
5. Explore some of Deja News's features.

Details

We assume you've already started the Web browser.

1   **Go to the home page for Deja News.**

✳Do It! Click on the location field, type **http://www.dejanews.com**, and press Enter.

Using this URL, we go to the home page for Deja News. The home page with the search terms entered appears in Figure 11.6. Remember, though, that Deja News may have changed its home page when you try this.

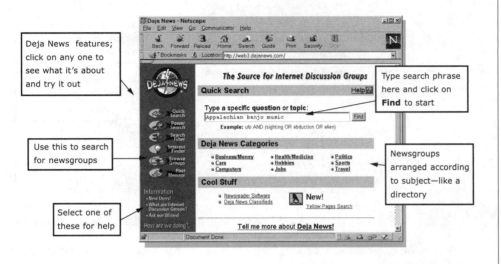

Figure 11.6—Deja News Home Page

2   Search for articles using the phrase **Appalachian banjo music**.

Do It! Type **Appalachian banjo music** just below **Type a specific question or topic** and click on the button labeled **Find**.

In Figure 11.6, we've shown where to type in the search phrase and where to click to start the search. You'll find that a "quick search" looks for articles that contain *all* the words in your search phrase, but not necessarily in the order you've typed them. Click on the hyperlink **Quick Search** to get some more information about how Deja News works. To search using other features or options, click on **Power Search**.

3   Browse the results.

Figure 11.7 shows the search results. At almost any other time, we would expect different results, so use these as a guide. There are 16 relevant articles retrieved from the Deja News database; if there are more, they appear 20 per page. For each article in the list, we have the date it was posted, its "score," the subject, the newsgroup to which it was posted, and the author's email address. For reasons of privacy, we've purposely not shown the entire email address of each author here. It does appear on the Web page, however. After the list of articles, near the bottom of the Web page (not shown here), there is a form to let you search again or refine your search. There is also a link to a larger database holding older articles. Click on the hyperlink **Help** for more information about interpreting the results.

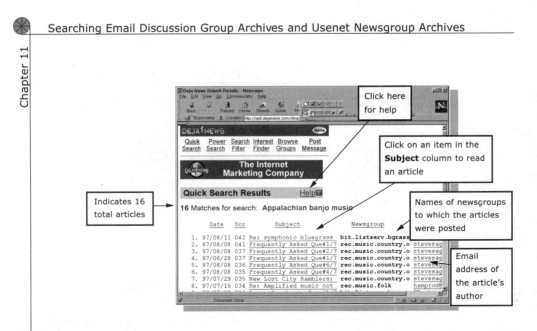

Figure 11.7—Results of Search Using the Phrase "Appalachian banjo music"

We can read any article, but let's look at the second one to be specific; it's a portion of a FAQ.

✳Do It! Click on the subject listed for the second article in Figure 11.7.

Clicking on the subject in the listing brings up a Web page that contains the article, as shown in Figure 11.8. This happens to be a portion of the FAQ for the newsgroup **rec.music.country.old-time**.

*Figure 11.8—Portion of the FAQ for the Newsgroup **rec.music.country.old-time***

If you want to read the article, then you can view this Web page in the same way as any other. You click on the icons across the top of the Web page to reach other articles in the current list or to return to the list.

Clicking on the icon labeled **View Thread** brings up a Web page in which the thread of related articles are represented as hyperlinks. You can read them and follow the discussion of a topic on Usenet. Try this with another article in the list, one that's not a FAQ. It's likely to be more lively.

Clicking on **Post Message** lets you post an article to the newsgroup of the current article. This comes with appropriate instruction and reminders from Deja News about appropriate uses of the service and etiquette. If you register with Deja News, you give them your email address and they send you a small file that identifies you to them whenever you contact their service. There's no fee involved, and Deja News says it won't use or sell your email address for commercial purposes.

Now we're going to return to the list of articles we found during the search.

✳Do It) Click on the icon labeled **Current Results**.

From there, you can read other items in the hit list or take note of the newsgroups and addresses listed.

4   Note the names of newsgroups and authors' email addresses.

Clicking on the icon labeled **Current Results** takes us back to the list of articles shown in Figure 11.7.

The listing includes the name of a newsgroup for each article. We can use our newsreader to browse any of these groups. Another way is to click on **Browse Groups** and then enter the name of a newsgroup in the frame on the page that appears. You'll get a list of newsgroups. Clicking on any one lets you browse the articles in the same way as you can with the current hit list.

The listing also includes the email address of each article's author. Clicking on the address brings up the Deja News "author profile" for that person. That's a summary of information from the Deja News database about articles posted by this author, including the number of articles and the names of newsgroups in which you can find this author's articles. You might want to save the author's email address to write for more information about your topic.

5   Explore some of Deja News's features.

Deja News has several features with which you can set criteria for searching and for reading or posting articles to Usenet. They're listed either along the top or down the side of each page. We won't go into all the details here. Instead, we'll list and briefly describe some of the features.

Deja News lists features that let you browse the Usenet hierarchies of newsgroups, read articles in a newsgroup, and post articles. Once you register, Deja News offers you many of the features of a newsreader.

There are several features for searching. We used **Quick Search** above. There's also **Power Search**, with which you can specify whether to use all or any of the terms in the search phrase, Boolean search expressions, the dates of articles, the number of items listed per page, and other options. You can also set a **Search Filter** that obtains matches only from specific newsgroups, authors, dates, and subjects. **Interest Finder** lets you search by topic and gives you a directory of newsgroups arranged by subject. **Browse Groups** lets you read messages from groups in which the newsgroups are arranged according to the Usenet hierarchy. You have to go through three Web pages, for example, to reach the articles in the group **rec.bicycles.off-road**. You can type the name of a newsgroup here to see if Deja News makes it available. There's also a link to a page from which you can post articles to Usenet.

The features page also contains links to extensive help in using and explaining Deja News and Usenet. One page that is worthy to note is "Search Language Help," **http://www.dejanews.com/help/help_lang .shtml**. That page gives all the details you need to form a search phrase using Boolean expressions, wildcards, parentheses, or near searching (when you want to look for words next to or near each other). You can also use expressions that allow for context searching, such as searching for a specific word in the newsgroup name or author field.

Take some time to explore these features. There's lots of useful information available about Usenet and lots of ways to use Deja News.

_____ End of Activity 11.2 _____

In Activity 11.2, we used Deja News to search the archives of Usenet articles. When you type in a keyword or phrase, a list of articles appears. You then select articles to read. You can also click on the author's address to see what other articles by that author are available. Deja News offers several other services, including a search for newsgroups and a good introduction to using Usenet, reading news, and posting articles.

Etiquette in a Discussion Group or a Usenet Newsgroup

Rules	Reasons
Spend some time getting to know the group.	When you first join a discussion group, take a little time to see the types of items discussed and the tone of the discussion. Read the articles in a newsgroup before posting. You may also find that the questions you have are currently being answered.
Write easy-to-read messages.	The material you write to the group should be grammatically correct, concise, and thoughtful. It's a lot easier to read something that is well written, and many group members may not have the time to deal with long-winded, incorrect writing that does not make a clear point. If the posting must go on for several screens, it's a good idea to summarize it and to invite others to ask you for more information.
When responding to something from the group, include only the pertinent portions of the original message.	Let's say that a group member starts a discussion and writes something about 40 lines long. You want to respond, but only to one portion of it. In your follow-up message, include just the portion that's relevant to your response.
When you ask group members any questions, post a summary of the responses you receive.	With this summary, everyone in the group benefits from the responses to your question. Naturally, this applies only if you get several responses and if the answers to the question are of general interest.

Posting or sending a message to the group is a public act.

Everything you write to the group may be distributed to all group members or posted worldwide through Usenet. If the group is moderated, your messages may be read first by the moderator and then passed on to the group. If you're working with a list that isn't moderated (most aren't), your messages go directly to the group. Don't embarrass yourself. A friend, relative, or supervisor may also be a member of the list.

Group members are people like yourself and need to be treated with respect and courtesy.

Respond to messages as if you were talking face-to-face. A member may be from a different culture, may not be familiar with your language, and may have different views and values from your own. Don't respond too quickly to something that upsets you, and don't criticize others too hastily or without good reason. It's better to think before you write than to be sorry afterward.

Avoid sarcasm and be careful with humor.

You are communicating entirely by your words. You don't have the benefit of facial expressions, body language, or tone of voice to let somebody know you're only kidding when you make a sarcastic remark. Group members will appreciate well-written, humorous pieces or responses, but be sure your writing will be interpreted that way.

Think about whether a response to a message should go to the group or to an individual.

Messages to the list should be of general interest. They may be requests on your part for advice or for help in solving a problem. You'll know the email address of the person who made the original request, and you can send a response to that person if it's appropriate.

If you're working with an email discussion group, remember to send messages going to the entire group to the list address. Send commands or requests to be interpreted by the software managing the list to the administrative address.

Over the years, several documents have been developed about proper Usenet etiquette. These are regularly posted in **news.announce .newusers**, **news.answers**, or **news.newusers.questions**. Here is a list of some that you ought to read:

- ❋ A Primer on How to Work with the Usenet Community
- ❋ Emily Postnews Answers Your Questions on Netiquette
- ❋ Hints on Writing Style for Usenet
- ❋ How to Find the Right Place to Post (FAQ)
- ❋ Please Read Before Posting
- ❋ Rules for Posting to Usenet
- ❋ A Weekly FAQ on Test Postings

Summary

Both email discussion groups and Usenet news are examples of group communication on the Internet. They're useful and valuable as sources of information for two reasons:

- ❋ The people who participate in them are a ready source of information.
- ❋ The groups often keep archives of files, FAQs, and periodic postings that can sometimes be retrieved and searched.

Email discussion group members communicate via email, with messages broadcast to all group members. In Usenet, people communicate via articles or files that are posted to Usenet newsgroups. Anyone with access to Usenet can access the articles. In both cases, messages can be read, replied to, or posted.

Several thousand discussion groups are available and active on the Internet. They may be called mailing lists, discussion groups, Listserv lists, or interest groups. Regardless of the name, each consists of a group of members anywhere on the Internet. This way, communities or collections of people can discuss items related to a common topic, find information about the topic, make announcements to the group, or ask questions and receive help from other group members. The large number of lists guarantees a wide range of topics. The groups are particularly useful to people who want to discuss issues with a large or diverse group. The groups extend any resources beyond a local site.

You send messages to the list by using the list address. Commands and requests for service are usually sent to the administrative address. For example, the list photo-l, which deals with a variety of topics related to photography, has **photo-l@csuohio.edu** as the list address and **listproc@csuohio.edu** as the administrative address. You use this second address to join a list, leave or unsubscribe from a list, request archived files from the lists, and get a list of the members of the list. Be sure you use the correct address when you communicate with the group or list. Most lists also have a person designated as the list owner, list administrator, or moderator. That person is in charge of the list, and you send him or her email if you have problems using the list or questions about the operation of the list. Some lists are moderated. Messages sent to the list first go to the moderator, who decides whether to pass the messages on to all group members.

The lists can be thought of as communities of people sharing common interests. There are generally accepted rules of behavior or etiquette for list members. These include providing appropriate, thoughtful, and concise messages to the group, providing a summary of the responses received in answer to a question, and communicating with other group members in a civil and respectful manner.

Several "lists of lists" and other documents related to using discussion groups are available as part of the World Wide Web. There are also services on the Web to find discussion groups and to search or retrieve groups' archives.

The news is a collection of messages called articles. Each is designated as belonging to one or more newsgroups. These articles are passed from one computer system to another. There are several thousand newsgroups, all arranged into categories. Users at a site can usually select any of the groups that are available and can often reply to, follow up, or post an article. Some estimates put the number of participants at more than forty million worldwide.

Usenet is a community of users helping each other and exchanging opinions. A code of behavior has developed. The rules are, of course, voluntary, but users are expected to obtain a copy of some articles about working with Usenet and to follow the rules. Several newsgroups carry regular postings of articles meant to inform the Usenet community. These are often found in the groups **news.announce.newgroups**, **news.announce.newusers**, and **news.answers**.

You use software called a newsreader to work with the articles and newsgroups in Usenet news. Several different newsreaders are available. The one you use will depend on your preferences and what's available on the system with which you access Usenet.

You'll probably find Usenet a valuable resource for information on a wide array of topics. It can be enjoyable to read and participate in the discussions. Services are available on the World Wide Web to search for newsgroups related to a specific topic and to search for articles that contain keywords or phrases.

Selected Terms Introduced in This Chapter

administrative address	interest group
archived	list address
article	listserv
cross-posting	lurking
discussion group	mailing list
group address	moderator

Network News Transport
   Protocol (NNTP)
newsgroup
newsreader
post

subscribe
thread
unsubscribe
Usenet

Exercises and Projects

Email Discussion Groups

1. Practice subscribing to or joining an email discussion group.
    One you can use for practice is test-listproc with the adminis-
    trative address **listproc@listproc.mwc.edu**. Send email to the
    administrative address with the message
    subscribe test-listproc *your-full-name*

2. Search for email discussion groups. Several sites on the World
    Wide Web let you search for and find the names of discussion
    groups. Using the ones below, come up with a list of three dis-
    cussion groups, along with the administrative address and list
    address for each.

    *   CataList
        http://www.lsoft.com/lists/listref.html
    *   Liszt, the mailing list directory
        http://www.liszt.com
    *   Publicly Available Mailing Lists
        http://www.neosoft.com/internet/paml
    *   Reference.COM
        http://www.reference.com
    *   tile.net/lists
        http://tile.net/lists

3. Using one of the discussion groups you found in the previous
    exercise, use each of the services listed above to search for that
    list. For each service, briefly describe the type of information it
    had available. Is there one service you prefer over the others? If
    so, why?

4. Search the archives of a discussion group in the following ways:
    a. Search using Web-based services at LWGate. Open the Web
        page for *NetSpace Mailing List WWW Gateway (LWGate)*,
        http://www.netspace.org/cgi-bin/lwgate. Take some
        time to become familiar with the facilities and services avail-
        able at that site. When you're ready, click on the hyperlink
        Search the NetSpace LWGate. That brings up a search
        form that you use to select a list. Type **medicine** and click
        on the **search** button. Now select any list, but you might
        want to try CBR-MED (Case-Based Reasoning in Medicine),

as it allows you to search its archives. Type in a phrase. The archives will be searched and a reply will be emailed to you. What did you receive? What file or files did you retrieve?

b. Search using the Web-based services at **listserv.acsu .buffalo.edu**. Open the Web page "List Archives at LISTSERV, ACSU.BUFFALO.EDU," **http://listserv.acsu .buffalo.edu/archives**. You can search the list archives of any of the discussion groups listed. When you search in the list archives, the results are displayed in the browser's window. Select a list based on your interests, and become familiar with searching the archives. What list did you select? What search phrase and options did you use for the search? What were the results?

Usenet News

5. Can you access Usenet news either by using your Web browser, as in the case of Netscape, or through some other program?

a. If so, what are the names of some of the newsgroups available?

b. What's in the newsgroup **comp.internet.net-happenings**?

6. Search the FAQs by using the Web page at Ohio State, **http:// www.cis.ohio-state.edu/hypertext/faq/usenet/top.html**.

a. Use the search phrase *restaurants vegetarian*. What were the results? Retrieve one of the FAQs.

b. Use the search phrase *restaurants for vegetarian*. You'll see you get many more results. Why do you think that's true?

c. Search the FAQs by either using the search form or going through the list. Retrieve a FAQ about something that you find interesting but that isn't associated with your work. Do the same for a FAQ that is related to your work. Which ones did you retrieve? Did you find them useful? Explain.

7. Search for newsgroups.

a. Use the search form for finding newsgroups at Liszt, **http://www.liszt.com/news**. Search for newsgroups dealing with each of these topics: child health, pet health, and mental health. What newsgroups did you find? What information does Liszt give about a newsgroup? Is it useful?

b. Use the search form for Usenet newsgroups at tile.net, **http://tile.net/news**. Search for newsgroups that deal with each of these topics: child health, pet health, and mental health. What newsgroups did you find? What information does Liszt give about a newsgroup? Is it useful?

c. Compare Liszt and tile.net in terms of using these services for keyword searching. Which do you prefer? Why?

8. As in Activity 11.2, use Deja News, **http://www.dejanews .com**, to search archives of newsgroups.

a. Search the archives for articles using the search phrase *Nobel prize literature*. Read the first five articles listed. What are they about? Which one do you find the most interesting? Explain.

b. For the article you found most interesting in Part a, click on **Author Profile** when the article is in the browser's window. What do you find out about the author?

c. Find an article that has a thread associated with it. A good choice would be one for which the subject starts with *Re:*. Select the article and click on the icon **View Thread**. How many articles are associated with the one you selected? Follow the thread of group discussion on the topic by selecting articles. Were any new issues or questions raised? Was anything resolved?

d. Now search the archives for articles on a subject you choose. Read some of the articles. If you think it's appropriate—according to the "Etiquette in a Discussion Group or Usenet Newsgroup" section in this chapter—post a follow-up message to the group or email a reply to the author for one of the articles you've found.

9. Use the URL **http://web3.dejanews.com/info/policy.shtml** to read the information Deja News has on its policies.

a. What do they say is the purpose of the author profile? Do you feel the author profile is proper? Do you feel that it is an invasion of privacy?

b. How can you prevent articles you write from appearing in the archives?

c. Summarize Deja News's position on Usenet and privacy.

10. Try some of the other Web facilities for searching Usenet archives. For each of the following, search with the phrase *Nobel prize literature*. Compare all the results, and compare each Web facility to Deja News.

a. Use AltaVista, **http://www.altavista.digital.com**, and select **Usenet** in the frame labeled **Search**.

b. Use Infoseek, **http://www.infoseek.com**, and select **Usenet** in the frame next to the button labeled **seek**.

c. Use Reference.COM, **http://www.reference.com**, and select **Usenet & Mailing List Archive** in the frame labeled **Search in**.

Chapter 12

Evaluating Information
Found on the WWW

As you've seen in previous chapters, you can find information on the World Wide Web on all sorts of topics. You've also seen that the information can come from different types of sources, such as online magazines and other periodicals, news agencies, government agencies, companies, nonprofit organizations, educational institutions, and individuals. Some of the information is available through email discussion groups, FTP, and Usenet newsgroups, but most of the information takes the form of Web pages. Information abounds; it's possible for anyone with the appropriate computer, the right software, and an Internet connection to make information available on the Web.

When we access or retrieve something on the World Wide Web, we need to decide whether the information is useful, reliable, and appropriate for our purposes. This is particularly true when we're using Web or Internet resources for research, which should be based on accurate, trustworthy, and authoritative sources. Of course, we need to assess the veracity of information from other sources as well, including printed material, broadcast media, and communication with individuals. Information that appears in print often has been reviewed and checked for correctness before publication, but outlandish stories, incorrect information, and hoaxes have certainly been published. Information on radio and television is usually checked for accuracy, but that's not always the case.

In this chapter, we'll look at some issues related to evaluating resources on the World Wide Web. The chapter will include these sections:
* Reasons to Evaluate
* Guidelines for Evaluation
* Information on the World Wide Web about Evaluating Resources

Reasons to Evaluate

We use the information we've found on the Internet or Web for a variety of purposes. Sometimes we use it for entertainment, recreation, or casual conversation. When we use the information for research, we have to be sure the information is reliable and authoritative. That puts us in the position of having to verify information and make judgments about whether it is appropriate. We need to think critically, as opposed to using information just because it's available to us or published on the Web.

In some situations, we don't have to do that work on our own. Some information is screened before it comes to us. When we retrieve information from an academic or research library, either by using the Web or by visiting in person, we rely on professional librarians who have evaluated and selected the material. Information in a database that's been prepared by a scholarly or commercial organization is often evaluated and checked for correctness before it's made available. Articles and reports published by scholarly organizations, research labs, and government agencies often go through an independent review process before being published. Some librarians and other information specialists have established virtual libraries on the Web where they review, evaluate, and list reliable sources of information on the World Wide Web. Here are some of those virtual libraries:

* Argus Clearinghouse
  http://www.clearinghouse.net
* Internet Public Library
  http://www.ipl.org
* Librarians' Index to the Internet
  http://sunsite.berkeley.edu/internetindex

It's useful to visit these sites to find information that's been reviewed by someone else. Still, when you deal with any information you find on the Web or in a library, it is up to you to be skeptical about it and to assess whether it's appropriate for your purposes. For example, if you want information before buying a CD player, then product announcements from manufacturers will give you some data, but the announcements will probably not be the right source for impartial brand comparisons. If you're researching techniques for advertising electronic consumer products, then the advertisements might be good resource material; if you are writing about the physics involved in producing sound from audio CDs, however, these ads may not be authoritative sources.

The nature of the Internet and the World Wide Web makes it easy for almost anyone to create and disperse information. People also have considerable freedom and variety in the formats with which they publish information on the Web. A person who wants to sell a product or disseminate propaganda can make material appear to be part of a well-researched report. A quotation attributed to English dramatist Thomas Dekker (1572?–1632?), a contemporary of William Shakespeare, is particularly applicable here: "A mask of gold hides all deformities." Thinking critically about information and its sources means being able to separate facts from opinions. We have to be able to verify information and know its source, we have to determine whether the facts are current, and we need to know why someone offered the data at all. After considering these issues, we can decide whether the information is appropriate for our purposes.

Regardless of where you access information—whether from virtual resources, such as the Web or the Internet, or from a real resource, such as a library or a database—don't be shy about asking a librarian or some other information specialist for help in evaluating it. Librarians, particularly reference librarians, have lots of experience and are very good at determining whether a resource is relevant, authoritative, and appropriate for your research needs. Additionally, you may want to check some of the guides we've listed in the section "Information on the World Wide Web about Evaluating Resources."

Guidelines for Evaluation

In this section, we will first list guidelines or criteria that you can use for evaluating information. Then, we will indicate how you can apply these guidelines to documents and other information that you retrieve from the Web or Internet.

Guidelines

To help you develop guidelines for evaluating sources, we will pose the sorts of questions you might ask when assessing information.

Who Is the Author or Institution?

❋ If an individual has written the resource, does it give biographical information about the author? That information could include any of the following: educational and other credentials, occupational position, institutional affiliation, and address.

❋ If an institution has written the resource, does it give information about that institution, including its purpose, history, and street address?

❋ Have you seen the author's or institution's name cited in other sources or bibliographies?

❋ What clues does the URL give you about a source's authority? A tilde (~) in the Web page's URL usually indicates that it is a personal page, rather than part of an institutional Web site. Also, make a mental note of the domain section of the URL, as follows:

❋ **.edu** educational (Can be anything from serious research to zany student pages.)

❋ **.gov** governmental (Is usually dependable.)

❋ **.com** commercial (May be trying to sell a product.)

❋ **.net** network (May provide services to commercial or individual customers.)

❋ **.org** organization (Is a nonprofit institution; may be biased.)

❋ If the page is part of a larger institution's Web site, does the institution appear to filter the information that appears at its site? Was the information screened somehow before it was put on the Web?

How Current Is the Information?

❋ Is there a date on the Web page that indicates when the page was placed on the Web?

❋ Is it clear when the page was last updated?

❋ Is some of the information obviously out of date?

❋ Does the page creator mention how frequently the material is updated?

Who Is the Audience?

❋ Is the Web page intended for the general public, or is it meant for scholars, practitioners, children, and so forth? Is the audience clearly stated?

❋ Does the Web page meet the needs of its stated audience?

Is the Content Accurate and Objective?

❋ Are there political, ideological, cultural, religious, or institutional biases?

❋ Is the content intended to be a brief overview of the information or an in-depth analysis?

❋ If the information is opinion, is this clearly stated?

❋ If information has been copied from other sources, is this acknowledged? Are there footnotes, if necessary?

What Is the Purpose of the Information?

❋ Is the purpose of the information to inform, explain, persuade, market a product, or advocate a cause?

❋ Is the purpose clearly stated?

❋ Does the resource fulfill the stated purpose?

Discussion and Tips

We will now discuss the criteria we have listed and indicate how you can verify information obtained from the Internet.

Who Is the Author or Institution?

If you're not familiar with the author or institution responsible for producing the information, you'll need to do some checking to determine whether the source is reliable and authoritative. You can't consider a resource reliable if you don't know who wrote it or what institution published it. If a Web page doesn't contain the name of the author or the institution, and if there are no hyperlinks to Web pages that give that information, then you should be suspicious of its content.

> **❋ Tip**
>
> Look for the name of the author or institution at the top or bottom of a Web page.

Being suspicious doesn't mean that you must disqualify the information. For example, the Web page "The VENONA Project," **http://www.nsa.gov:8080/docs/venona/ddir.html**, doesn't say who has sponsored the information. But if you look at the URL, you can see that the information is provided through the Web server with the Internet domain name **www.nsa.gov**. This indicates that it's supplied by a government organization, which means that it's usually suitable for research purposes. We'll do some more sleuthing in Activity 12.1, and we'll start with this Web page.

On the other hand, if the information is provided by a commercial site (its URL will contain **.com**, as in **www.greatplace.com**) or if it's on a personal Web page (its URL will contain a tilde, as in **mary.mwc.edu/~ernie**), then we may need to do further checking.

> **❋ Tip**
>
> To find out about the sponsor, go to the home page for the site that hosts the information.

Regardless of whether the Web page contains the sponsor's name, we can investigate further by looking for more information about the author or institution. For example, consider the document "CDT's Children's Privacy Issues Page," **http://www.cdt.org/privacy/children/index.html**. Looking at that Web page, we can see that the Center for Democracy and Telecommunications (CDT) has made it available. There are hyperlinks from that Web page to the home page for CDT. You can follow the hyperlinks to find out more about the CDT, or you can go to the home page by typing the URL **http://www.cdt.org**

in the location panel and pressing **Enter**. When you can't find your way to a home page or to other information, try using a search engine, directory, or other service to search the Web or Usenet.

❄Tip

To find further information about the institution or author, use a search engine to see what related information is available on the Web.

❄Tip

Use Deja News or another tool to search Usenet archives. That way, you can find other information about the author or institution. If an individual is the author, you can see what sorts of articles they've posted on Usenet.

If you're searching with Deja News, use the URL **http://www.dejanews.com**. Type the author's name in the search panel. If a list of articles comes up, click on the author's name in the Author column to read articles that the author has posted to Usenet. To read more about working with Deja News's Author Profile Help, use the URL **http://www.dejanews.com/help/help_ap.shtml**.

❄Tip

Remember that the Web is always changing and that your results may differ from those shown here. Don't let this confuse you. The activities are meant to teach you fundamental skills. These skills don't change, even though the number of results obtained or the actual screens may look very different.

Activity 12.1   Using a URL and Search Engine to Investigate a Resource

Overview

In this activity, we'll seek further information about a resource we've come across on the Web. Let's assume that we've found or retrieved the Web page shown in Figure 12.1. Its title is the VENONA Project, but it doesn't contain the name of the author or institution providing the information. To find more information, we will do the following steps:

1. Use parts of the URL to find further information about this resource.
2. Use a search engine to learn more about this resource.

Details

1   Use parts of the URL to find further information about this resource.

Here is the URL for the Web page shown in Figure 12.1:

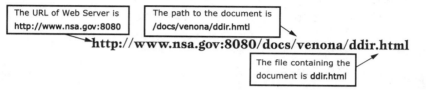

The URL of Web Server is
http://www.nsa.gov:8080

The path to the document is
/docs/venona/ddir.hmtl

http://www.nsa.gov:8080/docs/venona/ddir.html

The file containing the
document is **ddir.html**

We can see that the URL for the Web server that makes this document available is **http://www.nsa.gov:8080**. The path to the document is **docs/venona/ddir.html**. Finally, the name of the file containing the document is **ddir.html**.

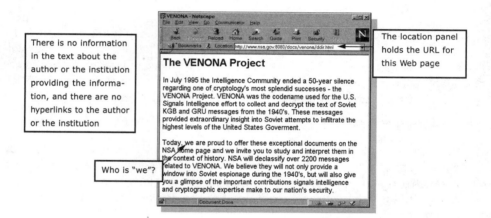

There is no information in the text about the author or the institution providing the information, and there are no hyperlinks to the author or the institution

The location panel holds the URL for this Web page

Who is "we"?

The VENONA Project

In July 1995 the Intelligence Community ended a 50-year silence regarding one of cryptology's most splendid successes - the VENONA Project. VENONA was the codename used for the U.S. Signals Intelligence effort to collect and decrypt the text of Soviet KGB and GRU messages from the 1940's. These messages provided extraordinary insight into Soviet attempts to infiltrate the highest levels of the United States Goverment.

Today, we are proud to offer these exceptional documents on the NSA Home page and we invite you to study and interpret them in the context of history. NSA will declassify over 2200 messages related to VENONA. We believe they will not only provide a window into Soviet espionage during the 1940's, but will also give you a glimpse of the important contributions signals intelligence and cryptographic expertise make to our nation's security.

Figure 12.1—Web Page for the VENONA Project

To obtain more information about the document, we'll first use the URL without the file name. That may give us a Web page with links to this document and to other related Web pages.

✻*Do It!* In the location panel, type **http://www.nsa.gov:8080**, and press **Enter**.

Another way to get the same result is to click on the location panel to the right of the URL. The panel will turn blue. Click again so that the cursor is just to the right of the URL (just past "html"). Use **Backspace** to erase characters until only **http://www.nsa.gov:8080** is left, and press **Enter**. The Web page in Figure 12.2 will be displayed in a few seconds.

Figure 12.2—Home Page for the National Security Agency

We see that the URL **http://www.nsa.gov:8080** has led us to the home page of the National Security Agency. The NSA has therefore made the information available. What is the NSA? The seal on the page leads us to believe it's an agency of the U.S. government. To find out more, we'll click on the hyperlink labeled **About NSA**.

Do It! Click on the hyperlink **About NSA**.

Clicking on the hyperlink brings up a Web page describing the NSA; we won't show it here. We read there that the NSA is a part of the U.S. Department of Defense. That indicates that the information we find at this site is authoritative.

Now we will try to find out more about the VENONA Project.

Do It! Click on the toolbar button labeled **Back** to return to the NSA's home page.

You should be back at the home page.

Do It! Click on the hyperlink **The VENONA Project**.

Clicking on this hyperlink takes us to the Web page for the project. We show a portion of this Web page in Figure 12.3. The page starts with such a large colorful image that you might mistake it for a commercial site advertising a movie.

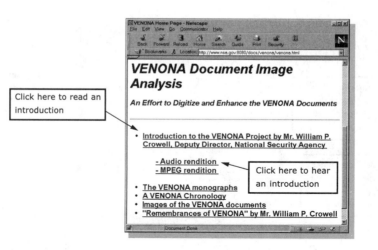

Figure 12.3—Home Page for the VENONA Project

We'll follow the first hyperlink to see what we can find out about the VENONA Project.

Do It! Click on the hyperlink **Introduction to the VENONA Project by Mr. William P. Crowell, Former Deputy Director, National Security Agency**.

Following that link takes us to the Web page we were first considering—Figure 12.1! Now we know the author, William P. Crowell, and the sponsoring institution, the National Security Agency. You can follow the hyperlinks on the VENONA home page (Figure 12.3) to find out more about the project.

2   Use a search engine to learn more about this resource.

First, we'll see what information we can find on William P. Crowell. We're going to use HotBot because it has the option to treat the search phrase as a name.

Do It! Go to HotBot's home page by typing **www.hotbot.com** in the location panel and pressing **Enter**.

We are now at HotBot's home page, as Figure 12.4 reflects. Enter the search query by following the next instructions.

Do It! Using the pulldown menu indicated in Figure 12.4, set the option to search for **the person**.

Do It! Type **William P. Crowell** in the search phrase panel.

Do It! Select **brief descriptions** as a display option.

We'll select this display option here, just so we can show more results listed in Figure 12.5.

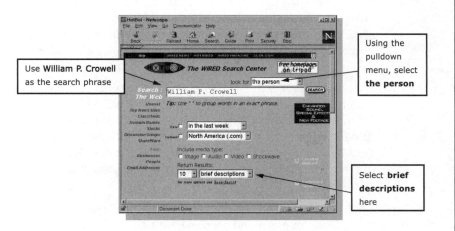

Figure 12.4—HotBot's Home Page with the Search Query Entered

Once the options and search phrase are set, we're ready for HotBot to search its database.

✳️ *Do It!* Click on **Search**.

Our results partly appear in Figure 12.5. Yours may differ.

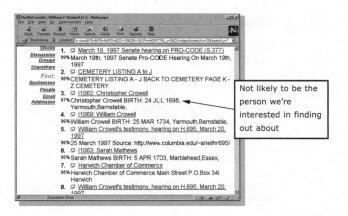

Figure 12.5—A Portion of HotBot's Search Results

Using HotBot to search for the person William P. Crowell gives several results. Some of the results listed in Figure 12.5 deal with people who lived in the seventeenth and eighteenth century, so they wouldn't be appropriate because the VENONA Project took place during the 1940s. You may wonder why the Web pages titled "1062: Christopher Crowell" and "1063: Sarah Mathews" turned up at all. Remember that search engines usually index the full text of a Web page. Therefore it's enough for the name William Crowell to appear anywhere on a Web page for the page to turn up in the list of results. Another item is a listing for a chamber of commerce, so it doesn't apply to the NSA's work. Checking some of the other links, we confirm that William Crowley was Deputy Director of the NSA and that he's particularly well qualified in the areas of cryptography and electronic intelligence gathering.

Now we'll use search engines to see if there's other information on the Web related to the VENONA Project. This will help us to evaluate the information available through the NSA. First we'll search HotBot's index for information about VENONA, and then we'll search using WebCrawler. Both use full-text indexing for documents, but they use different methods for relevancy ranking, so we're likely to see different results.

✸(Do It!) Go to HotBot's home page by typing **www.hotbot.com** in the location panel and pressing Enter.

✸(Do It!) Using the pulldown menu to the right of the word **look for**, as shown in Figure 12.4, set the option to search for all the words, any of the words, or exact phrase.

We have to use one of those search options since our search phrase is a word, *VENONA,* not a person's name.

✸(Do It!) Type **VENONA** in the panel as the search phrase.

✸(Do It!) Select **brief descriptions** as a display option.

Once the options and search phrase are set, we're ready for HotBot to search its database.

✸(Do It!) Click on **Search**.

The first few search results appear in Figure 12.6. Most of the links go to information provided by NSA. You'll want to check the first link, **VENONA—Soviet Espionage against the US Atomic Program**, to see if it's helpful. You should examine some of the others as well.

Now we'll use WebCrawler to see what information we can find about VENONA.

✸(Do It!) Go to WebCrawler's home page by typing **www.webcrawler .com** in the location panel and pressing Enter.

✸(Do It!) Type **VENONA** in the search phrase panel.

The Web page with searching options set appears in Figure 12.7.

Figure 12.6—Results of Search for Exact Phrase "VENONA"

Figure 12.7—WebCrawler Home Page with Search Query Entered

Once the options and search phrase are set, we're ready for WebCrawler to search its database.

✳*Do It!* Click on **Search**.

The first few search results appear in Figure 12.8. If we were to follow the first two, we'd see they are linked to the NSA, but there are several others listed that don't go directly to the NSA.

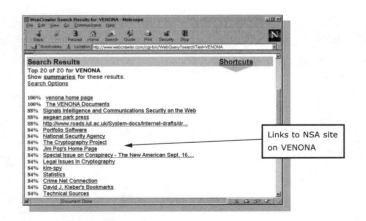

Figure 12.8—WebCrawler Search Results

Figure 12.8—WebCrawler Search Results

We leave it to you to explore and read some of the other links. Remember to think critically about and evaluate the information you find.

End of Activity 12.1

In Activity 12.1, we started with a Web page and used its URL to find the organization that published the Web page and to whom we could attribute the text in the Web page. We used HotBot to find information about the author. Then we used HotBot and WebCrawler to find additional information about the topic.

How Current Is the Information?

In some cases, it's important to know whether the information you're using is up-to-date. This is particularly true when you're using information that contains statistics. If the information is of the type that is frequently updated—for example, a FAQ or a news report—then try to be sure you have the most recent information. Check the date on the Web page, and if it's more than a month old, search for a more recent version.

A well-designed Web page indicates when the information was last updated, often at the top or bottom of the page. If that date isn't displayed, you may be able to find the date on which the Web page was last modified on the server. If you're using Netscape Navigator, click on **View** in the menu bar and select **Page Info**. That will tell you the date of the last modification to the file. If you're using Microsoft Internet Explorer, put the cursor on the Web page in the browser window. Then click the right mouse button and select **Properties** to obtain the same information. We show this in detail in Chapter 13.

❄ Tip

Check the top and bottom of a Web page for the date on which the information was last modified. If no date is present, look at **Page Info** if you're using Netscape, or **Properties** if you're using Microsoft Internet Explorer.

Email messages and Usenet news articles usually have the date on which the message was posted. This information is part of the message or it's in the header information, as shown here.

Date posted →

```
Subject: Re: Agape on the Internet: A Preach
From: Ernest C Ackermann <ernie@paprika.mwc.edu>
Date: 1997/03/30
Message-Id: <199703301552.KAA13690@eagle>
Newsgroups: bit.listserv.nettrain
```

Who Is the Audience?

Web pages are sometimes written to give information to a specific group: the general public, researchers and scholars, professionals in a specific field, children, potential customers, or others. Try to determine the intended audience, as that may have an impact on whether the information is relevant or appropriate for your purpose. Suppose you are preparing a report on sustainable forest management. An appropriate information resource, whether in print or on the Web, is one that is written for your level of expertise and for the expertise of your audience. The Web page "Forest Service Mission, Vision, and Guiding Principles," United States Department of Agriculture Forest Service, **http://www.fs.fed .us/intro/mvgp.html**, might be useful for a general overview of the issues and principles involved in forest management. On the other hand, the Web page "Alternatives to Methyl Bromide: Research Needs for California," **http://www.cdpr.ca.gov/docs/dprdocs/methbrom/mb4chg .htm**, is more appropriate for a specialized audience.

Is the Content Accurate and Objective?

Determining whether information is accurate and objective is easy if we can find corroborating sources for it. Before using information that makes claims or contains statistics, we need to be sure they can be substantiated. In the best situations, claims or statistics on Web pages are supported by original research or by hyperlinks or footnotes to the primary sources of the information. Sometimes, however, one has to check several sources to verify the accuracy and objectivity of a source. This can involve a lot of work, but it's worth it, because you end up with solid, factual results.

Take, for example, the following quotation:

Women make up more than half of the undergraduate enrollments in higher education for every racial/ethnic group in the United States. Among black students, women comprise more than 60 percent of the undergraduate enrollments. Foreign students are the exception; women comprise less than one-half of foreign undergraduate enrollments (45 percent). Students with disabilities make up about 6 percent of all students enrolled in postsecondary institutions; 5.7 percent of all students who major in S&E fields and 6.6 percent of students who major in non-S&E fields (NCES, 1995a).

This quotation has been taken from "Undergraduate Science and Engineering Students and Degrees," **http://www.nsf.gov/sbe/srs/ seind96/ch2_undr.htm#p1**, which the National Science Foundation published in December 1996. It may be viewed as accurate and objective, because it is part of a report that underwent a prepublication review by the National Science Foundation, an independent U.S. government agency. Furthermore, there is a citation—NCES, 1995a—for the statistics. Checking the included footnotes tells us that NCES is an abbreviation for the National Center for Educational Statistics. Enrollment figures are available through a hyperlink (not shown here) in the report.

The following statements are presented for contrast to show information that would likely be less reliable:

We're losing our freedom—with the government's help. Right now one out every four Americans legally owns a firearm, and yet the government is spending more than one-third of its budget to ban firearms. In 1996, only 1.25 percent of all deaths were attributed to the use of guns, but guns were used in over 83 percent of all crimes. The government is going after the wrong group. Most crimes—74.56 percent—are committed by illegal minorities. The government wastes billions of dollars ($2.7 billion in 1995) to keep guns away from Americans, but studies show that money would be better spent in supporting firearm safety training and increasing the size and effectiveness of the immigration service.

This is unreliable for several reasons; the statistics aren't corroborated, the language suggests an ideological bias, and none of the claims are supported by citations or footnotes. We wrote this to give a contrasting example; it doesn't represent our views or those of the publisher.

What Is the Purpose of the Information?

When you're evaluating information that you've found on the World Wide Web, the Internet, or in print, you need to consider its purpose. Information on the Web can be produced in a variety of formats and styles, and the appearance sometimes gives a clue to its intent. You probably know that information in a glossy brochure is usually produced with the intent of selling a product, concept, or cause. Similarly, Web pages aimed to market something are often designed in a clever way to catch our attention and emphasize a product. For example, see the home page for Ford in the United States at **http://www.ford.com/us**. Since there's considerable freedom in publishing information on the Web and the Internet, it's not too difficult to mask the purpose of information through its appearance. A person who wants to sell a product or promote a cause can present information in a format that makes it appear to be part of a well-researched report. It's your job, then, to concentrate on the content and to determine the purpose of the information so you'll feel comfortable using it for research or other purposes.

Activity 12.2 Applying Guidelines to Evaluate a Resource

Overview

In this activity, we'll apply the guidelines for evaluating information on the Web. If we were researching a topic related to teaching or distance education, we might come across a Web page called "Tools For Teaching: The World Wide Web and a Web Browser," **http://www.mwc.edu/ ~ ernie/facacad/WWW-Teaching.html**. This is the Web page we'll evaluate in this activity. We'll go through the guidelines by answering each of the following questions:

1. Who is the author or institution?
2. How current is the information?
3. Who is the audience?
4. Is the content accurate and objective?
5. What is the purpose of the information?

In this activity, we'll be able to obtain answers in a rather direct way. It's not always so straightforward, but this is meant to be a demonstration. In your own work, you may have to be more persistent and discerning. Don't be shy about asking for help when you need it.

Details

We'll assume your Web browser is already started. You get to the Web page discussed in this activity by typing in its URL, **http:// www.mwc.edu/ ~ ernie/facacad/WWW-Teaching.html**.

1   Who is the author or institution?

Figure 12.9 shows the beginning of the Web page we're considering. The author's name is at both the beginning and end of the page, as

shown in Figures 12.9 and 12.10. We can see that the author is affiliated with the computer science department at Mary Washington College.
The page has hyperlinks to the author's home page and to this college.
If we viewed his home page, we'd see that he's written at least two
books on using the Internet and World Wide Web and he has developed
several Web pages for the courses he teaches. If we followed the links
Department of Computer Science and **Mary Washington College**,
we'd see that he is a professor of computer science at a state-supported
college in Virginia. These help establish the author's credentials, which
influences our assessment of the resource we're considering.

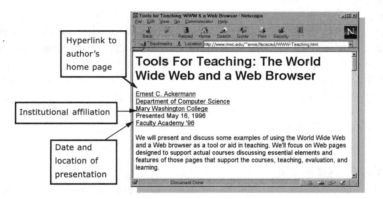

Figure 12.9—Beginning of "Tools For Teaching" Web Page

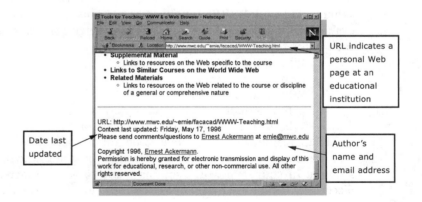

Figure 12.10—End of "Tools For Teaching" Web Page

We can search the Web for other information about the author or for
hyperlinks to resources that cite his work. One way is to use HotBot, as
we did in Activity 12.1, to search for the person Ernest Ackermann.
When this was tried, HotBot returned more than 300 results. Many
referred to pages he had written, several related to courses he teaches,
and more than 50 were from other sources citing his work.

Another way is to use Deja News to see what work of his is available on Usenet. The second activity in Chapter 11 showed you how to use Deja News to find information on a topic. You could find any newsgroups to which Ackermann posts messages by searching the Deja News archives; you would use **Ernest Ackermann** as the search string. Your results would likely be extremely different from any we would show here, because by default, Deja News searches a collection of articles that's at most a few months old. You could select an option to bring up entries going back a few years, but that's likely to give you postings in a wide variety of newsgroups. It may help to use Deja News's Author Profile for a summary of the names of newsgroups to which the author contributes. We'll try that now.

✳*Do It!* Go to the home page for Deja News by typing **http://www .dejanews.com** in the location field and pressing Enter.

✳*Do It!* Type **Ernest Ackermann** in the search form.

✳*Do It!* Click on the button labeled **Find**.

This starts the search using the Deja News database. Results will be displayed in a format similar to that shown in Figure 12.11. The first three articles were not posted by Ackermann, so we've hidden the addresses in Figure 12.11.

	Date	Scr	Subject	Newsgroup	Author	
Click on the author's	05/02	027	Re: bauer/landbauer	soc.genealogy.germa		Click on the
name to see the Deja	04/30	027	Re: Automatic positionin	comp.infosystems.ww		Subject to read
News Author Profile	04/22	025	Re: Automatic positionin	comp.infosystems.ww		the article
	04/20	029	Re: Changing Subject lin	comp.infosystems.ww	Ernest Ackermann	
	04/20	029	Re: How do I show HTML-c	comp.infosystems.ww	Ernest Ackermann	
	04/20	027	Re: Automatic positioning of	comp.infosystems.ww	Ernest Ackermann	
	10/02	025	Re: How to Destroy a Lis	bit.listserv.nettra	Ernest C Ackerm	

Figure 12.11—Excerpt of Deja News Search Results

To read any of the articles, click on the entry in the **Subject** column. For a summary of the newsgroups to which Ackermann has posted messages, click on the entry in the **Author** column. Reading some of the articles he's written and noting the newsgroups to which he posts may give you some clues about whether to consider his work as credible.

In this case, we see that Ackermann has posted several of the articles listed. Reading them, we can see that the first few are posted to **comp.infosys.www.authoring.html** and that the last is posted to **bit.listserv.nettrain**. If we think it's necessary, we can obtain more information about the newsgroups themselves by using tile.net or Liszt, as described in Chapter 11. The first group deals with writing or authoring Web pages, and anyone may post to it. Nettrain addresses issues related to training or teaching others to use the Internet and World Wide Web. It's a moderated group, so the posting goes through an initial screening to see if it's appropriate.

Searching for postings to Usenet tells us that the author is interested in writing Web pages and teaching and training people to use the Internet and the Web. This gives us a positive indication about the resource we've found, as it deals with a related topic—using the Web for instruction.

We can use the URL as a clue to a source's authority. In this case, the URL is **http://www.wmc.edu/∼ernie/facacad/WWW-Teaching .html**. The domain name **www.mwc.edu** ends with **.edu**, so the site hosting the page is an educational institution in the United States. If this were an educational institution in another country, the domain name would end with a two-letter abbreviation for the country and probably wouldn't have edu in its name. The tilde (∼) in the URL indicates that this page was most likely posted by the author, rather than being a Web page officially posted by the institution. Therefore, the URL alone tells us that this resource was published on the Web by an individual at an educational institution in the United States. To find out more, the best bet is to visit the Web site. Visiting the site with URL **http:// www.mwc.edu** and following appropriate hyperlinks would tell us that the institution is a liberal arts, state-supported college in Virginia. Since the Web resource deals with teaching, it seems appropriate for it to be available at such a site.

2   How current is the information?

In Figure 12.9, we see that the material about teaching with the Web was presented on May 16, 1996, and in Figure 12.10, we see that it was last updated on May 17, 1996. Any information about a specific technology may be relevant for about two years after the last update. Information related to the contents of Web pages or the teaching practices and methods applicable to teaching with the Web will probably be relevant for more than two years after the date of publication.

3   Who is the audience?

In Figure 12.9 we see the hyperlink **Faculty Academy '96**. Following that link takes us to a document holding the proceedings of Faculty Academy '96, which was held at Mary Washington College in Fredericksburg, Virginia. Reading through the proceedings, we see that the resource we're considering was presented at a conference about using technology in the instructional program at an educational institution. From this information and from reading the resource we're considering, we see that the audience consists of educators who want to use technology, specifically the World Wide Web, to support instruction.

4   Is the content accurate and objective?

As we read the Web page we're considering, we see that the language is not inflammatory. It is, in fact, rather objective. It lists several references, which may be checked to corroborate the information present. It also provides links to other Web resources on the same topic. We can conclude that the information presented is accurate and objective.

5   What is the purpose of the information?

The page states that it relates to using the World Wide Web and a Web browser to teach. Reading the Web page, which contains recommendations for using the Web as an instructional tool, we see that this is the case.

Conclusion

The Web page we're considering was written by a college professor with experience related to the topic. It's relatively current. Furthermore, it was presented at a conference related to using technology in instruction. We may conclude that it is an authoritative and objective source of information.

———————————— End of Activity 12.2 ————————————

In Activity 12.2, we used the guidelines in this chapter to evaluate a Web page. We used a variety of Web and Internet resources to establish the identity and suitability of the author, and we considered other issues related to whether the information was reliable and appropriate.

Information on the World Wide Web About Evaluating Resources

There are several good resources on the World Wide Web to help you evaluate information. They give in-depth information about critically examining documents that appear on the Web or in print, and they offer other guidelines and suggestions for assessing Internet and Web resources.

Guides to Evaluating Library Resources

❋ "Evaluating What You Have Found," University of Waterloo Library

http://library.uwaterloo.ca/howto/howto28.html

❋ "How to Critically Analyze Information Sources," References Services Division of the Cornell University Library

http://urisref.library.cornell.edu/skill26.htm

Brief Guides to Evaluating Web Resources

❋ "Evaluating the Documents You Have Found on the World Wide Web," Gillian Westera

http://www.curtin.edu.au/curtin/library/staffpages/gwpersonal/senginestudy/zeval.htm

❋ "Evaluating World Wide Web Information," D. Scott Brandt, Purdue University Libraries

http://thorplus.lib.purdue.edu/library_info/instruction/gs175/1gs175e/evaluation.html

❋ "Practical Steps in Evaluating Internet Resources," Elizabeth Kirk, Milton S. Eisenhower Library, Johns Hopkins University

http://milton.mse.jhu.edu:8001/research/education/ practical.html

❋ "Significance," Iowa State University

http://www.public.iastate.edu/~CYBERSTACKS/ signif.htm

❋ "Thinking Critically about World Wide Web Resources," Esther Grassian, UCLA College Library

http://www.library.ucla.edu/libraries/college/ instruct/critical.htm

Extensive Guides to Evaluating Resources on the World Wide Web

❋ "Criteria for evaluation of Internet Information Resources," Alastair Smith, Department of Library and Information Studies, Victoria University of Wellington, New Zealand

http://www.vuw.ac.nz/~agsmith/evaln/index.htm

❋ "Evaluating information found on the Internet," Elizabeth Kirk, Milton S. Eisenhower Library, Johns Hopkins University

http://milton.mse.jhu.edu:8001/research/education/ net.html

❋ "Kathy Schrock's Guide for Educators—Critical Evaluation Surveys," Kathleen Schrock

http://www.capecod.net/schrockguide/eval.htm

❋ "Evaluating Web Resources," Jan Alexander and Marsha Tate, Wolfgram Memorial Library, Widener University

http://www.science.widener.edu/~withers/ webeval.htm

Bibliographies for Evaluating Web Resources

❋ "Evaluating Internet Resources," Nicole Auer, Virginia Polytechnic Institute and State University

http://refserver.lib.vt.edu/libinst/evaluating.html

❋ "Evaluating Web Sites for Educational Uses: Bibliography and Checklist," Carolyn Kotlas, Institute for Academic Technology

http://www.iat.unc.edu/guides/irg-49.html

❋ "Information Quality WWW Virtual Library," T. M. Ciolek

http://www.ciolek.com/WWWVL-InfoQuality.html

� "Web Evaluation Techniques: Bibliography," Jan Alexander and Marsha Tate, Wolfgram Memorial Library, Widener University

http://www.science.widener.edu/~ withers/ wbstrbib.htm

Summary

The World Wide Web gives us access to a great variety of information on many different topics. When we want to use the information or resources we find on the Web for information or research purposes, we need to exercise some care to be sure it's authentic, reliable, and authoritative. We need to be equally cautious when we use information from other sources.

Print sources that are available to us through a research or academic library have often been put through a screening process by professional librarians. There are several virtual libraries on the Web, and it's useful to consult some of these libraries when doing research. Information in such libraries tends to be evaluated before it's listed. Plus, by consulting these libraries, we can also observe how librarians and other information specialists evaluate resources.

It pays to be skeptical or critical of information we want to use. It's relatively easy to publish information on the Web, and it can be presented in such a way as to hide its intent or purpose. Generally, as we evaluate documents, we also learn more about the topic we're considering. Assessing resources, then, makes us more confident of the information and helps us become better versed in the topic.

We need to use some general guidelines or criteria when evaluating information or resources. In this vein, we should ask the following questions about whatever information we find:

- Who is the author or institution?
- How current is the information?
- Who is the audience?
- Is the content accurate and objective?
- What is the purpose of the information?

Various strategies will help us find answers to the questions. Here are some of those tips:

- Look for the name of the author or institution at the top or bottom of a Web page.
- Go to the home page for the site hosting the information to find out about the organization.
- To find further information about the institution or author, use a search engine to see what related information is available on the Web.

❋ Use Deja News or another tool to search archives of Usenet articles. This way, you can find other information about the author or institution. If an individual has written the article, you can see what other articles they've posted on Usenet.

❋ Check the top and bottom of a Web page for the date on which the information was last modified or updated. If no date is present, look at Document Info if you're using Netscape, or Properties if you're using Microsoft Internet Explorer.

There are a number of Web resources that can help us evaluate information and that discuss issues related to assessing documents.

Exercises and Projects

1. Suppose you're preparing a report on astronauts' jet packs, which are known as SAFER. One way to obtain information on them is to search the Web using HotBot, **www.hotbot.com**, with the search phrase **jet pack + safer + astronaut**, with the option set to use **all the words**.

    a. Evaluate the first two resources using the criteria given in this chapter.

    b. If the report is going to be given to a sixth-grade class, select three appropriate resources from the list returned by HotBot. Why did you choose these?

    c. If the report is going to be given to a local group of engineers interested in the NASA space program, which resources would be most appropriate? Why?

2. The URLs of the following Web sites end with **.com**, so the Web pages available may be designed to sell or market a product. Determine which of the following are designed to sell or market a product. What's the purpose of each Web page? Justify your answer based on what's on the Web page or on the site that hosts the Web page.

    ❋ "Smokers: Protect Your Health with Vitamins"
      http://www.van99.com/smokers

    ❋ "HP ScanJet 5p scanner"
      http://hpcc920.external.hp.com/peripherals/scanners/sj5p.html

    ❋ "Esprit Development Corporation: C.D. Repair"
      http://www.cdrepair.com

    ❋ "The Compact Disc Player"
      http://www.philipsmagnavox.com/product/pa332cd.html

❋ "Netscape Communicator and Netscape Navigator"
**http://home.netscape.com/comprod/products/
communicator/index.html**

❋ "What's the story on Internet Explorer 4.0?"
http://www.microsoft.com/ie/press

3. Here's a collection of Web pages dealing with the issue of sustainable forest management. Write a short evaluation of each, focusing on whether the information is presented with a bias or with the intent to advocate a cause.

❋ "Guaranteeing the future of our forests through sustainable forest management"
**http://www.nafi.com.au/faq/management/
sustainable.html**

❋ "Sierra Club Policy: Public Lands Forest Management"
http://www.sierraclub.org/policy/forest.html

❋ "SFI, Principles for Sustainable Forestry"
**http://www.afandpa.org/Forestry/
principles.html**

❋ "Owens Forest Products: Forest Facts"
http://www.hdwds.com/forest_facts.htm

4. Here are some references to Web pages that address the issues of euthanasia and assisted suicide. For each reference, use the methods and guidelines we've discussed to write a brief explanation about whether the Web page contains information that is accurate and objective. In each case, be sure to identify the organization that's sponsoring the Web page.

❋ "Harvard Risk Management Foundation: Euthanasia and Physician-assisted Suicide"
http://www.rmf.org/w3415.html

❋ "Ohio Right to Life: Euthanasia: A Case of Individual Liberty?"
http://www.ohiolife.org/euth/liberty.htm

❋ "HLI Position Paper: Euthanasia"
**http://www.hli.org/issues/euthanasia/
euthanas.html**

❋ "Statement of the National Hospice Organization Opposing the Legalization of Euthanasia and Assisted Suicide"
http://nho.org/pasposition.htm

5. Here are the home pages for two organizations involved with issues related to smoking. Looking at the Web pages and some of the information available from the pages, determine whether one is likely to provide more authentic and reliable information than the other. Justify your answer.

   ❋ "Action on Smoking and Health"

   http://ash.org

   ❋ "The National Smokers Alliance"

   http://www.speakup.org

6. Here is a list of Web documents dealing with the issue of affirmative action. Using the guidelines in this chapter for evaluating Web resources, determine whether any of these provide reliable and objective information about the issue.

   ❋ "It's Genocide"

   http://www.africa2000.com/xndx/xaffirm.htm

   ❋ Affirmative Action

   http://www.buchanan.org/afirm.html

   ❋ "Statement by the AFL-CIO Executive Council on Affirmative Action"

   http://www.aflcio.org/estatements/affirmat.htm

7. Here are several Web resources dealing with the topic of gun control. When you're evaluating a document, you need to establish the name and credentials of the author or institution providing the information. In many cases, this helps determine the level of credibility or reliability. Do that for each of the following Web resources (some also appear in print).

   ❋ "Owning and using firearms"

   http://pocari-sweat.jprc.com/ ~ karl/firearms

   ❋ "Guns in America: The Statistics"

   http://www.aclu-sc.org/gunstats.html

   ❋ "Kids & Guns"

   http://www.gunfree.org/csgv/bsc_kid.htm

   ❋ "Memorandum on Arms & Freedom"

   http://www.mcs.net/ ~ lpyleprn/ls-memo2.html

   ❋ "The Racist Roots of Gun Control"

   http://www.cs.sonoma.edu/ ~ cramerc/ racism.htm

8. One virtual library with a clear statement of how items are selected and rated is the Argus Clearinghouse, **http://www .clearinghouse.net**. Go there and find information about how

sites are rated or selected. Compare the criteria they use to those we've discussed in this chapter. How do those sets of criteria compare?

9. Several directories rate and select Web pages. One site, *Lycos Top 5%* by Lycos, **http://point.lycos.com/categories**, uses the criteria at **http://point.lycos.com/categories/criteria.html**. Read the criteria they use and compare it with those we have offered.

10. The Web page "RB Red Alert Beauty," **http://homearts.com/rb/beauty/01rabef2.htm**, published by the popular magazine *Redbook,* contains information about dealing with skin conditions. Several physicians are given as references for the information. Using the methods demonstrated in Activity 12.1, see what information you can find about the physicians. Your intention is to verify that the information is authoritative.

11. In this exercise, we'll use some of the guides for evaluating Web resources to assess documents. As a sample document, use either "CDT Children's Privacy Issues Page," **http://www.cdt .org/privacy/children/index.html**, or "Tools For Teaching: The World Wide Web and a Web Browser," **http://www.mwc .edu/ ~ ernie/facacad/WWW-Teaching.html**.

   a. Evaluate the document using the "Internet Evaluator Checklist," which is available halfway down the Web page "Evaluating World Wide Web Information," D. Scott Brandt, Purdue University Libraries, **http://thorplus.lib.purdue .edu/library_info/instruction/gs175/1gs175e/ evaluation.html**.

   b. Evaluate the document using an appropriate checklist. You can find one on the Web page "Evaluating Web Resources," Jan Alexander and Marsha Tate, Wolfgram Memorial Library, Widener University, **http:// www.science.widener.edu/ ~ withers/webeval.htm**.

13
Chapter

Citing Web and
Internet Resources

When you write a research report, it's usually necessary to cite your sources. That way, others who read your work can check the resources you've used. They can view or read the original sources to check for accuracy, to see excerpts or ideas in the context of the original piece, or to obtain more information. You'll also want to cite resources to let people know where they can find information on the Web, whether you're preparing a formal research paper or writing email to a friend.

There are several guidelines and styles for citing works correctly. No one uniform style has been adopted or is appropriate in every case. The same situation exists for citing works that appear in print; you may be expected to follow APA or MLA style, for instance. You need to adopt a style for your own work and communications, and you should check with your instructor, boss, or publisher to see what citation style is required in a work you're preparing.

In the last few years, people have been citing resources that they find on the Web or through the Internet. The styles used for citing electronic works sometimes differ from those of citations for printed works, which have a long tradition of specific formats. Citations for works in print or on the Web have a number of common elements. These include the author's name, the work's title, and the date on which the cited work was published or revised.

In this chapter, we'll discuss the formats for different types of URLs and suggest citation styles for various resources. Specifically, this chapter will contain the following sections:
* URL Formats
* Styles for Citing Web Resources
* Information on the Web about Citing Electronic Resources

Unlike citations for printed works, a citation for a Web or Internet resource must have information about how to access it. That's often indicated through the work's URL (Uniform Resource Locator). In addition to telling you where to access a work, a URL serves to retrieve the work. For that reason, we have to be precise about all the symbols in the URL and about capitalization.

There are other differences as well. Works that appear in print— such as books, essays, articles, or songs—have a definite publication date associated with them. Documents in the Web sometimes include information about when they were first created or last revised, but not always. Add to that the fact that authors can revise work on the Web at any time. It may therefore be more important to cite the date on which a work was viewed or retrieved.

URL Formats

Everything on the Web has a URL, indicating where something is located and how to access it. We've seen lots of URLs throughout this text. Here are some examples:

http://www.loc.gov	The home page for The Library of Congress
http://vlib.stanford.edu/ Overview.html	The World Wide Web Virtual Library arranged by subject
http://home.netscape.com/ excapes/search	The Web page you see when you click on **Search** in the Netscape command toolbar
ftp://ftp.jpl.nasa.gov/pub/ images/browse	The NASA Jet Propulsion Laboratory directory of image files from JPL space missions

You'll find it helpful to think of a URL as having the following form:

how-to-get-there://where-to-go/what-to-get

You probably already know some ways in which URLs are used. For example, all hyperlinks on Web pages are represented as URLs. Entries in bookmark and history files are stored as URLs. You type in a URL when you want to direct your browser to go to a specific Web page. When you cite a resource on the World Wide Web, you include its URL. You'll also want to include the URL when you're telling someone else about a resource, such as in an email message. Here's an example:

If you haven't already seen this fabulous page, you must look at it. It's called "Business Researcher's Interests" and is hosted by @BRINT. The URL is:
> **http://www.brint.com/interest.html**

It's one of the best subject guides I've ever used.

That way, a friend reading the message could use her browser to go directly to the items you mention.

By providing the name of a Web server and the name of a file or directory holding certain information, a URL tells you how to retrieve the information; from the URL alone, you know which Internet protocol to use when retrieving the information and where it's located. If only a server name is present, as in **http://www.loc.gov**, then a file will still be retrieved. Web servers are configured to pass along a certain file (usually named **index.html** or **index.htm**) when the URL contains only the name of the server or only the name of a directory. Table 13.1 lists different types of URLs that you're likely to use when citing resources from the World Wide Web. The URLs are arranged by Internet protocol.

Resource or Service	Beginning of URL	Example	Description
Web Pages	**http://**	**http://nmaa-ryder.si .edu/artdir/treasures .html**	Selections from the Permanent Collection of the National Museum of American Art
FTP	**ftp://**	**ftp://ftp.jpl.nasa .gov/pub/images/ browse**	A directory of images from NASA Jet Propulsion Laboratory's public information FTP archive
Gopher	**gopher://**	**gopher://wiretap .spies.com**	Internet Wiretap

Table 13.1—Types of URLs Arranged by Protocol

It's important to be precise when you write URLs, because a Web browser uses the URL to access something and bring it to your computer. More specifically, the browser sends a request extracted from the information in the URL to a Web server. Remember, we're talking about having one computer communicate with another; as amazing as some computer systems are, they generally need very precise instructions. Therefore, you have to be careful about spaces (generally there aren't blanks in a URL), symbols (interchanging a slash and a period won't give appropriate results), and capitalization.

Here's an example. In Chapter 12 we examined the Web page called "Tools For Teaching: The World Wide Web and a Web Browser," with the URL **http://www.mwc.edu/~ernie/facacad/WWW-Teaching .html**. Replacing the uppercase T in Teaching with a lowercase t and writing the URL as **http://www.mwc.edu/~ernie/facacad/WWW- teaching.html** will cause the browser to give the following response:

```
404 Not Found

The requested URL /~ernie/facacad/WWW-teaching.html
was not found on this server.
```

That tells us that the name of the Web server, **www.mwc.edu**, was correct but that there was something wrong with the rest of the URL.

Styles for Citing Web Resources

When you're looking for the proper way to cite resources in a report or research paper, you must first see if there is a required or accepted citation style. If you're preparing a report or paper for a class, then check with your instructor. If you're writing for a journal, periodical, or some other publication (either in print or electronic form), then see if the editor or publisher has guidelines.

Proper format for citations from printed sources is very well established. Two commonly used formats are APA (American Psychological Association) style and MLA (Modern Language Association) style. Each of these organizations publishes a handbook or publication guide. At the time of this writing, however, neither organization has adopted a style that completely addresses citations for electronically printed works.

There are a number of issues involved in citing Web or Internet resources. For instance, they may be updated or modified at any time, they may not have a title or major heading, and they don't have page numbers. Thoughtful people have been working to expand existing standards. There are several very good guides to specific citation styles for electronic resources, and some are listed in the section "Information on the Web about Citing Electronic Sources" in this chapter. A few books have been published on the topic; the Internet Public Library has a short list in the books section of its Web page "Citing Electronic Resources," **http://www.ipl.org/ref/QUE/FARQ/netciteFARQ.html#books**. One of the first books written on this subject (it's been revised since it was first published) is *Electronic Styles: A Handbook for Citing Electronic Information,* Xia Li and Nancy Crane, Information Today, 1996. There is an accompanying Web site at **http://www.uvm.edu/~xli/ reference/espub.html**. Another is *Online! A Reference Guide to Using Internet Sources,* Andrew Harnack and Gene Kleppinger, Saint Martin's Press, Inc., 1997; there is an accompanying Web site at **http://www .smpcollege.com/online-4styles ~ help**.

There are some differences of opinion about the format of citations for Web and Internet items. Some say to include a URL in angle brackets (< >), and others do not. Some people advise including the place of publication if the Web resource is a copy of a printed work. Several say to put the date of last revision and to place in parentheses the date on which you accessed the document, whereas others do not make this recommendation. There is, however, considerable agreement on the basic information to be included in a citation to a Web resource. We need to remember that World Wide Web is a relatively new concept, and an even newer resource for researchers and other scholars. It's reasonable to expect some differences in style.

✴ Tip

When you have specific questions about citing Internet and Web sources, check some of the Web resources listed in this chapter, and be sure to check with whoever is going to be evaluating or editing your work.

You'll see that the guidelines for citations or references to Web or Internet resources all contain two dates: the date of publication or revision and the date of last access. The reason we need both dates has to do with the nature of digital media as it's made available or published on the Web. Works in print form are different from digital works; printed documents have a tangible, physical form. We all know we can pick up and feel a magazine or journal in our hands, or we can use a book or periodical as a pillow. It's pretty hard to do that with a Web page! This tangible nature of a printed work also gives an edition or revision a certain permanent nature. It's usually possible to assign a date of publication to a work, and if there are revisions or different editions of a work, it's possible to date and look at the revisions. If a new edition of a printed work exists, it doesn't mean that older editions or versions were destroyed.

The situation is different for Web documents and other items in digital form on the Internet, for several reasons. They don't have a tangible form. It's relatively easy for an author to publish a work (the work usually only needs to be in a certain directory on a computer that functions as a Web server). It's easy to modify or revise a work. Furthermore, when a work is revised, the previous version is often replaced by or overwritten with the new version. Because of this last point, the most recent version may be the only one that exists. The version you cited might not exist anymore. It is therefore necessary to include the date you accessed or read a work listed in a citation or reference. You may also want to keep a copy of the document in a file (save it while browsing) or print a copy of it to provide as documentation if someone questions your sources.

In some cases the first date of publication or posting on the Internet (not only the date of last revision) is important as well. A periodical was recently the focus of a $1 billion libel lawsuit. The suit was filed one year to the day after an article appeared in print format. It turns out the article was available online one day earlier than the print version. Since the statute of limitations for libel suits is one year after publication, lawyers for the periodical asked a trial judge to dismiss the case since the suit was brought a day after the article was first published. At the time of this writing, the case is still unresolved.

To find the date a work was last revised, see if the date is mentioned as part of the work. You'll often see a line like

Last modified: Wednesday, January 15, 1997

in a Web document. If a date of last revision isn't included, or if you want to verify the date, you can usually determine when the file holding the document or item was last modified. Here are some ways.

❊ If you're using Netscape Navigator, click on **View** in the menu bar and select **Page Info**. That will tell you the date on which the file was last modified, as well as the document's title, as shown in Figure 13.1.

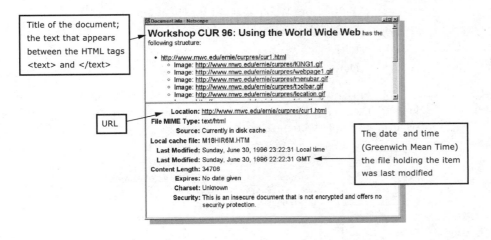

Figure 13.1—Netscape Document Info for a Web Page

❊ If you're using Microsoft Internet Explorer, with the cursor on the Web page in the browser window, click the right mouse button and select **Properties**. That tells the document's title and the date on which the Web page was viewed. Note that the date after **Modified:** is not when the source file was last modified, as shown in Figure 13.2.

Figure 13.2—Microsoft Internet Explorer Page Properties for a Web Page

Here, we'll give some models for citations. These models are meant to include the basic information needed to cite a work so that someone using the citation can access the resource. It would be presumptuous for us to claim to give definitive formats here. We will concentrate on describing ways to find the necessary information for a citation. For simplicity's sake, we won't put angle brackets around URLs and won't put the date of last access in parentheses.

Web Pages

A citation for a Web page contains certain parts in the following order:

- ❋ Name of author or authors—if known
- ❋ Title of the work—in quotes, if known
- ❋ Title of the Web page—in italics, if applicable
- ❋ Date of last revision—if known
- ❋ URL
- ❋ Date accessed

We will now show you how to examine Web pages so that you can identify these citation elements and write citations. Figure 13.3 shows parts of a sample Web page with its citation.

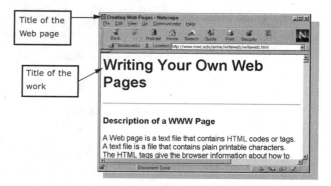

Ackermann, Ernest. "Writing Your Own Web Pages." *Creating Web Pages.* 23 Oct. 1996.
http://www.mwc.edu/ernie/writeweb/writeweb.html
10 Feb. 1997.

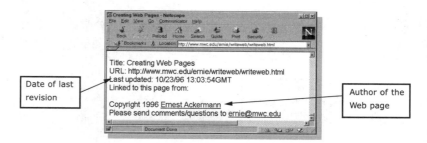

Figure 13.3—A Web Page and Its Citation

In the citation, note that the URL is on a separate line with no period at the end. We do this for clarity; we don't want a reader to think that a period is the last character in the URL. We'll follow this convention for the other formats we give in this chapter. Some authorities require the URL to be surrounded by angle brackets. This method would also clearly set off the characters in the URL.

We looked at the very end of the document to determine the author's name. Not every Web document includes the author's name. If it weren't part of the document, we wouldn't include it.

We found the date of the last revision at the end of the document as well. You could also determine that date by looking at Page Info or Properties, as we mentioned earlier.

We determined the work's title by using the major heading that appeared when we viewed the document with a browser. The Web page title, cited in italics, comes from the title at the top of the browser window. That's the same title that would show up as a hyperlink in the search results if you had used a search engine. The title is specified in the HTML source for the page and doesn't necessarily show up in the text of the document as you view it with a browser. The following is a portion of the HTML code for the Web page cited above. It's here in case you're curious about how the title of a Web is specified.

The exact text of the title of a Web page is surrounded by the tags < Title > and < /Title > in the HTML source for the page. The source for this page, for example, begins with

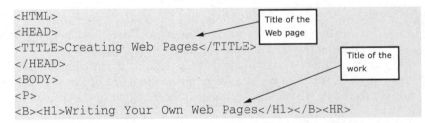

```
<HTML>
<HEAD>
<TITLE>Creating Web Pages</TITLE>
</HEAD>
<BODY>
<P>
<B><H1>Writing Your Own Web Pages</H1></B><HR>
```

If the Web page title is the same as the title of the work—see the Web page with URL **http://www.mwc.edu/ernie/vas96.html**, for example—then we would include only the work's title, and we would put it in quotes. If there is no apparent title of the work (in other words, no major heading), then we would include only the Web page title, and we would style it in italics. If there is neither a major heading nor a Web page title, then you'll have to come up with some descriptive title.

FTP Resources

FTP stands for File Transfer Protocol. Before World Wide Web browsers came into popular use, FTP was the most popular way to retrieve and send files from one computer to another on the Internet. Anonymous FTP allows people to retrieve files without supplying a "secret" login name or password. Hundreds of thousands of files on the Web are available by anonymous FTP. It's an efficient and reliable way to transfer files.

Within the context of using a Web browser, you often access a file through anonymous FTP by clicking on its name in a list of file names. You can specify a file that is available by anonymous FTP or an anonymous FTP site by using a URL. For example, the Electronic Frontier Foundation (EFF) makes many files available by anonymous FTP through the system **ftp.eff.org**—here the URL is **ftp://ftp.eff.org**. The ACLU Briefing Paper Number 5, "Drug Testing in the Work Place," is accessible using the URL **ftp://ftp.eff.org/pub/Privacy/Medical/aclu_drug_testing_workplace.faq**.

A citation for a file available by anonymous FTP contains certain parts in the following order:

- ❋ Name of author or authors—if known
- ❋ Title of the work—in quotes, if known
- ❋ Date of last revision—if known
- ❋ URL
- ❋ Date accessed

The work mentioned above would be cited in this way:

American Civil Liberties Union. "Briefing paper Number 5, Drug Testing in the Work Place." 19 Nov. 1992.
ftp://ftp.eff.org/pub/Privacy/Medical/aclu_drug_testing_workplace.faq
13 Feb. 1997.

Note that there are periods after each of the items, except for the URL, and that the URL is on a separate line.

If there's no obvious title for a file, as in the case of a file that holds an image, then use the file name as the name of the work. An example is the file that holds an image of Mars, cited in the following way:

"Mars1.gif." 16 Jan. 1995.
ftp://ftp.jpl.nasa.gov/pub/images/browse/mars1.gif
13 May 1997.

Gopher Resources

Two or three years before Web browsers became popular, Gopher was one of the easiest ways to retrieve information and access Internet services. Gopher lets you select items from a menu or list. Each item on a menu could be a file, an Internet service, or a link to another menu. Gopher was very popular because it was easier to navigate through the resources on the Internet than to use other tools, such as anonymous FTP. Because of its popularity, a great many documents were (and still are) available through Gopher.

You can access Gopher by using a Web browser. The URL for a Gopher resource starts with **gopher://**. For example, the URL for the Gopher server called AskERIC is **gopher://ericir.syr.edu**. AskERIC is the Internet-based education information service of the Educational Resources Information Center (ERIC).

When you cite a resource available by Gopher, as with other forms of citations, you use a URL. These are the items to include when citing a Gopher resource:

- Name of author or authors—if known
- Title of the work—in quotes, if known
- Date of last revision—if known
- URL
- Date accessed

Here's an example:

Shultz, Michael T. "Significant Figures." May 1994. gopher://ericir.syr.edu:70/00/Lesson/Subject/Math/cecmath.42 15 Feb. 1997.

All items except for the URL are followed by periods.

Email Sources

We'll discuss writing citations for two types of email resources: email sent to an individual and email messages distributed through a discussion group. The main reason for the distinction is that discussion groups usually keep past messages in archives so the message cited can be retrieved.

In either case, a citation will include the following items:

- Name of author
- Subject of the message—in quotes
- Date the message was sent
- Author's email address
- Date accessed

All of these are usually displayed by the software you're using to read email; these are available as standard headers in a message.

We alter this boilerplate format, depending on which type of email message we're citing. These are the items to include in the citation of an email message to an individual:

- Name of author
- Subject of the message—in quotes
- Date the message was sent
- *Type of communication: personal, distribution list, professional*
- Author's email address
- Date accessed

The italicized line represents the only addition to the standard format. Here are some examples of such citations:

Mills, C. "Getting gigs in Nashville." 13 May 1996. Personal.
cc@digicool.com
13 Dec. 1996.

Ackermann, E. "Working on post-tenure review." 02 Feb. 1997. Distribution list.
ernie@mwc.edu
04 Feb. 1997.

Hartman, K. "Changes in search engines." 13 Nov. 1996. Professional.
khartman@mwcgw.mwc.edu
21 Nov. 1996.

A citation for email that was generated in a discussion group or Listserv needs to include the discussion group's address. If the message can be retrieved through an archive, the citation needs to include the URL of the Web page that allows access to the archive. Here are the items included in a citation for an email message distributed through a discussion group:

- Name of author
- Subject of the message—in quotes
- Date the message was sent
- Author's email address
- *Address of discussion group*
- *"via" plus URL of archive—if known*
- Date accessed

Again, the italicized lines represent deviations from the standard format. Here's an example of this sort of citation:

Ackermann, E. "Re: Bookmark files with Netscape 2.0." 7 Mar. 1996.
ernie@mwc.edu
nettrain@ubvm.cc.buffalo.edu
via http://listserv.acsu.buffalo.edu/cgi-bin/wa?S1 = nettrain
14 Feb. 1997.

Usenet Articles

Usenet news consists of a collection of articles, each part of a specific newsgroup. The articles, like email messages, have headers that will give us the information we need for the citation. These are the items to include in the citation of a Usenet article:

- Name of author
- Subject of the message—in quotes
- Name of the newsgroup
- Date the message was sent
- Author's email address
- Date of access

Here's an example:

Ackermann, E. "Question about keeping Bay plant indoors." rec.gardens.
3 Dec. 1995.
ernie@mwc.edu
13 Feb. 1997.

Electronic Journals

In this section, we'll consider electronic journals that are accessible
through a Web browser. Since we can access FTP and Gopher resources
through a Web browser, this includes journals that are accessible by
FTP or Gopher. An article in an electronic journal can be cited very
much like any other WWW resource. If we're making a citation to an
article in a journal, then it's reasonable to include the journal name and
the volume and issue information. If you were citing a resource from a
printed journal, you would also include page numbers, but that does
not apply in this case. The URL gives the location of the article. The
citation, then, will include the following elements:

* Name of author or authors—if known
* Title of the work—in quotes, if known
* Title of the journal, volume number, issue number, and
  date of publication—in italics, if applicable
* Date of last revision—if known and if different from the
  date of publication above
* URL
* Date accessed

Here are two example citations of articles from electronic journals:

Harnack, A., and Kleppinger, G. "Beyond the MLA Handbook: Documenting Electronic Sources on the Internet." *Kairos: 1.2. Summer 1996.*
June 11, 1996.
http://english.ttu.edu/kairos/1.2/inbox/mla.html
10 Feb. 1997.

Agre, P. "Designing Genres for New Media: Social, Economic, and Political Contexts." *The Network Observer: 2.11. November 1995.*
http://communication.ucsd.edu/pagre/tno/november-1995
.html#designing
14 Feb. 1997.

Information on the Web About
Citing Electronic Resources

There are several very good Web pages with information about citing
Web and other electronic resources. The following two Web pages have
links to several other sources on the subject:

"Citing Electronic Sources," Tom Nickel

http://www.csbsju.edu/library/ internet/citing.html

"IPL Citing Electronic Resources," Internet Public Library

http://www.ipl.org/ref/QUE/ FARQ/netciteFARQ.html

The Web pages in this list contain information about specific styles for citations:

"Bibliographic Formats for Citing Electronic Information," Xia Li and Nancy Crane

http://www.uvm.edu/ ~ ncrane/estyles

"Citing the Sites: MLA-Style Guidelines and Models for Documenting Internet Sources," Andrew Harnack and Gene Kleppinger

http://falcon.eku.edu/honors/beyond-mla/#citing_sites

"CITING INTERNET-APA Style," Maryann Readal and Susan Goodwin

http://www.nhmccd.cc.tx.us/contracts/lrc/kc/ CitingElecSources-apa.html

"MLA Electronic Citation Examples—Internet/Westlaw," Peggy Whitley

http://www.nhmccd.cc.tx.us/groups/lrc/kc/mla-internet.html

"Columbia Online Style: MLA-Style Citations of Electronic Sources," Janice R. Walker

http://www.cas.usf.edu/english/walker/mla.html

These two Web pages contain good, thoughtful discussions about citing work from Web or other electronic sources:

"Citing Electronic Information in History Papers," Maurice Crouse

http://www.people.memphis.edu/ ~ mcrouse/elcite.html

"Electronic Style—What's Here," George H. Hoemann

http://funnelweb.utcc.utk.edu/ ~ hoemann/whats.html

Summary

Citing references or writing a bibliography is usually part of creating a research report. You provide citations so others may check or examine the resources used in the report. There are several agreed-upon styles for citing documents in print format. With the use of resources from the Web or the Internet, it becomes necessary to have a uniform format for citing these resources. This chapter presents a set of formats for documenting or citing information obtained from the Web or the Internet.

Citations to documents and other information found on the Web or Internet always include the URL, or Uniform Resource Locator. A URL includes the names of the Web server and the file or directory holding the information. The URL therefore tells you which Internet protocol to use to retrieve the information and where it's located. You need to be precise in terms of spelling and capitalization when writing a URL, as a computer will be interpreting it. We listed URL formats for common Web or Internet services.

There is no uniform agreement on how to cite information from the Web or Internet. Most suggest that a citation include the author's name, the work's title, the date the information was last revised, the date the information was accessed, and the URL. The date of access is included because it's relatively easy to modify information on the Web and the information may not always be the same as when it was accessed for research. We discussed methods for determining the date of access and the title of a Web document.

The chapter concluded with a list of Web resources that provide more information about citing sources and some suggestions for specific formats.

Exercises and Projects

1. Write a citation to the document in the Web with URL **http:// www.mwc.edu/ernie/curpres/cur1.html**.

2. Use anonymous FTP to retrieve the file **FAQs about FAQs** from **ftp.mwc.edu**. Here's one way to retrieve it: Go to the location using the URL **ftp://ftp.mwc.edu**, click on the hyperlink **internet.info/**, click on **usenet/**, and then click on **FAQs about FAQs**. Write a citation to that document.

3. In this exercise you'll get experience citing the same document that's available though Gopher and the Web.

    a. Go to the Gopher system at wiretap.spies.com, **gopher:// wiretap.spies.com**. Select **Government Docs (US & World)** from the main menu and retrieve a copy of the Electronic Communications Privacy Act. Write a citation for that document. The citation should reflect that you retrieved it using Gopher.

    b. Retrieve another copy of the **Electronic Communications Privacy Act** that's presented as a Web page. One way to do that is to use a search engine and to search for the phrase **Electronic Communications Privacy Act**. Another way is to go to the section of the Electronic Frontier Foundation's Web site "Legislation & Regulation Issues," **http://www .eff.org/pub/Legislation**, and to find the hyperlink to the Electronic Communications Privacy Act on that page.

4. Send yourself some email with a profound message. Write a citation for the message as if you were going to use it in a research report.

5. In Chapter 11, we mentioned that it is possible to search the archives of the email discussion groups hosted at listserv.acsu.buffalo.edu by starting with the Web page with URL **http://listserv.acsu.buffalo.edu/archives**. Go to that site and search the archives of HWY61-L for articles with *Allen Ginsberg* in the title. Select one of the email messages retrieved and write a citation for it.

6. In Chapter 11, we showed you how to use Deja News, **http://www.dejanews.com**, to search archives of Usenet articles. Search for articles about health care for pets. Select two of the articles and write citations for them.

7. There's an article titled "The Netizens and Community Networks" in the February 1997 issue of *Computer Mediated Communication*. Use a search engine to find the article, and then write a citation for it.

8. In Chapter 12, we discussed evaluating resources on the Web. One of the resources we discussed had the URL **http://www .nsa.gov:8080/docs/venona/ddir.html**. Write a citation for it.

9. Some search services allow the use of Boolean expressions and provide online help or tips. For each of the following services, find the portion of online help that tells how to use Boolean expressions, and write a citation to that resource:

   a. Excite, **http://www.excite.com**.
   b. WebCrawler, **http://www.webcrawler.com**.
   c. Deja News, **http://www.dejanews.com**.
   d. Argus Clearinghouse, **http://www.clearinghouse.net**.

10. There are other opinions about the proper way to write citations for works found on the Web and Internet. Retrieve and read through each of the resources below, and then write answers to Exercises 2, 3a, 5, 6, and 8 using the MLA style formats given.

   a. *Electronic Sources: MLA Style of Citation,* Li and Crane, **http://www.uvm.edu/~ncrane/estyles/mla.html**.
   b. *MLA-Style Models for Citing Internet Sources,* Harnack and Kleppinger, **http://www.arh.eku.edu/eng/harnack/ models.htm**.
   c. *MLA-Style Citations of Electronic Sources,* Walker, **http:// www.cas.usf.edu/english/walker/mla.html**.

Chapter 14

Putting It All Together:
Two Sample Research Projects

In this chapter, we will bring together most of the important skills introduced in this book. We'll accomplish this by doing two separate projects. The first one involves using several different types of search tools to research a broad topic that we'll narrow as we go along. The second project is also broad, but it is much more focused from the outset; we know what we need to find, and we'll look for it using an approach and resources that we won't have used in the first project.

We'll go through the following major steps involved in using the World Wide Web for research:
  * Search a Directory to Find Resources
  * Find and Search a Specialized Database
  * Formulate and Submit a Search Query to a Search Engine
  * Locate and Search a Library Catalog
  * Search a Usenet Archive
  * Evaluate the Resources Found
  * Cite the Sources in a Bibliography

Project 1—Finding Resources for a Research Paper

In the first project, we'll research the topic of women in computing. This topic is fairly broad. Although we aren't sure exactly what we want to focus on, we do want to know why there are so few women in this field. We'll start by looking at the topic broadly, and we'll narrow the focus as we go along. We may end up choosing a particular aspect of the topic that we didn't know about beforehand.

We'll go through the following major steps:
- A. Search a directory to find resources.
- B. Find and search a specialized database.
- C. Formulate and submit a search query to a search engine.
- D. Locate and search a library catalog.
- E. Search a Usenet archive.
- F. Evaluate the resources found.
- G. Cite the sources in a bibliography.

✳ Tip

Remember that the Web is always changing and that your results may differ from those shown here. Don't let this confuse you. The activities are meant to teach you fundamental skills. These skills don't change, even though the number of results obtained or the actual screens may look very different.

Activity 1-A   Search a Directory to Find Resources

Overview

Before starting this section, you may want to review Chapter 4. We'll need to find a subject guide for the topic. A subject guide lists several types of resources on a topic and can thereby provide an overview of the subject. The best place to obtain a subject guide is a directory or virtual library. In this project, we'll use a directory. Let's try one of the most comprehensive directories on the Web—Yahoo! Why? Because Yahoo! is so large, it is likely to have some Web pages on women in computing.

Follow these steps:
1. Go to the home page for Yahoo!
2. Search Yahoo! for the concept "women and computing."
3. Follow hyperlinks that appear to be helpful.
4. Bookmark a useful Web page.

Details

1   Go to the home page for Yahoo!

Do It! Click on the location field, type **http://www.yahoo.com**, and press **Enter**.

2   Search Yahoo! for the concept "women and computing."

You should be on Yahoo!'s home page.

Since we're going to do a keyword search, let's see what our options are.

Do It! Click on **options**, located next to the **Search** button on Yahoo!'s home page.

Do It! Under **Select a search method**, select **Matches on all words (AND)**.

Do It! Click on the circle next to **Web Sites**.

Do It! Type **women computing** in the search form and click on **Search**.

Your screen should look like the one in Figure 14.1.

Figure 14.1—Yahoo! Search Options Page

You could also get the same results by typing **women and computing** in the search query box on Yahoo!'s home page.

3   Follow hyperlinks that appear to be helpful.

The search results should appear, as in Figure 14.2. Scroll down until you find some Web pages that look interesting. There are several hyperlinks to investigate. Several Web pages do not turn out to be relevant. **Women and Computing** looks more promising.

Chapter 14

✳*Do It!* Click on **Women and Computing**, as shown in Figure 14.2.

Click on **Women and Computing**

Yahoo! category that **Women and Computing** falls under

Figure 14.2—Women and Computing Search Results in Yahoo!

Figure 14.3 shows a portion of the Web site that appears. Women and Computing is a subject guide and information page put out by the CPSR. By scrolling to the bottom of the page and clicking on **CPSR Home Page**, we find out that *CPSR* stands for Computer Professionals for Social Responsibility. The page has a collection of hyperlinks, called Gender Pages Index, on the topic of women in computer science, engineering, and related technical fields. Let's open the first Gender Page listed.

✳*Do It!* Click on **General Resources for Women**, as shown in Figure 14.3.

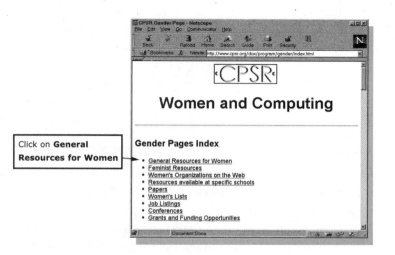

Click on **General Resources for Women**

Figure 14.3—CPSR's Women and Computing

The page that comes up appears in Figure 14.4 with the heading "General Resources for Women."

Select **Ellen Spertus' Women and Computer Science page**

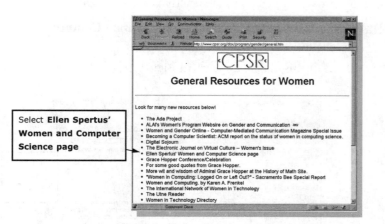

Figure 14.4—CPSR's List of General Resources for Women

We could try many of the hyperlinks listed under this heading. Let's try **Ellen Spertus' Women and Computer Science page**.

※Do It! Click on **Ellen Spertus' Women and Computer Science page**.

A portion of this page appears in Figure 14.5. "Women and Computer Science" is a subject guide with links to journal articles, associations, and other types of resources covering the subject of women and computer science.

Click on **Why Are There So Few Female Computer Scientists?**

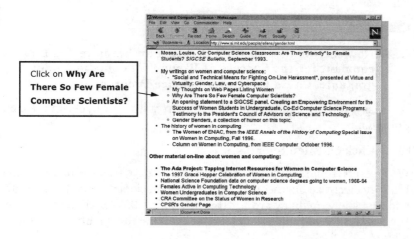

Figure 14.5—Ellen Spertus' Women in Computer Science Page

Notice in Figure 14.5 that Ms. Spertus has listed several hyperlinks to her own writings. The article "Why Are There So Few Female Computer Scientists?" appears to be exactly what we want.

✱*Do It!* Click on **Why Are There So Few Female Computer Scientists?**

An abstract of this article appears in Figure 14.6.

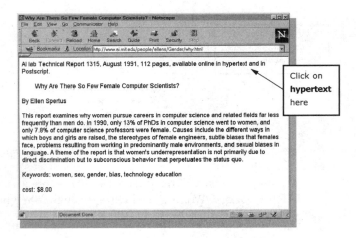

Figure 14.6—Abstract of the Article

The next step is to find out something about the author. You'll need to find a hyperlink that takes you to biographical information. In this example, you'll need to go back to the list of Ellen Spertus' writings that appears in Figure 14.5.

✱*Do It!* Click on the **Back** icon in the toolbar.

✱*Do It!* Now click on the hyperlink **Creating an Empowering Environment for the Success of Women Students in Undergraduate, Co-Ed Computer Science Programs**.

An essay should appear on your screen with the hyperlink **Ellen Spertus**.

✱*Do It!* Click on **Ellen Spertus**.

We find out from reading Ms. Spertus' home page that she obtained her Ph.D. in electrical engineering and computer science from MIT in 1997, and that she won an award for this article in 1991. By knowing something about the author, you can better evaluate the quality of the information.

✳*Do It!* Return to the abstract of "Why Are There So Few Female Computer Scientists?" by clicking **Back** on the toolbar twice, and then clicking on its hyperlink again.

Although the abstract provides useful information, we may want to read the entire article. We can do this by clicking on the word *hypertext,* as shown in Figure 14.6.

✳*Do It!* Click on **hypertext**.

You should now have the entire article.

4 Bookmark a useful Web page.

To save this hyperlink, you need to bookmark it so you'll be able to access it at a later time. (After the project is finished, you may want to go back and delete the bookmark. Refer to Chapter 2 for instructions on how to delete bookmarks.)

✳*Do It!* Point to **Bookmarks** in the location toolbar and click. Point to **Add Bookmark** and click.

If you were doing an actual research project, you'd probably want to explore all or most of the hyperlinks that have appeared so far. We'll move on, though, and try to find a journal article on the topic.

Activity 1-B   Find and Search a Specialized Database

Overview

We're looking for a database that indexes journal articles. As we discussed in Chapter 7, one of the best sources for such databases is the Internet Sleuth. We'll use the Internet Sleuth to find a journal article database, and then we'll search it, following these steps:

1. Go to the home page for the Internet Sleuth.
2. Use the Internet Sleuth's directory to find a database that indexes journal articles.
3. Open the CMP Technology Database.
4. Search for the keywords "women AND computer."
5. Bookmark an article.

Details

1   Go to the home page for the Internet Sleuth.

✳*Do It!* Click on the location field, type **http://www.isleuth.com**, and press [**Enter**].

You should now be in the Internet Sleuth, as shown in Figure 14.7.

Click on **Computers** here

Figure 14.7—The Internet Sleuth

2   Use the Internet Sleuth's directory to find a database that indexes journal articles.

The Internet Sleuth's directory is on the left side of the screen. Of the major subject headings, we could look under **Women** (a subheading of **Society**) and **Computers**.

✳*DoIt!* Scroll down until you find **Society**. Click on it. Then click on **Women**.

Scroll down the list of databases. Although there are several databases listed that may provide useful information, none of them specifically mentions indexing journal articles. Let's try **Computers**.

✳*DoIt!* Locate **Computers** in the directory and click on it.

3   Open the CMP Technology Database.

Scroll down the list of databases until you see **CMP Technology Database**. This database consists of more than a hundred thousand articles, as shown in Figure 14.8. We could search the database from the Internet Sleuth or we could click on its hyperlink and search the database directly. For this exercise, we'll search it directly.

✳*DoIt!* Click on **CMP Technology Database**.

4   Search for the concept "women AND computer."

The first thing to do in any database is to find out what search techniques are used.

✳*DoIt!* Click on **Search Help**.

From the help page, we learn that the CMP Technology Database's searchable index, called TechSearch, supports some simple search features, including the ability to AND words together. Although it's not explicitly mentioned, it appears that AND should be capitalized, since the example shows it in capital letters. Since we want articles with the words *women* and *computers* or *computer science,* we need to search the word *computer* by itself. There is no mention about whether the database supports truncation, so we'll try searching on the singular form of computer and see if the database automatically truncates the word for us.

✱*Do It!* Click **Back** on the toolbar.

You should now be back at the screen shown in Figure 14.8.

✱*Do It!* Type **women AND computer** in the search form, and click on **Search**.

Figure 14.8—Query "women AND computer"—CMP Technology Database

Several article titles will appear. Part of this list appears in Figure 14.9.

Figure 14.9—Journal Article Titles Found in CMP Technology Database

✳*Do It!* Scroll down the list until you see **Introducing girls to high-tech careers is 'Awsem'**. You'll need to go through several pages. Let's read the article.

✳*Do It!* Click on **Introducing girls to high-tech careers is 'Awsem'**.

The full text of the article appears and is partially shown in Figure 14.10.

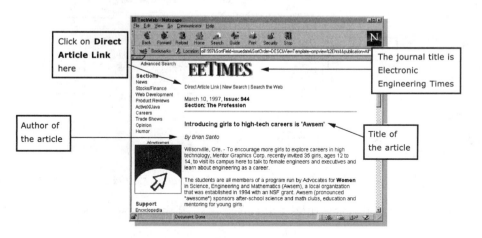

Figure 14.10—Full Text of an Article Found in CMP Technology Database

5   Bookmark an article.

This seems to be a useful journal article. Let's bookmark it for later use.

Since the primary reason we're bookmarking items we find is so we can show how to cite these resources in a bibliography, you may want to save this article with a shorter URL that is easier to deal with. This database allows this by providing a *Direct Article Link*. Let's try it.

✳*Do It!* Click on **Direct Article Link**, as shown in Figure 14.10.

Do It! Click on the URL that's provided.

Your screen should fill with the same article but with a different URL. Now we're ready to bookmark it.

Do It! Point to **Bookmarks** in the location toolbar and click.

Do It! Point to **Add Bookmark** and click.

Several other articles in the list look like they'd be appropriate. If this were an actual project, you would read them. After reading a few articles, you may be ready to formulate a search request and submit it to a search engine database.

Activity 1-C   Formulate and Submit a Search Query to a Search Engine

Overview

Before working on this section, you may want to go back and review Chapter 5. If you typed *women in computing* in a full-text search engine, you could easily get several thousand hits. With a few other keywords and a more pointed search, you can narrow the search considerably and retrieve more relevant results. In terms of the given topic, you may want to focus your research on how gender bias has affected career choices for women starting when they were schoolgirls.

For this part of the project, we'll use the basic search strategy that we introduced in Chapter 5. We'll follow the first nine of the ten steps. These are the steps to take:

1. Identify the important concepts of your search.
2. Choose the keywords that describe these concepts.
3. Determine whether there are synonyms, related terms, or other variations of the keywords that should be included.
4. Determine which search features may apply, including truncation, proximity operators, Boolean operators, and so forth.
5. Choose a search engine.
6. Read the search instructions on the search engine's home page. Look for sections entitled "help," "advanced search," "frequently asked questions," and so forth.
7. Create a search expression using syntax that is appropriate for the search engine.
8. View the results. How many hits were returned? Were the results relevant to your query?
9. Modify your search if needed.

Details

1   Identify the important concepts of your search.

We want to focus on the gender bias and stereotypes in our society that seem to thwart girls' abilities to study engineering and computer science later in life.

369

2   Choose the keywords that describe these concepts.

The main terms or keywords are *girls, gender, bias, stereotypes,* and *computer science.*

3   Determine whether there are synonyms, related terms, or other variations of the keywords that should be included.

Synonyms for girls: women, female.

Synonyms for computer science: computing, computers, engineering.

4   Determine which search features may apply, including truncation, proximity operators, Boolean operators, and so forth.

Synonyms are connected by OR because any of the keywords are acceptable in the results. *Computer science* should be searched as a phrase, and *stereotypes* should be truncated so that alternative endings to the word will appear in the search results as well. This is one example of how this search could be worked out:

❋   girls **OR** women **OR** female
    AND
❋   gender
    AND
❋   bias
    AND
❋   "computer science" **OR** comput* (truncating this will get computers and computing) **OR** engineering
    AND
❋   stereotyp* (to retrieve stereotypes, stereotypical, stereotyping, and so forth)

5   Choose a search engine.

We require a search engine that supports Boolean searching (both simple and nested), truncation, and phrase searching, so we'll use AltaVista.

❋⟨Do It!⟩ Click on the location field, type **http://www.altavista.digital .com**, and press ⟨**Enter**⟩.

6   Read the search instructions on the search engine's home page. Look for sections entitled "help," "advanced search," "frequently asked questions," and so forth.

Since our search requires the nested Boolean search feature, we'll have to use AltaVista's advanced mode. The advanced mode also provides a big search query box that makes it easier to type a multifaceted search query. To refresh your memory about how AltaVista's advanced searching works, we'll look at the search instructions.

(*Do It*) Click on the **Advanced** button.

Your screen will fill with the advanced search form.

(*Do It*) Click on the **help** button.

Read the instructions.

7   Create a search expression using syntax that is appropriate for the search engine.

Now that you've familiarized yourself with the search features, we're ready to formulate the search expression. Here is one way to express this search:

(girls or women or female) and gender and bias and ("computer science" or comput* or engineering) and stereotyp*

You can always modify your search at a later time. Let's see what Web pages this search expression retrieves.

(*Do It*) Click on **Back** to return to the advanced search page.

(*Do It*) Type the search expression in the box provided, as shown in Figure 14.11.

Make sure all of the parentheses are closed properly and that you spell the words correctly.

(*Do It*) In the **Ranking** field, type **girls**.

(*Do It*) Click on **Search**.

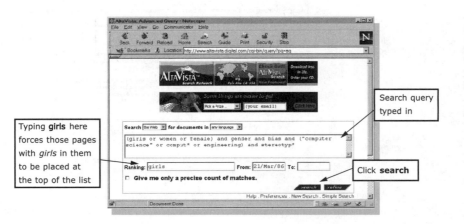

Figure 14.11—Search Query Entered in AltaVista's Advanced Search Mode

8   View the results. How many hits were returned? Were the results relevant to your query?

The results appear to be relevant to the query we entered, as shown in Figure 14.12.

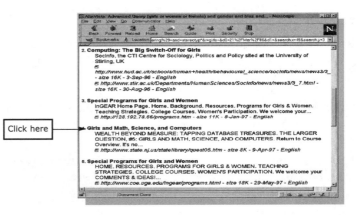

Click here

Figure 14.12—Prominent Search Results in AltaVista

Let's open a Web page to see how useful it may be.

✳*Do It!* Click on **Girls and Math, Science, and Computers**, as shown in Figure 14.12.

Part of this page appears in Figure 14.13.

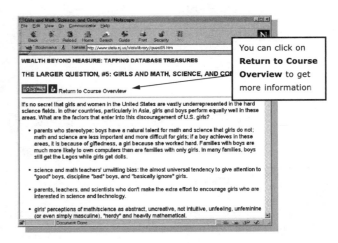

You can click on **Return to Course Overview** to get more information

Figure 14.13—Girls and Math, Science, and Computers

The New Jersey State Library published this page as part of a course designed for school library media specialists. How do we know this? When we click on **Return to Course Overview**, as shown in Figure 14.13, we find a course description and the name and biographical information of the person who created it.

This page will help our research, so we'll want to bookmark it for later use.

Do It! Point to the location toolbar at the top of the screen and click on **Bookmarks**.

Do It! Point to **Add Bookmark** and click.

9   Modify your search if needed.

If we wanted to modify the search results, we could go back to the search query screen and type in another keyword. We could also click on **Refine**. AltaVista would provide keywords. We could add those keywords and redo the search.

Activity 1-D   Locate and Search a Library Catalog

Overview

For this section, you may want to review Chapter 8. We'll find a Web-based library catalog and look for books about women in computing. Specifically, we want books on the gender bias against girls, as that seems to be one of the main reasons that more women don't go into computer and engineering fields. In order to obtain the largest number of books on this topic, we'll want to search a sizable library catalog, specifically one from a large research university. We'll follow these steps:

1. Open the location for webCATS.
2. Find a large university library catalog.
3. Search the ALADIN catalog for "women" and "computer science."
4. Browse the list.
5. Email a record that appears to be useful.

Details

1   Open the location for webCATS.

Do It! Click on the location field, type **http://library.usask.ca/ hywebcat**, and press **Enter**.

You should be at the webCATS home page, as in Figure 14.14.

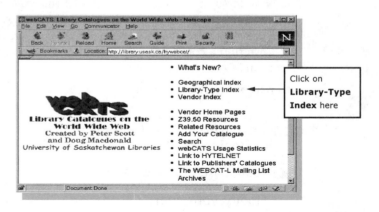

Figure 14.14—webCATS Home Page

2   Find a large university library catalog.

To find a university library catalog, we first need to open the Library-Type Index.

✳*Do It!* Click on **Library-Type Index**, as shown in Figure 14.14.

The screen will fill with different categories. You want to select the category for college and university libraries.

✳*Do It!* Click on **College and University**.

The screen will fill with the names of hundreds of colleges and universities with Web-based library catalogs. Scroll down until you come to George Washington University.

✳*Do It!* Click on **George Washington University (Washington, D.C.) (via Aladin)**, as shown in Figure 14.15.

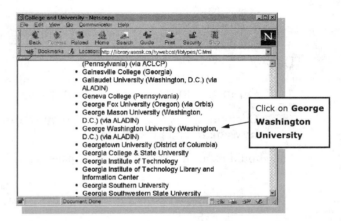

Figure 14.15—Partial Listing of College and University Libraries in webCATS

Your screen should look like the one in Figure 14.16.

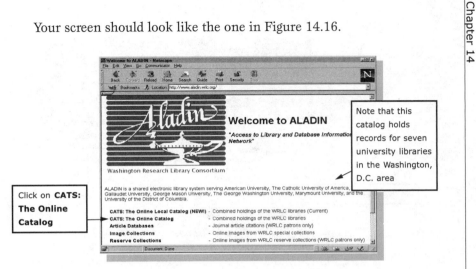

Figure 14.16—The ALADIN Catalog: Washington Research Library Consortium

3   Search the ALADIN catalog for "women" and "computer science."

Note that the ALADIN catalog holds library records for seven university libraries in and around Washington, D.C. Of the choices offered in Figure 14.16, you want to search the online catalog.

⁂Do It! Click on **CATS: The Online Catalog**.

You may get a screen with some text that explains the changes that are being made to this catalog. If you get this screen, simply click on **continue**.

You will now be at the ALADIN database search query screen, which appears in Figure 14.17. Since we aren't sure which subject headings are attached to books on this subject, it's a good idea to start with a keyword search. Make sure **Keyword(s)** is selected, as shown in Figure 14.17.

⁂Do It! Type **women computer science** in the box under **Enter search word(s) or phrase**.

⁂Do It! Click on **Begin Search**.

Figure 14.17—Keywords "women computer science" Entered in ALADIN Form

4   Browse the list.

Partial search results are listed in Figure 14.18.

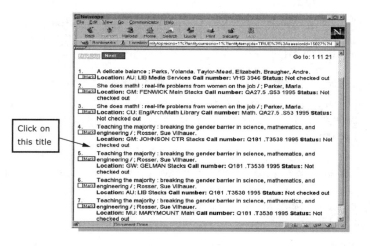

Figure 14.18—Results of Keyword Search in ALADIN

On the first page, a title that looks particularly useful is **Teaching the majority: breaking the gender barrier in science, mathematics, and engineering**. Note that a few copies of this book are listed. They are in different libraries. Next to **Location**, letters indicate which library holds the books. For example, GW is George Washington University, GM is George Mason University, and so forth.

To read a full description of this book, we need to click on its title.

※Do It! Click on **Teaching the majority: breaking the gender barrier in science, mathematics, and engineering**.

Figure 14.19 shows some of the descriptive information that has been included in this database for this book, which is a collection of several authors' writings on gender and the teaching of mathematics and other sciences. The contents section lists all the chapter titles and chapter authors. By reading the chapter titles, you can determine whether the book covers the type of information you're seeking. This book in particular seems to have some useful information.

The contents are the titles of chapters in the book

Figure 14.19—Detailed Information About the Book's Contents

5   Email a record that appears to be useful.

If you'd like to read this book, you'll need to see if your library owns it. If it doesn't, you'll want to request the book through an interlibrary loan or purchase your own copy. In either case, you'll need to document accurate information about the book, including the author, title, publisher, and date of publication. So that you don't forget something important or write something down incorrectly, you could bookmark the record or email it to yourself. To email the record to yourself, you'll need to go back to the previous screen and follow these steps:

✻Do It! Click on **Mark** next to the record, then click on **Show Marked Records** at the top of the screen.

✻Do It! Click **E-mail**, type your email address in the space provided, and click on **Submit**.

Activity 1-E   Search a Usenet Archive

Overview

Now we're ready to find out what other people have to say informally about women in computing. The best way to find out what's being discussed is to search a Usenet or email discussion group archive. For this project, we'll use Deja News, a search service that specializes in searching newsgroup articles. You may want to refer to Chapter 11 for more in-depth information about searching Deja News. This section will cover the process very briefly.

We'll follow these steps:

1. Open the location for Deja News.
2. Search for articles using the keywords "girls computers technology."
3. Browse the results and bookmark an article.

Details

1   **Open the location for Deja News.**

✳*Do It!* Click on location field, type **http://www.dejanews.com**, and press **Enter**.

The Deja News home page with the search terms entered appears in Figure 14.20.

2   **Search for articles using the keywords "girls computers technology."**

✳*Do It!* In the search form provided, type the following keywords, as shown in Figure 14.20: **girls computers technology**, and click on **Find**.

We want each of these words to appear in the articles. By clicking on **Help** at the top of the Deja News home page, and then clicking on the hyperlink **New Users**, you'll see some search examples to help you understand how Deja News works.

3   **Browse the results and bookmark an article.**

Figure 14.21 shows the search results, which list several articles. We've chosen not to show the authors' entire email addresses for privacy reasons.

Click on an item in the Subject column to read an article

Email address of the article's author

Figure 14.21—Results of Search Using Keywords "girls computers technology"

(*Do It!*) Browse the list and click on any articles that look interesting.

(*Do It!*) Bookmark an article of your choice.

Activity 1-F   Evaluate the Resources Found

Overview

We've gone through the most important research skills, and we've collected some Web pages that appear to be useful. Now it's time to go back to the pages we bookmarked and to look at them again. We'll evaluate their usefulness to our research and determine whether they are worthy of our project. You may want to refer to Chapter 12 before doing this activity. We've bookmarked four references in this exercise. If this were an actual research project, you'd want to read and evaluate each Web page carefully before citing it in your bibliography. To save space, we'll take one of the resources and run it through the evaluation criteria introduced in Chapter 12. We'll follow these steps:

1. Go to your bookmark list and select "Why Are There So Few Female Computer Scientists?"
2. Evaluate this resource using the evaluation guidelines.

Details

1   Go to your bookmark list and select "Why Are There So Few Female Computer Scientists?"

(*Do It!*) Point to the location toolbar and click on **Bookmarks**.

✳Do It! Drag the mouse down until you come to **Why Are There So Few Female Computer Scientists?** Click on the title.

Figure 14.22 shows the Web page that appears.

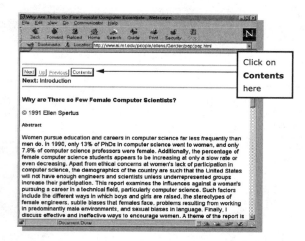

Figure 14.22—Why are There so Few Female Computer Scientists?

Before proceeding any further, scroll down the page pictured in Figure 14.22 and note that this paper is labeled **MIT Artificial Intelligence Laboratory Technical Report 1315**. We can also verify by looking at the URL that the author is affiliated with MIT.

To see the contents of the research paper, you can click on the hyperlink shown in Figure 14.22.

✳Do It! Click on **Contents**.

The paper's contents appear in Figure 14.23. These are hyperlinks to all the major parts of the paper.

2   Evaluate this resource using the evaluation guidelines.

Now that you have the paper on your computer screen, we'll go through the evaluation guidelines one by one.

Who Is the Author or Institution?

Earlier in the chapter, we found out that Ellen Spertus, the paper's author, is obtaining her Ph.D. in electrical engineering and computer science from MIT in 1997.

How Current Is the Information?

We can note from the page shown in Figure 14.22 that the paper's copyright is 1991.

Figure 14.23—Contents of the Research Page

✳️*Do It!* Scroll down the **Contents** page (Figure 14.23) until you find the hyperlink **References**, as shown in Figure 14.24.

✳️*Do It!* Click on **References**.

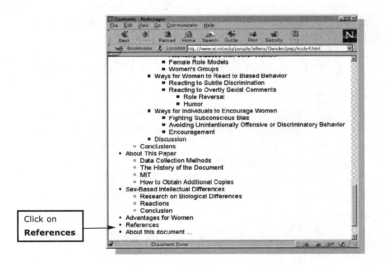

Click on
References

Figure 14.24—A Hyperlink to the References

You'll find that most of the references date from the late 1980s through 1991. When you cite this page in the bibliography, you'll need to state when the page was last updated. To determine this, access the **Page Info** screen in Netscape.

✳Do It! Click on **View** in the Netscape menu bar, and choose **Page Info**. This screen will indicate when the page was last modified.

Who Is the Audience?

Because the Web page is a research paper, it is explicitly intended for scholars and educators. As the paper was placed on the Web, we can infer, however, that Ms. Spertus has widened her audience to include students, parents, and anyone else who is interested in this subject.

Is the Content Accurate and Objective?

The author cites others' research in the thesis and gives each author a hyperlink, so you can go directly to the list of references at the end of the paper to the full bibliographic information of the cited author's work. Finding cites to others' research is a good indicator that the material is objective and well documented, not just the writer's opinion.

What Is the Purpose of the Information?

The intention is to document, with actual research, the reasons women are underrepresented in engineering and computer science. Acknowledging that women's underrepresentation in these fields raises ethical concerns, the author also points out that fuller participation from all segments of society would strengthen these fields of study. The paper's major purpose is to educate people about this situation and to offer solutions.

Activity 1-G   Cite the Sources in a Bibliography

Overview

Now you'll need to pull all of your resources together and cite them properly in a bibliography, or a webliography, as they're sometimes called. Here are the steps to follow:

1. Open your bookmarks.
2. Determine how to cite each resource properly.
3. Assemble the citations in a bibliography.

Details

1   Open your bookmarks.

✳Do It! While in Netscape, click on **Bookmarks** in the location toolbar, and move the pointer to the bookmarks.

✳Do It! Select each bookmark in turn, starting with **Why Are There So Few Female Computer Scientists?**

2   Determine how to cite each resource properly.

We'll use the guidelines from Chapter 13 to cite the resources properly.

Resource: Why Are There So Few Female Computer Scientists?

Type of resource: Web page

- ❋ **Name of author:** Spertus, Ellen
- ❋ **Title of the work (in quotes):** "Why Are There So Few Female Computer Scientists?"
- ❋ **Title of the Web page (in italics):** *Why Are There So Few Female Computer Scientists?*
- ❋ **Date of last revision:** 28 Jan. 1995 (To find this, click on **View** in the menu bar and select **Page Info**.)
- ❋ **URL:** http://www.ai.mit.edu/people/ellens/Gender/pap/pap.html
- ❋ **Date accessed:** 21 April 1997

Resource: TechWeb

Type of resource: Electronic journal

- ❋ **Name of author:** Santo, Brian
- ❋ **Title of work (in quotes):** "Introducing Girls to High-Tech Careers Is 'Awsem'"
- ❋ **Title of the journal, volume, issue, and date (in italics):** *Electronic Engineering Times, March 10, 1997*
- ❋ **Date of last revision:** Not available
- ❋ **URL:** http://www.techweb.com/se/directlink.cgi?EET19970310S0124
- ❋ **Date accessed:** 21 April 1997

Resource: Girls and Math, Science, and Computers

Type of resource: Web page

- ❋ **Name of author:** Kay, Linda
- ❋ **Title of the work (in quotes):** "Wealth Beyond Measure: Tapping Database Treasures"
- ❋ **Title of the Web page (in italics):** *Girls and Math, Science, and Computers*
- ❋ **Date of last revision:** 9 April 1997
- ❋ **URL:** http://www.state.nj.us/statelibrary/quest05.htm
- ❋ **Date accessed:** 15 April 1997

Resource: Usenet article of your choice (this is a sample citation)

Type of resource: Usenet article

- ❋ **Name of author:** Hartman, Karen

❈ **Subject of the message (in quotes):** "Girls and Mathematics"

❈ **Name of the newsgroup:** soc.feminism

❈ **Date the message was sent:** 13 April 1997

❈ **Author's email address:** khartman@mwc.edu

❈ **Date accessed:** 3 May 1997

3   Assemble the citations in a bibliography.

Now that we've determined the elements in each citation, we need to gather the citations into a bibliography. Remember the book we found in the ALADIN library catalog? Let's say we found a copy of the book, read it, and wanted to cite it in our bibliography. We would cite it properly by using a style manual and including a citation in our list of Web resources. You'll find that book included in the following list of sources.

Bibliography

Hartman, K. "Girls and Mathematics." soc.feminism. 13 April 1997. khartman@mwc.edu
3 May 1997.

Rosser, Sue V., ed. *Teaching the Majority: Breaking the Gender Barrier in Science, Mathematics, and Engineering.* New York: Teacher College Press, 1995.

Santo, Brian. "Introducing Girls to High-Tech Careers Is 'Awsem.'" *Electronic Engineering Times, March 10, 1997.* Date of last revision not available.
http://www.techweb.com/se/directlink.cgi?EET19970310S0124
21 April 1997.

Spertus, Ellen. "Why Are There So Few Female Computer Scientists?" *Why Are There So Few Female Computer Scientists?* 28 Jan. 1995.
http://www.ai.mit.edu/people/ellens/Gender/pap/pap.html
21 April 1997.

Project 2—Using the Internet for Market Research

This project focuses on how to use the Web for market research. Let's say you are a person who has come into some money. You want to make a sound investment, and you've always wanted to own a bookstore. You've read that one of the fastest growing areas in the country, specifically on the East Coast, is Fredericksburg, Virginia. All you know about the area is that it is 50 miles south of Washington, D.C. You want to research the following questions:

❋ How is the bookstore industry faring in the United States?

❋ Is the Fredericksburg, Virginia, bookstore market saturated?

❋ What types of people buy the most books? Couples with no children? Couples with children? Single people?

❋ What does the Fredericksburg area look like demographically? How many people live there? What is the population growth projected to be in the next few years? What is the educational background of the people there?

❋ What is the business climate of the area? What is the unemployment rate?

We'll look for this information by taking the following steps:
A. Search a virtual library.
B. Search a specialized database.
C. Perform a search in a search engine.
D. Evaluate the resources found.
E. Cite the resources found.

Activity 2-A   Search a Virtual Library

Overview

The best place to find free information about industries is through trade association Web pages. Such pages can provide a wealth of information about the industry they cover, gleaned from a myriad of sources to which you may not have access. Some association Web pages provide links to other related sites and resources, as well as publishing their own research.

There are several ways to find association Web pages. You could do a keyword search in a search engine. For example, you could search for **bookstores and association** or **"bookstore industry"**. It may be difficult, however, to find an association quickly using this method. The best place to go for a resource like this is a virtual library. Why? As you may remember, virtual libraries make it their priority to list specialized databases on the Web. They also try to list resources that will help people doing serious research.

In this part of our project, we'll search a virtual library for a database on associations, search this database, and find an association that involves the bookstore industry. We'll search the association's Web page for information about the bookstore market. We'll follow these steps:

1. Open the Librarians' Index to the Internet and search for associations.
2. Select "Associations on the Net," an Internet Public Library database.
3. Search for and select an association that involves the bookstore industry.

4. Browse BookWeb, the American Booksellers Association Web page.

5. Bookmark some useful information about the bookstore industry.

Details

1   Open the Librarians' Index to the Internet and search for associations.

Do It! Click on the location field, type **http://sunsite.berkeley.edu/ InternetIndex**, and press **Enter**.

We want to find any special databases that focus on associations. In this virtual library, we're only searching for words in the titles of Web pages, annotations, and URLs—not in the Web pages themselves.

Do It! Type **associations** in the form next to **Search words or phrase**, as shown in Figure 14.25.

Do It! Click on **Search**.

Figure 14.25—Librarians' Index to the Internet Home Page

Figure 14.26 shows the search results. Note that there is a database entitled **Associations on the Net**, which the Internet Public Library has assembled.

2   Select "Associations on the Net," an Internet Public Library database.

Do It! Click on **Associations on the Net**, as shown in Figure 14.26.

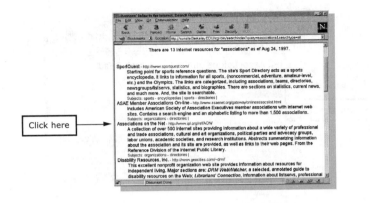

Figure 14.26—Search Results in the Librarians' Index to the Internet

3   Search for and select an association that involves the bookstore industry.

You should now be in Associations on the Net.

✷*Do It!* Scroll down until you come to a search form.

✷*Do It!* Type **bookstores** in the search query box and click on **Search**, as shown in Figure 14.27. (Since all the resources in this database are association Web pages, you don't need to type in the word *association*.)

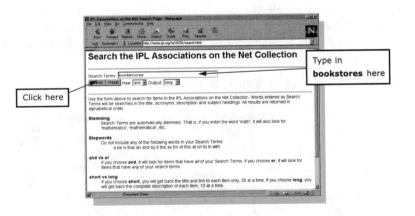

Figure 14.27—Associations on the Net Search Form

The search results appear in Figure 14.28. The first resource listed, **American Booksellers Association (ABA)**, looks like the Web page we've been seeking.

✷*Do It!* Click on **American Booksellers Association (ABA)**.

Figure 14.28—Associations on the Net Search Results

4   **Browse BookWeb, the American Booksellers Association Web page.**

Your screen should now show the home page of the American Booksellers Association's BookWeb. You'll need to scroll down until you see **Contents**. Since we want to find out something about the bookstore industry and we're not sure where to begin, let's try the Reference Desk.

✳*Do It!* Click on **Reference Desk**.

Figure 14.29 shows a picture of it. We'd like to find out if the Fredericksburg area is already one of the top U.S. book markets, so we are especially interested in the link to **Top U.S. Book Markets**, as shown in Figure 14.29.

✳*Do It!* Click on **Top U.S. Book Markets**.

Figure 14.29—Reference Desk Page of BookWeb

When your screen fills, you'll see a list of the cities with the number of bookstores in each, along with the 1992 sales in thousands of dollars. See Figure 14.30. For each sales amount listed, you would add three zeros to get the accurate amount spent on books for that particular year. The cities are ranked from highest to lowest sales figures. If we want to know if Fredericksburg is on the list, we need to use the Find in Page feature.

⟨Do It⟩ Click on **Edit** in the menu bar. Choose **Find in Page**.

⟨Do It⟩ Type **Fredericksburg** in the query box next to **Find what**.

⟨Do It⟩ Click on **Find Next**.

Figure 14.30—Using the Find Feature to Locate Fredericksburg

After you click on **Find Next**, the Find function will return with the message "Search String Not Found!" This means that Fredericksburg is not on the list of the top U.S. book markets.

⟨Do It⟩ Click **OK** to close the "Search String Not Found!" message box. Close the Find in Page dialog box.

Next, we want to see what other information BookWeb can give us about the bookstore industry. We need to go back to the Reference Desk page.

⟨Do It⟩ Click **Back** on the Netscape toolbar.

You should be back at the BookWeb Reference Desk.

⟨Do It⟩ Click on **IN FACT: Statistics from the ABA Research Dept**.

Figure 14.31 shows a partial listing of the information that is provided. Scroll down the page until you see a list of topics.

Click on **Projected Growth in Single-Person Households**

Figure 14.31—List of Research Topics on the Bookstore Industry

We could select several items, and if this were an actual research project, you'd want to select and read most of them. For our purposes, we'll choose one.

✸*Do It!* Click on **Projected Growth in Single-Person Households (7/29/96)**.

Your screen should look like the one in Figure 14.32. Note the significance of including single-person household statistical information in this Web page. Single people, or people living alone, tend to purchase more books than those in other types of households. The Web page also tells us that there is going to be an increase of single-person households in the next decade. Our picture doesn't show the source of this information, but if you scrolled down to the end of the page, you'd find that the U.S. Department of Commerce, the Bureau of the Census, and the ABA Research Department supplied these facts. This statistical information can give us clues as to what to look for in the next step, when we'll search for demographic data on the Fredericksburg area.

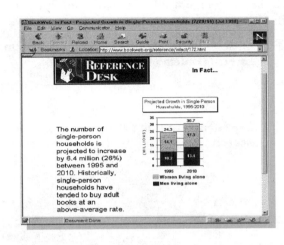

Figure 14.32—U.S. Census Statistics on Single-Person Households

5   Bookmark some useful information about the bookstore industry.

Before you leave this very useful site, you should bookmark it so you can return to it later and cite it in your bibliography. First, return to the home page.

Do It! Scroll down to the bottom of the page and click on **HOME**.

Do It! Now point to the location toolbar and click on **Bookmarks**.

Do It! Point to **Add Bookmark** and click on it.

Activity 2-B   Search a Specialized Database

Overview

While looking for marketing information about bookstores in BookWeb, we noted that some of the demographic statistics came from the U.S. Bureau of the Census. In this section, we will locate the U.S. Bureau of the Census database and search it for demographic information about Fredericksburg, Virginia. We'll follow these steps:

1. Return to the Librarians' Index to the Internet and search for demographic data.
2. Select the U.S. Bureau of the Census.
3. Search for demographic data on Fredericksburg, Virginia.
4. Bookmark the demographic information.

Details

1   Return to the Librarians' Index to the Internet and search for demographic data.

The best way to return to the Librarians' Index to the Internet is to type the URL for its location.

✻*Do It!* Click on the location field, type **http://sunsite.berkeley.edu/ InternetIndex**, and press **Enter**.

You should be at the home page for the Librarians' Index to the Internet, as shown in Figure 14.33.

✻*Do It!* Type **demographic data** in the search query box and click on **Search**.

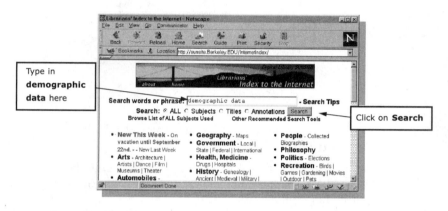

Figure 14.33—Librarians' Index to the Internet with Search Query Entered

2   Select the U.S. Bureau of the Census.

The search results appear in Figure 14.34. The best source on this list is the **U.S. Bureau of the Census**. Remember that much of the statistical information we found in the American Booksellers Association Web page came from the U.S. Bureau of the Census.

✻*Do It!* Click on **U.S. Bureau of the Census**.

Figure 14.34—Search Results with U.S. Bureau of the Census Selected

Your screen should look like the one in Figure 14.35. This is an official U.S. government Web page. The United States takes a census of population and housing every 10 years. The last one was done in 1990. Entire books have been written on the U.S. Census and how to understand it. We'll barely touch the surface here. Suffice it to say that having this information in digitized form will make it much easier for the public to find demographic information. Census information, hypertext, and graphical imaging go together quite nicely.

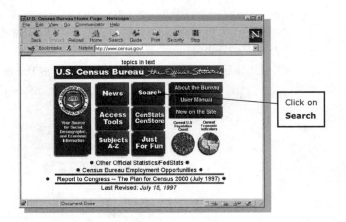

Figure 14.35—U.S. Census Bureau Home Page

❋*Do It!* From the U.S. Census Bureau home page, click on **Search**.

Your screen will fill with a lists of different types of searches you can do. We could do a place search, but for educational purposes let's try a map search.

❋*Do It!* Click on **Map Search**.

Your screen should look like the one in Figure 14.36. As Fredericksburg is in Virginia, we want to select Virginia, as shown in Figure 14.36.

❋*Do It!* Click on **VA**.

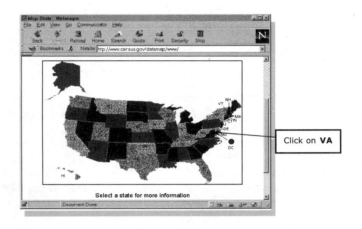

Figure 14.36—U.S. Census Bureau Map of the United States

3   Search for demographic data on Fredericksburg, Virginia.

Your screen will fill with a map of Virginia separated into parts. We know that Fredericksburg is 50 miles south of Washington, D.C., so we can make an educated guess that Fredericksburg would be in the state's northern section.

❋*Do It!* Click on the northernmost section of the map.

Your screen should look like the one in Figure 14.37.

Figure 14.37—U.S. Census Map of Northern Virginia

Note that Fredericksburg is an independent city surrounded by two counties: Stafford and Spotsylvania. If we want to find marketing information for the entire area, we'll have to look at statistics for these counties as well as the city of Fredericksburg, as it appears to be so small. In this project we're going to show what we found for the city of Fredericksburg only, but if this were an actual research project, you'd be wise to look in the counties as well.

※*Do It!* Click on **6**, as shown in Figure 14.37.

The screen that appears includes some hyperlinks that you can explore, as shown in Figure 14.38. We could look at a map of Fredericksburg. We could open a general statistical file about the city, a business and economic profile, and statistical tables. *STF* stands for *Summary Tape File.* Let's look at STF3A.

※*Do It!* Click on **STF3A**.

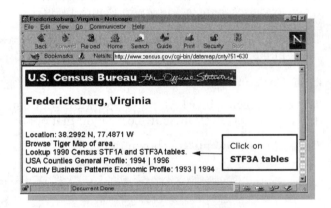

Figure 14.38—Data Hyperlinks for Fredericksburg, Virginia

Now you should see a long list of data elements, or tables, as shown in Figure 14.39. Each one represents a different census statistic. For example, P1 is the total number of people in Fredericksburg. If we wanted to know this amount, we'd have to check the box next to P1. For this example, let's find out how many people are in Fredericksburg. Remembering how the American Booksellers Association Web page mentioned that single people buy more books, let's also see how many single-person households there are.

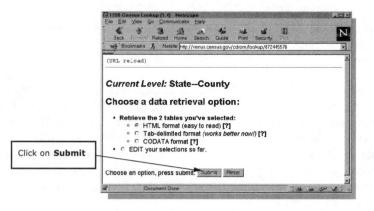

Figure 14.39—Selecting Data from Census Files

Do It! Click on **P1**, which represents the total number of people in Fredericksburg, as shown in Figure 14.39.

Do It! Scroll down until you come to **P16**, which represents the number of people in each household.

Do It! Click on **Submit**.

The next screen will ask you how you want your data to be retrieved. The default is **HTML format**. Leave it on that option.

Do It! Click on **Submit**, as shown in Figure 14.40.

Figure 14.40—Data Retrieval Options in Census Data Search

The data search results appear in Figure 14.41.

Figure 14.41—Results of the Statistical Data Search

4   **Bookmark the demographic information.**

You'll want to bookmark this information for later use. If you bookmark this page, however, your data won't be saved. Instead, you'll have
to go back to the table selection screen pictured in Figure 14.38 and
bookmark that screen.

✳*Do It!* Click **Back** on the toolbar until you are at the screen pictured
in Figure 14.39.

✳*Do It!* Point to the location toolbar and click on **Bookmarks**.

✳*Do It!* Point to **Add Bookmark** and click.

Evidently, we can find a great deal of marketing data for the
Fredericksburg, Virginia, area by exploring the U.S. Census Bureau Web
site. There will be questions, however, that census data won't answer.
You may need to search a state, city, or county government Web page to
find other types of information. For example, counties and other jurisdictions often have commissions or councils who research development
concerns in a particular area and then publish demographic and other
types of results. To find local information such as this, you'll probably
do best to use a search engine and search by keyword.

Activity 2-C   Perform a Search in a Search Engine

Overview

At the beginning of this project, we had a list of questions that we wanted
to answer. Thus far, we have found an association Web page with information about the bookstore industry. We have also found census data
about demographics, such as the number of households, the population's
education level, and other types of population-related questions. We still

haven't found a population projection for the Fredericksburg area, however. To find this particular statistic and detailed information about the area's business climate, it might be smart to use a search engine. We can type in the city's name and see what happens. We'll try that next. We'll follow these steps:

1. Open the location for WebCrawler.
2. Search for Web pages about Fredericksburg, Virginia.
3. Open StarWeb and follow some hyperlinks.
4. Bookmark a useful Web page.
5. Try to relocate the information by browsing in a search engine.

Details

1   Open the location for WebCrawler.

✳*Do It!* Click on the location field, type **http://www.webcrawler .com**, and press **Enter**.

We chose WebCrawler because it is a fast, full-text search engine that supports all the major search features: phrase searching, Boolean searching, and nested Boolean searching. We may need to use all of them.

2   Search for Web pages about Fredericksburg, Virginia.

✳*Do It!* Type **Fredericksburg Virginia** in the search form. We know that WebCrawler supports phrase searching by reading the help screen.

✳*Do It!* Click on **Search**, as shown in Figure 14.42.

"Fredericksburg Virginia" typed in

Click on **Search**

Figure 14.42—WebCrawler Search Form

3   Open StarWeb and follow some hyperlinks.

Figure 14.43 shows a partial list of results. Notice that several hyperlinks on the first page are for real estate agents.

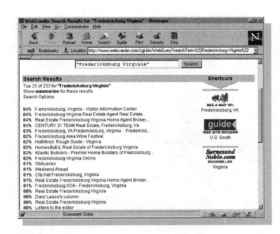

Figure 14.43—Results of WebCrawler Search

Let's try the first Web page that appears.

✳Do It! Click on **Fredericksburg, Virginia-Visitor Information Center**.

This Web page has several links to information about Fredericksburg. The Fredericksburg newspaper, the *Free Lance-Star,* may be a good place to start. Newspapers themselves can be a great source of information, not to mention all the hyperlinks that can appear there. Many newspapers will have the most current paper on the Web.

✳Do It! Click on **Fredericksburg Free Lance-Star**.

In the next few steps, keep in mind that Web research can take a lot of time. Many promising links don't yield good resources, and links that don't appear to be relevant often turn out to be exactly what you want. This project may make it look as if Web research is easy, but this is not always the case.

✳Do It! Click on the **Tourism** button, which is on the left side of the page.

Your screen will fill with a list of several tourism and travel hyperlinks. Many of these hyperlinks may help in locating information about doing business and living in the Fredericksburg area. For example, if you clicked on **Welcome to Virginia**, you'd be connected to the State of Virginia home page, which would have several links to state, county, and city government agencies.

✳Do It! Click on **Around the state**, as shown in Figure 14.44.

Chapter 14

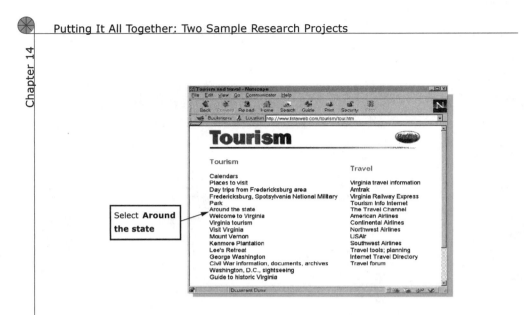

Figure 14.44—Tourism Hyperlinks in StarWeb

Once you're in **Around the State**, you'll notice that this is part of the **State of Virginia** Web site, as shown in Figure 14.45.

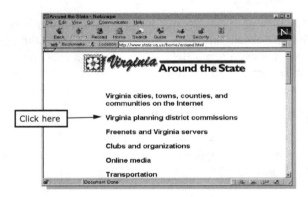

Figure 14.45—Virginia's "Around the State" Web Page

As we're trying to find local information, let's see if there are any planning district commissions in the area that interests us.

✻*Do It!* Click on **Virginia planning district commissions**.

Several hyperlinks will appear. Each one represents an area planning commission. If we didn't know anything about the area, we'd have to use trial and error to select the right hyperlink. We happen to know, however, that the Rappahannock River runs through the Fredericksburg area, and that the Rappahannock Area Development Commission is located in Fredericksburg.

✻*Do It!* Click on **Rappahannock Area Development Commission**.

Figure 14.46 shows a portion of the page that appears.

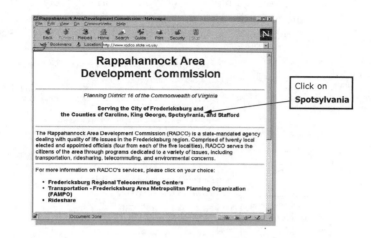

Figure 14.46—Rappahannock Area Development Commission Web Page

If we clicked on **City of Fredericksburg**, we'd go back to StarWeb. We can try clicking on several of the hyperlinks. Let's see what **Spotsylvania** has to offer.

Do It! Click on **Spotsylvania**, as shown in Figure 14.46.

After your screen fills, scroll down until you see **Why you want to do business here**, **Why you want to live here**, and the other hyperlinks shown in Figure 14.47. Each one of these hyperlinks gives you an incredible amount of information about the area. If you clicked on **Why you want to do business here**, you'd find all sorts of labor statistics, including the unemployment rate and tax information. Many of the statistics listed come from the U.S. Bureau of the Census, others are compiled by the state of Virginia, and others are provided by universities, commissions, and other entities.

Do It! Click on **Why you want to live here**.

Figure 14.47—Portion of Spotsylvania County's Economic Development Page

Your screen will fill with many more choices.

Do It! Click on **Housing**.

Do It! Click on **Population Profile**.

Do It! Click on **Profile**.

Figure 14.48 shows the population projection we've been seeking. If this were a real project, you would probably want a copy of the report done by the University of Virginia, Center for Public Service, which produced these statistics.

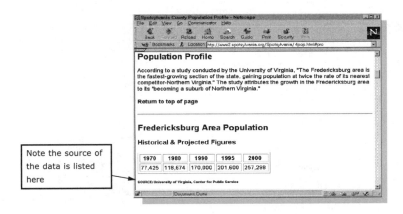

Figure 14.48—Population Profile for Fredericksburg Area

4   Bookmark a useful Web page.

Let's bookmark this page so we don't lose track of it.

Do It! Point to the menu commands at the top of the screen and click on **Bookmarks**.

Do It! Point to **Add Bookmark** and click.

5   Try to relocate the information by browsing in a search engine.

Let's do an experiment. Now that we know where the information is and what words are on the page, let's do a search in WebCrawler using words that appear in the Web page to see if we come upon this page again. First, open WebCrawler.

Do It! Point to the location field, type **http://www.webcrawler.com**, and press **Enter**. (You could also get to WebCrawler by pressing **Back** in the menu bar several times.)

Do It! In the search query box, type **Fredericksburg and "popula-tion profile"** (WebCrawler is case-insensitive, so we don't need to capitalize **population** and **profile**, even though they are capitalized on the Web page).

Do It! Click on **Search**.

Figure 14.49 shows the response we receive. This just goes to show you that a search engine isn't always able to find pages with the keywords you request. Sometimes serendipity and plain old persistence are needed to find the most important information on the Web.

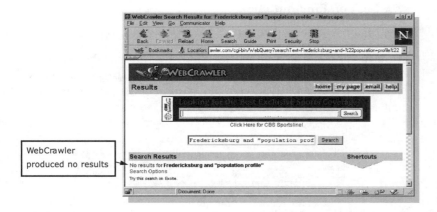

WebCrawler produced no results

Figure 14.49—WebCrawler Results

Activity 2-D   Evaluate the Resources Found

Overview

In this project, we bookmarked three references. We'll evaluate one of these resources, just as we did in the first project, by applying the evaluation guidelines introduced in Chapter 12. We'll follow these steps:

1. Go to your bookmark list and select "BookWeb: Home Page."
2. Evaluate this resource using the evaluation guidelines.

Details

1   Go to your bookmark list and select "BookWeb: Home Page."

Do It Point to the menu commands at the top of the screen and click on **Bookmarks**. Drag the mouse down until you come to **BookWeb: Home Page**.

Do It Click on **BookWeb: Home Page**.

2   Evaluate this resource using the evaluation guidelines.

You should be at the home page for the American Booksellers Association. We'll go through each of the guidelines for this Web page.

Who Is the Author or Institution?

It's evident when you get BookWeb up on your screen that it's put out by the American Booksellers Association (ABA), because its name appears just before **BookWeb** at the beginning of the Web page. We also know that the ABA is an organizational Web page, because it has *.org* in its URL. But we'd like to know more about it. Scroll down the page until you come to **Contents**.

✳*Do It!* Click on **Find out about**.

✳*Do It!* Click on **The American Booksellers Association**.

Part of the page appears in Figure 14.50. We find out that the association has existed since 1900 and is devoted to promoting the book-retailing industry. If you scroll down to the bottom of the page, you'll find an email address for the association, in addition to a street address.

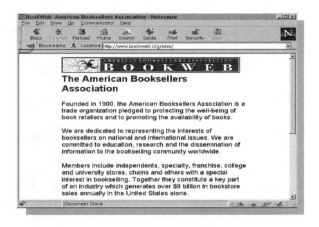

Figure 14.50—American Booksellers Association Web Page "BookWeb"

How Current Is the Information?

At the beginning of the Web page, there is a date that indicates when it was updated. It appears to be updated every weekday. To find out when it was last updated, you can click **View** in the menu bar and choose **Page Info**. This will tell you the date on which it was last modified. It may match the date on the first page.

Who Is the Audience?

The audience is clearly stated in the mission statement, which is partially shown in Figure 14.50. The audience consists of people who are involved in the book-retailing business. These would be bookstore owners and managers, as well as people in the book-publishing industry. From the looks of some features in the Web page, you could argue that this Web site is for any avid reader who loves books and bookstores.

Is the Content Accurate and Objective?

After looking at several of the statistical pages in the Reference Desk section, noting that all of them are properly cited, and noticing that everything in the site is attributed to a source, we can reasonably conclude that the content is accurate. BookWeb is an advocate of artistic freedom, however, as evidenced by its section on free expression. You can find a list of banned books in the United States, along with articles on censorship legal cases and other issues. This would make BookWeb subjective. The association isn't going to give both sides of the censorship issue, because it's in its best interest to show only one side, which is that expression in its purest form should be supported. This doesn't mean, however, that this resource can't be trusted. It's just something you should keep in mind.

What Is the Purpose of the Information?

The purpose, which is clearly stated in the mission statement and implied throughout the Web page, is to inform booksellers across the country about the state of the industry. Its purpose is to inform people in a timely manner about how the book business is faring and to present related issues.

Activity 2-E Cite the Resources Found

Overview

We'll look at all of your bookmarks now to determine their bibliographic format, according to the guidelines in Chapter 13. Here are the steps you'll take:
1. Open your bookmarks.
2. Determine how to cite each resource properly.
3. Assemble the citations in a bibliography.

Details

1   Open your bookmarks.

✱*Do It!* While in Netscape, point to **Bookmarks** in the location toolbar and move the pointer to the bookmarks.

✱*Do It!* Select each bookmark one by one, starting with **BookWeb: Home Page**.

2   Determine how to cite each resource properly.

We'll use the guidelines from Chapter 13 to determine the best way to cite these resources.

Resource: BookWeb: Home page

Type of resource: Web page

✱   **Name of author:** American Booksellers Association

✱   **Title of the work (in quotes):** "American Booksellers Association BookWeb"

❋ **Title of the Web page (in italics):** *BookWeb: Home Page*
❋ **Date of last revision:** 23 April 1997
❋ **URL:** http://www.bookweb.org
❋ **Date accessed:** 23 April 1997

Resource: Census Lookup (1.4)

When you open this bookmark, you'll have to look for the data again. Go back to the project and search for the same data elements you searched for earlier, and then cite the information that you need.

Type of resource: Web page

❋ **Name of author:** U.S. Census Bureau
❋ **Title of work (in quotes):** "1990 US Census Data"
❋ **Title of the Web page (in italics):** *Census Lookup (1.4)*
❋ **Date of the last revision:** Not available
❋ **URL:** http://venus.census.gov/cdrom/lookup/861845234
❋ **Date accessed:** 23 April 1997

Resource: Spotsylvania County Population Profile

Type of resource: Web page

❋ **Name of author:** Spotsylvania County Office of Economic Development, Spotsylvania, VA
❋ **Title of the work (in quotes):** "Population Profile"
❋ **Title of the Web page (in italics):** *Spotsylvania County Population Profile*
❋ **Date of the last revision:** 20 December 1996
❋ **URL:** http://www2.spotsylvania.org/spotsylvania/14pop.html#pro
❋ **Date accessed:** 23 April 1997

3   Assemble the citations in a bibliography.

Now that we've determined the elements in each citation, we can see what they'd all look like in a bibliography:

Bibliography
American Booksellers Association. "American Booksellers Association BookWeb." *BookWeb Home Page.* 23 April 1997. http://www.bookweb.org 23 April 1997.

Spotsylvania County Office of Economic Development, Spotsylvania, VA. "Population Profile." *Spotsylvania County Population Profile.* 20

December 1996. http://www2.spotsylvania.org/spotsylvania/
14pop.html#pro
23 April 1997.

U.S. Census Bureau. "1990 US Census Data." *Census Lookup (1.4)*. Date
of last revision not available.
http://venus.census.gov/cdrom/lookup/861845234
23 April 1997.

Summary

This chapter focused on two research projects that were very different
from each other not only in content but also in approach. The first was
a broad, open-ended topic in the sense that we had no clear expecta-
tions about the search results. We researched the topic of women and
computing with no idea of what we were going to find or how we were
going to narrow the topic as we went along. The second research project
was also broad but required a different approach. In that project, we
knew what we needed to find and looked for it. Our topic—marketing
data for the bookstore industry in Fredericksburg, Virginia—was much
more focused and required an almost formulaic approach.

The chapter taught us the following lessons:

❋ Research on the World Wide Web doesn't always follow a
systematic process. Sometimes you may start with a library
catalog, sometimes with a search engine.

❋ Most search engines claim that they index the full text of
every Web page, but this is not always the case.

❋ Guidelines for evaluating resources are just that—guidelines. If a particular site doesn't give both sides of an issue,
that doesn't mean it is unreliable. It's good for you to know
that there may be an underlying bias to the information
and that you should make allowances for this.

❋ Sometimes, finding information on the World Wide Web
requires a great deal of persistence.

The chapter brought together skills on how to find a specialized
database, how to search a library catalog, and how to find information
in a Usenet archive. You practiced evaluating resources and citing them
properly in a bibliography.

Exercises and Projects

Create a research project of your own, using the following checklist:

1. Search a directory or virtual library to find resources.
2. Find and search a specialized database.
3. Formulate and submit a search query to a search engine.
4. Locate and search a library catalog by subject or keyword.
5. Search a Usenet or email discussion group archive.
6. Evaluate the resources found.
7. Cite the resources in a bibliography.

Appendix

Annotated List of Selected Search Tools

In this appendix, we'll discuss various search engines and search tools in detail. We'll cover both general-purpose search engines and meta-search tools.

For each search engine or search tool, we will list the URLs of its home page, help page, and FAQ page, along with its output features. For search engines, we'll also identify the types of searches available, the sources to search, and the type of indexing used. For meta-search tools, we'll specify any special features. If the search tool allows for searching several sites concurrently (the parallel search tools), we'll also name the search engines contacted. Whenever an activity in the book has used the search engine or search tool, we will list it as an example as well.

Major Search Engines

This section will list some of the major search engines.

AltaVista

Created by Digital Equipment Corporation, AltaVista is one of the most popular and well-regarded search services on the Web. Two types of searching, simple and advanced, are available. AltaVista's home page begins in simple search mode. A hyperlink on each search or results page lets you switch from one type of searching to the other. Information about either type of searching is available if you click on the Help hyperlink.

In a simple search, only the implied Boolean operators + and - may be used. In an advanced search, you *must* use the Boolean operators AND, OR, or NOT to form search expressions. The term NEAR may also be used for proximity.

In either the simple or advanced mode, you can do phrase searching in which you enclose words in quotes. Furthermore, you can use * as a wildcard character. Finally, you can use capitalization to form a search phrase.

Both modes let you restrict the search to certain fields or portions of a Web page. AltaVista calls this *special functions*. A complete list of fields is available at either help page.

Search results are ranked by relevance in either mode. In the advanced mode, you can specify the ranking by requiring pages that contain certain words to be listed first. This doesn't include or exclude a page from the result; it only affects the ranking. You can specify that you only want links to pages that were indexed or modified during a specified time period. You may specify to see only a count of the results.

You can choose to have the results displayed in compact or standard format. In compact format, only a hyperlink to the title and a few words from the text of the Web page are displayed. In standard format, each result contains the title and URL as hyperlinks, the size (in bytes) of the item, the date it was last visited by the search engine robot, and the first few lines of text from the Web page.

AltaVista offers a *refine* feature, which helps to form search expressions and make the results more precise. Click on **refine** from any page of results. A graphical view (using Java) is available as well. The next Web page lists your expression along with synonyms for terms in the search phrase. By selecting terms you can require that the results include or exclude certain topics.

AltaVista lets you set and save preferences. That way every time you access AltaVista, you can start with the features, such as advanced search or graph view for refine, that work best for you. Click on the **Preferences** hyperlink to see the possibilities.

Home page:	**http://altavista.digital.com**
Help with simple searches:	**http://altavista.digital.com/av/ content/help_simple.htm**
Help with advanced searches:	**http://altavista.digital.com/av/ content/help_advanced.htm**
FAQ:	**http://altavista.digital.com/av/ content/about.htm**
Types of searches:	Keyword or phrase. Implied Boolean expressions in simple search, and full Boolean expressions in advanced search. Proximity, truncation, wildcards, case sensitivity, and field searching supported.
Sources to search:	Web or Usenet.
Indexing:	Full-text.
Output features:	Standard: hyperlink, URL, and text from the Web page. Compact: hyperlink only. Ranked only by relevancy in simple search. User can supply ranking criteria in advanced search.
Examples:	Activities 2.1, 5.1, 6.2; Chapter 14, Project 1.

Excite

From Excite's home page, you can search the Web, Excite Channels, Usenet, and magazines and newspapers on the Web. The home page also contains a link to City.Net; links to business information and maps; Instant Info, an online reference center; links to stock quotes, travel sites, and horoscopes; and ways to find email addresses, street addresses, and phone numbers. The channels are collections of information and ways to retrieve information based on a topic. Here are some examples: *News* is a search service and directory dedicated to magazines and newspapers that are available on the Web. *My Channel* is a personalized list of hyperlinks to news, weather, or entertainment information. *People* and *Chat* are collections of bulletin boards and chat rooms for online discussions, as well as access to search services for finding home pages, email addresses, and street addresses.

Search results are displayed 10 per page and ranked by a relevancy score. Links may also be arranged by site, so all the links from each Web site appear together. When results are displayed, you have the opportunity to select from a list of suggested words to add to the search phrase, but this performs a new search. Each result includes a hyperlink **Click here to perform a search for documents like this one**. These perform a new search for documents similar to the one selected. You can also select the **Power Search** hyperlink if it is available. The associated Web page contains several forms to help you create a search phrase by requiring some words, excluding others, and so forth.

You search Excite's index using keywords or phrases. The search tool is one of the few that uses concept searching. For instance, a term such as *young people* may result in links with terms such as *adolescents, juveniles,* or *children.* Excite also offers the implied Boolean operators + and -, and the Boolean operators AND, OR, and AND NOT. These Boolean operators *must* be typed in uppercase. Although Excite is case-sensitive, it lacks some of the capabilities of other search tools for forming search expressions; it doesn't have truncation, wildcards, or proximity operators, and it doesn't support field searching.

Home page:	**http://www.excite.com**
Help:	**http://www.excite.com/Info/searching.html**
FAQ:	**http://www.excite.com/Info/features.html**
Types of searches:	Keyword (concept search) and phrase. Boolean expressions allowed.
Sources to search:	Web pages (full text), Excite Web Guide, Usenet articles, selected news sources, or City.Net travel guide.
Indexing:	Full-text.
Output features:	Title (hyperlink), URL, summary, and a link to similar sites. Ranked by relevancy or site.
Examples:	Activity 6.3.

HotBot

HotBot has become one of the most highly regarded search engines on the Internet. Its home page lets you search the Web. Enter one or more keywords and select from a menu the way the keywords will be used in obtaining results: match all the words or any of the words; use the keywords as a phrase, name or Boolean expression; or return results with the keywords in the title. A URL can be entered in the search form, and HotBot will return a list of Web pages that contain links to the URL, provided you select **link to this URL** from the menu. You could restrict the date by asking for documents that were added to or updated in the index within a specific time period (click on **Date**). You can specify domains or geographical locations (click on **Continent**). Alternatively, you can specify that results contain certain media types, such as Image, Audio, Video, and Shockwave.

Results may be displayed from 10 to 100 at a time in brief or detailed format or as URLs. When results are displayed, you have the opportunity to revise the search words or phrase. HotBot includes a feature titled **SuperSearch**. It's an extension of the regular HotBot search interface. You use it to enter additional search terms, specify additional media types, and to be more precise about the time period and location of documents. It is very useful in constructing Boolean search expressions.

Hyperlinks on HotBot's home page take you to forms to use for searching Usenet archives, news sites, classifieds, domain names, stocks, lists of discussion groups, and collections of shareware. You can also follow links to pages you use to find businesses, people, and email addresses.

The home page also contains Wired Cybrarian, a directory of guides to information on the Internet. You can search entries at individual topic sites using HotBot. Wired Cybrarian is therefore similar to a collection of specialized databases.

To obtain help in using HotBot and answers to frequently asked questions, click on the button labeled **Help** on the home page. Several selections are available, including **Getting Started**—a quick and thorough introduction to using HotBot, and **Frequently Asked Questions**—a detailed explanation of HotBot's features and operation.

Home page:	**http://www.hotbot.com**
Help:	**http://help.hotbot.com, http://help.hotbot .com/intro.html**
FAQ:	**http://help.hotbot.com/faq/index.html**
Types of searches:	Keyword or phrase. Boolean expressions allowed.
Sources to search:	Web, Usenet, news sites, classifieds, domain names, stocks, discussion groups, and shareware.
Indexing:	Full-text.
Output features:	Full description: title (hyperlink), excerpt, URL, size, and date indexed. Brief: title (hyperlink), one-line excerpt.
Examples:	Activities 6.1, 12.1, 12.2.

Infoseek

From Infoseek's home page, you can search the Web, Usenet, news services, and company profiles. It also contains links to Infoseek channels, a collection of Internet and Web resources based on a topic. The Entertainment channel, for example, contains a collection of Web sites; links to movie, TV, music, and book reviews; news about the entertainment industry; and links to tickets and events. The home page also has links to a page you use to find street and world **maps** (provided by MapQuest); **Big Yellow**, a Web site that is primarily a listing of businesses on the Web (like the yellow pages in a phone book) but that also allows you to find people, look up email addresses, and search country-specific directories from around the world. There's also a link to a **reference** section that includes a forms-based interface to a dictionary and thesaurus.

You search Infoseek's index using keywords or phrases. You can search for a phrase by enclosing it in quotes. Only the implied Boolean operators + and - are available. Field searching is also available on the title of a Web page, the domain name of a site, or a full or partial URL.

Search results are displayed 10 per page and ranked by a relevancy score. You can hide the summaries. You can also arrange the links by site so that all the links from each Web site appear together. When results are displayed, you can begin a new search, but Infoseek makes it rather easy to restrict a search and increase its precision. You can modify the search phrase so that you search either through the current results or on the Web (the part in the Infoseek index).

Home page:	**http://www.infoseek.com**
Help:	**http://www.infoseek.com/ Help?pg = HomeHelp.html**
FAQ:	None available.
Types of searches:	Keyword or phrase. Implied Boolean expressions allowed.
Sources to search:	Web, Usenet, news services, email addresses, and company profiles.
Indexing:	Full-text, keyword.
Output features:	Title (hyperlink), summary, URL, and size. Can hide summary.
Examples:	Activities 3.4, 5.2.

Lycos

From Lycos's home page, you can search the Web; search for pictures (image files), sounds (audio files); personal home pages; books; stocks; and search the annotated listings in the Lycos directory by subject. There are also links to a number of directories and services available through Lycos, including **Yellow Pages**, a listing of companies on the Web; listings of news stories; **Companies Online**, a listing of Dun and

Bradstreet's information about companies; **Road Maps**, a search tool that obtains maps and driving directions to street addresses in the United States; a site to get weather information; a site that has links to several chat groups; and **Top 5% Sites**, a directory of the most popular Web sites. The home page also has links to the Lycos Web Guides—a collection of Web and Internet resources arranged into categories. A hyperlink to help is available on each page.

You can perform a simple search from the home page by typing in one or more keywords. The simple search finds sites that match any of the words. The results (10 per page) are ranked by relevancy; pages that match more of the terms rank higher. Lycos takes the words you give plus similar words to find Web pages. When results are displayed, you can modify the search terms, select related sites, or obtain a list of pictures (images, video) or sounds (audio) matching the search terms.

More sophisticated searches are available only if you select Lycos Pro by clicking on the hyperlink **Advanced Search**. In Lycos Pro, you can set search options to allow a match of any word (OR) or all words (AND). That also allows you to set some search parameters, but it does not give you the same capabilities for using Boolean operators that exist in other search tools. See the "Lycos Help" page for full details.

Display options can also be set from the advanced search page. You select the number of items, from 10 to 40, to be displayed per Web page. The results can be listed in summary form (hyperlinks only, along with a relative score), standard form (hyperlink, score, URL, and an excerpt from the Web page pertinent to your search phrase), or detailed form (standard, along with detailed information about the Web page, including the number of links it has to other Web pages, an outline, and an abstract or excerpt of the page).

Home page: **http://www.lycos.com**
Help: **http://www.lycos.com/help**
FAQ: None available.
Types of searches: Keyword. Implied Boolean expressions allowed. Can match all words (AND) or any words (OR). Boolean expressions allowed only with Lycos Pro's Java Power Panel. See the "Lycos Help" page for details.
Sources to search: Web, pictures, sounds, Top 5% sites, personal home pages, stocks.
Indexing: Full-text.
Output features: Summary: links only. Standard: title (hyperlink), excerpt, URL, size, and number of terms matched. Detailed: standard format plus outline, abstract, and number of links to external Web pages.
Examples: None.

Open Text

Open Text's home page has a form in which you enter keywords to perform a simple search. Select from a pulldown menu whether to use phrase searching or keyword searching, in which case Open Text returns results that match all terms. Its **Power Search** link lets you use Boolean and proximity operators to form a search expression. Open Text's links allow you to search selected newspaper articles on the Web, Usenet newsgroups (using Deja News), and email addresses (using WhoWhere). The page also contains links to **help** and **FAQ**. The FAQ page explains how Open Text differs from other search tools, such as Lycos, Infoseek, and WebCrawler.

There are two types of searches in Open Text: simple and power. The simple search either matches all words or searches for phrases. Once results are displayed, you have the option of choosing to **start a new search** or **improve your result**. Choosing the latter takes you to a form that lets you add another term to your expression. You can combine the terms using **And**, **Or**, or **But not**. Alternately, you can specify that your search expression be **Near** another term. You could ask Open Text to search for each term in the text, first heading, summary, title, or URL.

The power search lets you use Boolean expressions. It selects matches based on the nearness and order of the terms in a phrase and in the portion of the page (title, first heading, whole page, summary, or URL) it is searching. You can add more terms and operators to the search expression. When the results are displayed, you can again improve the search, making it more precise. By using Boolean expressions, proximity operators, and field searching, you can use an incremental approach to find what you need. The power search also allows for searches of current events, newsgroups (using Deja News), and email addresses.

Home page:	**http://index.opentext.net**
Help:	**http://index.opentext.net/main/ help.html**
FAQ:	**http://index.opentext.net/main/faq.html**
Types of searches:	Keyword or phrase. Simple search is the default on the home page; it matches all terms. Power search allows for Boolean and proximity operators. User completes the search expression using a form.
Sources to search:	Web, Usenet (Deja News), email addresses (WhoWhere), selected newspapers.
Indexing:	Full-text.
Output features:	Title, size, URL, and excerpt.
Examples:	Activity 5.1.

WebCrawler

WebCrawler was one of the first search engines available on the Web. It was started by Brian Pinkerton as a research project at the University of Washington and has since become part of Excite, Inc. WebCrawler works quickly, and it gives useful results. It also contains a good description of how it and other search engines work, and a very well organized help facility. The home page has a simple search form that can be filled in for simple keyword searching, phrase searching (enclose the words in quotes), or with expressions using Boolean (AND, OR, NOT) and proximity (NEAR, ADJ) operators. The home page also contains a collection of channels, each of which includes a directory of reviewed Web sites. There are also links to search services for **yellow pages** (GTE), **newsgroups** (Deja News), **people finder** (WhoWhere), **maps** (MapQuest), **weather**, **classifieds**, **horoscopes**, and **stock quotes**.

Results are displayed, 25 per page, ranked by relevance, and presented in brief format by default, with the title as a hyperlink. Clicking on the hyperlink to show **summaries** gives an excerpt from each page, the URL for the page, and a link to similar pages.

WebCrawler has a very easy-to-use and effective interface.

Home page:	**http://www.webcrawler.com**
Help:	**http://www.webcrawler.com/ WebCrawler/Help/Help.html**
FAQ:	None.
Types of searches:	Keyword, phrase, Boolean.
Sources to search:	Web.
Indexing:	Full-text.
Output features:	Title (hyperlink), excerpt, and URL. Can hide excerpt. User can set options.
Examples:	Activity 3.3, 12.1, Chapter 14, Project 2.

Other Resources

Here are some Web sites that have lists of hyperlinks to several general-purpose search engines, including the ones above. Take a look at some of these if you want to try some search engines in addition to the ones mentioned above.

Title of Web Page	URL
Beaucoup Search Engines—Category Page:General Engines	**http://www.beaucoup.com/ 1geneng.html**
Internet Search Tools (Library of Congress Explore the Internet)	**http://lcweb.loc.gov/global/ search.html**
Needle in a Cyberstack— the Info-finder: Search Engines	**http://home.revealed.net/ ~ albee/pages/search.html**

Search Engine Watch	**http://searchenginewatch.com**
Search Results for: Search Bots	**http://botspot.com/search/s-search.htm**
Yahoo!—Computers and Internet: Internet:World Wide Web:Searching the Web:Search Engines	**http://www.yahoo.com/Computers_and_internet/internet/world_wide_web/wearching_the_web/search_engines**

Comparison of Major Search Engines

The tables at the end of this appendix give a comparison of some of the major search engines. For each we list its search features, including a list of resources it has available, and then the output features.

Meta-search Tools

Meta-search tools allow you to use several search engines. Some sites merely list World Wide Web search tools with their search forms so you can search one at a time. These are called all-in-one search tools. If a meta-search tool allows you to search several search engines or directories simultaneously, it's called a parallel search tool. Many meta-search tools take your query, search several databases or search engines simultaneously, and then integrate the results. Some meta-search tools are good places to find lists of specialized databases. This section is an annotated list of meta-search tools. Some are all-in-one tools, and most are parallel search tools.

All-in-One Search Page

The All-in-One Search Page is a large collection of forms-based search tools arranged by categories, including **World Wide Web**, **General Internet**, **Specialized Interest**, **Software**, **People**, **News/Weather**, **Publications/Literature**, **Technical Reports**, **Documentation**, **Desk Reference**, and **Other Interesting Searches/Services**. After you select a category, you see a list of hyperlinks for the search services in that category, along with a simple frame for submitting a phrase for each tool. This easy-to-use interface was developed and is supported by William D. Cross. The goal is to provide a consistent interface to search tools from one location on the Web. That goal is met, but there is no search facility that locates resources within All-in-One. The only way to find a specific service is to browse the directory. For example, the search form for the Getty Information Institute is found under Publications/Literature.

Home page:	**http://www.albany.net/allinone**
Help:	None available.

FAQ:	None available.
Output features:	Either displays search result or search page for selected service.
Special features:	Forms-based search services arranged by categories.
Examples:	None.

Internet Sleuth

Internet Sleuth lists close to two thousand general-purpose and specialized searchable databases available on the Web. The databases are arranged by subject; the major headings are **Arts & Humanities**, **Business**, **Computers**, **Education**, **Employment**, **Environment**, **Government**, **Health**, **Internet**, **News**, **Recreation**, **Reference**, **Regional**, **Sciences**, **Shopping**, **Social Sciences**, **Society**, **Sports**, **Travel**, and **Veterinary/Zoology**. The home page, as well as the other pages, has a search form you can use to find databases or search tools listed by the Internet Sleuth.

A search form that lets you search several databases at once is included on the home page and in several of the sections. Internet Sleuth lists the most popular and useful search engines, including AltaVista, Excite, Infoseek, Lycos, and WebCrawler. Other categories on the home page that allow for parallel searching are **News**, **Business and Finance**, **Software**, and **Usenet**. For each search, you may specify a maximum search time. The selected search engines or databases are contacted, and the results are presented as if the searching were conducted at the search engine's home site.

Each search tool or database is represented by a hyperlink to the search page for the database, a brief description of the type of information it provides, and a search form that lets you initiate a search from the Internet Sleuth. In many cases, you'll also be able to set options or select types of resources using the form there. The entry for ArtsEdge, for example, allows you to search using phrases or Boolean expressions and to select one or more categories. Internet Sleuth is a good tool to use to find both general-purpose and specialized databases and search tools.

Home page:	**http://www.isleuth.com**
Help:	**http://www.isleuth.com/about.html**
FAQ:	None available.
Output features:	Each service or tool represented by a hyperlink and a form (usually with options) for submitting a query to the service.
Special features:	Search form on home page allows user to search for services available through the Internet Sleuth. Also allows for parallel search of several services.
Examples:	Activity 7.2; Chapter 14, Project 1.

Dogpile

Dogpile bills itself as a "friendly multi-engine search tool." It has a well-designed and easy-to-use interface. You type keywords in a search form on its home page, select whether to search the Web, Usenet, FTP archives, or news services, and then click on a button labeled **Fetch**. Dogpile then submits the keywords, assuming the words are connected by AND, to three search engines. It then displays the results. If it doesn't come up with 10 documents, then another three search engines are contacted. This continues until at least 10 results are obtained. You can request that other search engines be contacted even if 10 results are found.

You can use Boolean and proximity operators (AND, OR, NOT, and NEAR) in the keyword expression. If you use NEAR, then search engines that allow its use are contacted first. You can also use quotes and parentheses. If a search engine doesn't support these then they're removed before the search expression is passed to one of those.

The search engines and directories contacted for Web resources include AltaVista, Excite, Magellan, Lycos, WebCrawler, Infoseek, HotBot, and Yahoo! For Usenet searches, Dogpile contacts Reference.COM, Deja News, HotBot News, and AltaVista. Filez and FTP searches are contacted when you indicate you want to search FTP archives. When searching news services, Dogpile contacts Yahoo!, News Headlines, Excite News, and Infoseek News Wires.

The search options on the home page let you pick one category of resources to use to start the search and then to go to another category. For example you can choose to have Dogpile first contact Web search engines and then go to Usenet archives. You can set the order in which search engines and other resources are contacted by selecting **Custom Search** from any Dogpile Web page.

Dogpile works well, is well designed, and is easy to use. It's definitely worth considering if you want to use a parallel search tool.

Home page:	**http://www.dogpile.com**
Help:	**http://www.dogpile.com/notes.html**
FAQ:	None available.
Search engines contacted:	Twenty-five search engines, directories, and other resources.
Output features:	Results arranged by relevance according to each search engine or resource contacted.
Special features:	Keywords connected by AND is the default. Searching by phrase, Boolean expressions, or proximity operators.
Examples:	None.

MetaCrawler

MetaCrawler takes the keywords entered in a search form on its home page and simultaneously conducts a search using several popular search engines and directories. Those include AltaVista, Excite, Lycos, WebCrawler, and Yahoo! Keywords can be passed to the search engines as a phrase. They can be connected by *AND* (all the words) or by *OR* (match any of the words). MetaCrawler supports implied Boolean expressions using **+** and **-**, as well as phrase searching when the search string is enclosed in quotes. The top 10 results are taken from each search engine, and duplicates are eliminated. MetaCrawler displays results according to relevance. To do so, it computes a score based on the search engines' scores or according to location. It determines location from the domain names in results, including U.S. commercial, U.S. educational, North American, European, and other sites. MetaCrawler has the option **Power Search**; select it from the home page. The page that appears lets you set the location for searches, the number of results per page, the number of seconds to wait for the search to complete, and the number of results to get from each source. MetaCrawler gives relatively quick access to the most relevant results from several search engines. Read the MetaCrawler FAQ for details and updates.

Home page:	**http://www.metacrawler.com**
Help:	None available.
FAQ:	**http://www.metacrawler.com/faq.html**
Search engines contacted:	Six of the most popular search engines.
Output features:	Results arranged by location (domain name) or relevance. Duplicates eliminated.
Special features:	Searching by phrase, as well as AND and OR. Implied Boolean operators may be used. User may select **Power Search**.
Examples:	Activity 5.3.

SavvySearch

SavvySearch takes keywords entered in the search form on its search page and ranks the suitability of each of the possible search engines. The ranking, done by the software that controls SavvySearch, depends on which search engines will perform best based on the request, as well as the current load and availability of search engines. In ranking the search engines, SavvySearch puts them into groups, each called a *search plan*. SavvySearch performs the search with the first search plan and gives you the option of selecting another plan for a subsequent search.

You may select from a collection of sources and types of information, such as **Web Resources**, **People**, **News**, **Software**, and **Images**. When you search for documents that contain the query keywords, you can choose to use all the terms (AND), any of the terms (OR), or to do phrase searching. You can also specify how many results you want from each search engine; whether to display results in brief, normal, or verbose format; and whether to integrate the results. The results displayed include the title as a hyperlink, the URL, and the search engine used. Using normal or verbose format gives more information, including an abstract or description of each result. Choosing to display the results in integrated form eliminates duplicates and preserves relative rankings. Otherwise, results are arranged according to search engine. A final choice that SavvySearch presents is one of language; the search form is available in approximately 20 languages.

Home page:	**http://guaraldi.cs.colostate.edu:2000**
Search form:	**http://guaraldi.cs.colostate.edu:2000/ form**
Help:	**http://guaraldi.cs.colostate.edu:2000/ help**
FAQ:	**http://guaraldi.cs.colostate.edu:2000/ faq**
Search engines contacted:	A relatively large number (more than 20) available. Specific ones (three to five) contacted per search, depending on availability and other factors.
Output features:	Title as a hyperlink and search engine name always displayed. More information also available, including author, location, and brief description. Results may be displayed by the search engine used or integrated.
Special features:	User may specify sources and types of information, such as Web resources, people, news, software, and images. SavvySearch uses this, along with availability of search engines, response time, and other factors to determine a search plan (which search engines and resources to query). User can select another search plan.
Examples:	Activity 3.5.

SEARCH.COM

SEARCH.COM has put together a collection of more than a hundred searchable databases that are available on the Web. These are listed in two ways: by subject (more than 20 categories are listed from **Automotive** to **Travel**) and in alphabetical order (the A–Z List). To find a specific resource, you can use SEARCH.COM's internal search tool by clicking on **Find a Search** or using the URL **http://www.search.com/**

Find and browsing the sections. You could also browse the entire list by using the URL **http://www.search.com/Alpha/**.

Links are included for other services that search for people (using **Yellow Pages**), **Stock Quotes**, and **City Maps**. Entries within a category are represented by a one-line description, a hyperlink to a page at SEARCH.COM that contains a hyperlink to the search tool, a form to do the search at SEARCH.COM, a description of the type of information available, and some tips for performing the search. SEARCH.COM gives good coverage about the search tools available on the Web and emphasizes the information you need to use the tools effectively.

Home page:	**http://www.search.com**
Help:	**http://www.search.com/Help**
FAQ:	**http://www.search.com/About**
Output features:	Search form, description of search tool, tips for searching, and hyperlink to resource.
Special features:	Search services and databases arranged by category and in alphabetical order. Individual services selected with a search form.
Examples:	None.

Other Resources

Here's a list of collections of Web pages that have links to meta-search tools, including the ones listed above:

Title of Web Page	URL
All-in-One Search Pages	**http://www.voicenet.com/ ~ bertland/searchf/allinone.html**
Internet Search Tools (The Library of Congress: Multiple Resource Types)	**http://lcweb.loc.gov/global/ search.html#all**
Meta-Search Engines	**http://ds2.internic.net/tools/ meta.html**
Meta-Search Engines	**http://www.voicenet.com/ ~ bertland/searchf/ metasearch.html#meta**
Needle in a CyberStack— the InfoFinder: Multi- Search Tools	**http://home.revealed.net/ ~ albee/ #Multi**
Yahoo! Computers and Internet:Internet:World Wide Web:Searching the Web:All-in-One Search Pages	**http://www.yahoo.com/ computers_and_internet/ world_wide_web/ searching_the_web/ all_in_one_search_pages**

Search Engines

Search Features	AltaVista	Excite	HotBot	Infoseek	Lycos	Open Text	WebCrawler
Boolean	**Advanced Search:** AND, &, OR, |, NOT, !, and ( )	AND, OR, AND NOT, and ( ) Must be typed using uppercase	AND, &, OR, |, NOT, !, and ( )	No	**Lycos Pro:** Boolean only with Java form. AND, OR, and NOT	**Power Search:** form-based AND, OR, BUT, and NOT	AND, OR, NOT, and ( )
Implied Boolean	**Simple Search:** + and –	+ and –	+ and –	+ and –	+ and –	No	No
Phrase	Enclose in " "	Enclose in " "	Enclose in " "	Enclose in " "	**Lycos Pro:** use " "	Yes, form-based	Enclose in " "
Proximity	**Advanced Search:** NEAR and ~	No—uses concept searching	No—only phrase searching	No	**Lycos Pro:** ADJ, NEAR, FAR, and BEFORE	**Power Search:** NEAR	NEAR and ADJ
Truncation	Yes	No	No	No	Yes	No	Yes
Wildcards	Use *	No	No	No	No	No	Use *
Field Searching	Anchor, applet, domain, host, image, link, object, text, title, and URL	No	Link, domain, file extension, and geographic region	Link, site, title, and URL	No	First heading, summary, title, and URL	No

Table A.1—Search Features of Major Search Engines

423

Search Engines

	AltaVista	Excite	HotBot	Infoseek	Lycos	Open Text	WebCrawler
Case Sensitivity	Yes	No	No	Yes	No	No	No
Concept Searching	No	Yes	No	No	No	No	No
Limits	Advanced Search: date	None	Date and media type	None	None	None	None
Types of Resources	Web and Usenet	Web, Usenet, Excite Web Guide, maps, email addresses, and news sites	Web, Usenet, and news sites	Web, Usenet, news sites, email addresses, and companies	Web, pictures, and sounds	Web, Usenet, email addresses, and selected newspapers	Web

Table A.1—Search Features of Major Search Engines (continued)

424

Search Engines

Output Features	AltaVista	Excite	HotBot	Infoseek	Lycos	Open Text	WebCrawler
Relevancy Ranking	**Simple Search:** score **Advanced Search:** score and keywords	Score	Score	Score	Score	Score	Score
Annotations or Summaries	**Standard:** title, URL, and summary **Compact:** URL only *Count* only in **Advanced Search**	Title, URL, and summary	**Full:** title (hyperlink), excerpt, URL, size, and date **Brief:** title (hyperlink) and one-line excerpt	Title (hyperlink), excerpt, URL, and size	**Summary:** hyperlink **Standard:** summary and excerpt, URL, and size **Detailed:** standard plus outline and abstract	Title, size, URL, and excerpt	Title, excerpt, and URL; can hide excerpt
Sorting	Relevance	Relevance and site	Relevance	Relevance	Relevance	Relevance	Relevance
Modify Results?	Yes, use **Refine** option	Yes, add words to search; power search	Yes	Yes, search among results found	Yes	Yes	No, new search

Table A.2—Output Features of Major Search Engines

425

Appendix

Selected Directories

A directory, or subject catalog, is a collection of Internet and Web resources arranged in categories. There are many general-purpose directories on the Web, as well as lots of specialized ones. Here, we'll discuss some of the more popular and useful ones.

For each tool, we'll give the URLs for its home page, help page, and FAQ page. We'll also indicate whether or how the items in the directory are rated, whether entries are reviewed before being included, and whether it's possible to search the directory. In addition, we'll present the directory's output features and any special features. Whenever an activity in the book has used the directory, we will list it as an example as well.

Excite Web Guide

Excite, also discussed in Appendix A, provides Excite Web Guide, a general-purpose directory. Major topics include arts and humanities, travel, business, entertainment, and regional information. Excite reviews the resources and rates the best sites by attaching a star to them.

Excite Web Guide is a part of but not the same as Excite Channels. Like the guide, the channels are collections of Web resources arranged by subject, but the channels bring together different types of resources, including listings of Web sites, news reports, TV listings, Web tours, and chat rooms. Excite aims to be a guide to many types of information, in addition to providing a directory to Web sites. You can browse the directory or locate items using the search form that appears after you've clicked on a Web sites category.

Home page:	**http://www.excite.com**
Help:	**http://www.excite.com/Info**
FAQ:	None available.
Ratings:	Top sites are starred.
Reviews:	Items annotated, reviewed, and rated.
Searching:	Yes.
Output features:	Title (hyperlink), rating, and review of the content.

Special features:	Other specialized guides available include guides to cities (City.Net), a reference section, and a directory of news services. Also includes a link to bulletin boards and chat services and a general-purpose search tool.
Examples:	Activities 3.1, 6.3.

Galaxy

From Galaxy's home page, you can search the collection of reviewed and summarized resources that are part of the Galaxy directory. This includes hypertext, Gopher, and Telnet resources. Put together over the past few years by volunteers serving as "guest editors," the Galaxy directory has several thousand entries.

Galaxy also features a portion of **Professional Directory**, the subject guide designed for use by specialists or professionals in a field. It includes the categories **Business And Commerce**, **Engineering And Technology**, **Government**, **Humanities**, **Law**, **Medicine**, **Reference**, **Science**, and **Social Sciences**. The items in each subject area or subtopic are arranged into categories: academic organizations, collections, directories, discussion groups, government organizations, guides, nonprofit organizations, organizations, and periodicals.

When you browse the directory, you will only see the titles of resources listed in the form of hyperlinks. When you use the search form to search the directory, you will also see the following information: an excerpt summary, a list of words that appear frequently in the document, size, when it was last added to the collection, and where it can be found in the directory.

Home page:	**http://galaxy.einet.net**
Help with searches:	**http://galaxy.einet.net/howto.html**
FAQ:	None available.
Ratings:	None available.
Reviews:	Items reviewed. Excerpts available through search tool. Sections of guide managed by volunteer "guest editors."
Searching:	Yes.
Output features:	Items listed with title (hyperlink).
Special features:	Resources in a subject area arranged by major subcategories (if any), academic organizations, collections, directories, discussion groups, government organizations, guides, nonprofit organizations, organizations, and periodicals. List of resources accessible through Gopher and Telnet.
Examples:	None.

Infoseek

The Infoseek directory is a subject catalog produced by the same organization that provides the Infoseek search engine described in Appendix A. The major channels include **Automotive**, **Business**, **Careers**, **Computer**, **Entertainment**, **The Good Life**, and others. These topics are listed along with popular subtopics. Some categories—including **Business**, **Computer**, **Sports**, and **Personal Finance**—also have a hyperlink to relevant news headlines.

You access the entries by browsing the channels and clicking on a hyperlink for a subject area or topic. Each page of the directory (except for the home page) contains a forms-based search tool that you can use to search for entries within the current subject area. Alternately, you can use Infoseek's search engine to search resources on the Web. Each entry in the directory consists of the title (in the form of a hyperlink to the item on the Web), a description, the URL, and the size (in kilobytes) of the item. Some entries are marked with a check mark to indicate that they are especially recommended. Each page has hyperlinks to relevant entries in both Infoseek's specialized guides to news and business information and its directories to email addresses and other addresses.

Infoseek's home page includes a search form with which to search the Web, Usenet, news services, and companies. The search engine is described in Appendix A. It also contains links to **Maps**, **People**, **Reference Sources**, and **Big Yellow** (a Web site that, like the yellow pages in a phone book, primarily lists businesses on the Web but also contains ways to find people, look up email addresses, and browse directories from various countries).

Home page:	**http://www.infoseek.com**
Help:	**http://www.infoseek.com/ Help?pg = HomeHelp.html**
FAQ:	None available
Ratings:	Entries with one or two check marks are especially recommended.
Reviews:	Items reviewed and annotated.
Searching:	Search form on each page lists directory entries and allows user to search current subject area or the Web.
Output features:	Items listed with title (hyperlink), summary, URL, and size.
Special features:	Each page of the directory provides access to specialized directories for news, business information, maps, email and street addresses.
Examples:	None.

InterNIC Directory of Directories

The InterNIC Directory of Directories is a subject guide to Internet resources, products, and services. Supported by the National Science Foundation and AT&T, InterNIC is a network information center that registers Internet domain names. Information in InterNIC comes from contributions from the Internet community.

The major subject guide categories are listed on the home page, along with two forms-based search tools used to find entries in the subject guide. From the home page, you go to a listing of major topics by clicking on the hyperlink **Browse the Directory of Directories**. Approximately 30 main topics ranging from **Agriculture** to **World Wide Web Servers** are listed, including a topic giving recent additions to the directory. The topics also include services pertaining to the Web or Internet, such as **Bulletin Board Systems**, **Databases**, **FTP/Archive Sites**, **Mailing Lists**, **News Groups**, **Providers**, and **Training**.

Clicking on a hyperlink for a subject area or topic brings up a Web page listing more hyperlinks for each resource in that category. Selecting the hyperlink for a specific resource or service takes you to a page with information about the type of resource (category), keywords describing the content, a brief description of the resource, a hyperlink to the item, the dates it was last verified and updated, and contact information for the owner of the resource. This information is supplied by the information provider or the person suggesting the resource. Items within a subject area are arranged in alphabetical order without classification into subtopics. Each page listing a subject area or item contains a link to the Directory of Directories home page. The search tools allow access to two different tools for searching the directory, along with a link to help in using the tool.

Home page:	**http://www.internic.net/ds/dsdirofdirs.html**
Help:	**http://www.internic.net/internic.info/ dirofdirs.info**
FAQ:	None available.
Ratings:	None available.
Reviews:	Items annotated by information provider.
Searching:	Search forms available by clicking on a link on the home page.
Output features:	Titles are hyperlinks; resources are listed with a description of the resource, and keywords are used to index it.
Special features:	Contact information for the information provider, including email address, is included.
Examples:	None.

LookSmart

The LookSmart subject guide provides ways to browse the directory in a relatively unique manner. Instead of using the common practice of replacing a Web page each time a topic or subtopic is selected, LookSmart lets up to three levels of subjects be present on the screen.

There are relatively few main topics. They include **Computers & Internet**, **Reference & Education**, **Travel & Vacations**, and **Home, Family & Auto**. The topics and entries appear to provide practical information rather than resources appropriate for a research paper or topic. The directory is constructed so that a reasonable amount of individual entries (usually no more than 30) are displayed in a specific subject area. Individual entries consist of a title (which is a hyperlink to the resource) and a brief description.

In addition to browsing the subject guide, you can select the link **Search**. This allows you to do keyword searching for items through the LookSmart subject guide or to access the search facilities available through AltaVista. You can also select links in the "Personalize" section, which includes links to specialized collections in the following categories: **Your Town**, **News**, **Magazines**, **Shopping**, and **Software**. Each of these may be personalized—you select the resources that will appear.

Home page:	**http://www.looksmart.com**
Help:	**http://www.looksmart.com/h/info/ helpmain.html**
FAQ:	Links available on help page.
Ratings:	None available.
Reviews:	One-sentence description with each listing.
Searching:	User can search the directory using either LookSmart Search or AltaVista, a search engine that has teamed up with LookSmart.
Output features:	Title (hyperlink) and brief description.
Special features:	If Java features are selected, up to three levels of the guide are present on the screen as user moves through a subject area.
Examples:	None.

Lycos—Top 5% Web Sites

Top 5% Sites ("Best of the Web") is a subject guide to the best resources on the World Wide Web (according to Lycos). A written review and ratings in the categories of appearance, content, and experience accompany the full entry for each item. According to Top 5%, the categories may be interpreted as follows:

❋ Content: The strength, reliability, or uniqueness of the site's content.

❋ Design: The way in which the site is set up; originality of layout and presentation.

❋ Overall: Combines content and design factors.

The main subjects range from **Autos** to **Travel**, with a good selection of sites in each of the various categories. Entries are arranged by topics, with popular subtopics listed for each category. You access the entries either by browsing the directory or by using the search forms on each directory page to search the directory. On pages listing individual entries, the entries may be viewed in alphabetical order, arranged by date reviewed, or displayed by rating. Each directory entry consists of the title (a hyperlink to the Web item), a description, and a link to related sites. Each title is also a hyperlink to a complete review of the site. The detailed listing includes the title, the score in each of the rating categories, a written review of the site or resource, a hyperlink to the Web site, and a hyperlink to the area or areas of the subject guide that list the item. For some sites, there's also a link to a map giving the geographical location of the site creator. Each page has hyperlinks to the major categories in the directory.

The home page for Top 5% includes links to the Lycos search engine and a number of directories and services available through Lycos. These include the following:

❋ Yellow Pages, a listing of companies on the Web.

❋ TopNews, a listing of current news stories.

❋ StockFind, a search tool that obtains stock quotes.

❋ PeopleFind, a way to search for addresses and phone numbers supplied by InfoSpace.

❋ City Guide, a collection of links to cities in the United States.

❋ Companies Online, a listing of Dun and Bradstreet's information about companies.

❋ Road Maps, a search tool that obtains maps and driving directions to street addresses in the United States.

Home page:	**http://www.pointcom.com**
Help:	**http://www.lycos.com/help/top5-help.html**
FAQ:	None available.
Ratings:	Entries rated using a scale of 0 to 100 on content, presentation, and experience.
Reviews:	Detailed review of each site.
Searching:	User can do a forms-based search of the directory (Top 5%).
Output features:	Title (hyperlink), detailed review of the site (which contains a hyperlink to the site itself), and list of ratings. Items may be listed by date reviewed; in alphabetical order; or by ratings of content, presentation, and experience.
Special features:	Can search the whole Lycos index for sounds or pictures.
Examples:	None.

Magellan Web Reviews

The Magellan subject guide includes, for most entries, a description, a rating and contact information for each site. Magellan used to include more information regarding sites in the directory, but as the result of an acquisition by Excite, Inc., the Magellan directory has been replaced by what was Excite Reviews. In addition to browsing the reviewed sites, it's also possible to search the "old" Magellan directory for sites with a "green light"; these sites are suitable for anyone, not just "adult" audiences.

The subject guide's major categories are listed on the home page, and you can access subtopics by browsing the directory. Major topics in the directory range from **Arts** to **Sports** and include topics such as **Business**, **Entertainment**, and **Regional**. Web sites within a subject area are displayed according to ratings (1 through 4), and then alphabetically within a rating category. Each entry has a rating, a title (which is a hyperlink to the Web site), and a brief review of the Web site.

Home page:	**http://www.mckinley.com**
Help:	**http://www.mckinley.com/magellan/Info/advancedtips.html**
FAQ:	None available.
Ratings:	Most sites rated on a scale of 1 to 4. Sites also rated with the "Magellan green light" system regarding content intended for a mature audience.
Reviews:	Summaries and reviews included with many of the entries.
Searching:	Search tool with several options for searching rated and reviewed sites, "green light" sites only, or entire Web.

Output features:	Rating (most but not all sites are rated), title (hyperlink), and brief review. Within a category, sites are alphabetized by ratings.
Special features:	Search Voyeur—a changing list of 12 randomly selected real-time searches, and specialized guides, including a guide to cities, email and street addresses, horoscopes, maps, sports scores, stocks, and weather.
Examples:	Activity 4.2.

NetGuide: Your Guide to the Net

NetGuide's stated aim is to provide a comprehensive daily directory of what's available on the Web. To that end, the home page, **http://www .netguide.com**, offers links to a variety of services including a form to search the reviewed Web sites (all the entries are reviewed and rated before being included in the guide), and links to a set of comprehensive guides to information, tips, and events in a particular subject area.

The home page for the subject guide, **http://www.netguide.com/ Browse**, includes links to the major categories, as well as popular subcategories of the guide. Major categories include **Art & Culture**, **General Reference & News**, **Living**, **Science & Nature**, and **Sports**. The listings of Web sites within a subject area are displayed according to ratings (1 to 5 stars), and then alphabetically within a rating category. A listing of entries shows the rating, the title of a site as a hyperlink to the site, an excerpt from the review, and a hyperlink (**Site Details**) to a detailed review of the site. This detailed review contains the site's overall ratings along with scores for content, design, and personality. Other items noted are parental control (the possibilities include none, nudity, violence, and obscenity) and fees/registration (which applies to access to the site). The site details also contain the title of the Web site as a hyperlink to the site, the name of the information provider, and a detailed review.

The NetGuide site also supports some other guides, including **Today's Top Happenings** (links to daily top net/media events), **How to** (a collection of well-developed articles dedicated to using technology or accomplishing a general task on the Web, such as renting an apartment), and a reference section.

A relatively small number of guides or subject areas (ten, to be exact) are available on the home page, **http://www.netguide.com**. These topics range from **Computing** to **Travel**. Each guide is written and maintained by an individual and contains links to sites arranged in subcategories of the main topics of the guide. The home page for a guide also includes a featured site of the day, other featured sites, and new items in the category. This format presents a comfortable, relatively easy-to-use interface.

Home page:	**http://www.netguide.com**
Help:	**http://www.netguide.com/AboutUs**
FAQ:	None available.
Ratings:	1 to 5 stars based on content, design, and personality.
Reviews:	One-paragraph review with each listing. See **http://www.netguide.com/Browse**.
Searching:	Search form available on each page, giving the option to search this subject guide or to use Lycos to search for resources elsewhere on the Web.
Output features:	Items within a category displayed alphabetically by rating, title (hyperlink), link to a detailed listing, and one-sentence description or review. Each site includes detailed rating, information about cost and parental control, title (hyperlink), name of provider, and one-paragraph review.
Special features:	Links to other portions of NetGuide include **Today's Top Happenings** (links to daily top net/media events), **How to** (a collection of well-developed articles dedicated to using technology or accomplishing a general task on the Web), and a reference section.
Examples:	None.

WebCrawler Guide

WebCrawler is a search tool that incorporates channels in its organization. Part of WebCrawler's channels is a highly discriminatory collection of Web sites and other resources arranged in a subject directory called the Guide. This is the directory section of WebCrawler. The channels range from **Arts** to **Travel** and include **Computers & Internet**, **Health & Fitness**, **Relationships**, and **Sports**. All items in the Guide are reviewed and selected before being added to the collection. The aim is to provide a comprehensive collection of high-quality Web sites and other resources. The help for WebCrawler is very well written, and the site is easy to navigate. Each category entry has a link that allows you to search the Web for related resources using WebCrawler.

The listings within a subject area are arranged into subcategories. Entries in a subcategory are arranged into types of sites and have an accompanying list of Usenet newsgroups related to each topic. There is also a link that begins a search of WebCrawler's database of sites. The entry for an individual listing includes a hyperlink to the entry, a review of the site, a hyperlink that searches WebCrawler for similar sites, and links to take you to other entries in the category. This Web site is very well done and is highly recommended.

Home page: **http://www.webcrawler.com**
Help: **http://webcrawler.com/Help/Guide.html**
FAQ: None available.
Ratings: No ratings, but WebCrawler Select is quite
                exclusive.
Reviews: Each item reviewed.
Searching: Searching is not possible in the WebCrawler Guide.
Output features: Subject guide arranged by category; each item
                reviewed, annotated, and represented as a
                hyperlink.
Special features: Links from each category to related Web sites and
                related Usenet newsgroups. Links from each listing
                to related Web sites.
Examples: Activity 4.3.

Yahoo!

Yahoo! was one of the first subject guides or directories on the World
Wide Web and is undoubtedly the most popular and talked-about subject guide. Thousands of entries are submitted to Yahoo! by information providers or others and are included in the subject guide by the
Yahoo! staff. Each item is put into an appropriate category and listed as
a title, which is a hyperlink to the site, along with a brief description
(provided by the person recommending the site).

Yahoo!'s strengths are the number of sites listed and the organization of the site itself. There are several major categories, including **Arts
and Humanities**, **Education**, **Health**, **News and Media**, **Science**, and
Society and Culture. Each is divided into subcategories, and listings
include individual sites and links to other categories. Some of the major
categories also include a hyperlink **Xtra!**, which takes you to a list of
hyperlinks to daily news stories. There are no extensive reviews for
sites, and Yahoo! does not rate sites, but it does manage the entries by
selectively including them in the directory.

You can search for sites throughout Yahoo! or within the currently
selected category. All the categories include keyword searching, which
supports matching all words (AND), any word (OR), phrase searching,
wildcards (use * after a prefix), and limiting a search by date. After
performing a search, you can continue the search by using AltaVista,
using indexes titled **Headlines** and **Net Events**, or selecting another
major search engine from a list. Yahoo! also offers other services for
finding information, such as directories or subject guides with options
to search. These include **Yellow Pages**, **People Search**, **Maps**, **News**,
Stock Quotes, and **Sports**.

Yahoo! provides subject guides specific to Canada, France, Germany,
Japan, the United Kingdom, and Ireland, with listings in each country's
language. There are regional guides for some cities in the United States,
including Austin, Boston, Los Angeles, New York, San Francisco, Seattle,

and Washington D.C. Other subject guides include "Yahooligans! for Kids," "Yahoo! Internet Life," "Yahoo! Store," "Classifieds," "Today's Web Events," "Chat," and weather forecasts.

Yahoo! began early in the history of the World Wide Web (1994). It is relatively easy to use, provides much useful information, continues to be very popular, and has provided a model and high standards for other subject directories to emulate.

Home page:	**http://www.yahoo.com**
Help in general:	**http://www.yahoo.com/docs/info/help.html**
Help with searches:	**http://search.yahoo.com/search/help?**
FAQ:	**http://www.yahoo.com/docs/info/faq.html**
Ratings:	None available.
Reviews:	No written reviews. Items included only after approval by Yahoo!
Searching:	Search form available on each page, giving the option to search within current category, all categories, Headlines, Net Events, AltaVista, or another search engine.
Output features:	Title (hyperlink) and brief annotation.
Special features:	There are several regional or national editions of the guide and other special subject guides, including **Yellow Pages**, **People Search**, **Maps**, **News**, **Stock Quotes**, **Sports**, **Yahooligans! for Kids**, **Yahoo! Internet Life**, **Yahoo! Store**, **Classifieds**, **Today's Web Events**, **Chats**, and weather forecasts.
Examples:	Activities 1.1, 4.1, 7.3; Chapter 14, Project 1.

Other Resources

Here are some Web pages that contain hyperlinks to directories, including the ones we've discussed above:

Title of Resource	URL
Internet Search Tools (The Library of Congress)	**http://lcweb.loc.gov/global/ search.html#www**
Needle in a CyberStack—the InfoFinder, Directories and Guides	**http://home.revealed.net/ ~ albee/ pages/guides.html**
Yahoo! Computers and Internet:Internet:World Wide Web: Searching the Web: Web Directories	**http://www.yahoo.com/ computers_and_internet/internet/ world_wide_web/ searching_the_web/web_directories**

Appendix

Virtual Libraries

Virtual libraries are directories that contain collections of Internet or Web resources that have been reviewed and evaluated before they're included. For this reason, the resources tend to be useful, accurate, and authentic. Most of them are, in fact, selective subject guides. In many cases, you'll find that professional librarians staff and manage these virtual libraries.

For each item, we'll list the URLs for the home page, help page, and FAQ page. We'll also state the output features and any special features. Whenever an activity in the book has used the virtual library, we will list it as well.

Argus Clearinghouse

The Argus Clearinghouse bills itself as "The Internet's Premier Research Library." It is a collection of reviewed and rated Web guides to information about specific topics. The guides are not about a specific site; instead, they are about a certain topic.

The major Argus Clearinghouse categories range from **Arts & Humanities** to **Social Sciences & Social Issues**. The guides are arranged in a hierarchical subject arrangement, so you can browse the collection. It's also possible to search the collection using a form that permits two terms. These would be connected by AND or OR; truncation (use * after a prefix) is also an option. For assistance with searching Argus Clearinghouse, see the help page, **http://www.clearinghouse.net/ searchtips.html**.

Guides in the collection have been reviewed and rated by professional librarians. The rating system, a range of one to five check marks in each category, is based on the following criteria:

- Level of resource description
- Level of resource evaluation
- Guide design
- Guide organizational schemes
- Guide meta-information

The listing for a specific guide includes its title, a separate hyperlink to the Web resource, a list of keywords, the name of the guide's author or producer, the date it was last checked, the overall rating, and a rating in each category. You'll want to check Argus Clearinghouse when you're looking for guides to resources on the Web and Internet.

Home page:	**http://www.clearinghouse.net**
Help:	**http://www.clearinghouse.net/ searchtips.html**
FAQ:	**http://www.clearinghouse.net/faq.html**
Output features:	Topics arranged by category, each with a list of resources. Each item represented by title, hyperlink to resource, keywords, author's name and affiliation, date Argus Clearinghouse last checked resource, overall rating, and rating in each category.
Special features:	Searches full text of information pages, including titles, names of authors, institutions, and keywords.
Examples:	Activity 4.4.

Internet Public Library

The Internet Public Library (IPL) was created to give the Internet library services, including the accumulation, evaluation, selection, and classification of materials. IPL is staffed and managed by professional librarians; the project is hosted by the University of Michigan's School of Information. This virtual site is analogous to a real library in terms of its structure or architecture, its collection, and the services it provides.

The IPL home page, called the IPL Lobby, has hyperlinks to the Web site's primary sections, or divisions. These links are both embedded in images and visible as text. Lots of different resources and several types of activities and services are available through the IPL. Many of the guides can be searched, and most divisions have hyperlinks on their pages that encourage and help a patron—someone browsing the Web page—to ask questions of the IPL staff or the reference librarian. This is indeed a very useful and rich resource. The reference collection alone matches in quality (if not quantity) the resources available through other, commercial subject guides.

The major topics are the usual ones you'd expect to see in a library, such as **Reference**, **Arts & Humanities**, **Education**, **Health & Medical Sciences**, and **Social Sciences**. The listing for an individual entry includes a review and descriptive annotation, the title as a hyperlink to the resources, the author's name, and the subjects under which it is classified.

To help you find the information you need, the following charts have been provided to explain the unique organization of the IPL:

Division: Reference
URL: **http://www.ipl.org/ref**
Description: Three separate reference guides: Reference (a general
                 directory to reference sources), Associations on the Net
                 (a guide to professional and scholarly organizations on
                 the Web), and POTUS (a guide to the elections, presi-
                 dencies, and lives of U.S. presidents).

Division: Youth
URL: **http://www.ipl.org/youth**
Description: A resource for children ages four through fourteen.

Division: Teen
URL: **http://www.ipl.org/teen**
Description: A subject guide to useful and interesting Web sites for
                 teenagers.

Room: Exhibit Hall
URL: **http://www.ipl.org/exhibit**
Description: A "space" on the Web for people to display virtual ex-
                 hibits. One featured exhibit, any current exhibits, and
                 the permanent collection are listed.

Room: Reading Room
URL: **http://www.ipl.org/reading**
Description: Hyperlinks to more than 4,000 books and more than
                 1,300 periodicals, including newspapers, may be ac-
                 cessed by browsing or searching. The books are ar-
                 ranged by author, title, or Dewey subject categories.

Service: For Librarians
URL: **http://www.ipl.org/svcs**
Description: A collection of information and services for librarians
                 or other professionals who organize information.

Service: Directory & Tour
URL: **http://www.ipl.org/bldg.dir**
Description: Hyperlinks to all divisions, rooms, and services of the
                 IPL.

Service: Web Searching
URL: **http://www.ipl.org/ref/websearching.html**
Description: An annotated list with hyperlinks to search tools on
                 the Web.

Home page:	**http://www.ipl.org**
Help:	**http://www.ipl.org/about**
FAQ:	**http://www.ipl.org/about/iplfaq.html**
Output features:	Image-based and text-based interface to the main sections of the library.
Special features:	Thousands of items in the collection of reviewed resources. The IPL is presented as Divisions: Reference (annotated subject guides), Youth, and Teen; Rooms: Exhibit Hall and Reading Room (a collection of online texts, serial publications, and newspapers); and Services: For Librarians, Directory & Tour, and Web Searching.
Examples:	Activity 3.2.

Librarians' Index to the Internet

The Librarians' Index to the Internet is a directory to Web and Internet resources. Each entry is reviewed before being included in the collection. Entries are arranged by subject area, and individual entries are alphabetized within a subject area. These entries are well organized. An entry consists of the title as a hyperlink to the site, an annotation or summary of the site, and hyperlinks to the subject area or areas for an individual resource.

The subjects cover a wide range of topics. At one time called the Index to the Internet for the Berkeley, California, Public Library, the index has an understandable emphasis on a few topics of particular interest to residents of that region. The Librarians' Index to the Internet gives good coverage to a variety of resources on the Web.

You can locate entries by browsing the guide or by using a forms-based search tool. The tool allows you to search in the titles, subjects, annotations, or all fields of the entries. You may choose to search for a match to all or any of the search terms—in other words, a Boolean AND or OR, respectively. It's also possible to truncate words by including an asterisk (*) after a prefix.

Home page:	**http://sunsite.berkeley.edu/ internetindex**
Help with searches:	**http://sunsite.berkeley.edu/ internetindex/tips.html**
FAQ:	None available.
Output features:	Subject guides arranged by category. Items reviewed, annotated, and represented as hyperlinks.
Special features:	Can search by title, subject, annotation, or fields.
Examples:	Activity 7.1; Chapter 14, Project 2.

World Wide Web Virtual Library

The World Wide Web Virtual Library (WWWVL) was started in 1991 by Tim Berners-Lee, the person credited with the concept of the World Wide Web. It is staffed entirely by volunteers—experts, organizations, or other interested people who take responsibility either to create an entry for the library or to maintain a topic or subject area.

There are more than one hundred individual subjects ranging alphabetically from **Aboriginal Studies** to **Zoos**. The subject guides reside on several different computer systems throughout the world; the WWWVL is a distributed library. For that reason, and because the work is shared among many people, there's little uniformity in the format for the subject areas.

The URL **http://vlib.stanford.edu/Overview.html** takes you to the home page or **Subject Catalogue** for the WWWVL—information is arranged by subject. Two other views of the library or arrangements of the information are available: **Category Subtree, http://vlib .stanford.edu/Overview2.html**, in which the information is arranged as in a subject guide with primary topics and subtopics, and **Library of Congress Classification, http://vlib.stanford.edu/ LibraryOfCongress.html**, in which information is put into categories according to Library of Congress Standards.

The WWWVL is a good resource for guides to a variety of subject areas. It's been around since the early days of the World Wide Web, and it has a good reputation for the high quality of its resources and the demonstrated benefits of cooperative, volunteer work.

Home page:	**http://vlib.stanford.edu/Overview.html**
Help:	None available.
FAQ:	**http://vlib.stanford.edu/ coordination.html**
Output features:	Items arranged alphabetically by topic. No uniformity, because each category or topic is maintained by a volunteer, but each is meant to be a guide to all the major resources related to a specific topic.
Special features:	Besides alphabetical arrangement, there is a category subtree (subject guide) and sorting by Library of Congress classification.
Examples:	None.

Other Resources

Here's a list of collections of Web pages that have links to virtual libraries and to other Web resources:

Title of Resource	URL
Internet Search Tools (The Library of Congress)	http://lcweb.loc.gov/global/ search.html#www
MWSC Library Links to Virtual Libraries	http://www.mwsc.edu/ ~ libwww/ref2.html
Needle in a CyberStack—the InfoFinder	http://home.revealed.net/ ~ albee/
Yahoo! Computers and Internet: Internet:World Wide Web: Searching the Web: Indices to Web Documents	http://www.yahoo.com/ computers_and_internet/ internet/world_wide_web/ searching_the_web/ indices_to_web_documents

D
Appendix

Ways to Stay Current

The content of the World Wide Web is always changing, because tools, resources, and documents are added daily. Many of the tools and resources available for searching and conducting research are very good, but none of them is perfect. You'll want to keep informed of new and improved services. We'll list some ways to do that here. You can regularly visit the Web sites we'll name and read the articles in Usenet newsgroups that carry announcements. You'll also want to keep checking the Web sites that list search tools, directories, and virtual libraries since they sometimes mention new tools; we've mentioned these sites in previous appendices.

Web Sites Listing New Resources

This section contains an annotated list of resources to use to keep track of new Web sites.

Scout Report

The Scout Report lists new and newly discovered resources of interest to researchers and educators. It is a publication of The Internet Scout Project, which is part of the Computer Science Department at the University of Wisconsin. This project is also supported by InterNIC, the agency that registers Internet domain names.

Weekly issues of The Scout Report contain listings in three categories:

❈ Research and education
❈ General interest
❈ Network tools

Each listing contains the name of the resource, the URL as a hyperlink, and a written description. Instructions for getting weekly issues through a free email subscription service appear at the end of each issue. Instructions to access the weekly reports as Web pages, through Gopher, and FTP are also included.

The URL for the Scout Report is **http://www.cs.wisc.edu/scout/ report**. To receive the weekly issues by email, send email to **listserv@lists.internic.net**, and type

subscribe scout-report your-first-name your-last-name

as the body of the message. Substitute your first and last names for your-first-name and your-last-name, respectively.

What's New Web Sites

Several sites on the Web list new Web sites. Most of these are associated with directories or subject guides and list items that have recently been added. There's a category in the Yahoo! directory for sites that are dedicated to listing new Web sites. The name of the section, starting from the top of the Yahoo! directory, is Top:Computers and Internet: Internet:World Wide Web:Searching the Web:Indices to Web Documents:What's New. The URL is **http://www.yahoo.com/ computers_and_internet/internet/world_wide_web/ searching_the_web/indices_to_web_documents/what_s_new**. More than 40 sites are listed.

Here's a short list of "What's New" sites that you may want to check occasionally. You could add them to your bookmark or favorites list.

❋ **Librarians' Index to the Internet: What's New This Week**

A listing of sites added to the index, it's available as the hyperlink **New This Week** on the home page. The URL for the home page is **http://sunsite.berkeley.edu/ InternetIndex**.

❋ **Internet Scout Net-Happenings**

Archives of the articles posted to the Usenet newsgroup comp.internet.net-happenings and the corresponding email discussion group net-happenings. Each item lists a resource that's been submitted to the newsgroup or discussion group. Labeled with a category, announcements contain URLs and some descriptive information. Net-happenings is a service of InterNIC, the Net Scout project, and the list moderator, Gleason Sackman. The URL is **http://scout.cs .wisc.edu/scout/het-hap**.

❋ **What's New Too!**

A daily listing of new sites. Hundreds of items appear each day. Anyone may post an announcement, and all announcements are listed. It is possible, however, to customize the listings so you only see announcements in specific categories. The URL is **http://nu2.com**.

❋ **Yahoo!—What's New**

A listing of new sites added to Yahoo!'s directory. This Web page has links to a list of new sites for each of the past seven days, a list of Yahoo!'s daily picks, and a link to Yahoo!'s weekly picks. The URL is **http://www.yahoo .com/new**.

Email Discussion Groups Listing
New Web Sites and Resources

Email Discussion Groups for Announcements
of New or Changed Web Sites

The primary email discussion group or mailing list for announcing new or changed Web sites and other resources is net-happenings. Messages are submitted to the moderator, who then passes them on to the group. The messages are labeled with a category, such as BOOK, COMP, K12, or SOFT. This discussion group is also available as the Usenet newsgroup **comp.internet.net-happenings**. Archives are available and may be searched at the Web site *Internet Scout: Net Happenings,* **http://scout.cs.wisc.edu/scout/net-hap**. Net-happenings is a service of Internet Scout Project in the Computer Sciences Department at the University of Wisconsin-Madison, and the list moderator, Gleason Sackman. To join the list, send email to **listserv@cs.wisc.edu** and type

subscribe net-happenings your-first-name your-last-name

as the body of the message.

Email Discussion Groups for Announcements
of New Discussion Groups

The email group NEW-LIST carries announcements of new lists. To join the list, send email to **listserv@listserv.nodak.edu** with the message

subscribe new-list your-first-name your-last-name

Usenet Newsgroups Listing
New Web Sites and Resources

Newsgroups for Announcements of
New or Changed Web Sites

Two primary Usenet newsgroups announce new Web sites and resources. When people with access to Usenet submit announcements to the groups, the moderators post appropriate announcements. A description of each group follows.

comp.infosystems.www.announce
Each announcement is tagged with a keyword indicating the type of resource, such as ART, EDUCATION, RELIGION, SPORTS. The moderator does not permit announcements of any commercial Web site or Web sites with only local interest. A FAQ for the newsgroup is regularly posted to the newsgroup and is available as a Web page with the URL **http://boutell.com/~ grant/charter.html**.

comp.internet.net-happenings

Each announcement is tagged with a keyword indicating the type of resource, such as BOOK, COMP, K12, or SOFT. This newsgroup has an associated Web site that includes archives and searching at **http://scout.cs.wisc.edu/scout/net-hap**, and the articles in the newsgroup are also available through the email discussion group net-happenings. Net-happenings is a service of Internet Scout Project in the Computer Sciences Department at the University of Wisconsin-Madison, and the list moderator, Gleason Sackman.

news.announce.newgroups

This is the primary Usenet newsgroup used for announcing new newsgroups. This group also carries discussions related to creating a specific newsgroup. These include requests for discussions (RFD) about new newsgroups and a call for votes (CFV) to determine whether a newsgroup be established.

Glossary

administrative address The address to use to join an email discussion group or interest group and to send requests for services.

all-in-one search tool A tool that provides search forms for several search engines and directories all in one site. The tool also provides hyperlinks, which allow you to go to the services directly.

annotated directories Often referred to as virtual libraries, these directories have brief summaries, descriptions, ratings, or reviews attached to Web pages and subject guides.

annotation A brief summary or description of a Web page or of any work listed in a database.

anonymous FTP A means of using FTP to make files readily available to the public. If you start an FTP session with a remote host, you give the log in or user name anonymous, and enter your email address as a password. When you use a URL starting with "ftp://" and a domain name with a Web browser, an anonymous FTP session begins, and you don't have to enter a user name or password.

article A message or file that is part of a Usenet newsgroup.

attachment A file that is sent as part of an email message but that is not part of the main message. Usually images, programs, or word processor files are sent as attachments, because most email programs allow only plain text in the body of a message.

bibliographic database An online database that lists sources of information and describes the information but that doesn't include the text of the information itself. Some bibliographic databases are annotated, which means that there is a brief summary of each work listed.

bookmark A hyperlink that is saved in the bookmark list, a file in your browser. You can use bookmarks to keep track of favorite or important sites and to return there whenever you are on the World Wide Web.

bookmark list A list of hyperlinks to items on the World Wide Web.

Boolean searching Searching that uses Boolean operators (AND, OR, and NOT) in the search expression. Especially helpful in multifaceted or specific topics, Boolean operators help expand or narrow the scope of your search. A search for rivers OR lakes returns all documents with both words or either word in them. A search for rivers AND lakes returns documents with both words in them. A search for rivers AND

447

lakes NOT swamps returns only documents that mention both rivers and lakes but omits those that also mention swamps.

browsing The process of clicking from one hyperlink to another on the World Wide Web. You can browse indiscriminately, or you can do structured browsing, using a hierarchical subject list in a directory.

case sensitivity The ability of a search tool to distinguish between uppercase and lowercase letters. Some search tools aren't case-sensitive; no matter what you type, the tool only picks up lowercase matches. Search engines that are case-sensitive will strictly follow the search request; they'll return documents containing the words in the case in which they were entered in the search expression.

client/server The interaction between a system that requests information (the client) and another system that provides it (the server). The browser is the client, and a computer at the site that provides the information is the server.

commercial database A database that requires you to pay a subscription cost before accessing it. See also proprietary database.

concept searching A feature enabling a search engine to find synonyms in its database. When you type in a word or phrase, the engine automatically searches for the word or phrase you want, plus words or phrases that may mean the same thing. For example, if the word teenage is in your search expression, the search engine would also look for the word adolescent.

content area The part of a Web browser window that contains the current Web page, including images, text, or hyperlinks.

cross-posting Posting an article to more than one Usenet newsgroup.

default setting The configuration a search engine uses unless you override the setting by specifying another configuration. For example, in most search engines, the Boolean operator OR is the assumed relationship between two words unless you type AND between the words.

Dewey decimal classification system Originated by Melvil Dewey in the late nineteenth century, this classification system for library materials divides all knowledge into 10 different classes, which are then subdivided into several sets of subclasses. Within these subclasses, decimals reflect still smaller subdivisions. The Dewey decimal classification system is most prevalent today in public libraries, whereas most other types of libraries, including academic ones, use the Library of Congress classification system.

directory Topical lists of Internet resources, arranged hierarchically. Directories are meant to be browsed, but they can also be searched. Directories differ from search engines in one major way—the human element involved in collecting and updating the information.

discussion group A group that discusses a single topic via email messages. An individual subscribes to or joins a discussion group electronically, and all messages sent to the group are distributed to the members by email.

domain name The Internet name for a network or computer system. The name consists of a sequence of characters separated by periods, such as www.mwc.edu. The domain name is often the first part of a URL that follows "://". For example, the domain name in the URL http://www.ckp.edu/technical/reference/wsftp.html is www.ckp.edu.

downloading Transferring or copying a file from another computer (the remote computer) to the computer you're using (the local computer). This term is often applied to the process of retrieving a file from a software library or FTP archive.

duplicate detection An output feature of some search engines and meta-search tools that automatically filters out of your search results any URLs that are duplicated elsewhere in the results.

FAQ (frequently asked questions) A list of commonly asked questions and answers on a specific topic. A FAQ is often associated with Usenet newsgroups, but several search tools also include a FAQ file. This, and online help, is usually the first place you should look to find answers.

field Part of a Web page or bibliographic record that is designated for a particular kind of data or text.

field searching A strategy in which you limit a search to a particular field. In a search engine, you might search only the URL field. In a library catalog, you could search for items by author, title, subject, call number, or any other data element that was designated as a field. By narrowing the scope of searchable items, field searching helps to eliminate the chance of retrieving irrelevant information.

frames A browser feature that displays several Web pages in the browser's content area. Each frame has its own URL and controls.

freeware A software program that's available for use without any charge. This doesn't mean the program isn't copyrighted. Usually, the originator retains the copyright. Anyone can use it, but the program can't be legally sold or distributed without permission.

FTP (File Transfer Protocol) A means of transferring or sharing files across the Internet from one computer system to another.

FTP archive A collection of files available through anonymous FTP.

full-text database A database that contains the full text of the information it describes.

full-text indexing A search engine feature in which every word, significant or insignificant, is indexed and retrievable through a search.

Gopher A menu-oriented system that gives access to documents, files, and other Internet services, regardless of where they are on the Internet. The software for Gopher was created and developed at the University of Minnesota to allow users to browse and retrieve documents in a campus environment.

group address The address to use to send email to each member of a discussion group, interest group, listserv list, or mailing list.

GUI (graphical user interface) An interface that uses icons and images in addition to text to represent information, input, and output.

helper applications Programs used with a Web browser to display, view, or work with files that the browser cannot display. For example, Netscape Navigator can display graphic or image files in GIF or JPEG format. If you accessed an image of another type through a hyperlink, then your browser would need a helper application to display it. As another example, some Web browsers can work with several protocols but not with Telnet. If you activate a hyperlink that begins a Telnet session, a Telnet client that is separate from the Web browser must be used. The Web browser can recognize when it's necessary to use specific helper applications.

hierarchy A list of subjects in a directory. The subjects are organized in successive ranks with the broadest listed first and with more specific aspects or subdivisions listed below.

high precision/high recall A phenomenon that occurs during a search when you retrieve all the relevant documents in the database and retrieve no unwanted ones.

high precision/low recall A phenomenon that occurs when a search yields a small set of hits. Although each one may be very relevant to the search topic, some relevant documents will be missed.

history list A list of Internet sites, services, and resources that have been accessed through a Web browser during recent sessions.

hit list A list of results obtained from an online search.

home page The first screen or page of a site accessible through a Web browser.

HTML (Hypertext Markup Language) The format used for writing documents to be viewed with a Web browser. Items in the document can be text; images; sounds; or links to other HTML documents, sites, services, and resources on the Web.

HTTP (Hypertext Transfer Protocol) The standard protocol that World Wide Web servers and clients use to communicate.

hyperlink Words, phrases, images, or regions of an image that are often highlighted or colored differently and that can be selected as part of a WWW page. Each hyperlink represents another Web page; a location in the current Web page; an image, audio, video, or multimedia file; or some other resource on the World Wide Web. When the hyperlink is selected, it activates the resource that it represents.

hypermedia   An extension to hypertext that includes graphics and audio.

hypertext   A way of viewing or working with a document in text format that allows you to follow cross-references to other Web resources. By clicking on an embedded hyperlink, the user can choose her own path through the hypertext material.

implied Boolean operators   Using the characters + and - to require or prohibit a word or phrase as part of a search expression. The + acts somewhat as AND, and the - acts as NOT would in a Boolean expression. For example, the Boolean expression rivers AND lakes NOT swamps may be expressed as + rivers + lakes -swamps.

interest group   Group discussion and sharing of information about a single topic carried out via email.

Internet   The collection of networks throughout the world that agree to communicate using specific telecommunication protocols, the most basic being the Internet Protocol (IP) and transmission control protocol (TCP), and the services supplied by those networks.

keyword indexing   A feature in which each significant word in the entire document or record is indexed and retrievable by the search engine or computer program being used.

keyword searching   A feature in which the search engine or computer program searches for every occurrence of a particular word in the database, regardless of where it may appear.

LCSH (Library of Congress subject headings)   A list of standardized subject headings that are used to index materials by the Library of Congress. The subject headings are arranged in alphabetical order by the broadest headings, with more precise headings listed under them. Most academic library catalogs are searchable by subject heading as well as by keyword.

Library of Congress classification system   Designed originally for the Library of Congress in the late nineteenth century, this classification system is used by most academic and special libraries throughout the United States and in many parts of the world. It consists of 21 classes, each designated by a letter of the alphabet. Subdivisions are created by the use of other letters and numbers.

limiting by date   A search tool feature that allows you to limit search results to pages that were indexed after, before, or within certain dates.

list address   See group address.

Listserv   The type of software used to manage a listserv list.

listserv list   A type of discussion group, interest group, or mailing list.

location field   The pane on the browser window that holds the current document's URL.

low precision/high recall   A phenomenon that occurs during a search when you retrieve a large set of results, including many unwanted documents.

lurking   Reading the email or articles in a discussion group or newsgroup without contributing or posting messages.

mailing list   See discussion group.

menu bar   The sequence of pulldown menus across the top of the Web browser window. All browser commands are embedded in the menu bar.

meta-search tools   Tools that allow you to search either more than one search engine or directory simultaneously, or a list of search tools that can be accessed from that site. These two major types of meta-search tools are called parallel search tools and all-in-one search tools.

meta-tags   Keywords inserted in the meta-tag portion of the HTML source document by the Web page author. If Web pages don't have much text, meta-tags help them come up in a keyword search.

moderator   A person who manages or administers a discussion group, interest group, listserv list, mailing list, or Usenet newsgroup. In most cases, the moderator is a volunteer. Messages sent to the group are first read by the moderator, who then passes appropriate messages to the group.

modifying search results   Changing an initial search expression to obtain more relevant results. This can involve narrowing the results by field, limiting by date, adding keywords, subtracting keywords, and so forth.

nested Boolean logic   The use of parentheses in Boolean search expressions. For example, the nested expression ((rivers OR lakes) AND canoeing) NOT camping will first find resources that contain either the words rivers or lakes and the term canoeing, but not resources that contain the term camping.

newsgroup   A collection of Usenet articles arranged by topic. Some are specialized or technical groups (such as comp.protocols.tcp-ip.domains—topics related to Internet domain style names), some deal with recreational activities (such as rec.outdoors.fishing.saltwater—topics related to saltwater fishing), and one, news.newusers.questions, is dedicated to questions from new Usenet users.

newsreader   The software you use to read, reply to, and manage Usenet news.

NNTP (Network News Transport Protocol)   The standard protocol used to distribute Usenet news between computer systems on the Internet in a form that machines can read and computers can access.

OPAC (Online Public Access Catalog)   An electronic catalog of a library's holdings, usually searchable by author, title, subject, keyword, and call number. Thousands of OPACs from libraries all over the world are available on the World Wide Web.

parallel search tools   A search tool or service that takes one search expression, submits it to several search services, and returns selected results from each. This is an example of a meta-search tool.

phrase searching   The search feature supported by most search engines that allows you to search for words that usually appear next to each other. It is possibly the most important search feature.

plug-in   An application software that's used along with a Web browser to view or display certain types of files as part of a Web page. Shockwave from MacroMedia is a plug-in that allows the browser to display interactive multimedia.

PPP (Point-to-Point Protocol)   A standard protocol that allows a computer with a modem to communicate using TCP/IP.

proprietary database   A privately owned database that isn't available to the public and that is usually password protected. Universities, businesses, and research institutes are the institutions most likely to subscribe to this kind of database and make it available to their employees and students.

protocol   A set of rules for exchanging information between networks or computer systems. The rules specify the format and the content of the information, and the procedures to follow during the exchange.

proximity searching   A search feature that makes it possible to search for words that are near each other in a document.

reference work   A resource used to find quick answers to questions. Traditionally thought of as being in the form of books (such as dictionaries, encyclopedias, quotation directories, manuals, guides, atlases, bibliographies and indexes), a reference source on the World Wide Web closely resembles its print counterpart. A reference work doesn't necessarily contain hyperlinks to other resources, although it will often have hyperlinks within the document itself.

relevance   A measure of how closely a database entry matches a search request. Most search tools on the Web return results based on relevance. The specific algorithm for computing relevance varies from one service to another, but it's often based on the number of times terms in the search expression appear in the document and whether they appear in the appropriate fields.

relevancy ranking   A ranking of items retrieved from a database. The ranking is based on the relevancy score that a search engine has assigned.

results per page   A feature of some search engines that allows you to designate the number of results listed per page. Search engines usually list 10 results per page.

robot   See spider.

scroll bar   The rectangular area on the right side of the window that allows you to move up or down in the open document. You move by clicking and dragging it or clicking on the arrow at the bottom of the bar.

search engine   A collection of programs that gather information from the Web (see spider), index it, and put it in a database so it can be searched. The search engine takes the keywords or phrases you enter, searches the database for words that match the search expression, and returns them to you. The results are hyperlinks to sources that have descriptions, titles, or contents matching the search expression.

search expression   The keywords and syntax that you enter in a search form. With this expression, you ask a search tool to seek relevant documents in a particular way.

search form   The rectangular pane or oblong box that appears on the home pages of most search engines and directories. In this space, you enter a search expression.

shareware   Software that you are allowed to download and try for a specified period free of charge. If you continue to use the program after that time, you are expected to pay a usually modest fee to continue using the product legally.

SLIP (Serial Line Internet Protocol)   Software allowing the use of the Internet Protocol (IP) over a serial line or through a serial port. Commonly used with a modem connection to a service providing Internet services.

sorting   An option in some search engines that allows you to determine how you'd like your search results listed—by URL, relevance, domain or location, date, and so on.

spam   Unwanted and unsolicited email. The electronic equivalent of paper junk mail.

special collection   A collection of material, usually a separate collection of a large library, that focuses on a particular topic and covers it in great depth.

specialized database   A self-contained index that is searchable and available on the Web. Items in specialized databases are often not accessible through a keyword search in a search engine.

special library A library that focuses on the interests inherent in the institution it serves. Libraries in hospitals, corporations, associations, museums, and other types of institutions are all special libraries. In many cases, they are not open to the public. A special library's collection may be narrow in scope, but it will have depth within the specialty it covers.

spider A computer program that travels the Internet to locate such resources as Web documents, FTP archives, and Gopher documents. It indexes the documents in a database, which is then searched using a search engine (such as AltaVista or Excite). A spider can also be referred to as a robot or wanderer. Each search engine uses a spider to build its database.

status bar The bar or rectangular region at the bottom of the browser window that displays information regarding the transfer of a Web document to the browser. When the mouse moves over a hyperlink, the status bar shows the hyperlink's URL. When a Web page is requested, the status bar gives information about contacting and receiving information from a server. During transmission, the status bar displays a percentage that reflects how much of the document has been transferred. The status bar also indicates whether transmissions are occurring in a secure manner.

stop words Words that an indexing program doesn't index. Stop words usually include articles (a, an, the) and other common words.

structured browsing The process of moving through a hierarchically arranged Web directory, from a broad subject heading to a more specific one, until you find the desired information.

subcategory A subject category that is more narrowly focused than the broader subject category above it in a hierarchy.

subject catalog See directory.

subject category A division in a hierarchical subject classification system in a Web directory. You click on the subject category that is likely to contain either the Web pages you want or other subject categories that are more specific.

subject guide A collection of URLs on a particular topic. Most easily found listed in virtual libraries, they are also referred to as meta-pages.

subscribe To join a discussion group, interest group, listserv list, or mailing list. You use this term when writing commands to join such a group and to list a Usenet newsgroup on your newsreader.

syntax The rules governing the construction of search expressions in search engines and directories.

TCP/IP (Transmission Control Protocol/Internet Protocol) A collection of protocols used to provide the basis for Internet and World Wide Web services.

Telnet   Allows for remote login capabilities on the Internet. One of the three basic Internet services, Telnet allows you to be on one computer and to access and log in to another.

thread   A collection of articles that all deal with a single posting or email message.

toolbar   The sequence of icons below the menu bar. Clicking on a toolbar icon executes a command or causes an action.

top-level category   One of several main subjects in the top of a hierarchy in a directory's list of subjects.

truncation   The phenomenon in which you cut off the end of a word when creating a search expression. When given such a request, a search engine will look for all possible endings to the word, in addition to the root word itself.

unified search interfaces   Meta-search tools that allow you to use several search engines simultaneously.

unsubscribe   To leave, sign off from, or quit a discussion group, interest group, listserv list, or mailing list. You use the term when writing commands to end a relationship with a discussion group or to remove a Usenet newsgroup from the list of those you would regularly read.

uploading   Transferring a file from a local computer (the one you're using) to another, remote computer.

URL (Uniform Resource Locator)   A way of describing the location of an item (document, service, or resource) on the Internet and specifying the means by which to access that item.

Usenet news   A system for exchanging messages called articles arranged according to specific categories called newsgroups. The articles are passed from one system to another, not as email between individuals.

vendor   A company that markets online catalog systems to libraries.

virtual libraries   Directories that contain collections of resources that librarians or cybrarians have carefully chosen and organized in a logical way.

Web browser   A program used to access the Internet services and resources available through the World Wide Web.

white pages service   A search service available on the World Wide Web that finds the email or street address of an individual, business, or government agency.

wildcard   A character that stands in for another character or group of characters. Most search tools use an asterisk for this function. Although the wildcard is most often used in truncation, it can also be used in the middle of words (for example, wom*n).

WWW (World Wide Web)   The collection of different services and resources available on the Internet.

Index

DATE DUE

GAYLORD			PRINTED IN U.S.A.